Beyond the Alamo

Raúl A. Ramos

Beyond the Alamo

FORGING MEXICAN ETHNICITY
IN SAN ANTONIO, 1821–1861

Published in Association
with The William P. Clements
Center for Southwest Studies,
Southern Methodist University,
by The University of
North Carolina Press
Chapel Hill

© 2008 The University of North Carolina Press
All rights reserved
Manufactured in the United States of America

Designed by Michelle Coppedge
Set in Arnhem Blond and Esprit Black
by Tseng Information Systems, Inc.

The paper in this book meets the guidelines for permanence
and durability of the Committee on Production Guidelines for
Book Longevity of the Council on Library Resources.

Library of Congress Cataloging-in-Publication Data
Ramos, Raúl A.
Beyond the Alamo : forging Mexican ethnicity in San Antonio,
1821–1861 / Raúl A. Ramos.
p. cm.
Includes bibliographical references and index.
ISBN 978-0-8078-3207-3 (cloth : alk. paper)
ISBN 978-0-8078-7124-9 (pbk. : alk. paper)
1. Mexican Americans—Ethnic identity—Texas—San Antonio.
2. Mexican Americans—Texas—San Antonio—History—19th
century. 3. Mexican Americans—Cultural assimilation—Texas
—San Antonio. 4. San Antonio (Tex.)—Ethnic relations—
History—19th century. 5. Ethnicity—Texas—San Antonio—
History—19th century. 6. San Antonio (Tex.)—History—19th
century. I. Title.
F394.S2119M5163 2008
305.868'72076435109034—dc22   2007044845

cloth   12 11 10 09 08   5 4 3 2 1
paper   13 12 11 10 09   5 4 3 2 1

Dedicado a la memoria de mi abuelito,
   Raúl Ramos González,

y a la vida nueva con mi hijo,
   Joaquín Enrique Ramos Chiao

Contents

Illustrations, Tables, Figures, and Map

TABLES

FIGURES

MAP

Acknowledgments

This project has gone through its share of fits and starts and exists because of the timely intervention of grants, keen observations, and camaraderie. The Ford Foundation provided the initial investment in my academic career. My project first took shape during a year as a Charles Gaius Bolin Fellow at Williams College. Joel Wolfe and K. Scott Wong saw its early promise. Several mentors guided its transformation at Yale, especially John Mack Faragher, Howard Lamar, Gilbert Joseph, David Montgomery, and Mario Garcia. The Mellon Foundation supported the first of many drafts. Archivists and librarians opened the doors to documents. I benefited from the staffs of the Beinecke Rare Book and Manuscript Library at Yale University, the Benson Latin American Collection and Center for American History at the University of Texas, the Texas State Library and Archives, Archivo General del Estado de Coahuila in Saltillo, Texas, the Local History Collection at the Houston Public Library, and Special Collections at the University of Houston.

The concepts in the book matured while I was at the University of Utah, where the history department and the Ethnic Studies Program supplied a nurturing place to grow. L. Ray Gunn, Eric Hinderaker, Rebecca Horn, Wesley Sasaki-Uemura, Ron Coleman, Paul Johnson, and Larry Gerlach protected my time and encouraged my development. Armando Salinas and Rudy Guevarra each spent a summer researching the project. Megan Armstrong, David Igler, Janet Theiss, Beth Clement, Bruce Dain, and Katheryn Stockton created a social community to rival the beauty of the Wasatch Mountains. I'm most grateful for my ally Susie Porter.

The final push took place during my year as the Summerfield Roberts Fellow in Texas History at the William P. Clements Center for Southwest Studies at Southern Methodist University. The year proved invaluable for the intense focus on the book. David J. Weber, Sherry Smith, and Andrea Boardman made the year possible. Steve Stern, Beth Haas, and Paul Lack supplied new perspectives to the project, along with Greg Cantrell, Roberto Calderón, Martin Padgett, and Marsha Weisiger. I came in contact with the Clements Center again through the Continental Crossroads project organized by Elliott Young and Sam Truett. Elliott, Sam, and the other collaborators offered new ways to recast my project. While in Dallas, I bonded with Alexis McCrossen and Adam Herring, who time and again knew what was needed to get past obstacles.

The history department at the University of Houston created a space that seriously engages the politics of Chicano/a history. All my colleagues have promoted this project, especially Guadalupe San Miguel, John Mason Hart, Joe Glatthaar, and Xioping Cong. A special group of graduate students and faculty has come together at Houston under *la colectiva*. Tatcho Mindiola and the Center for Mexican American Studies generously supported a year of research through the Visiting Scholar Program and continue to provide a strong community on campus. Publication was supported by a University of Houston Small Program Grant. Best of all, I came to Houston with Luis Alvarez and Marilyn Espitia—and Monica Perales arrived soon after—and knew right away I could finish my project here.

I am also the beneficiary of my connection with a larger community of Chicano/a and Tejano scholars. At various stages in my career, I gained from the insights of Frank de la Teja, George Sanchez, Vicki Ruiz, David Montejano, Ramón Gutiérrez, Ernesto Chavez, Steve Pitti, Omar Valerio, Miroslava Chavez, and John McKiernan-Gonzalez. I fondly remember the sense of a shared project I felt while presenting at a poorly attended panel in Atlanta with Omar, Miroslava, and George. I kept running into Mitch Duneier at the right time to get some needed perspective. In Houston, Pat Kelley shared his interests and his home. Completion of this project came about through thoughtful shepherding by Chuck Grench, Katy O'Brien, and the staff at the University of North Carolina Press. I thank Jim Crisp and Ernesto Chavez for their close reading.

I suppose I gathered many of my ideas about family networks and regional connections from my families. My extended family became a sounding board and support network. I owe my foundations to my mother, Margarita Ramos Petz, and my father, Raúl Ramos Lopez, with his wife Hilda. My sisters, María, Ana, and Veronica, created a web of support through rough times. Leticia Campos, Elva and Roque Yañez, and Florence and Raymond Chiao expanded my core family. My life is made rich by my chosen siblings—Josh Goldfein, Cathy Bowman, Brad Eastman, Sebastian Hardy, and Jonathan Holloway. I am grateful that in my freshman year, unseen forces put me in a dorm room with Ed Fraunheim. Ed created the category of critical friend, and he carried that out by reading the entire manuscript at least twice.

Taking on this sort of project and committing to a life in academia was possible because of the unique combination of idealism and realism modeled by two mentors. At Princeton, Michael Jiménez provided political and spiritual inspiration. He concretized the connection between studying the past and improving the present. He is greatly missed. When I decided to become a historian, David Gutiérrez took me on as a research assistant. With Dave, I first understood that insight comes from leaving my comfort zone and pushing my limits. Dave never stopped pushing, and I always know he is there at the end of the day with a cold beer.

No one lived with this project more than my partner, Elizabeth Chiao. She shared the frustrations and the breakthroughs and also knew that it was always more than just a job. She listened patiently as I went over my latest ideas while walking Josie and Buddy. As she threw the tennis ball, her observations forced me to clarify my thoughts. Her patience continued when we picked up and moved, tearing at our deep roots each time. Our son, Joaquín Enrique, was born into this project. His laughter and perseverance brighten the rainiest Houston day.

Beyond the Alamo

Forging Identity in the Borderlands

SITUATING SAN ANTONIO DE BÉXAR

At midnight on the night of September 15, 1835, church bells began to ring all through the town of Béxar. They signaled the beginning of festivities marking Mexico's independence from Spain. The schedule of events for the next morning was read aloud before a large gathering of the town's citizens. Soldiers carried flags and banners to the governor's quarters to position them for the coming day's parade. Behind those banners, town leaders organized a ceremony that was composed of "all citizens without distinction of class."[1] The commemoration temporarily lowered barriers between military and civilian, elite and poor. Many of those present that night carried memories of the insurgent battles that had taken place in Béxar in 1811 and 1813.[2] As a result, the evening events took place with the "utmost solemnity."[3]

At dawn on the morning of the sixteenth, Domingo de Ugartechea, commander of the town presidio, called his troops to order, and a salvo of shots rang out to announce the beginning of the daylong celebration. By nine that morning, military and civil authorities, along with their employees and other citizens, formed a procession as they entered San Fernando Cathedral. The parish priest of Béxar offered a mass of thanksgiving to bless the upcoming celebration. By four in the afternoon, the entire town assembled around the two plazas to participate in or cheer on a parade and convocation in honor of Independence Day. With the organizing committees at the podium, the soldiers and citizens formed another procession around the plazas. The processions also included several floats leading up to the featured cart decorated by a committee headed by Erasmo Seguín, a prominent Bexareño, as Mexicans in San Antonio de Béxar were known.[4]

Seguín's committee selected "a beautiful young girl," a beauty queen or *reina*, to ride on the float. The committee chose an ornate gown for her, "of a manner alluding to the dress of indigenous people, our progenitors in the Americas."[5] By including these symbols in the highest celebration of their nationalism, Bexareños acknowledged the indigenous aspects of Mexican identity. It is unclear from the description of that parade what specific style of dress the *reina* wore; it was probably modeled on the clothing of a local indigenous group of *indios civilizados*, or a variation of Tlascaltecan clothing.[6] After a full day of masses, speeches, and parades, the citizens of Béxar gathered again that evening in both of the town's plazas to dance the night away at a large fandango, or ball.

The festivities obscured the deep rumblings afoot at the time. Tensions between the Mexican government and Anglo-American immigrants living in the eastern region of Texas had reached a crescendo in the wake of the Law of April 6, 1830, which had effectively ended legal American immigration. The *vecinos*—Spanish citizens—of Béxar celebrated without acknowledging the increasing divide within their ranks over how best to deal with the growing Anglo-American insurrection. Only a few months following this Independence Day celebration in 1835, the self-proclaimed Army of Texas took over Béxar and its mission-turned-presidio, the Alamo. The action set in motion a successful Anglo-led movement to have Texas secede from Mexico. September 16, 1835, would be the last time Independence Day was celebrated in Mexican Texas.

It would not, however, be the last Mexican independence celebration in San Antonio. Mexican Independence Day is still commemorated and other symbols of Mexican national and ethnic identity persist in present-day San Antonio. This book tells the story of that continuity and of the transformation of identity in the region. It is the story of the cultural and political persistence of Bexareños in the face of American expansion. A transformation took place during those years; Bexareños went from their dominant political position in 1821 to a largely subordinate, nascent ethnic minority by 1861. While their social status changed, they maintained an identity based on their experiences before and during Anglo-American expansion. They forged this identity at the crossroads of nations and the juncture of multiple cultures. More than a story of cultural survival, the Bexareño case exemplifies the ways identity is both transmitted and transformed under changing social conditions during national and social shifts.

The Mexican independence celebration in 1835 serves as a microcosm of the multiple issues raised by analyzing this period through the Bexareño lens. First, the festival commemorated the birth of the Mexican nation. Did all participants take that to mean the same thing? Second, the *reina* from the principal float was dressed as an Indian. How did her costume link her, the town, and the nation to the region's indigenous peoples and cultures, if it all? Third, the event's organizers came from the elite families of Béxar. How did their participation shape or reflect their social position in the town? Fourth, the festival took place in locally meaningful places such as the cathedral, the military plaza, and the main plaza. What relation and weight did local identity have in the construction of a Mexican national identity? And finally, few Anglo-Americans were present or participated, yet they made up at least three-quarters of the population of Texas. How did the backdrop of Anglo-American immigration and American political pressures affect the development of Bexareño society?

Perhaps the most striking question regarding the celebration is raised after realizing that many of the Bexareños celebrating Mexican Independence that day joined the Anglo-American-led secession movement months later. Tracing the activities of Tejanos—Mexican Texans—before and during the war of Texas secession puts into relief national identities and also local interests. What led Tejanos to celebrate Mexican Independence one month and then participate in a rebellion against their nation in the next? Ultimately, nationalism meant something different to Tejanos, particularly in Béxar, where people also identified themselves by such categories as social standing and family connection. In short, there is no single or simple answer to understand Bexareño motivations in 1835. The following narrative pieces together the complex world around Bexareños to reconstruct the social context in which their actions made sense. To do so means focusing the story on Béxar and Bexareños in order to examine the nature of cross-cultural contact between Bexareños, indigenous groups, and Anglo-American immigrants and analyzing the meaning of nationalism and ethnicity during a period when these identities were fluid and in transition.

While situating Tejanos at the center of the narrative exposes the interconnections between peoples and cultures in the region, doing so involves recasting the way histories of nineteenth-century Texas have been told. In the same way that leaving the big city lights of New York or Mexico City makes nighttime stars in the sky more visible, moving the focus away from Anglo-Texan heroes and instead on Tejanos makes relationships between people and institutions more apparent. This narrative attempts to make sense of the interconnections among Tejanos, Anglo immigrants, indigenous inhabitants, and state and religious institutions. To do so requires steering the narrative away from once-central places, events, and people, such as the battle of the Alamo, Texas independence, and Sam Houston. In this telling, the Texas Revolution is better described as the war of Texas secession, and Erasmo Seguín and his son Juan play larger roles in the region's political and social formation than does Stephen F. Austin.

This study analyzes the history of the region by reframing the events and concepts significant to Tejanos in Béxar. The changes in this period fall into a larger trajectory of shifting national boundaries beginning in the late Spanish colonial period through American westward expansion. Plenty of interpretations of Austin's or Houston's words and actions appear in the historical record. This study begins by asking what Tejanos thought of the events and world around them and how they strove to fit into that world. Through the focus on Béxar, Austin and Houston enter into a socially complex region rather than a blank slate; the relationship between Anglos and Mexicans is part of the region's long development instead of a new place where Mexicans are bit players.

The relative abundance and availability of Anglo-American sources has resulted in a history of Tejanos largely shaped by Anglo assumptions and observations structured within the larger periodization of American history. The Tejano role in American history often only appears in relation to events significant to that narrative. In that view, Tejanos either supported the Texas Revolution or fought against it, since, from the American point of view, they could identify only with either Texas or Mexico and not both. Putting Tejanos at the center of this study complicates national identity by taking into consideration the larger historical trajectory of which Tejanos were a part. Theirs was not an either/or choice between Mexico and the United States but a matter of local survival and persistence in the long history of previous challenges to their community.

Significant barriers hinder the task of completely reconstructing nineteenth-century Tejano identity. Material, temporal, and political circumstances have combined to obscure the thoughts and daily lives of ordinary Tejanos. Rarely do documents surface that clearly state their beliefs or ideas regarding identity. The few available sources serve a limited use once the researcher sorts out the biases and ulterior motives of individual authors or interpreters. The lasting effects of Anglo-American colonization on the history of the region appear in the representations of Béxar as a sleepy town prior to its separation from Mexico.[7] These depictions of Béxar relate to the narrative common in histories of Texas today, which casts Anglo-Americans as the bearers of progress and Mexicans as the keepers of old folkways. Indeed, many cities and states in the American Southwest continue to promote their romantic, lazy, "Old Mexico" roots. An analysis of Tejano culture and society for the period needs to step beyond these predefined categories and to explore the complexity of these and other symbols and documents. Over the decades, a gap has appeared between the story of San Antonio and Texas history presented to tourists and the truly dynamic and complex culture and history of the region's people.

Growing up in San Antonio, I observed how historical symbols and narratives could favor one story or identity to the exclusion of another. The Alamo name and image seemed to appear everywhere I looked, but despite its commercial uses around town, visiting the Alamo was a serene, mysterious experience. Our teachers and the docents told visitors that they stood at the "shrine" of Texas liberty. These visits left a powerful mark on me—in my daily life, I was surrounded by reminders of the past. Yet the simple stories behind these historical symbols and their power in Texas popular culture and myth didn't square with my own complicated background.

My parents met in the northern Mexican city of Monterrey and moved to San Antonio just before they had my sisters and me. My paternal family, Ramos, has deep roots in Mexico's northeastern region, particularly in the state of Coahuila, extending back to the eighteenth century. My maternal grandparents, Petz, immigrated to Mexico from Hungary, taking advantage of the industrial growth of the region in the mid-twentieth century. These two sides of my family projected both a long connection to the region's past and a sense of global contacts and multiple ethnic identities. What it meant to be Mexican was a difficult question for me to answer, especially in a society where Anglo-Americans defined "Mexican." That definition implied a homogeneous and stagnant identity rather than the complex, multigenerational, and integrated identity I noticed; that definition cast the United States as the nation of immigrants and Mexico as an exporter of immigrants. Where did my family fit in that immigrant scheme? The Alamo came to feel stale and frozen in an arbitrary moment in time: 1836. The dominance of the Alamo story also overlooked the conflicting sentiments felt by the majority Mexican-origin population of the city.

Fortunately, I didn't have to look too far beyond the Alamo to find other historical reminders predating the Texas Republic. San Antonio has five missions extending southward along the San Antonio River. Depression-era projects reconstructed other historical sites commemorating early Spanish settlers at La Villita and colonial governance at the Governor's Palace. Growing up in San Antonio provided me with a rich historical landscape that enabled me to begin to make sense of my own past. Buildings and symbols of history were in abundance. Still, I lacked a way to put it all together. The Alamo left little room for the multiple histories overlapping the city and its surrounding region in time and place. It took leaving home for the East Coast, with its own political and historical perspectives, to make me take an interest in rewriting these stories. I began to consider writing a narrative that would spring from the Mexican point of view while making sense of the multiple, intersecting peoples and their histories in the region.

To tease out the multiple layers of identity and ethnic entanglements, I decided to follow the effects of several national transitions on the Mexican population of San Antonio de Béxar, from Mexican independence to American annexation. Bexareño experiences serve as the pivot-point that connects the peoples traversing and institutions established in the region during that period. While this narrative centers on the Mexican population of San Antonio, Bexareño identity and society is better understood in relation to other societies and within a broader national and transnational context. This situational approach avoids the uncritical and homogenous portrayal of Bexareños that might result from focusing on them exclusively. Rather, describing connections with other cultures and ideas outside of their homes reveals a community with a richly varied social world. These connections also highlight the complexity of the region and the greater significance of the Bexareño story beyond Texas and the American Southwest.

Telling the story of Bexareños in a variety of social and political contexts makes their experiences examples of identity formation in a cross-cultural frontier. I use identity and identity formation as the principal tools with which to examine the meaning and impact of these contacts with other cultures and changes in political status in the region. Identity, far from being inherent or passed down from generation to generation unchanged, is constantly being re-created in response to and in conversation with the changes in the world.[8] Bexareños carefully negotiated the changing cultural and political landscape, carving a path that connected their past with the new challenges that lay in their future. Their experience expands the debate around identity formation in American history, one formerly characterized by either assimilation or ethnic persistence among immigrant populations.[9] While they were not immigrants, Bexareños eventually had to contend with dwindling political and social power while attempting to keep their community intact. Bexareño identity itself is complex and contradictory, making this term difficult to use uncritically.

This study concentrates on two interrelated categories of identity to unravel Bexareño identity: nationalism and ethnicity. The case of San Antonio in the nineteenth century presents difficulty in defining and pinning down these two categories of identity. At various points in this story, numerous possible answers emerge to the question of ethnic or national identity for Bexareños and other people who played a significant role in the region. Were they Mexicans, or mestizo, or Español, or Tejano, or Texan, or American? How does looking at identity provide insight into events, the history of cross-cultural contact, and American history and Mexican history generally? A focus on national and ethnic identity can answer these questions and others by laying out the parameters and context where people met.

The meaning of nation in 1821 differed in many ways from current uses of the term. The nation-state had only recently come into existence in Europe and the Americas when Mexicans began to imagine their own nation.[10] "Nation" at that time had a closer connection to the symbols and structures of the colonial empire than to altogether new societies and ideologies. Bexareños not only participated in the transformation from Spanish colony to Mexican nation but did so with firsthand knowledge of American growth and expansion across the border. Between 1821 and 1861, Bexareños lived under five flags, which complicated the meaning of nation even further. Given the frequent changes of government during this period, nationalism for Bexareños focused less on official symbols and articulations, such as flags and laws, and more on locally established cultural and ideological practices. The nature of those practices drives this narrative—in other words, actions taken by Bexareños in their local sphere provide insight into the changing meaning of nation for them.

These practices shift attention back and forth between nationalism as defined by the Mexican state and proto-nationalism as performed by regional communities.[11] Local and regional identities, such as Bexareño,

Tejano, or Norteño, themselves constitute variants or subsets of nationalism. As a result, these identities, while related to nationalism, do not meet the complete scope and breadth necessary to be considered national identities. They nevertheless constitute crucial elements that together with wider political and social identities make up the "imagined community" of nationalist sentiment.[12] In referring to Tejano identity as proto-national, this study does not claim that it was on a course toward separate nationalism but rather emphasizes elements of nationalism beyond those officially defined by the state or that describe a single identity.

Like nationalism, ethnicity also held different meanings for Bexareños and shaped their responses to their rapidly changing social and political landscape. While Mexican ethnic identity appears more familiar to us after American annexation of Texas, Bexareños already had a complex system of social and cultural identity dating to the first Spanish colonies among indigenous peoples. American expansion into Texas added yet another layer to that set of social arrangements. The constant change in social and cultural identities over time makes establishing a consistent definition of ethnicity for Bexareños difficult. Generally, ethnicity means a social identity based on ancestry along with a variety of cultural factors, such as religion, language, nation, and race.[13] This narrative weaves together two strands of ethnic identity running through this period in Béxar. First, as Mexicans on the frontier, Bexareños carved an ethnic identity out of a wide range of indigenous and European identities spanning from central Mexico to the northern plains. Second, Anglo-American social and political dominance in Texas forced Bexareños to reconfigure their notions of ethnic identity and national affiliation.

Béxar's location in the borderlands of Mexico and later in the United States shaped the development of nationalism and ethnicity, and this study provides examples of the issues surrounding identity formation and cross-cultural contact in a borderland region. The term "borderland" refers to a relationship of a region to two or more nation-states and thus begs the question of what nationalism looks like on the border of a nation. Historians have begun to note the significant transformation taking place in the region during this period. Juan Mora-Torres proposes a systematic examination of borderlands regions by describing a "frontier to border" transformation.[14] Elsewhere, Jeremy Adelman and Stephen Aron chart a transition from "borderlands to *bordered* lands."[15] In both these cases, the relative fluidity and exchange of the early period in these zones of cross-cultural contact give way to rigidity and political and economic exploitation. The analysis used by these historians also emphasizes the colonial desires of empires to dominate frontier people and regions while overlooking local voices and responses to social change.

Examining the social practices and political affiliations of Bexareños during this period highlights the local aspect of national identity. Historian Peter Sahlins uses the borderlands between France and Spain in the seventeenth century to propose a framework for understanding the interaction between local and national identities. Sahlins writes, "National identity—as Frenchmen or Spaniards—appeared on the periphery before it was built there by the center. It appeared less as a result of state intentions than from the local process of adopting and appropriating the nation without abandoning local interests, a local sense of place, or a local identity."[16] In the case of the Pyrenees borderland, nationalism was part of the local identity because of internal reasons as much as an externally imposed ideology. Sahlins makes sense of the relation between nationalism and localism by introducing the idea of concentric circles of identity that ripple outward from the village.[17] Such a geographic and social system developed around Béxar, albeit on a smaller scale.

Historian Richard White has proposed yet a third way of approaching borderland regions through his use of the term "middle ground."[18] White's middle ground describes the broad set of ideas and interactions constructed between two disparate cultures, in his case between indigenous peoples and French colonists in the Great Lakes region. Middle ground refers to the time and place where cross-cultural interaction took place, as well as the ideological and cultural terms needed for that exchange to succeed. White offers historians a way to incorporate radically divergent worldviews into a narrative of conflict and cooperation in early colonial America. Cultural contacts taking place in early-nineteenth-century Béxar were numerous, and middle ground provides a framework to consider those Mexican, indigenous, and Anglo-American social interactions.

These approaches to borderland research, focusing on state formation, local practices, and cultural constructions, have raised the level of analysis of this field.[19] Using such methods to study Béxar in the nineteenth century allows me to examine the evolution of ethnic and national identity with an eye to the larger borderland region. Such approaches have already been combined, in a sense, through the development of the field of Chicano/a history. Chicano/a historians bring a similar analysis of colonialism at the national and community levels, emphasizing the subaltern response to oppression. Chicano/a historians emerged as a challenge to American history, questioning silences when it came to Mexican people and writing history not bound by traditional categories and periods.

Chicano/a history has been instrumental in shaping my view of what had become a master narrative in Anglo-American history in Texas and the American West. Beginning in the 1950s, Chicano/a historians began to develop a criticism of leading scholars, pointing out the absences and biases in their version of the history of the Southwest. Whether it was the Texas Rangers, the economic boom in the region, docile Mexican labor, or peaceful American expansion, existing narratives were questioned by Chicano/a historians and cultural critics who proposed new ways of looking at the past.[20] These historians, directly and indirectly, were in conversation with political movements of the time and responded to demands by students and local communities to provide a way to place their ethnic-Mexican world within a larger historical tradition largely absent from academia.

Recent reflections and reconfigurations of Chicano/a and Latino/a studies have explored the larger explanatory possibilities found in this approach. These historians and cultural critics combine identity politics and critiques of economic and political subordination with narrative re-telling to produce a new social history of the Americas. They propose analyzing motivation and historical agency through the creation of identities, communities, and political movements. For instance, George J. Sanchez's work on Chicanos/as in Los Angeles links political and social movements to cultural elements of identity such as music, religion, and ethnic organizations.[21] While conceptually, this study falls into the broader field of Chicano/a history, several problems arise in relation to its applicability. Since much of this story takes place before American annexation, it is uncertain whether the term "Chicano/a" would adequately describe Bexareños. The approach is useful, nevertheless, since Chicano/a history combines the articulation of a group identity in the context of colonial expansion.

Placing Bexareños at the pivot-point of the story rather than focusing exclusively on them connects the wide variety of peoples and ideologies converging in Texas during this period. Bexareño experiences in nation-state formation, during which they negotiated with indigenous groups and Anglo-American immigrants at the same time, provide a fertile context for historians to compare several nineteenth-century transformations. Viewed as a chapter in Mexican history, Béxar is featured in the northern expansion of New Spain's domain, developing simultaneously and separately from Chihuahua, New Mexico, and California. Mexican historians situate Béxar within the larger narrative of Spanish colonial settlement and frontier relations with nomadic indigenous groups. Prior to Anglo-American expansion, Béxar in many ways paralleled the social and economic development of other Spanish colonial outposts. The region's missions and military presidios connected settlers with the indigenous population. Béxar's location on the rim of the vast Comanche empire provided Comanche leaders with a place to trade and raid within their economic system. Finally, the history of Béxar also exemplifies the development of the Mexican nation-state in the frontier.

Yet even within Mexican literature, the case of Texas and other northern territories touches on a politically and culturally sensitive chapter in Mexican history. In a recent article, Cuauhtémoc Velasco describes Mexican resistance to writing the history of American westward expansion, despite the fact that Americans have little trouble writing Mexico's history.[22] Velasco notes that this discrepancy "results as much from the resources each nation has dedicated to research and writing the past, as . . . [from] the focus and the questions that take priority: in the United States the frontier explains the nation and in Mexico it threatens it."[23] Traditionally writing in American history, Chicano/a historians directly confronted this contradiction head-on. Their work has pointed to the arbitrary divisions set up by national histories by raising questions about the construction of nationalism during American colonial expansion.

The Bexareño experience resulting from American westward expansion is significant to American historians as well. Anglo-American families and their slaves migrated from southern states into the region during Mexico's first decade. Mexican participation in and reaction to this immigration can be better understood through the actions of Bexareños. Their story transforms American history in several ways—in particular, it challenges typical ways of describing immigration. Americans have seldom been labeled immigrants, and their immigration into Texas has followed that trend. More than a rhetorical oversight, depicting the United States as a sender country inverts the discussion of the motivations and ideology behind American westward expansion and territorial acquisition. Eventually, after Anglo-Americans established political power in Texas through annexation, the Bexareño story then turns to the social and cultural incorporation of an ethnic minority population into the American political body. When I started looking at the history of Béxar in the nineteenth century, nations came and went through the town, leaving people to make sense of these rapid changes. I propose using Béxar and the lives of Bexareños as a starting point to reconcile the division between Mexican and American national histories.

In the last twenty years, historians of the American West have also concentrated their efforts in untangling the way power has been deployed and maintained over people and the environment in the process of conquest and expansion. They joined the analysis already underway in Chicano/a history and applied it to other situations, such as the subordination of indigenous peoples and the reconfiguration of land and nature for economic production. Categories such as the middle ground described by Richard White or the market in captives told by James Brooks have expanded the area where cross-cultural contact is found. As such, the question is not so much of domination and subordination but of negotiation, collaboration, misunderstanding, and opportunism. Béxar provides similar examples of complex interactions in the borderlands that result in brokering, negotiating, and alliance building.

This book is divided into two parts. Part 1 uses the first three chapters to examine 1821, taking stock of the multiple changes underway at independence. The chapters set up three social "worlds" coexisting in the region and affecting the development of the others. Chapter 1 examines Tejano participation in Mexican independence, which gave meaning to nationalism on the frontier. Tejano motivations during this period are analyzed through the categories of prestige and social standing. The relative independence found in the far frontier also facilitated and perhaps encouraged Tejano participation in the Mexican insurgency. While still acting with local concerns, Tejanos began to consider national debates as they affected their situation. Tejanos were engaged in the Mexican national project but in terms set by their local interests. By the same token, their location on the borderlands affected the composition of their insurgent army and introduced an ethnic element, as seen in the companies of Anglo-American mercenaries fighting alongside Mexican insurgents.

Chapter 2 situates Tejanos along a broad spectrum of indigenous identities. This chapter expands the traditional narrative of *mestizaje*, or racial mixing, to include the other uses and meanings of the word "Indian," such as mission Indians, eastern migrant tribes, and nomadic groups like Comanches. The third chapter introduces Anglo-American immigration into the layered development of Tejano identity. The chapter shows how Tejanos gained an identity as "cultural brokers" between the new Anglo-

American population and the Mexican state, thus increasing the importance of both ethnicity and nationalism. While the changes ultimately had a deleterious affect on Tejanos, this period should be described in terms of the possibilities present before Tejanos. When Béxar's elites encouraged Anglo-American colonization, they drew on the desire for personal and regional wealth. Early cross-ethnic alliances formed along class lines and held out the promise of a "smooth" transition to prosperity. Indeed, northern Mexican settlers believed that an Anglo-American work ethic might transform Texas into a vibrant economy.

Part 2 follows the development of ethnicity and nationalism through Texas secession and American expansion up to the U.S. Civil War. External events coupled with internal developments strained the delicate balance Tejanos crafted after independence. The chapters in part 2 recast well-known events of that period—tensions with the Mexican government, Texas secession, the battle of the Alamo, the Republic of Texas era, and the U.S.-Mexico War—through their impact on Tejanos. The chapters present a narrative arc of Tejano decline, resurgence, and persistence in the face of changing conditions and difficult and oppressive circumstances.

Chapter 4 traces the rapid succession of changes that took place as Anglo-American colonists immigrated in large numbers and brought their own demands to the Mexican government. The chapter concentrates on anti-colonization laws passed by the Mexican legislature as a response to Anglo-American immigration. Mounting pressures from immigration and the response to it from the centralist Mexican government began to limit the possibilities of a peaceful prosperity and instead hardened lines of differentiation. Chapter 5 then describes the war of Texas secession, which ultimately closed the door on the carefully negotiated cross-ethnic future Tejanos had imagined. Afterward, class mattered less and ethnicity and race set the terms of the Texan social order. Even while war raged in Béxar, Tejanos held out the belief that their actions supported the federalist cause in Mexican politics. Secession limited the ability Tejanos had to directly and publicly connect with issues affecting the Mexican state.

Chapters 6 and 7 trace Tejanos' social and political reorganization while Anglo-Americans consolidated their hold on Béxar and Texas. In general, Tejanos carved out a space within the dominant framework of ethnicity during the Texas Republic and American annexation periods. Local Bexareño society and culture gave way to ethnic organizing, often uniting Tejanos across class. More specifically, Tejano political culture was situated within a larger system of racial and ethnic differentiation that led to social and economic marginalization. Chapter 6 examines these changes from the perspective of Mexican military incursions into San Antonio de Béxar in an attempt to reconquer Texas. Chapter 7 ends the narrative in antebellum San Antonio where Tejanos found new ways of participating in regional politics and continued to maintain the social and cultural integrity of their community.

At key points during this period of transition, from Mexican independence to the American Civil War, Bexareños articulated stances regarding Mexican national identity, referencing Mexican national debates regarding the form of nationalism. In these cases and later, those debates involved historically specific issues that Tejanos were aware of. Thus, the label of "Mexican" is itself part of an ongoing discourse that uses the language of the time. Tejanos understood being Mexican through the lenses of their place and time. As such, the Tejano activities described in part 2 refer to Mexican nationalism through the context of the federalist/centralist debates of the time. Being northern provincials seeking greater autonomy, Bexareños allied with federalist leaders and situated their actions in those terms. The several hundred Tejanos who fought in the Army of Texas did so with these debates in mind and with the interests of their community in sight. An analytical conclusion applies the lessons learned from Béxar to the growing literature in transnational history, reflecting on the importance of local historical development to understand global processes, such as constructions of ethnic and national identities.

Prologue

Life in a Norteño Town

Most nineteenth-century travelers approached Béxar from the south along the main road, the Camino Real, with a sense of relief and wonder. The relief came from arriving at a town safely after days of traversing the brush country, exposed to the possibility of attack from one of a variety of indigenous groups controlling the area, such as the Comanche or Lipan Apache. Indeed, immediately upon arrival, most Mexican travelers attended mass at San Fernando Cathedral. Writing in the eighteenth century, Juan Agustín de Morfi noted, "We went to the parish church to genuflect, to give thanks to Our Holy Father for the joy of our arrival."[1] The sense of wonder came from noting Béxar's relatively lush oasis in comparison to the harsh desert of northern New Spain. Later, a Mexican official writing about his view of the landscape surrounding the town commented, "The hills and valleys are gradually sloped, of low elevation, and covered in low-lying vegetation appearing like an amphitheater, dropping out occasionally in the form of uncovered banks of limestone."[2] He then added, "I imagined myself transported to those long ago times which are lost in the darkness of history."[3]

Texas, 1820–1836

San Antonio River with Mission San José y San Miguel de Aguayo in the distance, ca. 1869. (Courtesy of the San Antonio Conservation Society Foundation, Raba Collection)

Such was the reaction of arriving in the remote town of San Antonio de Béxar, a frontier town situated in the borderlands between two colonizing empires. Béxar's landscape possessed qualities typical of other frontiers, such as remoteness, indigenous threats, scarcity of natural resources, and a harsh climate.[4] Its location on the borderlands meant that visitors approached Béxar from both the north and south. Yet the presence of the town and the persistence of its inhabitants amazed all visitors equally.

On May 5, 1718, newly appointed governor of Texas Martín de Alarcón and his expedition chose a spot on the banks of the San Antonio River and San Pedro Creek to establish a mission, San Antonio de Valero, and a town,

Villa de Béxar.[5] Thirty Spanish soldiers and their families from Alarcon's expedition served as the first settlers of the town. The founding of Béxar initiated the establishment of several missions along the San Antonio River. Béxar served as the civilian and military corollary to the missionary colonization effort. The town received an early population boost when fourteen families migrated at royal expense from Spain's Canary Islands in 1731, ensuring the permanence of the settlement.[6] The settlers named their colony San Fernando de Béxar.

By 1778, when Morfi accompanied Teodoro de Croix on his inspection of the northern regions, it was estimated that Texas contained about 3,000 citizens in and around its three towns—Béxar, La Bahía, and Nacogdoches—and at least half of these resided in Béxar.[7] The population for Béxar and most of the province stagnated at that level around 1790, after several years of fluctuation. By 1800, the entire Provincias Internas, which included present-day Texas, Coahuila, Nuevo León, and Tamaulipas, contained a population of approximately 82,000, of which 3,500 to 4,000 lived in Texas.[8] A census taken in December 1795 listed the population of Béxar at 1,487, including its surrounding missions and barrios.[9] An estimate produced by Governor Manuel Salcedo in 1809 listed "1,700 souls" in Béxar and 3,122 for the entire province.[10] But large discrepancies in the exact population of the province appear through various reports. For instance, Father Miguel Ramos Arizpe put the total population of the province of Texas closer to 7,000 in his report of 1811.[11] The period immediately following independence led to the next expansion in the town's population, which doubled in population by 1834, when American traveler J. C. Clopper estimated between 3,000 and 5,000.[12]

The citizens and government officials of the region deemed populating Texas and the entire northern provinces a significant problem, and a successful solution eluded them. The town suffered from harsh climate and land, along with the isolation and danger endemic to Mexican frontier communities of the time. Nevertheless, enough people lived there to sustain the town while others on the frontier, such as San Sabá and Río Grande, disappeared. Indeed, by the mid-nineteenth century, Béxar grew to be a vital economic and political center. More important, it served as the most visited and supported outpost of Spanish and Mexican authority on the frontier, situating it squarely at the intersection of competing national interests throughout the nineteenth century. While not technically on the political borderline, Béxar stood as the first and largest Spanish colony Anglo-Americans crossed when traveling to Mexico. In this regard, Béxar shared aspects of frontier and border life with Santa Fe but with even closer geographic ties to the central government.[13]

Internal migrations within the northern region of New Spain accounted for a significant portion of the population of towns in the region. In Béxar, for instance, the census of 1793 indicated that 9 percent of its population migrated from some other part of the Provincias Internas, almost half coming from Saltillo and Monclova in Coahuila.[14] Another 4 percent of the population migrated from other villages within Texas. Those migrating from within the provinces were primarily identified as Español, or Spaniard, as opposed to mestizo, mulatto, or *indio*. From Nacogdoches, in northeastern Texas, census reports identify similar figures regarding migrants within the region. Marriages between people of the same region account for a portion of these migrants, as they appear frequently in church records.[15] These migrations and marriages present Béxar as a town socially interconnected with the hinterland.

Despite the advantages of living on the frontier, Bexareños and others in northern New Spain experienced extreme difficulties on a daily basis. Many observers commented on what they called a Norteño character, grounded in the experience of living on the vast Spanish frontier.[16] Writing in 1811, Father Miguel Ramos Arizpe, the representative from the Provincias Internas de Oriente to the Cortes in Cadiz, Spain, found that the difficulty of subsistence on the northeastern frontier shaped aspects of its inhabitants' identities. "This [agriculture] is, Sir, the most common occupation of the inhabitants of these vast and rich provinces. Agriculture has in general formed their character," began Arizpe's comments on the "quality" of the region's colonists, "and as they have been employed day and night in the honest and systematic cultivation of the soil, from which alone they derive their sustenance, they are truly inflexible to intrigue, virtuously steadfast, haters of tyranny and disorder, justly devoted to true liberty, and naturally the most inclined toward all the moral and political virtues. They are very much devoted also to the liberal and mechanical arts."[17] Ramos Arizpe's description of the inhabitants of the Provincias Internas held them up as model subjects, grounded in practical, beneficial, and almost nascent democratic ideology. He shared many of the beliefs on the links between culture and environment discussed by Thomas Jefferson and, decades later, by Frederick Jackson Turner regarding the character of colonists on the Anglo-American frontier.[18] But, unlike Jefferson and Turner, who said the agrarian frontier character shaped American culture, Ramos Arizpe never claimed that Norteño identity reflected back on Mexican culture and

San Pedro Springs in San Antonio, 1869. The city council made the springs a park in 1852.
(Courtesy of the San Antonio Conservation Society Foundation, Raba Collection)

society to the south of the frontier. Ramos Arizpe's description of Norteños as "haters of tyranny and disorder" and "inclined toward all the moral
and political virtues" stands in contrast to historical accounts characterizing them as indolent and bound by an authoritarian system, a legacy of
the Black Legend of Spanish colonization.[19] The necessities of eking out a
living on the northern frontier required that colonists make on-the-spot
decisions to solve daily problems rather than wait for a central authority
hundreds of miles away to dictate procedure.

In the first century since its founding, Béxar developed an economy
based principally on three staples: ranching, military, and trade.[20] Initially,
ranching and agriculture supplied cattle and corn for both local subsistence and presidial troop support. In the late eighteenth century, Béxar
developed a small-scale beef, hide, and tallow trade with Saltillo.[21] Ranching methods limited the size of the trade since Bexareños primarily "har-
vested" livestock from *mesteño* cattle in the hinterlands. More important,

the economic activities of Bexareños played a large role in forming their culture and frontier identity.

Ramos Arizpe's comments emphasized his belief that the environment shaped identity and culture. This environmental explanation also included other features of the frontier life, mainly contact with indigenous peoples. As a result, Ramos Arizpe suggested that Norteños were naturally stronger, physically and mentally, than other Mexicans. This strength involved all aspects of their life. He continued, "With this combination of such excellent qualities, which result from the celestial climate and are cultivated by such honest occupations, each citizen becomes a worker, each worker a soldier, and each soldier a hero that is worth a hundred ordinary soldiers."[22] Beyond citizen/soldiers, Béxar served as an outpost for the Spanish military, with garrisons stationed in the region to engage indigenous groups and to establish a presence for the Crown on the frontier.

Ramos Arizpe took these observations directly to the centers of colonial power in Spain in 1811 in an effort to increase political autonomy in the region. At that time, Texas made up one of four provinces in the Provincias Internas de Oriente, the eastern half of the Provincias Internas. The other three were Coahuila, Nuevo Reino de León (later Nuevo León), and Nuevo Santander (later Tamaulipas). These four provinces would later become four states in the Mexican Republic and remain states, with slightly different borders, to the present day.[23] In 1768, Don José de Gálvez proposed establishing a *comandancia* over the northern territories of New Spain, given that the land's size and distance from Mexico City merited additional attention and support.[24] On August 22, 1776, the Crown named Teodoro de Croix commander general of the Provincias Internas, giving him command independent of the viceroy over the entire northern territories. Frequent changes in governing structure led to local dissatisfaction. Unlike other residents in New Spain, the region's inhabitants had to go to one place for military concerns, another for political and diplomatic matters, and still another for religious dealings.[25]

Dissatisfaction with Spain also came as a result of the region's distance from the center of the colonial economy and its proximity to an expanding colonizing empire across the border. Regarding this first factor, Ramos Arizpe contended that "the most shameful monopoly of all European merchandise is carried on there."[26] The distance from Mexico City itself did not matter as much as the costs accumulated by each stage of transporting goods to the frontier. The expenses added to the already high risk associated with living on the frontier and kept Mexicans from migrating north-ward. Ramos Arizpe detailed the process alienating the region's inhabitants: "The foreigner profits, the merchant of Cadiz profits, that of Vera Cruz profits, that of Mexico profits, that of Saltillo profits, and that of each one of the interior places profits; and only the unfortunate and unhappy consumers of the Eastern Internal Provinces suffer the dreadful weight of so many duties, so many excise taxes, so much freight costs by sea and land, so many and such enormous profits."[27] Economic hardships such as these cut across class, making life difficult for merchants and peasants alike. Not only did costs rise but income from frontier production failed to keep pace, sending Norteños into a spiral of dependence. Ramos Arizpe asked rhetorically, "Of what advantage can it be to the hungry to have flour if it costs him more than the whole is worth to make it into bread?"[28] The resulting disparities and exploitation would only result in a situation where "the nation or province will always remain in a state of servitude, precursor perhaps to its total decline."[29] Beyond being merely an obstacle, these inequalities defined the northeastern provinces and its inhabitants. Regional identity arose not only from the expense of living in the north but also through comparison to the rest of the colony. Resentment and a sense of entitlement resulted from the gains the colony and Crown made at the misery of Norteños.

Colonial policy on the borderlands only intensified the regional complaints by cutting off a potential avenue for relief. The woodland areas in northeastern Texas provided cover for a vibrant contraband trade with Anglo-Americans and indigenous groups. Ramos Arizpe noted the influence this trade would have on the provinces: "The Spaniards are mere spectators to these extraordinary and profitable resources in which the native Indians and Anglo-Americans carry on a great trade."[30] Tobacco, furs, guns, and stolen livestock dominated this illicit trade. Tejanos could purchase these and other merchandise for a lower price and in shorter order through Louisiana than through Tampico. While the extent of this trade never reached the proportions of Santa Fe's, Béxar stood near a central hub of these transactions.[31]

The influence of the border varied by location within the Provincias Internas. To the north of Béxar, some Mexican colonists participated in an active contraband trade with French, American, and indigenous peoples. Those transactions buffered them from some problems facing the remainder of the region. Nacogdoches proved to be a convenient place where Spanish subjects could carry out these activities, since it was not under the close supervision of the Spanish government. Nacogdoches itself served later as an escape hatch for members of the insurgent independence movement in 1811 when many of those fleeing authority traveled to this northern sector of the provinces. The economy in settlements closer to the Gulf of Mexico also differed from those in the interior. Ports served as entry points for goods and people, and imports usually cost less at these points. Nevertheless, the Crown frowned upon illicit trade, and the collection of duties remained a major concern until the end of the colony.

With potential profit from the Anglo-American trade came the possibility for Anglo-American interventions and conquest. Norteños witnessed the westward march of the United States, bringing the American border to Texas after the Louisiana Purchase in 1803. The idea of a buffer frontier became more important, and the number of Spanish soldiers in Texas increased. Ramos Arizpe remarked, "As a result of the pretension of the Anglo-Americans on the borders between Louisiana and Texas, the troops of Coahuila, aided by seven hundred militiamen of Nuevo Leon and Tamaulipas, . . . marched to Texas and to its frontier at the end of 1805."[32] These soldiers changed the character of Béxar by militarizing the town and increasing the population with their families.

Ramos Arizpe and others believed that increasing the population would solve this border problem as well as reduce the danger of attacks by indigenous peoples. The call went out for more migration by people from the south. Ramos Arizpe declared populating the provinces an "advantageous [project] to the province of Texas that so much needs the industrious workers, and necessary to the nation for the preservation of that important province."[33] But environmental barriers and the struggles of life on the frontier hindered migration.

People trickled into Texas and Béxar in the early nineteenth century. True to the nature of a borderlands frontier, not all the migrants or visitors came from the south. Traveler J. C. Clopper's observations from the 1830s emphasized the wide varieties of cultures and languages resulting from Béxar's location. "The traveler hears around him a confusion of unknown tongues," wrote Clopper, "the red natives of the forests in their different guttural dialects—the swarthy Spaniard of a scarce brighter hue—the voluble Frenchman—a small number of the sons of Green Erin—and a goodly few of Uncle Sam's Nephews or half expatriated sons—he feels himself now for the first time in his life a stranger truly in a foreign land and enters a door for a short residence that he may discover more of this people."[34] While Clopper's comments came after massive Anglo-American colonization north of Béxar, the frontier character of the town's border-lands already included Spanish, Indian, French, and some American voices through trade and occasional settlement.

In these ways, early-nineteenth-century Bexareños already stood at the crossroads of nation-states, cultures, and economies. Given the regional sentiments described by Ramos Arizpe, how did Béxar develop in this Mexican, Anglo-American, and indigenous nexus?

Part I

Three Worlds in 1821

Each citizen becomes a worker, each worker a soldier, and each soldier a hero that is worth a hundred ordinary soldiers.
—Father Miguel Ramos Arizpe, speech before the
Cortes de Cadiz, November 7, 1811

Chapter One

Making Mexico

INSURGENCY AND SOCIAL ORDER IN BÉXAR

On September 27, 1821, military officials in Béxar lowered the Spanish flag flying over the presidio in Béxar and raised the Mexican flag in its place.[1] The solemn and orderly transfer belied the contentious and often violent rebellion, known as the insurgency, of the preceding decade. On two separate occasions, in 1811 and 1813, insurgents and royal troops had clashed in and around Béxar, affecting the lives of people in the entire region. While the insurgency in Béxar had links and parallels to the greater independence movement in Mexico, it also took on distinctive local characteristics. Those differences stemmed from Béxar's location in the Mexican borderlands and the town's social order, based on Spanish notions of prestige. The year 1821 marked the start of a new period for Bexareños as citizens of the Mexican Republic, even while they continued the colonial social order based on family prestige.

The transition in 1821 is important not just for the change in official national identity but also because of the decade of turmoil that preceded it, starting with the rebellion in 1811. That period of violence revealed elements of the town's social order and the underlying connection between local culture and incipient nationalism. But larger questions remain: what explains Bexareño decisions to support either the insurgency or the Crown or to avoid conflict altogether? To understand Bexareño choices requires an analysis of the extent of dissatisfaction with Spain, the incentives encouraging independence, the decreased barriers to rebel, and internal support for the insurgency. While insurgency provided ideological support for independence on a national scale, local concerns shaped the protests raised by Tejanos and the form of their protest.

The Tejano social order based on family and prestige drove the local response to independence in Béxar. Individuals from the Navarro, Veramendi, and Ruiz families participated in the insurgency for a variety of reasons, from economic to ideological. A brief look at their involvement in this period leading to independence in 1821 illustrates to what extent the insurgency was largely a family affair. José Antonio Navarro joined the rebel cause, as did his uncle Francisco Ruiz.[2] Forty years later, Navarro wrote about this period, noting, "[Mexicans] did not understand the reasons for the rebellion of the priest Hidalgo as [anything] other than a shout for death and war without quarter on the *gachupines*, as the Spaniards were called."[3] Another participant in the rebellion, Juan Martín de Veramendi, married José Antonio's sister, Josefa. Yet these family ties did not easily translate to political affiliation, as the royalist defenders included José Antonio's brother José Angel Navarro.[4]

Two local issues in particular became important at this point and continued to shape Béxar's history after 1811. The first was the social structure informing action and power in the town. The structure itself can be understood through the acquisition of prestige by elite families to maintain their influence and status in the town. Second, Béxar's location on the borderlands placed pressures on its citizens that were different from those experienced by Mexicans in other regions. Proximity to the United States and to indigenously controlled territories fueled the rebellion while raising the stakes of its outcome. Tejanos became skilled at navigating between these borderlands communities and eventually used those interactions as a means to build family prestige within Béxar. This chapter uses the two very different rebellions in 1811 and 1813 as a window into the Bexareño social world and its connection to early Mexican national identity. The two rebellions followed a trajectory connecting established social foundations, defined by prestige, with new cross-cultural relations to Anglo-Americans and indigenous peoples. The 1811 rebellion revealed elements of the existing social hierarchy and the tense relationship between frontier Mexicans and the Spanish Crown. The 1813 rebellion added a layer of ethnic contact, since Anglo-Americans participated in the battles and many Bexareños relied on indigenous support after the war. These developments along the lines of prestige and cultural contact established patterns and practices that shaped the history of the region from independence in 1821 and beyond.

The movement for Mexican independence in the northeast revealed both the nature of region in relation to the rest of the nation and some differences of opinion on how to achieve independence. Insurgent activity produced few large battles in the northeast provinces of New Spain. Nevertheless, differences with royalist officials and peninsular natives living in the region created deep animosity and fueled the movement in the Provincias Internas de Oriente. The insurgency laid the groundwork for the northern region's inclusion in the Mexican nation, despite its often tense and exploitative relation with Mexico City. Mexican independence in 1821 extended the reach and power of the nation-state right up to the northern borderlands. Violence during the early insurgent years demonstrated Spain's tenuous domain over these frontier areas.

Attempts to understand Mexican independence as a broad national movement have failed to explain the diverse development and operation of the insurgency in each region. Father Miguel Hidalgo's initial drive to create a broad-based rebellion among the peasantry faltered as he left the Bajio region on the way to Mexico City.[5] In some areas, such as San Luis Potosi, royalist elites received extra support from rural villagers during the insurrection. Hidalgo never raised a unified revolt under a single ideology in his actions of 1810–11. Instead, the insurgency became a protracted war fought on many fronts and for a variety of reasons. Recent historians have turned to studies of the provinces of Mexico to understand the dynamics of the insurgency and Mexican independence.[6] Events in Béxar and Texas add a unique element to those regional case studies by introducing the border to the insurgency.

Northern Insurgency: Casas in 1811

Every morning, the people of Béxar awoke to the sound of reveille assembling the troops of the presidio.[7] But on the morning of January 22, 1811, secret plans disrupted the daily routine as reveille instead signaled the start of an insurgent plot to arrest the Spanish governor, Manuel Salcedo, and the

The Spanish Governor's Palace door after restoration, 1930. (San Antonio Light Collection, UTSA's Institute of Texan Cultures, No. 1037-I, courtesy of the Hearst Corporation)

military commander, Lieutenant Colonel Simon Herrera, and assemble the soldiers under new leadership. Juan Bautista de las Casas, a retired military officer, took control of those troops and declared himself and Béxar under the command of the newly formed Insurgent Army of America. Two town leaders, the heads of two local elite families, marched alongside Casas on the way to free insurgent messengers from the Alamo prison: Gaspar Flores and Francisco Travieso, the *alcalde* (or mayor) of Béxar. Flores and Travieso's presence gave legitimacy to the coup in the eyes of Bexareños and signaled the deep ambivalence many Tejanos felt about their allegiance to the Spanish Crown.

Travieso recounted his observations of and involvement with Casas and the revolt of 1811 during Casas's trial for high treason. According to Travieso, the soldiers and citizens of Béxar believed rumors that Salcedo and Herrera planned to permanently relocate troops stationed in town to Río Grande, abandoning the defense of Texas and leaving it open to attacks from Indians and Anglo-Americans. Travieso mentioned that "the citizens were equally obliged to render services in the defense of their country; . . . it would be a strange thing, that others from elsewhere were defending their country while the natives looked on indifferently in the case that affected them much more."[8] Travieso's opinion revealed the strong local interests motivating the actions of insurgents in Béxar. During the trial, Travieso claimed that his actions served to aid the colony, Crown, and church by protecting Béxar and Texas from Indians and foreign invaders. Travieso also believed his actions were required to protect the settlers in Texas. As a result, he and other insurgents imprisoned royal authorities and confiscated their property. While Travieso may have obscured some of the reasons for participating in the rebellion for fear of incriminating himself before the government tribunal, his statement underscored the local motivations that influenced many participants in the insurgency in Béxar and in other parts of northeastern Mexico. In this case, the threat of indigenous attacks motivated the rebellion in part.

Before Casas had initiated his revolt, news of Father Hidalgo's proclamation of independence and armed uprising against Spain had reached the northern provinces of New Spain, the Provincias Internas, soon after the Grito de Dolores, Hidalgo's declaration from a church bell tower on September 15, 1810. Hoping to cut off support for the rebellion early, Governor Salcedo called on the inhabitants of the Texas capital to publicly declare their allegiance to the Crown and to their religion.[9] Salcedo attempted to dispel rumors of abandoning Texas and listed the successes of the Spanish government. But unrest continued to spread in the northeast and in Béxar, primarily through the efforts of former military officer Mariano Jiménez. With close ties to Hidalgo, Jiménez organized the insurgent movement in the northeast, from San Luis Potosi northward to the four provinces.[10] Salcedo arrested two alleged agents of Jiménez's plotting to spread the revolution to Béxar. Soon after his coup, Casas moved rapidly to ally with Jiménez as he took control of Béxar.

Jiménez's insurgency occupied several major cities in northeastern Mexico, including Saltillo and Monclova. As Hidalgo and his collaborator Ignacio Allende's losses began to mount in central Mexico, they grew increasingly dependent on the base Jiménez built in the north as an escape to regroup for a later attack. But the inhabitants of northern Mexican towns provided tepid support for the insurgency and likewise provided little resistance to the counterinsurgency that would crush Jiménez and Hidalgo. Insurgent occupation of Béxar provided a crucial link to weapons and mercenary manpower from the border with Louisiana. In this way, the location in the borderlands served both as a resource and as an escape valve for the rebellion, giving the insurgency unique significance in the northern provinces.

Casas's occupation of Béxar lasted for only a short period, from January 22 to March 2, 1811, but his actions brought inhabitants from the northeastern reaches of the Mexican frontier into the national struggle for independence from Spain. Subdeacon Juan José Zambrano led the counterrevolt against Casas in Béxar, using a variety of emissaries to aid the resistance against the wave of insurgent activity in northeastern Mexico. The reestablishment of royalist government in the provinces culminated in an ambush at the Wells of Bajan on March 21, where Jiménez, Hidalgo, and Allende were captured. While the rebellion appeared to be a small skirmish in the larger insurgency, these activities on the northern frontier brought Spanish attention to the potential support insurgents could gain from the connection to the American frontier.[11]

While the actions of the Spanish military commanders in the north quelled the first flash of insurgent revolt in Mexico, unrest continued in the region, albeit in a less organized fashion. Again, Béxar served as the main site for rebel activity. And once again, members of the Travieso family played a role in the rebellion. This time, the participants in the second rebellion, two years later in 1813, availed themselves of the region's economic and political advantages to an even greater extent. In turn, increased numbers of Bexareños now put their lives and futures on the line for the chance to establish an autonomous government.

Casas's revolt in 1811 might appear as a footnote in Hidalgo's larger insurgency movement, yet it also served as a crucial first step that expressed displeasure with specific officials or policies of the Spanish government affecting Béxar.[12] Many features of Casas's actions give the impression that the revolt was primarily a dispute between military commanders. The lack of direct, active participation by the citizens of Béxar precludes calling these events part of a larger social revolution. While Casas set out to confiscate the property of Europeans in Béxar, his revolt lacked any stated ideology and never attempted to restructure society in a comprehensive way.

Nevertheless, the readiness of Bexareños to revolt against royal government officials suggested a growing sense of dissatisfaction with the viceregal government and perhaps the desire for increased political autonomy. To this point, the inhabitants of Béxar easily and rapidly accepted Casas's usurpation of power. But they just as quickly turned on Casas during the installment of a governing junta led by Zambrano. During the revolt and the counterrevolt, the soldiers of the garrison never raised their weapons against their declared leaders or even broke their assembled ranks. How should the citizens' quickness to support winners be interpreted? Were they, as Jesús F. de la Teja has suggested, "not interested in supporting lost causes but rather hoped to preserve and protect the town's interest"?[13]

While practical considerations surely dominated the thinking of Bexareños during these tumultuous moments, the events around them raised questions and possibilities regarding their government and their place in the nation. Two events illustrate the concerns circulating among the citizenry during those days. The first involves a hearing carried out by Lieutenant Miguel Diaz de Luna to investigate reports of rebellious statements shouted in public; the second appears in Governor Salcedo's appeal to Bexareños to disregard Hidalgo's rebellion and to quell any thoughts of insurrection.

On December 11, 1810, reports circulated that ranch hands from Francisco Pereyra's ranch entered Béxar and raised a ruckus by shouting anti-Spanish epithets.[14] The governor rapidly convened a hearing to determine the veracity of these reports and investigate the spread of insurrectionist sentiments in Béxar. Bystanders allegedly overheard the teamsters yelling, "Vivan los peones, y mueran los gachupines!" The teamsters expressed their disdain of *gachupines*, the word used generally for foreigners and specifically for Spaniards. Yet their slogan was ambiguous, combining a class-based attack on local elites with hatred of Spaniards. On December 19, Salcedo's appointed examiner declared his findings inconclusive.

Nevertheless, two weeks later, Governor Salcedo felt compelled to address the town to discredit the propaganda emanating from the Hidalgo rebellion and to reaffirm support among the general population for the Spanish Crown.[15] Speaking to the "Loyal Inhabitants of the Province of Texas," Salcedo urged Bexareños to "prepare with me to build an opposition to that band of infidels, expatriate sons and cowardly soldiers led down a cliff by a criminal caudillo," and to turn in people suspected of spreading the insurrection in town. While Salcedo's response might not have been directly related to the recent investigation of Pereyra's ranch hands, his comments addressed tensions he must have noticed among Bexareños. He first set out to dispel the rumor that the Spanish planned to abandon Texas by moving the military to Río Grande, thus allowing France or the United States to occupy the province. Salcedo suggested that the rumor was part of Hidalgo's plot to overthrow the government, or that Hidalgo might be an operative of the French.

The largest part of Salcedo's address, though, concentrated on extolling the virtues of Spanish rule over Texas and building allegiance to the king among the citizens of Béxar. Regarding Europeans, Salcedo continued, "It cannot be disputed . . . that they have always looked out for you . . . that they have worked alongside you in this beautiful land, sharing in the fruits of their sweat; they undertake the schooling of your children, and guard your haciendas and mines; and lately, they suffer the harshest and heaviest tasks of their duties, . . . and through this means [share] a most sacred and secure trust with you over the arbitrary birth of this or any other land."[16] He emphasized that every European in America was committed to the land like it was their own country, adding that citizens had elected him to represent Texas in the Cortes in Cadiz over local creoles.[17] Salcedo's rhetoric linked the experiences of native Mexicans with immigrant Spaniards, emphasizing these connections over any economic or political benefit possibly derived from independence. By bringing up working the land and teaching children, Salcedo suggested that difference of birthplace paled in comparison to the experiences over the years of toiling on the same land. Finally, Salcedo arrived at his primary critique of Mexican independence: "You want Independence: well, ask yourselves, are you sure you will enjoy it with the disorder which will exist after they vomit the venom of discord; and if the ambition of that same person who now motivates you does not oppress you with the chains of higher taxes, to make up for the bounty, welfare and guarantees of the sweet Spanish government[?]What nation has treated more generously conquered lands and what harm has she caused in this empire?"[18] Salcedo's statements attempted to raise doubts in the minds of Bexareños regarding their desires to change the status quo. No matter how discouraging the existing situation, Salcedo noted, hardships would only increase without Spanish support and largess. His direct language concerning independence indicated that people were discussing the topic among themselves in the province.

These two events, the investigation and Salcedo's speech, more than Casas's rebellion itself, display early evidence of national concerns seeping into the conversations of Bexareños. As quickly as they supported Casas, Bexareños and their representatives in the governing junta jumped to declare their allegiance to Spain and the king. Eventually, Salcedo returned to govern once again, enjoying as much popularity as before by winning another election to represent the region in Cadiz. While Casas paid with his head, the Spanish government absolved all other participants in the rebellion.

Prestige in the Insurgency

At first glance, insurgent battles, rebellions and counterrebellions, evacuations during hostilities, executions, desertions, and changing political leadership during the early nineteenth century give the appearance of chaos and disorder in Béxar. While dealing with political conflicts to the south, Bexareños also engaged in trade and negotiations with indigenous groups to the west and Anglo-Americans to the east. The instability created by the insurgency strained Tejanos' resources and lives, complicating survival on an already difficult frontier. While these external factors suggest that life in Béxar might have been disorderly, Bexareño society was on the contrary rather ordered and well structured. Social hierarchies and interrelationships introduced by colonists and forged on the frontier provided a means to survive these changes and on occasion to end up in a better position after these events. Prestige served as the key element structuring society during this era. The establishment and maintenance of prestige not only dictated the social order but also facilitated Bexareño interactions with various external groups, namely the neighboring indigenous groups and colonizing Anglo-Americans. Building and maintaining prestige among colonial elite families in Béxar took place in much the same way as in other communities throughout New Spain. Much can be learned by looking at research on these other notable families across the region to understand the importance of prestige in Béxar.

Prestige held currency in Tejano society in ways the individual categories of honor and class do not completely capture. The attainment and maintenance of prestige occupied a significant role in elite family strategies. Prestige not only defined these families as notable vis-à-vis the town population but also marked their position within the elite social world. Historians working on Latin American elites have described these networks as institutions critical for the transition out of colonialism. In their collaborative work on notability in Latin America, historians Diana Balmori, Stuart F. Voss, and Miles Wortman have elevated the concept of family history to a level at times on par with other key institutions in Latin America. They note: "But because of the relative vacuum of sociopolitical structures in the nineteenth century and through their own creative adaptations to it, they created a network that functioned as a social organization in its own right. [These families] may be the pivot around which Latin American history moved from the late colonial period through the early twentieth century."[19] In the case of Béxar, prestige among elite Tejano families had the added task of facilitating interactions with Anglo-Americans and indigenous groups on the northern Mexican frontier.

The values wound up in prestige involve a wide variety of public and private elements of social life. Social standing was publicly gauged and effected through several colonial institutions, mainly the Catholic church and local and state government. Privately, elite families used marriage to create alliances with other local and regional elites to extend their domain. These practices built around prestige shaped Béxar's social order and influenced the ways Bexareños engaged the world outside. For example, prominent Bexareño Francisco Ruiz had a sister, María Josefa Ruiz, who married the merchant Angel Navarro in 1783.[20] Navarro and Ruiz had several children, including José Antonio Navarro, who with his uncle Francisco Ruiz took leadership roles in Béxar and Texas.

While family history has generally played an important role in the field, it has mostly been limited to anthropologic interest in questions around culture and the formation of national identity.[21] Balmori, Voss, and Wortman define notability through the establishment of family networks that are "associations of families allied through business, marriage, spatial proximity, and later through membership in organizations."[22] Their analysis relies on charting the development of these family networks through three generations, each generation growing in status and importance to the region. As the Spanish colonial regime collapsed in the mid-nineteenth century, they note that the second generation assumed the duties of the state.[23] Local power through municipal posts, such as *corregidor* or *alcalde*, eventually translated into regional and sometimes national power for the families in their study. The Seguín family, led by patriarch Erasmo Seguín, gained prestige and importance in Béxar through these private and public means.

Along with their public presence, notable families also extended their status through marriage with other local and regional elites. Through a process of diversification, marriages were seen as a way to firm up or improve wealth and social standing in the community. As Balmori, Voss, and Wortman point out, "The alliances were often complementary: those with mercantile holdings married those with land; those with land wed those with capital or urban properties, a military command (which sometimes implied access to new land for settlement) or a political post. These combinations were crucial."[24] Several historians have detailed the development of elite family networks for several states in Northern Mexico.[25] In each of these case studies, families or groups of families amassed power and regional prestige to levels that required attention by national institutions. Marriages between elite families served as a basis for strengthening political power and expanding the economic reach of these families.

Since prestige functioned at the family level, it allowed women to play a significant role in amassing and keeping power. While men presented the public and political face of the family almost exclusively, women used their position to handle the everyday business of influence in the community. María Josefa Becerra, Erasmo Seguín's wife, became involved in domestic and political affairs in Béxar during Don Erasmo's frequent trips to Saltillo and Mexico City as part of his public positions. Doña María Josefa often passed information from Erasmo to other officials in Béxar during these trips.[26] Her importance in the family also came from her relation to prominent Bexareño Gaspar Flores. Flores, who was mayor and councilman on several occasions, was her uncle.

The disruption caused later by the 1813 rebellion exposed Béxar's social order and its reliance on these well-established practices around prestige. With elite Tejano families such as the Traviesos and Seguíns taking prominent positions during the early insurgent battles, Béxar's social order dictated how the rebellion spread in town and the ways Bexareños dealt with the consequences. As was the case with both the 1811 and 1813 insurgent battles, the movement to rebel was organized outside of Béxar and Texas; however, the movements connected with people and ideas inside Bexareño society. The success and failure of the movements relied on their ability to garner support from Tejano elites. Being Mexican elites themselves, Casas and another northern insurgent leader, Bernardo Gutiérrez de Lara, each recognized these points of entry into the social world of Béxar.

When Casas paraded his troops before the town in 1811, he marched with Travieso and Flores at his side. Their participation was necessary since Casas came from outside the town and region. Without their presence, Casas would have been an invader, imposing his will on the town regardless of his anti-Spanish motives. Local elite participation was more than symbolic; it plugged Casas into the existing social order in Béxar. Members of the general population opened themselves up to Casas because they understood their role in the rebellion in relation to the social hierarchy implicit in prestige. Elite status was built up through a wide variety of connections with non-elites, including employment, patronage, and *compadrazgo*. Important families often served as godparents to children in numerous families. In this way, *compadrazgo*, or godparentage, created another constituency supporting elite families.

The following description of broad participation in Gutiérrez's rebellion in 1813 makes this point even more clearly. The social breakdown of insurgent activity through home type suggests that at least two-thirds were not elites. Their decision to join the insurgency along with the Béxar elites needs to be seen in the context of social order. In other words, just because these Bexareños were rebelling against Spain didn't mean they were abandoning the social relationships forged over decades on the frontier. Instead, those social relationships encouraged and shaped Bexareño participation. Undoubtedly, many non-elites joined Bexareño elites because of their deep ties. This came despite the sizable Anglo-American participation in Gutiérrez's rebellion. Again, what could have been perceived as a rebellion from outside gained importance internally through the participation by elites.

Finally, the social order remained in place after the rebellions and continued to serve as the gateway for politics in Béxar. Erasmo Seguín's rapid reinstatement in town governance despite his position against Spain demonstrates government recognition of prestige for maintaining authority. Several years into the insurgency, as Spanish resources for the frontier defense dwindled, the same elites who had raised arms in 1813 paid the salaries of the presidial soldiers. Ultimately, the smooth, unremarkable transition to independence in 1821 was testament to the resilience of Béxar's social order and its ability to assimilate political changes. That ability would be tested repeatedly over the following decades.

Resurgent Insurgents: Gutiérrez de Lara in 1813

While the 1811 rebellion provided some insight into Béxar's social order, a second rebellion two years later exposed even more of the town's social structure and its deep links to incipient nationalism. Insurgent forces relied on Texas since its border location provided access to munitions and mercenaries. While Hidalgo, Allende, and other leaders failed to reach the frontier to regroup their rebellion, other insurgents managed to use the northeastern borderland to continue harassing the royalist government. In late 1812, the northeastern provinces witnessed renewed attacks, but unlike the previous rebellion, the royalist counterattack came stronger and more violently. Also, the insurgent movement had gained a larger base of support among civilians as well as military officers. More people lost their lives or were forced into hiding in this second wave of rebellion. The regional commander, General Joaquín de Arredondo, replaced the cooperative spirit between Spanish and Mexicans expressed by Salcedo with demands for strict loyalty and obedience to the Crown and the Spanish government.

In 1813, Béxar found itself once again occupied by insurgents claiming independence from Spain.[27] The new leader, Bernardo Gutiérrez de Lara, born in Revilla, Nuevo Santander, spent most his life in the Provincias Internas. Gutiérrez initiated his independence activities during the failed Casas and Jiménez rebellions of 1811. After the defeat of Jiménez, Gutiérrez headed to northeastern Texas, outside of Nacogdoches, to discuss the benefits of a free Mexico with the local indigenous tribes. While in the territory between the United States and Spain, Gutiérrez witnessed the growing interest among Anglo-Americans to migrate into Texas and establish an independent republic with closer mercantile ties to the United States.

In January 1812, Gutiérrez traveled to Washington, D.C., passing through Tennessee and Kentucky along the way. While in those states, Gutiérrez received even greater support in the form of volunteers for any expedition he might want to undertake in Texas. Once in Washington, Gutiérrez met with Secretary of State James Monroe to request American troops in order to establish a republic in Texas. The American government made an offer to aid Gutiérrez in liberating Mexico but under the condition that the western border in Louisiana would be extended to the Río Grande, making Texas part of the United States. Gutiérrez stood his ground regarding Texas, emphasizing that fact in subsequent writings. While on the East Coast, Gutiérrez also met with Cuban exile José Alvarez de Toledo. Toledo held similar aspirations for the independence for Cuba and had already established contact with Miguel Ramos Arizpe regarding autonomy for the Provincias Internas.

Gutiérrez left Washington without troops but with important contacts in Louisiana to help establish his army. Basing his operations in Natchitoches, Louisiana, Gutiérrez gathered a force of mostly Anglo-American mercenaries led by Agustus Magee, who had recently resigned his commission as lieutenant in the United States Army. In August 1812, the "Republican Army of the North," comprising mostly Anglo-American soldiers and a significant number of Mexican deserters from the Spanish military, invaded the frontier outpost of Nacogdoches. While occupying Nacogdoches, Gutiérrez and Magee regrouped and increased their forces while sending revolutionary propaganda to Béxar and towns along the Río Grande. Gutiérrez prepared the way for his advancement southward by informing insurgents of his plans.

Before advancing to Béxar, though, Gutiérrez and Magee occupied the presidio of La Bahía on November 7, 1812. Once again, Spanish troops split and either joined the rebel army or retreated to Béxar. At La Bahía, Gutiérrez met resistance from the royalist army led by Salcedo and Herrera. Several soldiers turned against the royalist army, hastening the royalist retreat to Béxar. Magee died during the occupation of La Bahía, elevating Samuel Kemper to a leadership position with Gutiérrez. The forces advanced to Béxar in late March 1813, again meeting opposition from Salcedo at the Salado River, thirteen miles southeast of Béxar. Governor Salcedo's troops lost at the battle of Salado, retreating to the presidio in Béxar and leaving their supplies for the insurgent army to take.

Gutiérrez approached Béxar on April 1, 1813, forwarding the terms of surrender to Salcedo on his way into town the next day. Salcedo asked that the citizens of Béxar be treated well and not be unduly taxed or looted by the occupying forces. He also requested that his army be allowed to leave Béxar to retreat to Spanish-held towns to the south. Gutiérrez agreed to the conditions but denied Salcedo permission to leave with his troops. Gutiérrez arrested Salcedo and Herrera upon entering the town and ordered them sent to Matagorda Bay to later be incarcerated in the United States. However, the insurgents executed Salcedo and Herrera just outside of Béxar.

The executions of Salcedo and Herrera raised suspicions among the Anglo-American soldiers of the occupying force. The actions of Gutiérrez in the early days of the invasion also discouraged their support of the rebellion. Soon after the capture of Béxar, Gutiérrez wrote a declaration of independence and a constitution for the new republic. While the declaration echoed many of the concepts introduced to Gutiérrez by his Anglo-American advisors, two aspects of the constitution made his American supporters especially nervous. The first stated that Texas formed "a part of the Mexican Republic, to which it remains inviolably joined."[28] The second involved the constitution's stated objective of continuing Spanish-style government in the new republic. Gutiérrez named himself president with ultimate authority over the decisions of the appointed governing junta.

The occupation of Béxar lasted from April through August 1813, ending with the defeat of Gutiérrez's Republican Army of the North in a battle with General Arredondo's forces at the Medina River on August 18. While he held Béxar, Gutiérrez continued to attempt to spread the insurgency through the northern provinces and met with limited success in several towns on the Río Grande. But he never persuaded any Spanish governors or other leaders to join his movement. Disaffection with Gutiérrez grew among Anglo-Americans as they became discouraged by his governing style and among Mexicans when they heard rumors, leaked by José Alvarez Toledo's agents, that Gutiérrez planned on giving Texas to the Americans.[29] Eventually, Gutiérrez lost power, and Toledo led the army in its final battle at Medina.

Arredondo defeated the insurgents so thoroughly that he drove them out of Béxar and sent his officer from Laredo to chase those fleeing beyond Nacogdoches. Almost two hundred families escaped from Béxar northward. Arredondo imprisoned many others, executing 327 insurgents within two weeks and confining their families to barracks. During the counter-insurgent sweep of the northern portion of the territory, 71 insurgents were shot and hundreds others captured. Arredondo's counterrevolution ensured that Texas would remain Spanish territory until the consummation of Mexican independence in 1821. But Arredondo's peace came at the cost of the lives of a large portion of the province, leaving the remaining population to rebuild their town and livelihood for almost a decade. Despite the insurgent defeat, the events of 1811 and 1813 brought Béxar, Bexareños, and the frontier into the debate for national sovereignty. Bexareños relied on and reinforced existing social networks in the process of staking those claims.

Lessons from Insurgent Defeat

The differences between the insurgent occupation of Béxar in 1813 and the previous revolt in 1811 left evidence of the social dimensions of the rebellion. First, the second rebellion included significant participation by Anglo-Americans, which provides clues about Tejano attitudes toward Anglos in the independence process. Were Gutiérrez and other insurgents simply naive about Anglo-American intentions after the war, or did Anglo participation fit within an existing continuum of cooperation and exchange between Tejanos and Anglos? Tejano engagement with Anglo-Americans reinforced elements of a social hierarchy based on prestige by empowering notable *vecinos* to negotiate tensions. Second, more Béxar *vecinos* fled the 1813 royalist counterattack than in 1811. In their trail, they left a snapshot of the cross-class nature of Bexareño insurgent involvement. Both observations indicate a shift in the attitudes and social makeup of those who had sought independence two years earlier.

Anglo involvement in this rebellion began with Gutiérrez's trip to Washington while he prepared for the rebellion in Texas. During his journey to the U.S. capital, Gutiérrez witnessed American excitement for participation in his army. Gutiérrez wrote later, "I found them [Americans] all attentive to our just cause. . . . The rest of the people, principally in Kentucky and Tennessee, but did not even want me to proceed, wishing me to remain there, and saying that they would make up a considerable army of volunteers."[30] While Gutiérrez might have believed that the idea of justice motivated these Americans, he also undoubtedly observed their desire for land in Texas; as noted above, Secretary of State Monroe directly asked Gutiérrez to deliver Texas to the United States.[31] Though Gutiérrez swiftly turned down the offer, American designs on Texas lingered through Gutiérrez's entire campaign. Gutiérrez blamed American aspirations for Texas for the growing opposition to his plan to spread the revolt beyond Béxar. He felt that the governing junta "allowed themselves to be deceived by those refined rascals whose crooked methods and innumerable intrigues I well knew."[32] Gutiérrez interpreted Anglo opposition to liberate all of Mexico to be based on the difficulty of separating Texas from what would be an independent Mexico.

Suspicion of Anglo motivations surfaced in voices from both sides of the rebellion, as seen when Governor Salcedo attempted to keep Tejanos from joining the revolt. His 1812 address following the capture of Nacogdoches by insurgent forces emphasized the Anglo-American role in the rebellion.[33] He mentioned a request received from the viceroy for troops "to defend our Holy Religion and to keep your property free from taxes and free from the grasp of ambitious foreigners." Salcedo then described the Anglo threat principally in religious terms. He declared "before the Almighty" that he would

> die before allowing His sacred temples and Divine Images [to] be [defiled] by the Lutherans and the rest of the heretics and Protestants, who try to seduce you from your loyalty and Catholicism. This same declaration should be made with me by all those who are Catholics and vassals of Fernando VII. Flee, then, from our ranks cowards and traitors and reunite with the band of heretics which only come to fulfill their ambition for the silver and gold of this Kingdom: go live among them lawlessly, without fear of God; and deliver yourself to all matter of sins; but await the indubitable drubbing from the Highest to die full of misery, desperation and worthlessness from Heaven and earth.

Salcedo's comments transformed the insurgents' desires for independence into a moral dilemma. By draping his plea in religious language, Salcedo concentrated on the close link Tejanos maintained between Catholicism and their political identities.[34] Rather than simply demonizing Anglos, and thus only employing nationalist sentiment, Salcedo's statements used a language and system of symbols more easily accessible and understood by Tejanos at the time. However, Salcedo also emphasized the notion circulating among some in Béxar that Anglos held values antithetical to their own. He labeled Anglos as land- and moneygrubbing and warned Tejanos not to be fooled by their promises. Salcedo's assessment of Anglo-American character, while not held by all Tejanos, needs to be situated in the spectrum of Tejano representations of Anglos. By linking the Gutiérrez rebellion to American expansion, Salcedo preyed on existing Tejano skepticism of Anglo-Americans in their midst.

Anglo-American participation in the 1813 rebellion introduced the problem of how ethnicity would figure into national identity. While Béxar's location on the borderlands with the United States meant Bexareños had existing commercial and personal contact with Anglo-Americans, the insurgency added nation-building to the incentives for contact. Though grounded in the colonial experiences between Spaniards, indigenous peoples, and other Atlantic groups, independence temporarily expanded the possibilities for inclusion into Mexican identity.

Salcedo urged Bexareños to fight against the insurgency for a second time in an address to "the defenders of the Mexican Kingdom." He noted their heroic stand on March 2, 1811, exonerating them from their earlier disloyalty. Salcedo concluded, perhaps overly optimistically, that "I will receive the necessary aid to direct our operations; if you are obedient to the Government orders and disclose the traitors which intend to perpetuate things contrary to the public tranquility: I am sure that if these things are done we shall triumph over the enemies of Religion and Nation." Despite his requests for supplies and troops, Salcedo received few reinforcements from the government.[35] Ultimately, many Bexareños put aside their doubts regarding Anglo-Americans to participate in the insurgency with Gutiérrez.

Insurgents like Gutiérrez and others joining his forces also decided to ignore their doubts about American designs on Texas. While Tejano participants might have weighed Anglo cooperation against the risk of losing Texas, they nevertheless chose to join with Anglos to resist Spain. It should be noted, though, that cooperation only extended as far as the battleground; for example, Mexican insurgents appointed only two Anglos to the seven-member governing junta.[36] The battleground itself became a segregated place when, in his final defeat at the Medina River, Toledo divided the insurgent forces into separate Anglo and Mexican units.[37]

Many of those Bexareños who participated in the insurgency left behind their property and possessions when they retreated from Arredondo's counterattack. In a report to Cristóbal Dominguez, the governor of Texas, José Antonio Saucedo and Luis Galán listed the names of owners of abandoned houses and land.[38] The names on the list identified participants in the insurgency in Béxar beyond the vocal leaders and provided clues to their socioeconomic status by noting the type of home each insurgent owned. The list identified only those compelled to leave the city as a result of their role in the uprising. Bexareños sympathetic to the insurgency but not overtly participating in the revolt probably remained on their land and did not appear on the list. Nevertheless, a clearer picture of the shape and appeal of the insurgency in this region of New Spain appeared through the report.

Saucedo and Galán's list contained ninety-two names, including five female homeowners, and details regarding landholdings and type of house, usually either a *casa de piedra* (brick house) or a *jacal* (a structure built from natural material from the local surroundings).[39] A few houses stood out from these two styles, especially the *casa de madera* (wooden house) on the higher end of the building spectrum and the *chamacuero* (hide house) on the lower end. Two-thirds of those listed left behind a *jacal*, and the number grows to three-quarters with the inclusion of *chamacueros*. The other

The Veramendi Palace, ca. 1870. (UTSA's Institute of Texan Cultures, No. 81-500, courtesy of Thomas W. Cutrer)

quarter lived in the stronger structures, primarily in the *casas de piedra*, with five living in *casas de madera*.[40] Several of those who left behind these sturdier buildings probably owned multiple houses or *jacales* along with their primary residence.

The distribution of evacuated dwellings suggests that non-elite Bexareños made up a high percentage of the insurgents. But at least twenty-four of those who left the city belonged to the elite, who abandoned a great amount of wealth. Thus, the leaders of the insurgency in Béxar apparently counted on a significant base of support among all social classes in the city. More important, these segments of society developed enough resentment toward the Crown to act upon their sentiments. The insurgency movement in Béxar could not be simply classified as either an elite replacement of authority, since many members of the lower classes participated in the movement, or a popular revolt, since several elites had prominent roles. Ultimately, the number of individuals on Saucedo and Galán's report constitutes less than 10 percent of the entire town population.

The insurgents who left Béxar in August 1813 moved to a variety of places north of town. Some went to Nacogdoches, a town held by rebels only a few

Children standing in front of a typical jacal *in San Antonio, 1889. (Courtesy of the San Antonio Conservation Society Foundation, Raba Collection)*

days longer than Béxar. Others entered the United States and took temporary residence in Natchitoches or New Orleans. And some availed themselves of friendships with Indian tribes in the north, spending their time in Indian settlements, or *rancherias*. In all these cases, insurgents benefited from the porous and fluid nature of the borderlands region. Arredondo recaptured the capital of Texas, but the Spanish government could not control all aspects of life in the hinterlands.

While Arredondo reconquered the province swiftly and decisively, killing many of the high-ranking rebels, he crafted compromises to govern effectively. By the following month, Arredondo began issuing pardons to most participants in the rebellion.[41] Many accepted his offer and began trickling back into Béxar soon after the dust had settled. While Arredondo denied pardons to such prominent citizens as those in the Arocha, Travieso, Veramendi, and Seguín families, exceptions became the rule. Erasmo Seguín returned within the next year, not only asking for a pardon but also appealing charges of sedition on grounds that insurgents coerced him, under duress, to sign letters supporting Toledo.[42] Seguín sought the pardon in order to continue his commercial relationship with his business in Saltillo.

Seguín managed to negotiate his way through the complex political situation in the northern provinces. Time and again, he used his knowledge of the prevailing social climate to maintain leadership positions in Texas. After the rebellion of 1813, Seguín had fled Béxar to Natchitoches in Louisiana, leaving behind a *casa de piedra* and some cattle. But eventually, Seguín regained his political status in Béxar. For example, he served as a court official by deposing witnesses in a case brought by a woman to regain the house she had fled after Arredondo's counterrevolt.[43] Juana Martinez left Béxar with her husband and sons, leaving behind a house and some agricultural land with water allotments. After royalists recaptured Béxar, Governor Dominguez gave her house to the widow of a soldier killed in combat. Martinez claimed that she and her family had fled for their lives based on rumors of Arredondo's retribution.

Arredondo used pardons in a variety of ways throughout the region. In February 1815, Arredondo issued an order giving amnesty to deserters from the army living in the hinterlands around Saltillo.[44] Arredondo gave the troops fifteen days to return and substituted the usual penalty with community service. As a stronger incentive, deserters captured after the deadline would be sent to serve in the military of Texas for ten years, or for eight years in Veracruz. Arredondo allowed most Mexicans to return, although not without a lengthy cross-examination to give their pretext and demonstrate loyalty to the Crown.[45] Most did so and in the process rebuilt and reconstituted Béxar's social world.

From August 1813 until Mexican independence and the transfer of power to Agustín Iturbide in 1821, the Provincias Internas de Oriente remained relatively free of the large-scale uprisings seen in the first three years of the insurgency. Arredondo frequently mentioned the "tranquillity" of the region in his public decrees.[46] But peace came at a considerable price for Arredondo, requiring him to spend three-quarters of his military budget on Texas over the three other provinces under his command.[47] In a letter to the viceroy, Arredondo expressed fear that the other provinces, finding themselves in the same state of poverty and danger, would protest the budget.

Regardless of the amount spent by Spain on the military in Texas, conditions improved little after the devastating conflict in 1813. In May 1814, the commanding officer of Béxar wrote to Arredondo to describe the deplorable condition of the town.[48] The letter commented on the woeful state of Béxar's inhabitants, noting that most of them seemed unwilling to even plan for the future, "taking advantage of what they can to scrape by for daily sustenance." He complained that the troops of the regiment under his command ate only meat, and only occasionally a tortilla. Troops stationed in towns throughout the four provinces relied on local citizens to supply them with many of their daily supplies. During lean years, inhabitants often volunteered food and mules to maintain the military presence in town.

In Béxar, inhabitants believed their situation was so distressing that supplying the army became a larger burden than they could bear. On February 1816, the Ayuntamiento (town council) of Béxar reiterated that the town's poverty prevented them from supplying the army with meat.[49] Furthermore, the army burdened Bexareños by asking them to supply firewood for the hospital and provide carts and mules on demand. The Ayuntamiento added, "The few inhabitants which remain in town [after the restoration of the royalist government] have been left to supply the troops of the garrison with meat, when even their own homes have been so depleted of beef that it requires much more work to acquire the amount needed for the troops." The Ayuntamiento also noted the difficult situation brought upon the town by frequent Indian attacks at its outskirts.

Arredondo justified his expenditures on the military in Texas as necessary to repel Anglo-American filibusters and inhibit contraband on the border.[50] Anglo-American military excursions loomed over the region throughout this period before independence, affecting Arredondo's policies. Incursions led by James Long, Henry Perry, and other American and French mercenaries required constant vigilance by Spanish authorities. During the cross-examination of an insurgent seeking a pardon, the government sought to know the activities of Americans on the border.[51] The informant replied, "In the port of Natchitoches, there is a small fort and about 200 troops which had recently arrived. . . . I heard talk that the Americans had the desire to rescue or make of their land up to the Rio Grande." Maintaining the frontier of the empire proved to be Arredondo's biggest undertaking. These local networks and connections between Tejanos and Anglo-Americans only grew as the insurgency in Texas raised the possibilities of further contact. Béxar's social order based on prestige and negotiation facilitated these connections with Anglo-Americans, and later with indigenous groups, on the frontier.

In the waning years of the empire in Mexico, Arredondo began to understand the complexities of the province's problems. He realized that paying soldiers would not solve Mexican merchants' demand for contraband and wealth from the United States.[52] He proffered his solution, writing, "The province will be protected through other means, such as the opening of a port on the Gulf of Mexico, increasing the population. They will bring with them the arts and industry, commerce and prosperity which is offered by that other vast and ferocious nation." Arredondo's formula for improving the province through increased population echoed Ramos Arizpe's statements at the Cortes ten years before. Population and colonization would continue to be significant issues in the development of Texas, although the development often followed unforeseen lines.

Social Order after Independence

Despite the turmoil caused by the battles in 1811 and 1813, Bexareños kept their social order largely intact through independence in 1821. Instead of having their social practices disrupted, Bexareños relied on them to weather the changes that came with independence. Independence resulted in a power shift from the Crown to local leaders and institutions. That shift made existing hierarchies and other modes of interaction critical to making the Mexican nation-state meaningful at the local level and to forging a connection to the nation.

In the years after 1821, Mexico underwent a series of political changes that brought Bexareño social and political leadership into the nation-state building process. Agustín Iturbide's government ran into opposition as elites from around the nation demanded more input through a legislative system. Iturbide abdicated his position in 1823 just as a convention had been called to write a federalist constitution. This period between Iturbide's departure and the formal ratification of the constitution in 1824 left the nation in the hands of local leadership. These changes allowed more regional elites to take political positions. For instance, Bexareño José Antonio Saucedo's support for the Crown brought him into the local government.[53] After independence, Saucedo rose to govern Texas as *jefe politico* and to institute policies based on his life on the frontier.

On March 23, 1823, leaders from every institution in Béxar signed an oath promising not to obey any further orders from Iturbide.[54] The letter contained fifty-five signatures from representatives of "the honorable Ayuntamiento, the state Capital, the Officers of troops and the barracks, the honorable Clergy and all the Citizens signed below." The letter not only provides a snapshot of leadership in Béxar but also reveals male dominance in the public political sphere prevalent at the time. A directory of power appears in the signatories; among them were José Felix Trespalacios, general commander; the Baron de Bastrop, mayor; Miguel Arciniega, José María Sambrano, José Antonio de la Garza, Erasmo Seguín, Gaspar Flores, José Cardenas, Angel Navarro, and Ygnacio Villaseñor, city officials; Juan Martín de Veramendi,[55] customs official; Francisco Ruiz, Indian administrator; Father José Antonio Díaz de Leon, overseer of missions; José Flores, José Antonio Navarro, José María Delgado, Joaquín Saenz, Francisco Ariola, Juan José Zambrano, Ignacio Chavez, and José Antonio Salinas, citizens; and Mariano Rodríguez, Juan José Sanchez, Martín Cuello, José Antonio Saucedo, and Juan N. Almonte, military officers. These men held public positions in the community and maintained extensive family connections in the larger region. Their ability to assert authority at a moment when national political structures seemed absent demonstrates the interaction between prestige and maintaining social order.

While the insurgency exposed the social elements of Béxar's innerworkings through politics and prestige, other categories of identity also figured into structuring the social order. Like much of the rest of Spain's American colonies, Bexareños also distinguished among themselves along lines of race, caste, and religion.[56] Perhaps the principal distinctions made at the time lay somewhere between European and Indian identity. The next chapter develops that range of social identities in greater detail. Yet prestige implied more than political and economic power, as seen through the significance of honor and purity in the social scheme. Recent work on the *gracias al sacar* (purchased legitimations) in colonial Latin America has introduced the central role legitimacy and race played in the way elites situated themselves in the social order.[57] In the colonial period, holding public office often required proof of legitimate birth granted by the Catholic church. It appears that court battles over legitimacy decided political and economic power. Statutes regarding *limpieza de sangre* ("cleaning blood" or "pure blood") raised additional barriers to approval, including faith, race, ancestry, and good standing in the church.[58] It is through one of these cases of *limpieza de sangre* that these values among the elite of Béxar on the eve of Anglo-American colonization first surface.

Limpieza de sangre procedures originated in fifteenth-century Spain as a tool in the crusade against Jews.[59] These hearings certified the subject's social standing along several broad lines, including race and legitimate birth. In order to establish this, several witnesses introduced testimony vouching for their knowledge of the subject's case. Witnesses were asked questions regarding the subject's parents, grandparents, appearance, and conduct in the community. Evidence of a *limpieza de sangre* hearing in Béxar in 1824 demonstrates that these practices continued beyond the colonial period. The case also shows the continued interest in maintaining good standing in a defined, legalistic manner among the Tejano elite.

The Béxar case was presented by Mariano Rodríguez, a "vecino de esta Ciudad," in the name of his son, José María Rodríguez. At the time, José María was attending the seminary in Monterrey.[60] Rodríguez presented documents and asked five Bexareños to testify to the validity of his marriage to María de Jesús Carbajal and that they were from their town. Being married to a member of the Carbajal family meant having a higher status, as it was one of Béxar's founding families.[61] The witnesses also had to verify that Rodríguez's parents were "noticeably white people and of clear birth, cleansed of all bad races of Moors, Jews, Negros and Mulattos, and they were Christians and not recent converts to the Holy Catholic Faith."[62] They were also asked to verify that the family had not been sanctioned or corrected by the Catholic church. While Rodríguez's petition involved church requirements for seminary attendance, questions of purity of blood reveal attention to racial concerns.

The *limpieza de sangre* hearing serves as a point of convergence for several elements defining prestige for elite families. First, interest in ancestry and legitimate birth emphasize the importance of status and marriage for past and present generations. Inquiry into the status of parents and grandparents were used to prove the status of the subject and, by extension, perpetuate these values into future marriages. As historian Ann Twinam points out, legitimate birth functioned as a baseline requirement for public office and social standing in colonial New Spain.[63] Second, attention to the grandparents' race underscored the caste elements of social status. Yet, the process required only testimony as to the race of the grandparents and not any kind of documentation. This suggests that racial categories themselves were fairly pliable in this point in Mexican history. Third, requirements of good standing in the Catholic church added an element of propriety policed by the church. Not only was legitimate birth necessary, but continued observance of the rules of Catholicism were also required. Finally, by asking for the testimony of five Bexareños, the petition added the element of notable family networks or an elite community. Rodríguez included testimony by Vicente Gortary, Clemente Delgado, José Antonio de la Garza, José Flores, and Manuel Jiménez in the document. Their participation gives a sense of the interrelations among these families in maintaining prestige.

The social world of Bexareños developed in the borderlands as an extension of Spanish colonial society. Like much of Latin America, their social order depended on a shared understanding of prestige built on wealth, political importance, personal connections, *compadrazgo*, and race. As a frontier town, Béxar incorporated additional factors in its social order. Frequent exchange with indigenous groups in the region combined with a variety of internal Indian identities resulted in a broad yet fluid range of identities centered on an Indian past and present.

Local manifestations of national independence movements reveal as much about the structure and operation of the town as they do the broader geopolitical forces affecting life there. In the case of Béxar, the rebellions in 1811 and 1813 happened because of several internal and external factors. Social networks based on prestige provided a ready structure for insurgent politics to operate with relative ease. Be it insurgents or royal authorities, the acquisition and maintenance of power in Béxar rested in the hands of a handful of elite families. Those families in turn established and maintained their status by building their prestige within the community and by controlling outsiders' access to the town.

The following two chapters provide further evidence of the importance of prestige to make sense of Bexareño motivations in this period. Beginning with relations to indigenous groups and continuing through Anglo-American immigration into Texas, Béxar's elites used their abilities to negotiate with various groups to improve life in the region as they saw fit. *Limpieza de sangre* cases show the interdependence of social order with racial hierarchy. In the course of maintaining their social standing, Tejano elites asserted a national—and later ethnic—identity related to the extension of the Mexican nation-state into the borderlands.

We desire to be together as one people,
and share the same sympathies as our Mexican
brothers, and we should never go back on our promises.
—Cherokee chief, letter to Indian commissioner
Peter Ellis Bean, July 2, 1828

Chapter Two

Indigenous Identities

LOCATING "LO INDIO" IN THE TEJANO WORLD

When prominent Bexareño Francisco Ruiz presented his report to General Manuel Mier y Terán on Indians living in the Department of Texas in 1828, his observations carried the weight of a native of the region and an individual involved in indigenous relations as an agent and soldier. His notes distinguished between dozens of indigenous groups with an eye toward the possibilities of peace and alliance or war. Of the Lipan Apache, Ruiz wrote, "In my opinion, the southern Lipans [Apache] are the most cruel of all the barbaric nations I know. . . . I have been told by some of these Indians that they sometimes eat those they kill in war."[1] By describing them as cannibals, Ruiz depicted Apaches as cruel and barbaric. His words also enlarged the cultural gulf between Apaches and Mexicans by marking the Apaches as dishonorable in warfare and, by extension, unmasculine.[2] While Ruiz's general comments focused on indigenous groups living in the Béxar hinterland, Ruiz wrote from within the context of Béxar and its significant mestizo and mission Indian population.

Portrait of Francisco Ruiz. (UTSA's Institute of Texan Cultures, No. 86-184, courtesy of Mrs. Ruby Hermes)

How might Ruiz's social and personal context have shaped his thoughts on indigenous cultures?

Ruiz's activity among indigenous groups illustrates the complexity of relations between Mexicans and Indians. After the insurgent defeat in 1813, many rebel Tejanos fled northward out of Béxar and into the large part of the province occupied by indigenous peoples. This land, sometimes called

"Comanchería" by Mexicans after its most populous indigenous group, provided an anonymous and safe haven for rebels escaping the reach of the Spanish military. As an active Mexican insurgent, Ruiz lived among the Comanches for eight years until independence.[3] Later, he used his connections to and knowledge of Comanches to serve as the Indian commissioner in Texas for the Mexican government. His ties to Comanche people might explain his harsh depiction of Apache people in his report, since Comanche groups were often at war with them.

Reports coming back to Spanish officials in Béxar and to General Joaquín de Arredondo in Monterrey located Ruiz and other insurgents hiding out in the hinterlands around Nacogdoches in 1814.[4] The Spanish government feared that these insurgents would unite with other rebels living in the United States or with indigenous tribes to mount another attack on the capital of Texas. While the reports never identified a new movement, they mentioned the commerce and treaties established between the northern groups, such as Comanches, and Ruiz and his fellow insurgents. Later descriptions of Comanche culture by Ruiz suggest that his relationship with them extended beyond trading, perhaps to include living in the Comanche camp for a lengthy time or even marrying into a Comanche family.

Ruiz's stay among the Comanches contradicts general portrayals of them as wild, violent savages, intent on killing or enslaving any non-Comanche.[5] The historical record, however, suggests a much more complex picture. Ruiz's friendship with Comanches came not as an anomaly but as a result of an Indian policy initiated by the Crown in the eighteenth century and continued in effect by Bexareños. Ruiz's actions during this period appear more significant after noting his status as one of two Tejano signers of the Texas Declaration of Independence in 1836 and later as a senator in the Texas Republic legislature. Born in Béxar in 1783, Ruiz cultivated relationships across cultures and nations, situating himself as a broker on the frontier. Ruiz's success in this complex social world required a deep understanding of the cultural nuances existing among these peoples. Growing up in the frontier town of Béxar afforded Ruiz the opportunity to learn this rich context by example.

Bexareños' lives were immersed and embedded in a broader indigenous world. That world extended from the intimacy of intermarriage and *mestizaje* to wars and the diplomacy of peace treaties with nomadic groups.[6] While the meaning of the term *indio* differed, indigenous identification appeared almost everywhere. Just what "Indian" meant varied over place and time, to the extent that in 1821, *indio*, "Indian" in Spanish, held several meanings specific to Béxar and the Mexican north. Interaction with and incorporation of indigenous peoples play as central a role in Mexican identity as slavery and race do in American history.[7] It is worth laying out the interrelations between Mexican and Indian worlds in the 1820s to understand the contextual nature of identity.

The decline of the mission system in Béxar ushered in a new era in the indigenous world. By the 1820s, Bexareños and indigenous groups could no longer be considered strangers. Almost three centuries had transpired since the first recorded contact between Spaniards and indigenous peoples took place in Texas, when Alvar Nuñez Cabeza de Vaca spent years living among them.[8] In 1821, Bexareños, many of whom considered themselves mestizo, or mixed Indian and Spanish, were making treaties with nomadic groups, incorporating migrant groups from the east and assimilating converted Indians from the local missions. Violence often defined indigenous relations with Mexican colonists, especially when Comanche and Apache groups were involved. While establishing peace with nomadic groups dominated the politics of Indian diplomacy in the early nineteenth century, this relationship occupied but one place on a broad spectrum of Mexican relations with indigenous peoples. Yet, all these relationships were not equal. They took place simultaneously in a system best understood as a network of meaning and identification.

The network of indigenous identities and relations can be roughly grouped into four categories, each situated like concentric circles emanating outward from Bexareño society (see figure 2.1). Placing these multiple identities on a single chart underscores the importance of context and situation in defining indigenous identity. The inner circle represents Bexareño society itself and the social categories of *casta* identification. *Casta*, literally "caste," provided the larger social meaning for the spectrum of racial categories found between *indio*, mestizo, and Español in colonial Spain. The second circle refers to indigenous groups who entered missions and Béxar society through a variety of other means, such as bonded servitude. Many of these groups lost or subverted their separate group identity over the decades of integrating. The third circle represents a category that developed over the early nineteenth century with the arrival of indigenous groups migrating into Texas in advance of American westward expansion. Groups in this circle, such as Cherokee people, had already spent decades negotiating with the American settlers and their government. Many of those migrants

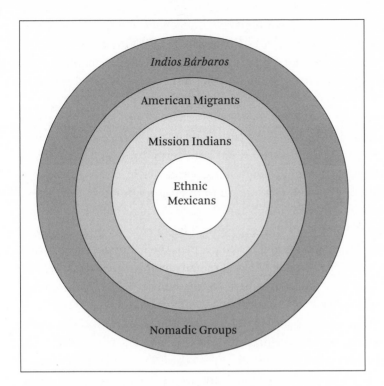

Figure 2.1. Concentric Circles of Indigenous Identification

took advantage of their familiarity with Euro-American ideas and politics to carve out a place for themselves in east Texas. The fourth circle includes groups that appeared more socially and culturally distant from Bexareños and participated in frequent and often violent interactions. These groups, such as the Comanche, were by and large nomadic.

The limit to this concentric circle approach is that it places Bexareños at the center of analysis, obscuring the actions and motivations of indigenous peoples. The sheer number of individual indigenous groups would raise the problem of multiple centers and narratives in this study. Furthermore, the vast majority of sources providing information on these groups depend heavily on European-based observers or extrapolation from anthropological and archaeological studies. But because this is a history of Mexicans in Béxar, the relationships laid out in this schematic at best provide a window into the lives of indigenous peoples through the perspective of the townspeople. Bexareños themselves are implicated in the social and cultural stratification resulting from indigenous identity. Placing Bexareños at the center raises questions about their own indigenous identity through *mestizaje* and situates them as part of a spectrum while also being a point of reference. Did the colonial legacy present in central Mexico manifest itself in the northern frontier? In what ways did the centuries of racial mixing in Mexico affect the ways Tejanos treated indigenous peoples in the region?

The concentric circles not only locate various groups along a spectrum of indigenous identity but also map out relative "distances," both physical and cultural. At the innermost level, the term "Mexican" itself was in flux and undergoing rapid change at independence in 1821. At this point in time, the state turned its attention to the incorporation of indigenous communities and mestizo people into the Mexican body politic. Even while the nation-state found ways to expand its idea of citizenship to include a broad range of indigenous and mixed peoples, the historical construction of Mexican ethnicity along the lines of Indian identity meant this would be a complicated incorporation at best. On the outer level, nomadic groups and so-called *indios bárbaros* (barbarous Indians) stand farther out, both geographically, on the periphery of colonial settlements, and culturally, even from indigenous-identified Mexican citizens.[9] The levels of identity themselves are blurred and overlap at the edges. The categories provide a way to figure out positions of various groups relative to each other rather than a rigid classification system.

An examination of Mexican relations with indigenous groups in Texas during the late colonial and early national period reveals many of the cultural and ideological roots of Tejano attitudes toward indigenous peoples. Most Tejanos avoided or feared Indians. Fear and conflict created a siege mentality in frontier towns, leading to what has been called an "Indian fighter" ethos among Spanish colonists.[10] Labeling Tejanos "Indian fighters," though, detracts from the full extent of their relations with and attitude toward indigenous groups. While violence undoubtedly existed between Tejanos and indigenous groups, trading alliances and the security of diplomatic overtures led Tejanos to continue the policy of negotiation started by Spanish officials.[11]

Mexican independence prompted local Tejano elites to take a more active role in preserving peace and security in the region. Through this role, Tejanos began to develop two significant aspects of their political identity: autonomy and the ability to negotiate across cultures. Early-nineteenth-century Indian policy figured prominently in aspects of Tejano ideology relative to the rise of the Mexican nation-state. Political stances taken by Bexareños, such as support for Mexican federalists and for foreign immigration, serve as examples of other ways regional autonomy and cultural brokering influenced local culture.

Elite Tejanos' interest in forging a secure frontier arose from their desire to see their province prosper. At the turn of the nineteenth century, an official from Chihuahua emphatically noted, "Population is the central point where all plans must be rooted."[12] Increased numbers of citizens in the provinces would both spur commerce and industry and secure the territory from encroaching Anglo-American interests. But the largest impediment to reaching these goals was the difficulty in establishing a lasting and stable peace with the indigenous tribes of the land.

Any analysis of Spanish, and later Mexican, relations with the indigenous peoples of the region must also take into consideration the multitude of tribes and family groups of indigenous peoples encountered by the colonists coming north from Mexico. Broad generalizations about Mexican-Indian relations obscure the complexity of this interaction and the historical variations in contact between different tribes.[13] Anthropologist Edward H. Spicer notes, "Although direct resistance was a universal reaction to contact with the Whites, it did not always come first. There were many tribes whose first reaction was one of friendly curiosity and there were others who sought the advantage of alliance with the Spaniards, or later with Anglo-Americans, against Indian enemies."[14] Spicer's suggestion, that relations with each tribe should be seen as historically specific, underscores the wide variety of experiences between Mexicans and Indians in nineteenth-century northeastern Mexico. The diversity of this task is made even more difficult by the numerous tribes present in northeastern Mexico. Cecilia Sheridan's research into early colonial settlements among these groups found up to 822 distinct peoples.[15]

Generations of historians have studied and characterized the Spanish conquest of the New World and the effect it had on the indigenous peoples.[16] The experience of conquest and colonization in Mesoamerica took a divergent form from that in the northern colonial settlements. Cultural differences between indigenous peoples along with the region's distinct environment contributed to these variations. As historian Vito Alessio Robles notes of the peoples of the Mexican northeast, "These Indians were completely different than those that the Spanish encountered on the central plateau and on large parts of both coasts . . . but none of [these studies of the conquest] considers the special conditions encountered by Spaniards in the northeast of Mexico."[17] Instead of *mestizaje* and the *encomienda* labor system, colonial officials developed a policy of Indian relations employing missions and the military.[18] Sheridan characterizes Spanish colonization among indigenous peoples in the north as an incomplete or stunted version of the rapid change that took place in central Mexico.[19]

Mexican colonists constructed their own categories to understand Indian cultures, distinguishing between tribes beyond the classic binary characterizations of *indios bárbaros* and *indios civilizados* (civilized Indians). Generally, *civilizado* implied conversion to Catholicism, along with acculturation to Spanish manners. Several Mexican observers of the time wrote lengthy descriptions of the Indians of the northeast and, in most cases, made specific distinctions between these groups.

One of these commentators from Béxar, Juan Antonio Padilla, reported on the "customs, habits and modes of life" of the barbarous tribes of Texas in 1819.[20] Within the category of barbarous, Padilla divided his report into two groups of tribes, friendly and hostile.[21] He listed sixteen tribes under "friendly nations," led primarily by the Caddo, and six under "hostile nations," with the Comanche and Lipan Apache most prominent. Regarding the Caddos, Padilla wrote, "Considering the fact that they are heathens, the moral customs of these natives are good, since they are not ambitious like the Comanches nor deceitful like the Lipanes."[22] Padilla's distinction between barbarous tribes complicates simple classifications such as *bárbaro* or *civilizado*, implying instead a gradation of social and cultural markers. Armed with a more detailed understanding of indigenous cultures, frontier Mexicans attempted to create peaceful coexistence in Texas. Forging treaties and restraining military force would test the limits of these definitions of Indian types and cultures.

More than a century after contact between the Indians of northern Mexico and the Spanish government, the nineteenth-century government policy attempted to continue several successful patterns from the eighteenth century. Colonial officials, most from the ranks of the military, found that gift-giving and diplomacy produced longer peaceful periods at a lower cost than military expeditions. However, changes in the social and political landscape shaped by both Anglo-American westward expansion and environmental limitations made the balance struck at the end of the eighteenth century much more difficult to maintain.[23] Yet, the experience of negotiating with Comanche groups indicates the centrality of Béxar in shaping these relationships.

Watercolor of a Comanche family by Lino Sánchez y Tapía, a member of General Manuel Mier y Terán's Comisión de Límites, 1828. (Courtesy of the Gilcrease Museum, Tulsa, Oklahoma)

A Comanche Treaty

Mexican independence presented Tejanos and the Mexican government with the opportunity to renew or establish improved alliances with indigenous groups in the north. Comanche people were the most dominant group in the region at the time, extending their influence over other indigenous groups as far south as San Luis Potosí.[24] A treaty between Mexico and Comanche chiefs in 1822 serves as a good measure of the direction Mexicans sought to take in their relations with indigenous groups.

Over three days in March 1822, Francisco Ruiz met with over five thousand Comanche people, including "the principal chiefs, captains and elders."[25] Discussions took place mainly between Ruiz and Pisinampe, a respected elder among the Comanches. During the negotiations, Pisinampe frequently turned to the assembled Comanches, who would then vote on what action to take. Ruiz emphasized that his government was not the Spanish but rather the Mexican nation, with "a native Emperor."[26] The conference resulted in a fourteen-point treaty between Comanches and the Mexican government, covering a variety of issues ranging from the treatment of captives to trade.

The Comanche leaders selected Chief Guonique to travel to Mexico City to sign the treaty. The first item of the treaty addressed the central subject of the meeting, the establishment of peace. It stated, "There will be perpetual peace and friendship between both nations: all hostilities of all sorts will end, and all that occurred during the Spanish reign will be forgotten."[27] The next items returned all captives who desired to be returned and set up an alliance to protect the frontier against hostile tribes or foreign invasion, including foreign explorers.[28]

Two items reflected and reaffirmed the central place of Béxar for carrying out the relationship spelled out in the treaty. Item 8 placed Béxar at the center of the new alliance: "*The Comanche will only practice trade in Béxar*, their merchants traveling there by public roads and under the direction of a chief held accountable for damages caused, and with a passport granted with the Emperor's seal: Mexicans will do likewise when they enter into the land of the Comanche."[29] The careful delineation of trading procedures indicates that fear of attacks persisted among Mexicans, despite this declaration of peace. The treaty even specified which goods each side would provide in trading. Item 12 designated a Comanche interpreter to live in Béxar, monitoring all relations.

The final item established a scholarship for twelve Comanche youth, who would be educated in Mexico City every four years. The Comanche youth would learn "to practice the arts and sciences and once they have been instructed, return so that their Nation in this way will become civilized and educated."[30] When the treaty is reread with this final item in mind, it casts the entire document as a project to bring indigenous peoples into the Mexican liberal project underway after independence. The plan assumed that educating several Comanche men in Enlightenment thought would change Comanche culture, bringing it closer to Mexican culture.[31] The items relating to Béxar made the town a literal border crossing by situating the oversight of movement and trade between Mexicans and Comanches there. The treaty conformed Comanche people and culture to a shape closer to Mexican society, or at least treated them more like another enlightened nation.

The treaty Ruiz brokered surpassed the peace won through a gift-giving relationship initiated by the Spanish during the previous decades. This treaty also demanded more personnel and resources to succeed, two things in short supply on the northern frontier after independence. Most significantly, the treaty practically relinquished control of the territory northwest from Béxar to Comanche groups. Mexican officials seemed willing to cede direct authority over the land in exchange for security and controlled access.

While the negotiations occurred under the authorization of the Mexican government, local efforts took on greater importance in the first decade of the new peace. Bexareño support for the deal, for instance, appears through a complaint lodged by José Antonio Navarro in the name of Juan Cortes of Nacogdoches in 1823.[32] Navarro, a prominent *vecino*, demanded the Mexican government compensate Cortes for over one thousand pesos given to Francisco Ruiz during his negotiations with the Comanches and Lipan Apaches. The money went specifically toward gifts for the two groups. While Cortes eventually received his reimbursement in 1828, his decision to put up the money demonstrated his interest in seeing the establishment of peace. The loan also indicated how much the process of making peace demanded the participation and even leadership of local elites.

While the 1822 treaty between the Mexican government and Comanche leaders seemed to indicate a sea change in relations between the two groups, the short-lived peace and subsequent waves of violence and transgressions require situating the treaty in a broader narrative of Indian/Mexican relations. The 1822 treaty serves as a window into what was possible while also revealing the complex relation to indigenous peoples Bexareños had developed over decades. Conversely, indigenous peoples, especially Comanche groups, picked up on changes in the Bexareño political and economic situation through independence and afterward. They sought to exploit these changes and continue to find ways of enhancing their trade networks and livelihood on the plains.[33]

For Francisco Ruiz and other Tejanos, establishing ties with Comanche peoples served as just one, albeit critical, relationship with and to indigenous groups in the region. Ruiz's capacity as Indian commissioner also led him to negotiate with migrant groups, such as the Cherokee entering to the northeast of Béxar. The town of Béxar defined itself with the incorporation of other groups through the area missions. Finally, Tejanos were implicated on a variety of levels in the construction of a Mexican identity that included a historical connection to *mestizaje*.

The First Circle: Mestizaje *and Mexican Ethnicity*

While situating Mexican identity at the center of this schematic might imply that it was a stable, homogenous, and fixed identity, the opposite is the case. Mexican identity arose out of the colonial relationship between Spain and the many indigenous groups throughout the territory. Unlike most other European colonial projects in the Americas, Spain's conquest and settlement among indigenous peoples resulted in a wide variety of Mexican subjects under a spectrum of identities. These identities combined elements of race, caste, gender, ethnicity, and class situated in a complex social order that varied over time and region. The main complicating factor in this new calculus of identities can be attributed to the frequent and socially defined offspring of mixed indigenous, African, or European parentage known as *mestizaje*, literally "mixing."

Usually referring specifically to the result of Spanish and Indian mixing, "mestizo" occupied a broad range of meanings often codified by the state or church.[34] Colonial Spanish society developed a complex system of terms used to define the results of *mestizaje*, expanding beyond the three categories of Spanish, Indian, and mestizo. Historians have noted the existence of over thirty categories of mixture resulting in a complex caste system throughout Latin America.[35] These *casta* categories regulated elements of daily life such as marriage, work, religion, and social status in general. In the northern frontier of New Spain, however, *casta* categories were much more fluid and played a less significant role in structuring society.[36]

Texas census records from the late eighteenth and early nineteenth centuries usually indicated the *casta* of the population being counted. Most records labeled persons as Español, mestizo, or *indio*, with a few other permutations of Indian and Negro, including mulatto. In all cases, the labels were used fluidly and were often self-ascribed and arbitrary.[37] Since these census categories serve as markers, their deeper meaning is more difficult to fathom. While these categories alone do not constitute an identity or a claim to an indigenous facet of Tejano identity, they do show a state interest in recording Indian subjects. Placing these census figures in the larger context of indigenous categories throughout the region provides a way to begin to understand what it might have meant to identify as *indio* or mestizo.

Census figures for Béxar present a picture of *mestizaje* as an unreliable substitute for race.[38] The January 1, 1820, census of the barrios of Béxar labeled nearly 59 percent Español of the total population of almost 1,600

TABLE 2.1. Census of Béxar, January 1, 1820

Barrio	Spaniards	Mestizos	Indians	Other[a]	Total
Valero	285	108	63	19	475
Sur	272	14	123	53	462
Norte	314	197	45	5	561
Laredo	68	0	7	22	97
Total	939	319	238	99	1,595
%	58.8	20.0	14.9	6.2	

Source: Residents of Texas, 1782–1836 (San Antonio: University of Texas Institute of Texan Cultures, 1984), 2:153–84.

[a] "Other" includes the categories listed as "Negro," "Mulatto," "Coyote," "Genizaro," and "Europeo."

(see table 2.1).[39] Of the remaining population, 20 percent were mestizo and 15 percent *indio*, with the final 6 percent indicating mulatto, coyote, or Negro. Using the census figures alone would leave the impression that Bexareños were mostly Español, or Spanish, in race and social standing. Combining the outsider observations of Anglo-Americans with the census figures raises questions regarding the relative meaning of *casta* definitions. "Spanish" or "Indian" held different social and physical meanings depending on the observer's culture and location. Additionally, census-taking required a certain degree of self-identification, possibly resulting in some upward *casta* mobility. These figures might also reflect a new ordering of social hierarchy on the frontier, where *indio* held a higher status than in other regions in Mexico, resulting from the proximity to nomadic tribes in the north.

The 1820 census also identified at least twenty-seven different marriages between people of different *castas*. These marriages involved all the *castas*, with no general trend toward the status of the husband or wife. In most cases, the children of these marriages took on the *casta* of mestizo or mulatto. But in one case, that of Alexandro Mansolo and Tomasa Montalbo, the marriage between a mestizo male and a Spaniard female produced Spanish children. Furthermore, the census of 1820 does not list any permanent Anglo-American residents. Recent studies suggest that fluidity and heterogeneity in Béxar resulted in racial leveling, thus decreasing the importance of *casta*.[40] This might explain the lack of precision and consistency in the application of the census category.

Along with these cases, the example of Pedro Huizar in the eighteenth century underscores the arbitrary nature of *casta*, usually due to its self-classification. In 1779, Huizar, a carpenter and surveyor, is listed as a mulatto.[41] Two decades later, in the 1798 census, Huizar carries the title Don in his entry, an honorific indicating elevated social status and sometimes used as a substitute for race.[42] While *casta* classifications seem fluid, the upward mobility appearing in several cases suggests that the classification nonetheless mattered. Perhaps Béxar's position on the frontier permitted more leeway regarding these classifications.[43] But distance did not reorder the social hierarchy placing Español above mulatto or *indio*.

Bexareños defied generalization in terms of their racial composition, although racial categories of the era were employed in official business such as court cases and the census. One eighteenth-century traveler described the Bexareño elite as "a ragged band of men of all colors."[44] The fluidity of Bexareño *casta* identity underscores the dynamic qualities of ethnic and racial identification in nineteenth-century Mexico and Latin America. As a result, it is difficult to strictly categorize Mexican identity as completely separate from Indian identity. The ethnic and racial classification of any Mexican community has to be situated in a specific time and place to make sense of the meaning of these terms. As such, while *indio* held one meaning within Mexican society in the context of *mestizaje*, it also held another meaning in the context of other indigenous groups in the northern frontier.

The Catholic church also actively participated in forming and maintaining connections to indigenous identity. *Limpieza de sangre* cases served as one place where the church made decisions on an individual's racial identity through a court proceeding. The cases illustrate the arbitrary nature of racial identity, as racial status could be contested and redefined through this procedure. While few instances of these cases remain from the period, their existence further supports the fluid nature of ethnic identity in late colonial and early national Mexico.[45]

Limpieza de sangre cases provide evidence of a direct intervention by the church in matters of individual identity. While census records and government documents employed categories defining people within a range of indigenous identities, Béxar society as a whole developed an internal order mediating between these external institutions. While such documents help reconstruct identity for Bexareños, a broader regional view brings additional context. The church changed the social landscape of the region in an even larger way when it established a system of missions along the San

Antonio River. The missions functioned as an avenue to incorporate various area indigenous groups into Béxar.

The Second Circle: Mission Indians

Beginning in the eighteenth century, Spanish colonial authorities constructed a chain of missions and presidios northward into Texas, reaching to the Louisiana border. The location of these frontier institutions reveals their multiple purposes: to establish the Spanish presence in the frontier, to incorporate the local indigenous peoples, and to lay the groundwork for civilian colonization of the region. Franciscan missionaries founded the first permanent mission along the San Antonio River in 1718 with the founding of San Antonio de Valero.[46] Subsequently, Franciscans built four more missions to the south along the river. The missions, and the presidio San Antonio de Béxar built near San Antonio de Valero, provided a basis for the settlement of families of Canary Islanders and for the founding of the villa of Béxar in 1731.[47]

Ideally, the missions were meant to attract indigenous peoples to the grounds, convert them, and bring them into Spanish civilian life in the span of twenty years. Once completely "reduced," the mission would revert to secular, or civilian, status as a parish church in the town. In practice, the secularization process took longer than two decades, and even then missions came to a complete end only by government decree. The missions began their secularization in April 1793, with the distribution of mission lands to the "native Christians of San Antonio de Valero."[48] The remaining missions secularized that year, but lack of parish priests forced Franciscans to continue to preach among the indigenous population, resulting in a partial secularization. The Mexican government legislated full secularization in 1823, completing the process of land distribution in the area around Béxar. Secularization delays resulted not only from lack of church resources but also from droughts and indigenous abandonment.[49]

Missions affected social and economic life in Béxar and the region. They were set up to function like self-sustaining units, with agricultural and pastoral land tied to each mission. Mission Indians lived in and around the mission and provided the labor to keep them in operation. Far from simple frontier outposts, missions ran like complex enterprises with a diverse set of assets.[50] The church not only owned the building and the mission grounds but also controlled riparian water rights to the rivers adjoining the land, groves and farms near the mission, and vast tracts to the east and

Mission Nuestra Señora de la Purísima Concepción de Acuña after secularization, 1868. (Courtesy of the San Antonio Conservation Society Foundation, Raba Collection)

south for ranching.[51] The land, labor, and production controlled by these missions made the outcome of secularization critical to Béxar elites.

Initial attempts at secularization in 1793 faltered in part from missionary awareness that mission Indians might lose out in the transfer process. Franciscans hesitated to sell off lands and fully integrate their subjects into the local market. Some of these fears were realized when mission lands were finally distributed and Béxar elites used personal connections to acquire mission tracts meant for mission Indians. Government officials continued to deal with the fallout of secularization years after the first missions closed. For instance, in 1826, mission Indians from Mission San Francisco de la Espada petitioned the political chief, José Antonio Saucedo, to recover title to homes on the mission lands.[52] Saucedo passed the petition on to the governor in Saltillo along with his recommendation to grant the land to the Indians. Later, Anglo-American speculators bought these tracts and accumulated smaller indigenous plots in a land speculation move.[53]

Secularization implied the incorporation of the converted indigenous population into Spanish civil society.[54] Incorporation thus suggests the disappearance of difference between indigenous groups and between colonist and native. Gilberto M. Hinojosa and Anne A. Fox have commented, "The secularization of the missions undoubtedly contributed to a blending of different groups into San Fernando [de Béxar]."[55] Even after secularization, though, identification as Indians continued. Census records from 1820 contain the self-identified categorization, or quality, of *indio*, mestizo, coyote, or Español with the names of the families of Béxar.[56] The missions themselves maintained their status as barrios within the city's jurisdiction. Such designations appear in census reports, and a large number of people identified themselves as *indio* in the southern section of town where most of the missions were located (see table 2.1).

Through secularization of the missions, separate tribal or group identification by mission Indians all but disappeared.[57] The distinction mission Indians made between themselves and local indigenous groups might explain their choice of the category mestizo instead of *indio* in the census reports coming from the northern and Valero sections of Béxar. The full impact of indigenous integration on the construction of concepts of ethnicity among Tejanos remains to be more fully explored.[58]

By 1823, the dissolution of the missions meant that mission Indians now lived outside the confines and oversight of the Catholic church and Franciscan priests. While their historical differences meant they were not quite ethnic Mexican, they were certainly not *indios bárbaros* of the Comanche type either. Many remained living in the area around the mission buildings. The buildings themselves fell into disrepair and their stones used for construction around Béxar.[59] Even though they stopped functioning in 1823, the missions of San Antonio de Béxar retained symbolic value, helping to define the image and history of the town. The social legacy of the missions also remained a presence through the incorporation of a mission Indian identity in Béxar. That identity served to situate other indigenous identities in the local context.

The Third Circle: American Migrants

While Bexareños in the early nineteenth century had built a deep and complex social relationship with indigenous peoples in the local missions, they also had a more recent history of contact with indigenous migrants from American territories. These groups sought land and sanctuary in Texas in order to escape the pressures of American westward expansion. Dominated in numbers by Cherokees, American migrants introduced new indigenous groups to Mexicans, groups that were neither local nor hostile. These migrants had over a century of history with Anglo-American colonists in the American South, during which they appropriated European customs and diplomatic skills, often to protect their diminishing rights and landholdings. Their history also resulted in Tejano suspicion of Anglo-Americans and westward expansion.

The first significant wave of eastern migrants into Texas came soon after the Louisiana Purchase. In a letter to Nemisio Salcedo, Antonio Cordero describes a request by Cawshatta Indians to settle in Texas. Salcedo writes, "After setting forth their ancient vassalage, their loyalty to our king, and the disdain with which they look upon the seduction of the American government, [they stated that] the object of their visit firstly [was] to request permission for the main tribe . . . to move to the place where they are living."[60] Whether Cordero added the criticism of Americans by noting their "seduction" in order to support his request for land, or the migrant chief stressed it in the meeting, American westward expansion provided the background for these and other meetings and treaties. Along with Cherokees, other groups entered Texas from the east during this period, most notably Chickasaw, Shawnee, and Pascagoula groups.[61]

After 1821, government officials out of Béxar continued to negotiate the entrance of migrant indigenous groups. Of all the tribes' agents with whom Francisco Ruiz and Peter Ellis Bean made treaties, Cherokee people practiced a form of diplomacy most recognizable to them. Like several other tribes, Cherokee groups migrated into northeastern Texas in the early nineteenth century in order to avoid Anglo-American westward expansion. Their experiences in trade and war with Anglo-Americans led to a sophisticated diplomatic culture headed by a war and diplomacy chief.[62] Furthermore, Cherokee leaders crafted alliances with other migrant tribes in the area, permitting them to broker settlements with Mexican agents.[63]

This broker role appeared in a meeting between Bean and several local Indian tribes held to sign a peace treaty on July 2, 1828, in Nacogdoches. The tribes, led by Cherokee chiefs, included members from the Shavano, Kickapoo, Delaware, Alabama, Nabadache, Ainais, and Cawshatta groups. They sat around a buffalo robe with the Mexican representatives and smoked a peace pipe. The speeches made by the Indian chiefs emphasized their desire to live in the Mexican nation and their feelings toward Mexicans.[64]

After ceremonial dances, the war and diplomacy chief for the Cherokees stood up and spoke. "It has been twenty moons since we smoked the peace pipe with our Mexican brothers," he stated, "and we desire to be together as one people, and share the same sympathies as our Mexican brothers, and we should never go back on our promises."[65] The chief went on to describe the treaties Bean had brokered with the Tawankawas and the Wacos for both the Mexican government and the Cherokee group. While suspicious of the sincerity of the Tawankawas and Wacos concerning peace, the Cherokee chief reaffirmed his trust in the Mexican government.[66] A Shavano chief echoed these sentiments when he spoke next. "I have heard what my Cherokee brothers have had to say and their word is good," said Piedra Negra. "We are red men and know nothing beyond what we think in our heads. We have traveled a long distance to this Nation, searching for the Mexicans, and they have received us like brothers and we should be honest men."[67] This testimonial by the Shavano leader sought to establish goodwill in the negotiations taking place on the blanket.

Piedra Negra emphasized the importance of working this new land when he continued, "We do not want to live lost in the prairie like other tribes. . . . These lands are good to those who work them; but those who do not work will always be hungry and he and his woman will be naked and their children will be thieves."[68] In this part of the testimonial, Piedra Negra linked the situation of his group with that of other American migrants. These groups feared being "lost in the prairie," a reference to both the Plains groups already inhabiting land to the west and to the established agricultural practices these migrants possessed. Settlement in Texas held out the possibility of stability for these migrant groups.

Other examples continue to situate Cherokees in a unique position in the Texas borderlands. In 1826, political chief José Antonio Saucedo received contradicting reports on the supposed danger posed by Cherokee groups, especially by one of their chiefs, Richard Fields. At one point, Saucedo believed Fields had organized a massive insurrection on the border. Later, Fields denied these charges and signed a peace treaty with Saucedo in 1827, leading to the above treaty in 1828. Of the first treaty, Saucedo noted, "The affection we have shown them and the shelter and protection of our Government resulted in the manifestation of their sentiment in favor of the Mexican Republic that they recognize as mother."[69] Much like the Anglo-American immigrants, Saucedo seemed to suggest that these indigenous groups could eventually become citizens of the new nation.

Without delving into the beliefs and culture of these tribes or the sincerity of their overtures, the proceedings between the Cherokees and the Mexican representative exemplify the development of Mexican/Indian relations from their origins in the late-eighteenth-century policy of gift-giving. Tejanos had to contend with an increased number of different tribes as Anglo-Americans pushed their civilization westward. In fact, Anglo-American colonists had already established numerous settlements near these tribes by the time of the 1828 treaty. Mexican efforts not only kept a general peace with the tribes but also aimed to keep Anglo-American colonists from resorting to vigilante attacks against these indigenous groups.

While the migrant groups possessed a facility with Europeanized modes of diplomacy and communication—at least more than nomadic groups to the west did—they differed greatly from mission Indians. These groups had limited exposure to Spanish language and culture and Catholicism. The land in which they requested to settle lay far from Béxar, rather than in the town itself where mission Indians lived. In a larger sense, American migrant groups formed the first wave of eastern immigration, introducing Anglo-American ideas of race and Indian people merely through their presence in Texas.

Negotiations with migrant groups can be considered a balancing act started by the Spanish government in the northern frontier. After independence, these efforts gave way to a series of brokered alliances and treaties designed to maintain peace and security in the region. The sheer number of different cultures Tejanos faced when constructing this arrangement suggests the complexity of this task. One U.S. Department of State agent mentioned at least thirty distinct tribes in his listing of the indigenous population of Texas, a population he calculated to be almost 10,000 in 1827.[70] Directives from Mexico City could not possibly have set out all the actions taken by Tejano agents. Rather, their participation in crafting these relations sprang from their experiences living in the frontier region. The American migrant groups added to the unique and nuanced cultural context of the frontier. In particular, the border with an expanding American empire added a dimension to indigenous identity not found in other regions of Mexico.

The Outer Circle: Nomadic Groups

While Bexareños attended to treaties with American migrants, the secularization of mission Indians, and their own social hierarchies, relations with nomadic groups, primarily Comanche and Lipan Apache, dominated Indian policy locally and nationally. The 1822 Comanche treaty discussed earlier stands as an example of how relations with these groups achieved some level of balance. More likely than not, though, nomadic groups were thought of as dangerous marauders befitting their title *indios bárbaros*. The gap between Béxar's ethnic Mexican community at the center of this schematic and the outer circle occupied by nomadic Indian groups appeared most often in opinions on the obstacles and dangers of colonizing the northern provinces.[71]

Comments in Juan Antonio Padilla's report of 1819 show that violence largely defined his idea of *indio bárbaro* culture. About Comanches, Padilla wrote that they were "treacherous, revengeful, sly, untrustworthy, ferocious, and cruel, when victorious; and cowardly and low, when conquered. They are inclined towards rapine and murder of their fellow-beings, sparing the lives of the young and of the women in order that they may teach their wicked customs to the former and satisfy their lust with the latter. Like cowards, they mutilate the bodies of the dead and, sometimes, they eat their prisoners after torturing them to death."[72] Padilla's brutal depiction of Comanche culture left little room for negotiation between Mexican and Comanche leaders. He not only deemed them untrustworthy but also portrayed them as living uncivilized lives. After all, for Padilla, they were killers and cannibals. Padilla and other Bexareños could point to the long history of violent conflict with Comanche groups. One of the most prominent attacks occurred in 1757, at San Sabá mission.[73] Franciscan missionaries founded the mission far to the northwest of Béxar in a brief and unsuccessful attempt to convert and colonize Apache people. Comanche raiders attacked the mission, killing scores of Apache residents and the friars.

In response to these dangers, Spanish colonial officials developed what one historian called the "frontier colonial apparatus" to foster a secure and stable environment receptive to further colonization of the north.[74] Using presidial detachments of soldiers, military commanders crafted a system of threat and reward to negotiate a peaceful equilibrium with the nomadic groups. Making this task more difficult, colonists entered into a landscape where the various nomadic groups held competing interests and continuously fought or formed alliances among themselves. Reactions to attacks varied between military and diplomatic.

These responses might seem contradictory when practiced by one commander. José Antonio Saucedo, upon hearing of a meeting between Waco and Tahuacano Indians near Nacogdoches, responded by calling for a strong military strike to achieve a wider effect across the entire frontier. He suggested "a decisive premeditated strike that would make them know the superiority of our weapons."[75] Saucedo paired this exhortation with a request for more rifles and manpower for the frontier areas. In a later letter

Watercolor of Comanche warriors by Lino Sánchez y Tapía, a member of General Manuel Mier y Terán's Comisión de Límites, 1828. (Courtesy of the Gilcrease Museum, Tulsa, Oklahoma)

to the military commander of Texas, Saucedo went beyond calling for one military hit, instead proposing "to the higher Government, if they wish, that in order for this important part of the federation to achieve the peak of abundance that its inhabitants practice without disruption, the most sure method is to exterminate the Nations that cause us such damage, putting in effect a campaign from points around New Mexico, Coahuila and Texas with a thousand cavalry soldiers."[76] In this case, he responded to reports of a meeting between Comanche, Aguaje, Tahuacano, Talmayace, and Waco groups who seemed to be planning an all-out war. Despite these problems, Saucedo continued the long-held Béxar practice of giving monthly gifts to

Comanche groups as they came peacefully. When local funds for these gifts ran low, he asked for additional funds from the government or temporary support from local elites.[77]

By the middle of the eighteenth century, the growing civilian population living in the Provincias Internas de Oriente required Spanish officials to take more concerted and decisive steps to establish peaceful relations with the nomadic indigenous groups in the region. Decades had passed since the establishment of the mission system in Coahuila and Texas, and while many indigenous groups settled in these communities, most remained in their *rancherias* and continued their lives on the plains. Despite living in separate places, tensions constantly arose between Mexican colonists and indigenous groups. It became clear that more active steps on the part of Spanish officials, especially within the military, would be required to create a climate in the region favorable to increased Mexican settlement.

These treaties extended to all the towns and outposts in the Provincias Internas, but they didn't wholly account for the different relations between indigenous groups from region to region. For instance, many of the treaties discussed by historian Elizabeth A. H. John involved the Comanche groups around Santa Fe and Chihuahua. Comanches themselves have been categorized into at least three narrower groups. One of these groups inhabited the region northwest of Béxar. Spanish officials in Texas and Coahuila crafted their own treaties with this Comanche group, treaties that didn't necessarily coincide with others made with Comanches farther to the west. These differences led to the appearance of treaty transgressions by Comanches when one group would steal or kill a colonist during the peace signed by another group. Nevertheless, Spanish officials developed a sense of the Comanche culture sophisticated enough to differentiate between the eastern and western Comanche groups. In one letter from 1819, for example, the comandante general of the Provincias Internas de Occidente informed the governor of New Mexico of military plans against the eastern Comanche. He asked the governor to meet with the western Comanche leaders to explain the situation and tell them the actions would not be against their people.

Creating peace in Texas occasionally took larger efforts than gift-giving as Spanish officials negotiated treaties with neighboring groups. The establishment of peace with Oso Ballo, a Comanche leader, in Chihuahua in 1811 provides an example of the beliefs and methods for carrying out these negotiations.[78] A report of the treaty reached officials in Béxar to inform them of the agreement. A key element of the report establishes the scope of Oso Ballo's authority, describing him as the "captain" of the Yamparica tribe within the alliance of western Comanches. This specificity suggests an understanding of the complexity of Comanche leadership and alliances among the Spanish. The report notes Oso Ballo first received a large medallion to distinguish his leadership and to pay respect. Finally, Béxar officials were reminded to maintain the flow of gifts Comanches had grown to expect. The report states, "I urge you to keep in mind the importance of not failing to keep in store the items the Indian Nations have grown accustomed to receive; for if it occurs, grave consequences of a large magnitude would come about. Take every measure to easily, securely and quickly acquire the necessary articles."[79] Ultimately, any peace treaty crafted between the Spanish and these groups required a continuation of gift-giving.

Through gift-giving and peaceful overtures, Tejanos worked to forge a relationship with various nomadic indigenous groups in the region. Regarding Comanche relations, John notes, "Tejanos traveled freely into the Comanchería to hunt and to trade; Comanche families came routinely to trade and visit at San Antonio de Béxar. There, eastern Comanches received the crown's annual treaty presents, and some Comanches formed personal friendships with San Antonians that proved useful in troubled times."[80] These sorts of contacts coincided with Comanche values important in establishing mutually trustworthy relations. John adds, "Visiting was a vital component of Indian friendships and unstinting hospitality a prime value in Indian cultures. Reciprocity was important."[81] Table 2.2 demonstrates the material dimension of this reciprocity between Bexareños and indigenous people in their hinterland.

Municipal officials in Béxar maintained detailed records of the goods exchanged with the visiting tribes. These records permit the reconstruction of the cycle of visiting and gift-giving over the course of a year. While fewer people came to Béxar in the winter months, records show a greater amount of meat delivered as gifts as the weather turned colder. Perhaps most telling of the degree of trust built by these visits appears in the amount of gunpowder granted in a few visits. Presumably used for hunting, Spanish officials gave gunpowder without fear of it being used in attacks against Spanish colonists.

Comanche people reciprocated Tejano actions by supporting hunting and trade expeditions in the region, as well as later providing a hideout for insurgents. John describes one example in 1803, when 130 Bexareños rode into the Comanchería to hunt buffalo.[82] Comanche people provided the hunters with shelter and guides and even tended their horses during the

TABLE 2.2. Indian Gifts Presented in Béxar, 1807

Month	Number Visiting	Value (in Pesos)	Cattle	Meat (Lbs.)	Gunpowder (Lbs.)
January	159	216	9	156	1
February	97	58	1	760	0
March	138	106	1	988	50
April	164	665	15	260	0
May	156	210	2	580	1
June	342	500	29	730	0
July	626	1,150	50	204	0
August	256	571	16	1,044	0
September	24	133	3	530	0
October	250	350	17	1,016	15.5
November	10	11	0	144	0
December	76	143	2	1,120	0
Total	2,298	4,113	145	7,532	67.5

Source: Bexar Archives, University of Texas, Austin.

expedition. During the Republic era, Bexareños relied on these contacts in exploring the possibility of joining with the Santa Fe trade.

These gifts not only established peace but also led to other benefits for the colonists. One came in the form of information and warnings from Comanche people about threats. In December 1811, a "Capitancillo," or junior captain, of the Comanches named El Sordo rode into Béxar with three others to inform authorities of potential raids against Béxar by the Tahuallare and Tahuacano tribes.[83] Such reports also pointed to fears and uncertainty about maintaining carefully crafted peace, especially as rebellion against the Crown spread through the nation. Funds and personnel were turned to fighting the insurgents, and in turn, insurgents used newly created rifts to fight against royalists. The advice from Chihuahua regarding peace with Chief Oso Ballo might have sprung from a desire to maintain secure relations with indigenous peoples while fighting the insurgency. Additionally, insurgents relied on and manipulated their connections with indigenous groups to continue their movement against the colonial government.[84] In the case of Béxar, many insurgents fled after its recapture by royalist troops and sought refuge in Comanche camps.[85]

When insurgents were forced to live in closer proximity to Comanches, they increased the earlier contacts initiated by gift-giving and trade. By independence, Bexareños managed to establish something of a relationship with Comanches enabled by the 1822 treaty. While this relationship didn't mean Comanche and Mexican people experienced daily contact, they did have much more frequent contact and raised expectations. However, Comanche raids and Tejano counterraids frequently broke this tentative peace. Furthermore, Comanche groups continued to keep great numbers of Mexican captives up until the 1830s, with estimates ranging into the hundreds.[86] The meaning and long-term impact of these raids do not have to be seen as entirely negative. As historian James F. Brooks has suggested, many Mexican captives assimilated into life in Comanche families. Raids and attacks themselves say more about the larger empire of trade the Comanche groups built in the entire Southwest, of which Béxar was but one corner.

Where Did the Indians Go?

The possibility of Mexican captives living in Comanche families raises the idea of closer contact between Mexicans and nomadic indigenous groups, despite the distances suggested by the model presented in this chapter. In a sense, the depiction of identities as concentric circles has come full circle. While *mestizaje* has been internalized into the Mexican national story, the case of Texas in the nineteenth century suggests multiple, simultaneous narratives. The diversity of indigenous identities, locations, and forms of contact requires a closer look at each interaction between Mexican and Indian to get a sense of the connections made and the resulting relationship. The example of Béxar provides insight into the process of ethnic creation in the nineteenth century.[87] The spatial and cultural distance between and among Mexicans and indigenous peoples emphasizes the importance of these relations for identity formation. Rather than constructing identity in opposition to another people, Bexareños found their identity relationally. The range of indigenous identities in nineteenth-century Texas provides the necessary context to situate numerous relationships.

For most indigenous peoples, the grounds and result of that contact with Tejanos were not equal. The best evidence of that inequality appears in the silences and disappearance of indigenous peoples from the Mexican and Anglo-American histories of Texas after 1836. Secularization of the missions in 1823 started the process of Indian "disappearance" in Béxar. The mission Indians lost much of their separate identity after the Catholic church and the Franciscan missionaries relinquished control of the mission and turned over its landholdings and water rights to them.[88] While many mission Indians continued to live in the area, other Bexareños moved in and began to buy up land. Over time, connection to the mission or to an earlier indigenous identity was pushed further back and, after Anglo-American colonization, replaced with an ethnic identity. Personal stories and family narratives of that connection remain as faint echoes to this day.[89] Those memories and *testimonios* provide current generations with a connection to the land in San Antonio that preceded Anglo-American conquest.

By 1821, Mexicans and indigenous peoples constructed a complex social world full of problems and possibilities. Anglo-American immigration into Texas disturbed the balance by adding population pressures and a third perspective on indigenous relations.[90] Anglo-American immigration also overshadowed indigenous peoples in the historical narrative. It remains a struggle to show evidence of indigenous voices after 1821, including this retelling.

When indigenous voices appear in Anglo narratives, they often surface in conjunction with Mexicans. During the Texas Republic period, Cherokee people were accused of allying with Mexicans in a revolt known as the Cordova Rebellion. Recent evidence points to even greater Comanche participation in the U.S.-Mexico War.[91] After 1848, indigenous peoples appear as thieves and rustlers, stealing on the American side and taking cover in Mexico. In all cases, it has been difficult to account for the thousands of indigenous peoples living in Texas in 1821. Some remained, others fought, and still others migrated once more. Many became Tejano, intermarrying with Mexicans and becoming ethnic Mexicans outright. Perhaps the answer to the loss of context and nuance of the indigenous elements of Tejano identity lies in the radical restructuring of identities resulting from American expansion into Texas.

*If I thought my advice would have any weight, I would say
to Texas, you must all harmonise [sic] with Béxar and Goliad,
that is with the Mexican population. If they petition for a State or
Territory and are seconded by the rest of Texas, the petition will
be granted, and I am equally certain that no petition of this
kind will succeed that is opposed by that population.*
— Stephen F. Austin, letter to Samuel M. Williams,
January 12, 1834

Chapter Three

American Immigrants

COLONIZATION AND TEJANO IDENTITY

In 1821, Stephen F. Austin organized the first foreign land grant colonization of Texas, with the goal of emigrating 250 families from the United States. Austin's settlement project would not have succeeded, or for that matter even started, without Tejano support and encouragement. Tejano political leaders ushered through legislation at the state level and smoothed over obstacles as they arose. Austin's relationship with Erasmo Seguín, the patriarch of the Seguín family, symbolizes the depth and interdependence of contact between Mexicans and Anglo-Americans generally. While the details of their political contacts extended beyond the local level, their personal relations revolved around exchanges involving both their entire families. Tejano elites facilitated the influx of Anglo-American immigrants into Texas by effectively functioning as cultural brokers between Anglo-Americans and Mexican government officials. Doing so set in motion a variety of shifts in Tejano identity and social structures affecting Tejanos' place in the world around them.

The Seguín-Austin friendship shows how cultural brokerage took place.

Austin's brother James spent several months learning Spanish in the Seguín household. Austin himself learned Spanish and became very adamant about the need for colonists to know the language while living in Mexico. He would goad his brother to keep working on his Spanish, even writing to him in Spanish. The next year, James stayed with their sister in the United States, but Austin continued to encourage him with his Spanish. Of his brother's stay in Béxar, Austin later wrote, "I owe something to Don Erasmo—he refused to receive pay for the time my brother staid [*sic*] here, and I have always staid here in my visits to Béxar and he would never receive pay."[1] On other occasions, Seguín's son Juan Nepomuceno spent time learning English with Austin at his home northeast of Béxar. These contacts reveal the personal nature of cultural exchange between elite families centrally involved in both sides of the immigration process. Their cultural and political relations were critical to larger transformations taking place during Anglo-American colonization in Texas as it started simultaneously with Mexican independence. Over the next decade, Anglo-American immigration rapidly and dramatically reoriented the demographics of the region. As a result, the meaning and importance of ethnicity changed during this period along with recently formed concepts of nation.

The story of Anglo-American colonization in Texas is a story of American immigration to Mexico. Within a decade, Anglo immigrants outnumbered the existing Mexican population in Texas almost ten to one, by some estimates.[2] Like other narratives of foreign immigration to the United States, this migration exposes the gray area between assimilation and cultural resistance while demonstrating evidence of ethnic enclaves and multiple nationalisms.[3] The politics and dynamics of immigration in general often speak to ideas of nation and culture held by the receiving society. As a result of Anglo-American immigration to Mexico, Tejanos articulated their position on issues of nation and culture, a task made more difficult by their recent independence from Spain and relative lack of state presence or control. This immigration story also takes a different turn from the typical narrative: Tejanos lost the power to define immigration over time instead of maintaining their dominance as the receiving culture.

While Bexareños forged a new nation after independence and redefined their relations to indigenous groups in the early nineteenth century, a third social world emerged in Texas through the process of colonization. Beginning in 1821, political and legal avenues were in place to promote the immigration of hundreds of foreigners into the territory, mostly Anglo-Americans from the southern states.[4] Led by Austin, southerners immigrated to Mexico as part of a broader movement for land in Texas. Their project succeeded due in great part to overlapping sets of goals and values held by both Anglo-American leaders and elite Tejano families. The areas of overlap encouraged colonization in the early period but represented only the tip of the respective cultures and larger regional and economic interests. Along with the significant fact that men primarily mediated cultural relations, the story of Anglo-American immigration in Texas revolved around shared notions of honor, prestige, and masculinity.

Anglo-American colonization in 1821 provided a short-term benefit for both southerners and Tejanos. The rapid influx of southerners during colonization tested the depth and power of these similarities, straining relations between Anglos and Mexicans. Tejano elites acted as cultural brokers, initially by encouraging Anglo-American immigration and later by mediating between them and the Mexican state, as the state asserted increasing control of the frontier.[5] By taking on the role of cultural brokers, Tejano elites attempted to maintain influence in the future of their region while keeping their prestige intact. The magnitude of differences in ethnic identification and nationalism between Anglo-Americans, Tejano settlers, and the rest of Mexico proved to be a large obstacle for Tejano elites to negotiate.

By acting as cultural brokers, Tejanos functioned in a manner similar to that in other frontier societies. Historians have more often employed this concept when describing indigenous relations with Anglo and French colonists in North America.[6] In these cases, a subgroup of the local culture serves as an intermediary or go-between to pave the way for more wide-scale commercial and social interactions. More than just interpreters, cultural brokers develop the ability to circulate in different cultural contexts. Anthropologist Eric Wolf explains the significance of cultural brokers, noting that "they stand guard over the crucial junctures or synapses of relationships which connect the local system to the larger whole."[7] In this case, elite Tejanos "translated" Mexican political culture while building social ties to Anglo-American elites. Like indigenous cultural brokers in other areas, Tejanos occasionally extended those ties to family and intermarriage.[8] Yet through the intimate engagement with two worlds, Tejanos also faced potential contradictions and conflicts inherent in their position as buffers.

Erasmo Seguín's central role in the success of Austin's colony exemplifies the mechanics and meaning of being a cultural broker. Seguín's political and social prominence in Béxar and northern Mexico enabled him to engage in negotiations with Austin. Seguín had participated in early insurgent actions against the Spanish government during Mexican independence. Even after his insurgent activity, Spanish officials granted him an important political post in the government of Béxar just before independence. The political positions held by Seguín and his family provided them with access to the legislative process and to influential people at the local, state, and national levels.

Seguín family ties to the region made them strong promoters of economic expansion in Béxar and northern Mexico, and they advocated allowing foreigners into Texas to rapidly and inexpensively increase its population and productivity. The Spanish government appointed Seguín as the envoy to present Moses Austin with the first land grant to settle in Texas in 1821.[9] While Austin died before receiving word of the government's contract, his son Stephen took up the land grant and initiated a long friendship with Seguín.

The Seguín-Austin relationship reveals the nuances of Tejano self-identity during a period of rapid changes, raising the possibility of cooperation and coexistence on the Mexican frontier. In the years between 1821 and 1830, the Anglo-American population of Texas increased at an explosive rate. From those years forward, the lives of Tejanos and Anglos would be inextricably tied together, though not always as equal partners. Examining the involvement of the Tejano elite in the process of Anglo-American colonization reveals a concrete example of the ebb and flow of ethnic identity. The year 1821 marked a time when ethnicity became a more prominent element of Tejano identity in Béxar, since there was now another large and noticeably different ethnic group living nearby.

Anglo-Americans affected Tejano ethnicity and ideas of nation through a combination of cultural traits, commercial relationships, and political participation. A close examination of the politics that introduced Anglo-Americans to Texas shows the significance of ethnic identity to the personal relationships between elites. In this chapter, Anglo-American immigration into Texas is first placed within the broader context of American westward expansion and southern politics and culture. Anglo-American immigrants moved to Texas for reasons apart from Mexican interests. Next, the colonization system that integrated Anglo-Americans is described. Finally, the chapter examines the extent and meaning of elite Tejano participation in colonization by looking at individual Bexareños and their activities during colonization. For these elites, what started as a self-interested project to advance the economic viability of Texas led to a more sustained role as cultural brokers. As such, this chapter views politics as both a barometer and instigator of ethnic difference.

Most Tejanos directly involved in the colonization process held political positions in the Mexican government. As a result, the politics of Anglo immigration into Texas reflected the sentiments of both Tejano elites and Mexican politicians in the interior of the nation. Yet the policies of the Mexican government during this period also affected ethnic identity by increasing the foreign population living in Texas and later by opposing Anglo immigration. Tejanos had an economic interest in increasing the population as well as a personal connection with some colonists.[10] Their support of colonization also suggests that Tejanos entered into a deeper relationship with Anglo-Americans that went beyond commerce, one that unintentionally elevated the importance of ethnic and national identity over regional benefits.

Anglo-American colonization in Texas proceeded in two stages, divided roughly at 1828. From 1821 to 1828, elite Tejanos and Anglo migrants largely cooperated in *empresario* colonization ventures to populate Texas. Biographies of elite Tejanos show a variety of involvement in the Anglo-American project. The next chapter addresses the subsequent period, from 1828 to 1834, when conflict between Mexican officials and Anglo colonists stemming from anti-Anglo colonization laws forced Tejanos to negotiate between the two groups while experiencing rapidly diminished status in the region. Acting as cultural brokers became untenable for elite Tejanos. Changes in the latter period constricted Bexareño ethnic choices and highlight the complex social context that pushed the northern Mexican culture and ideology toward a more distinct ethnic social position relative to Anglo-Americans.

During this early wave of Anglo-American immigration, Tejanos, in their desire to improve Texas, exhibited their strong regional identity. Yet at key moments, the significance of being culturally and politically Mexican appeared in stark contrast to the regional identity. Tejanos had to come to terms with their national identity at an early stage of the Mexican Republic's history. Understanding Mexican nationalism for Tejanos in Béxar requires the consideration of their social and political position.

Marriages, commercial ties, and social friendships between leading Anglos and Tejano elites allowed Tejanos to act as cultural brokers between the recent immigrants and the nascent Mexican government. Acting as a cultural broker meant employing insider knowledge to facilitate contacts between Anglo-Americans and Mexican officials. These early years of Anglo colonization also initiated a process where Anglos and Tejanos began to form views and concepts of each other within the context of their existing ideas of race and social hierarchy. Being a cultural broker was neither easy nor always safe for Tejanos. The risk undertaken by Tejanos grew as Anglo-American tensions and Mexican government demands increased. Tejanos struggled to negotiate these pressures in order to keep alive their aspirations for the growth and success of the region. In the midst of this struggle, Tejanos from the elite sector of society maintained a deep-rooted notion of honor and valor, developed over the decades of building the frontier colonies.

Colonization and Open Possibilities

Throughout the colonial period, Spain shunned bringing large numbers of foreigners into their frontier settlements.[11] But in 1821, on the eve of independence, the governor of Texas, Antonio Martinez, granted Moses Austin land and the franchise for three hundred Catholic families to be settled on the Brazos River.[12] The grant came in the context of years of filibustering and contraband trade by Anglo-Americans. While Martinez and some Tejanos had many reasons to mistrust Anglo-Americans, changes took place both among the Tejano elite and in the Mexican political climate to encourage immigration. Austin's grant became the basis for a set of colonization laws that established the *empresario* system, structuring immigration and migrations into Texas.

Under the *empresario* system, a land contract would be granted to an individual to settle between 150 and 800 families, though 300 families was more common. Each family received one *labor* of land to cultivate or one *sitio* to raise livestock.[13] The *empresario* received as compensation five *labores* and five *sitios* for each hundred families. He also directed the recruitment and movement of families onto his land grant, vouching for the character of his settlers. Governor Martinez stated his goal for the *empresario* system in Austin's contract, writing, "The most flattering hopes may be formed, that the said province will receive an important augmentation, in agriculture, industry, and arts, by the new emigrants, who will introduce them."[14] Along with the character requirements, Martinez stipulated that immigrants would become loyal Spanish subjects, willing to defend the territory "against all kinds of enemies."

Permitting Anglo-Americans to enter Texas was considered a necessary

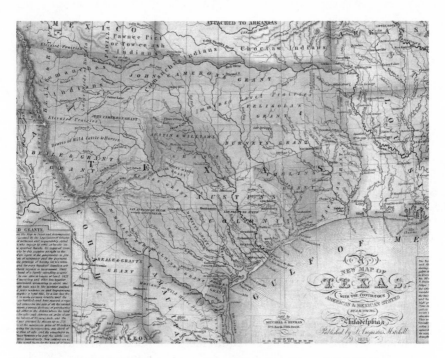

"*Map of Texas with the Contiguous American and Mexican States, 1835,*" *showing* empresario *land grants. (Map Collection, Archives and Information Services Division, Texas State Library and Archives Commission, 0023a)*

evil or worthwhile risk, with the benefits coming from increased economic production, increased population, and perhaps a new loyal citizenry. Frequent conflicts with indigenous groups in the north continued to strain local resources. Despite decades of missionary efforts, Mexicans never could enforce their social order on the indigenous people as a whole, due in large part to the low colonist population. With renewed expansionist pressures coming from the east after the Louisiana Purchase, Spanish government officials realized they needed to establish larger, loyal settlements in Texas in order to secure their claim to the land.[15] Some immigration started early as a few Anglo-Americans living in Louisiana during its Spanish possession took advantage of laws permitting Louisianan migration into New Spain after the Purchase.[16] Immigration pressures gave way to filibustering and demands for American annexation after 1803. The direct language defining the Texas border and Spanish domain found in the Adams-Onís Treaty of 1819 in many ways came in response to these pressures.

Elite Tejanos stood to gain economically from their plan to colonize Texas with Anglo-Americans. If the vast territory of Texas could be turned

American Immigrants   87

into productive farm and ranch land, Tejanos could benefit from their importance to the Mexican nation. Tejanos also considered the strategic importance Texas held as a border state between Mexico and the United States. Cooperating with Anglo-Americans would potentially provide stronger trade connections and make Texas a commercial center for economic exchange between the two countries. Tejano merchants saw only benefits of acting as brokers in this international transaction.

Uncertainty by royal, and later Mexican, officials over Anglo-American immigration resulted in character requirements codified in the colonization laws. Immigrants needed to provide proof of good character for permission to settle in Texas. The colonization law passed in 1825 by the Coahuila y Texas legislature stated that colonists needed to "prove their Christianity, morality, and good habits by a certificate from the authorities where they formally resided."[17] But the practice of religion never became a significant issue in the *empresario* grants. While Mexico mandated Catholicism as the only publicly celebrated religion, people in the land grants spent many years without even a priest assigned to their parish. Yet the inclusion of these character requirements not only acknowledged the risks of Anglo-American immigration but also reinforced status and gender beliefs held by elite Tejanos. These cultural values appear more clearly in letters of support written on behalf of Anglo *empresarios* discussed later in this chapter.

By encouraging Anglo-American immigration, these Bexareños suggested a broad definition of local identity in the context of recent Mexican independence. Instead of challenging Mexican nationalism by encouraging immigration, colonization encouraged Tejanos to expand the bounds of what it meant to be Mexican. Closer examination of individual Tejano actions as cultural brokers in the process shows a wider variety of motivations and a complex reconfiguration regarding who could be Mexican. While Tejanos almost always called American immigrants by the ethnic term *Anglo Americanos*, the traditional inclusion of Europeans in elite Mexican families and society in general fit within this notion of being Mexican. Elite Tejanos might not have sensed a great divide between their cultures, but the same could not be said for Anglo-American immigrants.

While Anglo-Americans immigrated to Texas with specific ideas about race and society, they held few general opinions about Mexicans.[18] Any impressions they had in 1821 related in part to experiences with the Spanish government in Florida and Louisiana. Southerners also held ideas about race, class, and civilization broadly. These concepts appeared in their treatment of indigenous groups in the South, such as Cherokees, and their complex system of labor based on slavery. During the first decade of colonization, Anglo-Americans developed ideas about Mexicans that incorporated these existing notions of class and race.

In his study of Anglo views of Mexicans, historian James E. Crisp questions the assumption that these colonists arrived in Texas with preconceived stereotypes.[19] While they did hold ideas about race, it was unclear how they would be translated into interactions with Tejanos. For Crisp, ideas about the Catholic church and Spanish monarchy more strongly influenced Anglo expectations of Mexican society than did assumptions about biological race.[20] Southerners also transported a complex set of social arrangements around class and honor that shaped their contact with Mexico's social order. Southern elites found themselves on familiar territory when they first met with Tejano elites.

One area where Mexicans did encounter racial ideas from Anglo migrants appeared in their attitudes regarding indigenous peoples. As noted in the previous chapter, early indications of Anglo westward migration toward Texas came through the arrival of several indigenous groups complaining of Anglo mistreatment. Cherokee leaders in particular referred to Anglo-American deceit in their attempts to coexist in the American South.[21] While Anglo-Americans held complex attitudes toward indigenous groups, there existed a broadly held belief in the biological inferiority of Indians.[22] Negative views of Mexicans by Anglos also focused on indigenous aspects of Mexican identity. These views were limited by social class, thus exempting most elite Mexicans from being stereotyped. The most well documented example of these elite connections appears in the friendship forged between Stephen F. Austin and Erasmo Seguín and their families.

For Tejanos, the beginning of Anglo-American immigration to Texas in 1821 held out the promise of a prosperous future. Open possibilities outweighed hesitation over American desires to annex Texas. Bexareño elites found a group of *empresarios* in Austin and other Anglo-American elites who appeared as motivated farmers willing to improve their struggling region. As Mexicans in a new nation, these immigrants, though culturally distinct, entered at a time when the meaning of Mexican nationalism and the presence of the Mexican state were in flux and in the process of consolidation. Immigration raised the possibility of building a multi-ethnic frontier state, one that could become nationally significant and powerful.

Gone to Texas: The Meaning of Southern Immigration

Despite earlier American designs on Texas, Tejano elites took an active role in encouraging Anglo-American colonization in Texas. From a global perspective, the introduction of Anglo-Americans into Spanish Texas appeared during a risky time for New Spain. Political tensions with Americans surrounding frontier issues loomed large in the minds of Spanish administrators. Problems arose in multiple areas, including contraband trade with merchants from Louisiana, filibustering expeditions led by Americans, and arguments by American politicians regarding the rightful claim to Texas.

The dispute over the claim to Texas, while diplomatically resolved by the Adams-Onís Treaty, played an important role in the political imagination of Anglo-Americans immigrating into Texas. In other words, the existence of a popular belief in Texas colonization opened the idea of immigration to southern Americans. Anglo-American claims to Texas had a significant effect on shaping the relations between incoming Anglos and resident Tejanos—not to mention between Anglos and the thousands of indigenous peoples living in the region—by encouraging massive westward migration by southerners.

The introduction of *empresario* grants in 1821 initially changed daily life very little in Béxar, especially since the Anglo-American colonists and their lands were in the vast hinterland to the east. Though few Anglo colonists moved into Béxar, Bexareños played a decisive role in advocating for the colonization laws and supporting their implementation. The eventual immigration of thousands of Anglo-Americans changed the already complex racial and ethnic landscape of Texas while introducing a new economic and political system. Tejanos became more adept at brokering disputes that arose between the Mexican government and these colonists. Tejanos employed many of the ideological and political tools acquired from their negotiation of the complex indigenous society in Texas. Once again, elite Tejanos organized the form of those negotiations while cementing their status and prestige within Tejano society.

Southern immigrants into Mexico thought differently of Texas than did the Tejanos or Indian inhabitants they came in contact with. For many southerners, especially those occupying the elite sectors of their society, Texas fit into a regional ideology around land and society. Expanding southern society and its economy into Texas held out the possibility for personal advancement and for strengthening what was perceived as an embattled region and culture.[23] The fact that Texas belonged to Mexico was not enough to stop this southern version of the "American Dream." Texas offered the opportunity for many southerners to start over, especially those deep in debt or with legal problems.[24] The first waves of immigrants were primarily made up of upland southerners without slaves.

Land was the central goal and organizing principle defining southern aspirations for Texas. Being predominantly an agricultural economy, the South relied on adding land to the productive base for economic expansion. Southerners imbued land with even greater meaning as generations passed on and American politics changed. As families handed down farms and plantations to their children, fewer landowners had access to the wealth of their ancestors. Scarcity of land in the South coupled with the politics of slavery implicit in westward expansion put Texas squarely in the southern sense of progress.

The abolition of the slave trade in 1807 raised the stakes around the sectional politics of American westward expansion. The language of progress and civilization surrounding westward expansion already included an implicit racialized definition of America and Americans.[25] Concepts of wild land, free of civilization, rendered indigenous and Mexican societies inferior. While most Americans agreed on the deficiencies inherent in the existing western societies, they disagreed on which version of American society and economy should be transplanted. Northerners believed a free labor system should dominate over the new territories, ensuring the welfare of laborers in their states. For southern politicians, westward expansion required the protection of their system of bonded labor to ensure the asset value of their slaves.

Opening Texas to westward migration under the southern ideology fit nicely with previous attempts at incorporating the state. The recent experiences of the Louisiana Purchase in 1803 and the acquisition of Florida in the Adams-Onís Treaty served to minimize the significance of the national ownership of colonized territory. After all, the Louisiana territories and Florida had also been held by other nations when the first American migrants began to occupy them.[26] The example of Florida fueled interest in immigration to Texas and attracted capital for land speculation from banking centers in New York and London. But instead of dealing with European colonial governments, as was the case with Florida, Anglo-Americans immigrating to Texas came in contact with Mexico, a creole nation-state at its earliest stage, and with its aspiring local elites. Shared cultural and economic values between southerners and Tejanos, particularly around ideas of land, aristocracy, and bonded labor, opened avenues of contact between the two groups.[27]

While Texas lacked the expansive haciendas located in other regions in Mexico, it shared the social importance placed on land ownership and labor relations tying workers to elites. Even though the eventual restrictions on slavery created obstacles to southern colonization, Tejano elites practiced other forms of bonded labor, particularly peonage. Peonage generally dominated agricultural areas and was present to a lesser extent in the municipalities. Mexican labor somewhat mimicked racial aspects of slavery through the elaborate caste system. According to census records and letters, some Tejanos also owned slaves.[28]

Tejanos and southerners shared elements of the aristocratic culture and social structure found among their landed elites. While very rare, a few elite families in Béxar owned enslaved people. These cases are limited to the colonial period and disappear from the record after 1821. Most notably, Erasmo Seguín appears in the 1820 census as owning a mulatto slave named María Juliana Cureste.[29] Two other heads of families also held slaves according to this census, namely Mariano Lopez and Luis Galán.[30] Lopez's household included an eighteen-year-old enslaved servant named María Rosa de la Rosa. Three years later, on July 19, 1823, she received her emancipation along with an unspecified payment and the right to own property.[31] In another case that same year, an enslaved "Negro Anglo-Americano" named Phil received his certification of emancipation when his owner, Charles Myers, was caught stealing livestock.[32] This handful of cases shows that while hardly widespread or significant to the local economy, slavery was recognized and practiced by elite Tejanos. That emancipation came quickly and easily in 1823 is further evidence of the minor role it played in Béxar's economy. But its presence and practice provided a critical connection point between Anglo-American immigrants and their Tejano supporters.

Honor resonated deeply in both Tejano and southern societies. Notions of honor played a central role in both of these aristocratic cultures, though the origins and development of honor differed between the two groups. It structured family, social status, and religious beliefs. The roots and function of honor varied between the peninsular Spanish origins of Tejano frontier honor and the British agrarian basis of southern honor.[33] Yet both valued the formal demands of masculinity and patriarchy undergirding their ideology and culture. An unwritten code of behavior and deference supported the wealth and prestige held by landed elites.

Economic motivations to colonization went along with these ideological similarities. Bexareños spent much of their time eking out a living in the harsh, isolated borderlands frontier. Ranching and farming provided little more than subsistence for the town, especially since frequent droughts often depleted livestock holdings. It was into this setting that the first Anglo-American *empresarios* arrived, promising to bring hundreds of families to increase the wealth of the region. For many Bexareños, the potential benefits of establishing new trade routes and making their region more economically valuable to Mexico City outweighed the perceived risks of allowing Anglo-Americans to settle in their province. Furthermore, the colonization laws included provisions that would in theory weed out rebellious Anglos and attract only industrious and thus "honorable" immigrants.

Elite Tejanos benefited economically from their ties with Anglo colonists by gaining an expanded market for merchandise. For instance, on November 27, 1828, José Antonio Navarro ordered gunpowder and three hundred pounds of coffee from Stephen F. Austin in exchange for some mules and horses.[34] In his letter, Navarro noted the lack of these items anywhere in Béxar. During the colonization period, Tejanos would trade for goods from the Anglo colonists in order to maintain their storehouses in Béxar. Historian Andrés Reséndez has noted that Ramón Músquiz and the Seguín family "not only had developed extensive trading networks comparable to those of their Anglo counterparts . . . but also dominated local politics and were very influential in matters of land distribution."[35] Cultural brokerage thus carried both economic and social status incentives.

Mexican land grants and the *empresario* system attracted Anglo-American immigrants into Texas.[36] Understanding this process and Tejano involvement in Anglo colonization provides insight into the changes that took place within Tejano ideology during this early period. Anglo-American colonization tested the strength of the nascent Mexican Republic at its borders. In light of increased Anglo-American colonization, Tejanos continued to define their regional identity but also realized the growing importance of being Mexican and of strengthening their identification with the new nation.[37] A close inspection of elite Tejanos acting as cultural brokers reveals elements of these dual objectives. For most of them, these objectives fit in the normal demands of building and maintaining status and prestige within Béxar society.

Béxar Elites and Colonization

Bexareño society reflected the social and gendered divisions between elites and lower classes prevalent throughout Latin America. These two societies circulated in very separate spheres, with most social interactions limited to exchanges within the groups. Tejano elites held their own fandangos, intermarried among their own families, organized the official town festivals, held most elected offices, and lived in their own neighborhoods. Even elite homes differed in their construction and furnishing, with the wealthy living in stone homes. Most of all, elite Tejanos developed their own variety of Norteño culture based on notions of honor and lineage. Tejanos also appeared to use honor, social status, and political connections to establish prestige and gain positions of leadership in the town and region.

The names of Tejanos who held government positions and were appointed to commissions repeat time and again from the turn of the century to 1835 and beyond. Among the elite family names of Béxar were Seguín, Navarro, Veramendi, Ruiz, Arciniega, Flores, Padilla, and Músquiz.[38] Most of these families came to Béxar in the mid- to late eighteenth century, some tracing their roots to the Canary Islander colonists. By the nineteenth century, most of these elite leaders had been born in Béxar, making them natives of the town. These families socialized together, aided each other in economic ventures, and facilitated marriage between elites. For example, Juan Martín de Veramendi, born in Béxar, married Josefa Navarro, also of Béxar. Veramendi worked with Erasmo Seguín to secure the Austin contract and went on to be the town customs collector and later deputy to the Mexican National Constitutional Congress in 1823.[39] Occasionally, the circle was expanded to include elites in other northern towns.

Deeply embedded in the Norteño elite idea of social status was the concept of honor. In contrast to southern honor, Mexican honor was rooted in Iberian culture and took on a unique frontier form in northern New Spain. Along with the idea of honor through family lineage, Tejanos added bravery and autonomy, as experienced during the insurgency and battles with indigenous groups. Bexareños articulated those ideas during the Anglo-American colonization period by using the language of honor to endorse *empresarios* before the state legislature. By supporting immigration, Tejanos expressed their sense of connection with the cultural values introduced by elite southern men.

Elite connections with Anglo-Americans and other Europeans were already underway before colonization. Several cases of non-Spanish Europeans and Americans becoming citizens in Béxar appear in records decades before this period. For instance, the Baron de Bastrop, one of Béxar's most prominent citizens and political figures, emigrated from the Netherlands. In the colonial period, Tennessean Peter Ellis Bean and Irishman Samuel Davenport both immigrated to Texas and became influential officials in the provincial government.[40] Both Bean and Davenport served as Indian agents to the indigenous peoples living in north Texas. Bean became further Mexicanized when he took a commission in the Mexican army and married a Mexican woman in Jalapa.[41] Anglo-Americans and Europeans took advantage of existing cross-national elite societies, such as the Masonic lodges, to establish early social ties. Tejano political leaders used the lodges as ideological headquarters and as a proxy for political parties.

Occasionally, non-Mexicans immigrating into Texas married Mexican women and lived culturally Mexican lives. But few Anglo-Americans married to Mexicans lived in Béxar prior to 1821. The 1820 census does not list any such marriages. Only after Anglo-American immigration, and especially after Texas became an Anglo-American Republic, do the intermarriage rates rise. These cases of Anglo-Americans and Europeans entering elite Norteño society provide evidence of a flexible notion of Mexican identity in the early nineteenth century.

Perhaps one explanation of why elite society could cut across cultural lines came from the existence of *mestizaje* in Mexican society. While the strict caste system broke down in the late colonial era, mixing of races and cultures implied in *mestizaje* provided a starting point for considering Anglo-Americans as future Mexicanos. Like Spaniards, Anglo-Americans could consider themselves European, in contrast to those who were indigenous or were of African origin. This is not to say that Spaniards saw themselves as equally white, given the complex racial and ethnic history of Spain.[42]

Masculinity also served as a significant factor in the relationships between elite Tejanos and Anglo-American *empresarios*. Overlapping ideas of gender and masculinity provided another tool for Tejanos to employ in their position as cultural brokers. The discussion of marriage above introduces one arena where these ideas of manliness appeared to influence the form of interethnic contact by adding a gendered dimension to that interaction. Other exclusively male spaces, such as Masonic lodges or legislative bodies, also served as places where a shared understanding of a gendered social order facilitated contact and contracts. Reséndez has researched the extensive Anglo-American reliance on freemasonry to establish contacts with Tejano government officials.[43]

It is worth returning to Stephen F. Austin and Erasmo Seguín's relationship to further examine the various elements of elite male contact and cooperation. Born in Béxar in 1782, Seguín held prominent positions in Béxar government and society.[44] At the age of eighteen, he married María Josefa Becerra, the daughter of a Spanish officer. In 1807, Seguín received his first public post as the postmaster of Béxar. As the postmaster, Seguín maintained close contact with the events and orders emanating out of the state capital in Saltillo as well as from Mexico City.

Seguín maintained the viability of Moses Austin's *empresario* contract through the transition of Mexican independence by bringing up the proposal again to the new government. He also passed along the strongest recommendations in favor of Stephen F. Austin and his colonists as they made their way to Texas. Regarding the colonists, Seguín wrote to the governor of Coahuila y Texas: "I am informed, [they are] of highly respectable families—[entertain them] in the best manner possible. Therefore I notify you so that you may, if you think desirable, have suitable lodgings prepared for them for the four or five days they will stay in the capital."[45] Austin realized he had an ally in Seguín and trusted him with defending the interests of *empresarios* in political matters. A strong bond formed between the Seguín and Austin families, perhaps because Austin quickly recognized Seguín's stature in the Tejano community.

Seguín, along with Baron de Bastrop, advised Austin in the early stages of establishing his colony.[46] In August 1821, Seguín discussed the possibilities and limits of setting up a system to regulate trade with indigenous peoples living around the colony.[47] Over the next decade, the Seguín and Austin families developed a close friendship on a personal level as well. As mentioned earlier, Stephen's brother James would stay with the Seguíns when he would come to Béxar. Seguín's wife, María Josefa Becerra, also participated in strengthening the bonds between the two families, writing to pass on messages from Erasmo or to invite Stephen Austin and his family to Béxar. The tone of Becerra's letters implies a neighborly intimacy suggesting the families had spent time visiting.[48] On September 20, 1824, Becerra wrote to Austin, "I have not lost hope that we can go visit your family when José Erasmo returns from Mexico City. The same Mr. Austin [Stephen Austin's cousin] informed me of the passing of your mother of which I send my deep condolences and we share that sentiment with your entire family. All our family greet you with the same warm regards [*cariño*] as we always do, offering ourselves at your disposal."[49] Becerra's letter reveals much about the emotional bonds shared between the two families. It also demonstrates the family-wide project involved in cultural brokering and prestige building. Husbands and wives and sons and daughters all participated in these relationships.

Austin managed the most successful *empresario* contract in Texas, quickly fulfilling his original grant for three hundred families by mid-1824. He later received several more land grants and fulfilled the quota of families each time. Austin continued to benefit from his friendship with Seguín while he built his colony.[50] Seguín represented Texas in the Constitutional Congress of 1824, advocating for colonization in the new laws of Mexico. Seguín also lobbied heavily to gain an exception from the ban on slavery for Texas, perhaps with the understanding that Anglo-Americans required slavery for their agricultural production. His motivation for such a request came from more than an interest in colonization, however; as noted earlier, census records show Seguín's household included a mulatto slave.[51] Still, correspondence between Seguín and Austin during the Congress demonstrated Seguín's interest in the success of the colonizing venture.

Early in the Constitutional Congress, Seguín wrote to both Austin and Bastrop regarding the progress made on Texas issues. Regarding slavery, Seguín stated, "I will present everything that comes to mind in favor of your colony . . . whether it be those [slaves] brought by colonists or those born in the territory."[52] Seguín placed himself on the colonization committee of the Congress, increasing the influence he could have in advancing his position. A few months later, Seguín commented on his lobbying efforts regarding colonization. He wrote Bastrop to tell Austin "to be in the secure knowledge that while I am in Mexico City, his colony has a protector, and when I leave I will know to leave an agent as interested as we are towards the business he requires with the Congress and the General Government."[53] By the end of the Congress, the constitution allowed for colonization by foreigners and permitted states to assign *empresario* grants. Regarding slavery, Seguín managed to get an exception for Texas, but the issue would not die easily. The next chapter explores the ways slavery became a wedge between Anglo colonists and the Mexican government in the years leading to secession.

Aside from Austin's colony, another example of Tejano participation in the Anglo land grant process appears in the *empresario* petition of Reuben Ross and in the aid he received from Juan Antonio Padilla. Ross, an American, first came to Texas in 1813 as a colonel in Bernardo Gutiérrez de Lara's insurgent campaign to capture Béxar from the Spanish royalists. Although Ross returned to the United States, he publicized the benefits of cheap land in Texas and obtained an *empresario* contract. Padilla served as his principal advocate before government officials.[54] Not a native of Béxar, Padilla came to the town in 1810 as an officer in the Spanish military.[55] He kept his connection to Béxar while becoming involved in official posts in the Provincias Internas. After independence, Padilla served as a representative from Béxar in the state legislature over several terms in the 1820s.

Padilla wrote a personal recommendation for Ross, whom he called Colonel Ross, emphasizing his bravery in fighting for Mexican independence. Padilla stated, "The aforementioned Colonel Ross, because of his valor and disposition, won victory for the Republican Army in the battle of Rosillo, which destroyed the provincial troops and allowed the capture of the capital of Béxar. It is also known that in the heat of battle, he fought hand to hand against Lieutenant Colonel Don José Montero of the royalists, one of the most intrepid officials of that battle."[56] Padilla concluded by stating that Ross's behavior during the occupation of Béxar was characterized by "honor, probity and fairness." These comments conveyed the values Tejanos held as important during the nineteenth century. In particular, his comments serve as an example of honor through valor in battle, a trait deemed important to frontier men. Padilla provided Ross with both a strong endorsement and access to the state legislature.

In another letter to the governor of Coahuila y Texas, Padilla elaborated further on the potential benefits to Texas if Ross were granted the *empresario* contract.[57] Ross requested a grant for settling four hundred families in the triangle between the Red River and the Sabine River. Padilla claimed bringing these industrious families into Texas would not only improve the land but also slow down the rampant contraband trade on the Texas and Louisiana border. Furthermore, Padilla believed the location of the grant in the lands of the Comanche people would hinder the trade of arms from Americans to the indigenous peoples and the trade of stolen horses and mules from Comanches to Americans.

While the Mexican and state governments deliberated over Ross's land grant, a filibuster led by an Anglo-American, Haden Edwards, broke out in Edwards's grant. This event harmed Ross's efforts and dampened the effect of Padilla's lobbying, since government officials suddenly grew reluctant to encourage more Anglo-American colonization. State officials also worried that the expenses of protecting colonies so deep in Comanche territory would be prohibitive.[58] Nevertheless, in 1826, Ross received a grant to settle one hundred families.

Before he could begin to operate his colony, Ross died. But the following year, John Cameron, a Scottish immigrant, took up Ross's grant to bring families to Texas. In 1827, he sought a grant for two hundred more families, half migrating up from other provinces of Mexico and the others from Europe.[59] By this point, the Mexican government responded positively to any contract that brought families other than Anglo-Americans into Texas. Cameron received his grant for two hundred additional families the next year.

By 1828, Padilla became much more involved in the general politics of colonization and also developed a personal relationship with Stephen F. Austin. Throughout the following two years, Padilla provided legal and political advice to Austin regarding his colony and state politics. Much of his connection with Austin seems to be based on their mutual membership in York Rite Freemasonry. In a letter dated January 12, 1828, Padilla warned Austin of the arrival of General Manuel Mier y Terán on his inspection of Texas, adding, "He is dangerous for those who do not know his Masonic opinions. He assures not to belong to any rite, but that is a lie, his is Scottish [rite] and a worshiper."[60] Further Masonic ties appeared when Padilla received a request from Austin to open a Masonic lodge in San Felipe de Austin.[61]

From his post as secretary of governance in Saltillo, Padilla forwarded news of significance to the colonization movement to Austin. In August 1828, Padilla wrote Austin a lengthy legal explication of property rights under Mexican law and suggested a manner in which to present his colony in order to incorporate Galveston Island.[62] In other letters, Padilla sent Austin news of political events in Mexico, especially during General Antonio López de Santa Anna's rise to power. But he also provided constructive criticism to the colonists, mentioning their lack of Spanish language and culture. He wrote to Austin, "Inform the gentlemen of the Ayuntamiento [of San Felipe de Austin] for me that now that they are members of the 'gran familia Mexicana,' they would be better served to adopt the virtues of being Mexican, and never the vices."[63] By early 1829, Padilla returned to Béxar and continued his correspondence with Austin.

Padilla's ties with Anglo-American *empresarios* suggest that honor and social status overcame possible political and racial conflicts. Padilla functioned as a cultural broker by serving as the contact point for Americans seeking land and for Mexican officials making demands. Places such as the Masonic lodges became a middle ground for shared beliefs among elite men as well as for making deals. Like Seguín, Padilla also supported and sponsored Anglo-American immigration into Texas. In doing so, Seguín and Padilla began to include Austin in the established Mexican patterns of familial notability and prestige.

Anglo colonizers also received a boost from the work of Bexareño José Antonio Navarro. Through his political involvement on the state level, Navarro managed to provide favorable legislation to promote colonization. Later, as land commissioner, Navarro assisted in maintaining Green De Witt's colony. Born in Béxar in 1795, Navarro became a self-taught lawyer and went on to hold several positions in local and state elected office.[64] His mother, María Josefa Ruiz, was the sister of Francisco Ruiz, the Indian commissioner of Texas. This puts him squarely in the network of notable families of Béxar. Navarro participated in the insurgency in Béxar and later became a vocal supporter of secession and annexation to the United States.

As a member of the Congress of Coahuila y Texas, Navarro and other Tejanos negotiated a loophole to allow Anglo immigrants to bring slaves into Texas. Colonists could circumvent Mexican law through a clause that honored labor contracts established on foreign soil before immigration into Mexico occurred. Navarro wrote to Austin from Saltillo, "Assure our compatriots that my heart goes out to them, . . . all our wishes and efforts are and will be used for the benefit of this Department."[65] Austin used Navarro's exemption for slave labor and even prepared a standardized form to give his colony's immigrants so they could bring slaves.[66]

Upon the conclusion of his term, Navarro returned to Béxar but continued his relationship with Austin on a personal and business level. On November 27, 1828, Navarro requested a list of goods to purchase from Austin. He prefaced his order with a note of friendship, stating, "I am very passionate and I cannot ignore my friends and therefore I am always here at your disposal."[67] Two years later, Navarro took another official post, with the De Witt colony. Through the state legislature, De Witt had obtained his grant on April 15, 1825, to settle three hundred families, about the same time as did a large group of *empresarios*. It is unclear whether Tejanos aided him at this point in the process. But in January 1831, the governor appointed José Antonio Navarro land commissioner to the colony.

As commissioner, Navarro was not only charged with the distribution of land titles to incoming colonists but was also granted the power to survey

the land to be subdivided.[68] Moreover, Navarro's duties included review-
ing the character recommendations of potential colonists and adminis-
tering the oath of allegiance to Mexico upon their immigration. Navarro's
involvement with the De Witt colony came at an important time for the
colonization project. As will be discussed below, Mexican government officials had become increasingly suspicious of Anglo-American immigration
and began placing restrictions on their entry.

From his position as the political chief of the administrative Department of Texas, Ramón Músquiz held a considerable amount of power, not
only to influence policy but to choose whether or not to carry out the laws.
Fortunately for Stephen F. Austin and other Anglo-American *empresarios*,
Músquiz proved to be a vociferous and competent advocate for their interests locally and at the state level.

Born in Béxar around 1797, Músquiz carried out his office with the goals
of increasing the population of Texas and of setting the tone for harmo-
nious relations between all inhabitants of the department, regardless of
nationality.[69] Músquiz began his political carrier in Monclova, as the postmaster of that town. He moved back to Béxar in 1823 to establish a trading
business while remaining politically active. His appointment as political
chief, a position that made him the de facto governor of Texas, occurred on
January 1828, and he served until 1834. Músquiz frequently corresponded
with Austin, which created a strong administrative link between Austin's
colony and Texas.

In several of his letters, Músquiz was critical of the development of
Austin's colony. Noting the difficulty in conducting government business
with the colony in a letter from January 22, 1828, Músquiz admonished
Austin, "It is certainly a disgrace that the Citizens making up [the colony]
do not speak Castillian [Spanish], the lack of which cannot be avoided,
and I console myself by your sentiment they are men of probity and common sense."[70] Statements such as these by Músquiz suggest that Tejanos
sought to use their cultural broker roles to advise and influence both Anglo-
Americans and Mexican officials, thus shaping the development of the
northern frontier.

In that month, Músquiz also appointed Gaspar Flores land commissioner
for Austin's colony. It seems Austin preferred Juan N. Seguín, Erasmo's son,
but Músquiz disregarded Austin's wishes.[71] On occasion, when government
officials might decide against a request by Austin, Músquiz would try to
soften the blow by recommending alternatives to Austin. When the govern-

ment turned down Austin's petition for land in a coastal area, as prohibited by the colonization laws, Músquiz advised him about other land he might find agreeable.[72]

In cases when Músquiz agreed with Austin, he lodged official complaints to state and federal authorities, attempting to get a policy changed or rescinded. On an official trip to Saltillo, Músquiz tried to get the Coahuiltexan legislature to pass a law suspending the payment of foreign debts by immigrants in Texas until 1840.[73] Austin had proposed the idea in June 1828 in order to provide relief for his colonists.[74] Músquiz succeeded in securing this exemption for Austin, but not without overcoming some resistance by legislators. Músquiz also used his connections to present Austin's idea to open a port on the Brazos to Governor José María Viesca.

While Músquiz dealt well with the business of governing Texas and overseeing the colonization process, all his diplomatic skills were put to the test when tensions rose after a series of anti-colonization laws in the years after 1828. It was at that point that Músquiz's support of Austin weakened, while he maintained his standing in the Mexican government.

Other Tejanos figured into the success of the Anglo colonies in Texas by acting as land commissioners and supporting favorable legislation. Miguel Arciniega and Gaspar Flores both functioned as land commissioners for Austin's colony and aided the colonization process in other ways. A native of Béxar, Flores rose quickly in the ranks of political leadership in that town. He was elected to the position of mayor, or *alcalde*, over several terms from 1819 to 1834. In January 1828, Músquiz appointed Flores land commissioner, a position with direct oversight of the *empresario* program.[75] Early in his tenure, Flores experienced delays, lasting through the summer, in moving to San Felipe de Austin. By January 1829, soon after arriving in San Felipe, Bexareños elected Flores municipal *alcalde*, and he continued his correspondence with Austin while in this position. Austin considered Flores such an ally that he suggested Governor Viesca appoint Flores commissioner of colonization after the arrest of Juan Antonio Padilla in 1830.[76]

Miguel Arciniega also served a time as both land commissioner for Austin's colony and *alcalde* of Béxar. Arciniega used his position in the state legislature in 1828 to lobby in favor of slavery by honoring prior labor contracts for immigrants.[77] He also seems to have corresponded with Austin, with whom he had an established friendship, during the years of his colony, even while he served as *alcalde* of Béxar after Gaspar Flores. After his tenure as *alcalde*, Músquiz appointed Arciniega land commissioner to Austin's colony on November 13, 1830.[78]

Other Bexareños, such as José Antonio de la Garza, José Casiano, Manuel Ximenes, José María Sambrano, and Ignacio Arocha, also became involved in the politics of Anglo colonization in Texas. As Tejano elites in Béxar, they held an interest in the economic and political future of Texas. As inhabitants of the Mexican frontier, they also experienced the most immediate effects of the Anglo-American immigration. Tejano participation in Anglo-American immigration provides a window into their efforts to shape the social and economic world around them at the beginning of the Mexican nation. These actions take on added significance in light of the relative absence of the Mexican state in this border region after independence.

Brokered Identities

The above examination of elite Tejano participation in the Anglo colonization of Texas shows the content and nature of Tejano culture and identity during Anglo-American immigration. Tejano support of Anglo *empresarios* and immigration reveals the contours of Tejano culture relating to honor, lineage, and citizenship, particularly where these ideas converge between Mexican and American cultures. By including Anglo-Americans in the future of Texas, elite Tejanos expanded their idea of who could become Mexican while maintaining their culture and nationality. Also, in fostering Anglo-American colonization, these Tejanos carved out a position as cultural brokers between the immigrants and the Mexican government, continuing efforts made over the previous decades with indigenous peoples. Unlike the relations forged with indigenous peoples, Tejano brokers shared the social status of elites with Anglo *empresarios*. While both these elite groups shared social goals, the broader populations, Anglo-American and Mexican, differed along ethnic lines and perhaps in their long-term goals as well. One difference began to develop as more non-elite southerners entered Texas. At that point, Mexican government officials began to think of Anglo-American immigration as a problem, putting the Tejano position of cultural brokers in jeopardy.

Maintaining familial prestige and regional power played a strong role in motivating elite Tejanos to support Anglo immigration despite any cultural barriers. The initial period of Anglo colonization required tacit Tejano support to ensure its success. The most articulate echoes of that support appear in letters attesting to the good character of Anglo land grant applicants. These letters not only reveal Tejano endorsement of Anglo immigration but also the meaning and significance of certain values within Tejano culture. Early colonization laws required immigrants to demonstrate their "Christianity, morality, and good habits." The meaning of morality and good habits is evident in letters written by both Seguín and Padilla. Along with these references to character, Tejano support of colonization also exposed the meaning of lineage, honor, and masculinity in their culture. The emphasis on character, prestige, and honor continued the development of a distinctive Mexican frontier identity initiated in the colonial period.[79]

Subtle undertones of the importance of class and status appear in examples of Tejano concepts of propriety found in letters they wrote to Mexican officials in Saltillo and Mexico City. In his letter to Antonio Martinez, governor and political chief of Texas, Erasmo Seguín referred to Austin and his colonists as being from recommended families. In his endorsement of Austin, Seguín relied on references of lineage and aristocracy to outweigh or allay any fears of permitting rebellious Anglos to colonize Texas. Throughout this period of Anglo colonization, Tejanos emphasized the merits of individual Anglo-Americans in order to counter perceived threats of American conquest. The personal friendships between many elite Tejanos and elite Anglo-American families deepened these one-to-one contacts. Tejano use of family prestige and lineage also coincided with the elite Mexican cultural notions of aristocracy and honor.

Honor and masculinity also appear in other recommendations of Anglo-Americans, such as Padilla's support of Colonel Ross. In this case, though, Padilla listed Ross's bravery and valor in battles against the Spanish army during the insurgency and his merits as a fighter for Mexican causes instead of using family and bloodline to vouch for his good character. Ross could be trusted not only to remain loyal to the Mexican nation but also to fight against threats to Texas. Padilla's employment of terms of valor and violence links the idea of good character to frontier experiences of Indian fighting.[80] Although organized citizen excursions against indigenous peoples occurred less frequently in Texas than in other parts of Mexico, Tejanos still valued those traits among their *vecinos*.

While honor, lineage, masculinity, and prestige describe the content and continuity of Tejano class culture, Tejanos during this period developed a functional aspect of identity through their roles as cultural brokers. Tejano elites developed the ability to negotiate and access to this negotiation largely as a result of their social development in Béxar, on the borderlands between a distant and nascent Mexican state and expanding Anglo-

American commercial interests. Furthermore, these actions provide clues to the motivations behind Tejano actions during the nineteenth century. Cross-ethnic alliances forged along class lines articulated a local version of Mexican nationalism. Anglo-Americans were potential Mexican citizens, and supporting their colonization effort was not yet seen as anti-Mexican.

Tejano support of Anglo colonization of Texas also demonstrated several aspects of the rise of ethnic identity in the changing borderlands frontier. Given their uneven connections to the colonization process, most Tejanos in Béxar served as cultural brokers by living in the contact zone between Anglo-Americans to the north and the remainder of Mexico to the south. Few Tejanos approached the high level of interaction or strong relationship found between the Seguíns and Austins. The examples of Padilla, Navarro, Músquiz, and others show that interethnic contact took place in capacities other than friendship, such as through official government channels. Nevertheless, the actions of these Tejanos occurred in the upper levels of Tejano society, the negotiation of culture and commerce being a hallmark of elite status.

Anglo-Americans faced a large cultural and ideological distance when they requested land from Spanish and Mexican government officials. Austin made clear his understanding of the significance of Tejanos to the success of the Anglo colonization project when he wrote, "I would say to Texas, you must all harmonise [sic] with Béxar and Goliad, that is with the Mexican population."[81] Although Austin wrote his statement in 1834, it should be considered the culmination of years of Anglo reliance on Tejanos to smooth their immigration into Texas. As Anglo colonization increased and the politics of living on the Mexican frontier changed, the role of Tejanos as cultural brokers constantly shifted. New pressures surfaced from continued non-elite Anglo-American immigration and growing opposition to the colonization policy by the government in Mexico City. Tejanos reacted to these tensions by carving a space as negotiators but later ended up in a situation of accentuated ethnic identification.

By the end of 1828, Mexican political opinions began to turn against the *empresarios*, Anglo-American immigrants, and the colonization laws in general. A revolt by *empresario* Haden Edwards in December 1826 stirred controversy and suspicion within the Mexican government. After having been granted a contract in 1825, Edwards refused to follow a Mexican law regarding land claims made by Mexicans already living within his grant.[82] The Mexican government subsequently revoked Edwards's contract in June

1826. Edwards and his disgruntled colonists proceeded to occupy Nacogdoches and declare the Republic of Fredonia on December 16. Austin feared that repercussions of Edwards's revolt would tarnish the image of his colony before Mexican authorities. To prevent this, Austin circulated a resolution to several other colonies pledging allegiance to the Mexican government and opposing the Edwards rebellion.[83] Austin wanted to clearly depict Edwards as the exception to Anglo colonist sentiments. By January 21, 1827, Mexican troops joined by Anglo volunteers easily managed to quash Edwards's revolt. Edwards found little vocal support for his anti-Mexican views among the other Anglo-American *empresarios*.

But the troubles in Nacogdoches did begin to raise suspicions among Mexican officials generally. After receiving a report about election problems in Nacogdoches, the political chief of Texas in Béxar, José Antonio Saucedo, commented, "If the *empresarios* and colonists are not obligated to respect and follow the Laws of their adopted Nation, then this will be made more difficult after the settlement of greater numbers, and who knows if they will separate from the State and adhere to those of their native nation with all the land they occupy."[84] He repeated such warnings on other occasions, imploring his superiors in Saltillo and Mexico City to take notice of the deteriorating situation on the frontier of his native Texas.

Edwards's revolt did damage the Anglo colonization project by raising old fears of Anglo-Americans among the Mexican authorities. While Anglo-American filibustering expeditions littered the Texas past, most Tejanos and Mexicans acted as though that period had come to an end. As time went on, Tejanos began to walk a thinner line between Anglo immigrants and Mexican political sentiments. Their actions between 1829 and 1832 demonstrate the manner and extent of that balancing act. Moreover, external events, such as the secession in 1835 and the U.S.-Mexico War in 1846, affected the course of identity formation, raising the importance of ethnicity, despite early Tejano efforts to the contrary.

In retrospect, the colonization project and permanent Anglo-American settlements marked the emergence of distinct ethnic identity among Tejanos. Two factors contributed to the development of ethnicity at this time: the emergence of national identity with the Mexican state and the voracious desire for land among southerners. The efforts and desires of both the Mexican state and American southerners forced Tejanos to play their hand during moments of crisis and conflict. Elite Tejanos sought an active role in encouraging immigration and mediating subsequent friction.

The shape and meaning that ethnic identity took during this period varied for Tejanos and Anglo-Americans alike. In the way the concentric circles of indigenous identity outlined in the previous chapter situated Tejanos in a spectrum of contacts, the relationship Tejano elites had with Anglo immigrants was different from their relationship with other Mexicans. Most Tejanos in Béxar and south Texas experienced infrequent contact with these immigrants through the 1820s. The lasting impact on their daily lives and identity took place in subsequent decades. Likewise, aside from *empresarios* and a few other merchants, most Anglo immigrants had few interactions with Mexicans.

As the primary bridge to the Anglo-American world, Tejano elites had a significant effect on the shape ethnic identification took in the Anglo/Mexican relationship. Much of that impact occurred by passing on cultural and social structures inherent in the Tejano social world. Anglo-American immigrants could, in part, racialize peonage, since it so closely resembled their treatment of enslaved blacks. The two social worlds, Tejano and Anglo-American, briefly followed parallel trajectories in Texas. As part 2 of this study shows, those worlds fractured and diverged precisely when nation began to matter.

Part II

Becoming Tejano

The political situation of the Mexican Texans, is now very difficult and compromised, and we all miss very, very much that the State government has not yet dictated any orders to preserve even a simulacrum of the laws and respect towards authorities that they are responsible for.

—José María Balmaceda, April 6, 1833

Chapter Four

Disrupting the Balance

COLONIZATION TROUBLES, 1828–1834

O n April 25, 1831, Father Refugio de la Garza, Béxar's longtime priest, wed the Anglo-American immigrant James Bowie and Ursula de Veramendi.[1] Veramendi's parents, Juan Martín de Veramendi and María Josefa Ruiz de Navarro, each came from notable families. Josefa's brother Francisco Ruiz had served as an important official during the Spanish and Mexican periods. Angel Navarro and Juan Francisco Bueno acted as *padrinos*, or godparents, to the ceremony and thus connected the couple to the broader elite community through *compadrazgo*. While questions remain about Bowie's truthful representation of his past, his marriage to Veramendi immediately opened doors and opportunities for him to benefit financially. Martín de Veramendi and others provided Bowie with cash and access to pursue business ventures, most of which failed. Tragedy cut short the marriage when Ursula, along with her parents and children, succumbed to the devastating cholera epidemic of 1833–34.[2] Afterward, Bowie became more involved in Anglo-Texan uprisings throughout Texas, ending in his death at the battle of the Alamo. The Bowie-Veramendi marriage brought together the social dynamics that had been underway in Béxar for a decade by linking Tejano cultural brokerage with family prestige and immigration. It reveals the reliance Anglo-Americans placed on Tejano social networks, a need made more important for the success of the *empresario* colonization system.

Of all the *empresario* contracts granted in Texas, Stephen F. Austin's proved to be the most successful. Austin's relatively close ties with the Seguíns and other Tejano elites provided him with an advantage over other *empresarios*. He achieved unparalleled access to the Tejano power structure and frequently asserted himself in regional politics. Austin stood alone as the dominant *empresario*, completing two different contracts, while twenty-five other *empresarios* failed to fulfill their quotas.[3] Few others took the time to learn the Mexican political system and Spanish language as well as Austin.[4] And when an uprising threatened the province, as was the case with the Edwards rebellion, Austin proved his loyalty to Mexico by taking up arms in support of the Republic.

Tejanos quickly noticed that Austin was the most industrious and adaptable of the *empresarios*. None approached his ability to befriend elite Tejanos, and he was the only one to integrate his colony into the Department of Texas, as the administrative region was known in the state of Coahuila y Texas. Despite modest success by *empresarios* other than Austin, the colonization laws still attracted thousands of immigrants to Texas from the United States during the 1820s and into the 1830s. While many immigrants entered Texas through the *empresario* program, a large number eschewed official procedures and immigrated illegally. As a result of this demographic wave, Anglo-American immigrants transformed the borderlands and subsequently Tejanos' social context.

Within a decade, the total population of Texas increased tenfold, from roughly 2,000 in 1820 to 21,000 in 1834.[5] But the population of Béxar remained fairly stagnant, in one account even decreasing from approximately 1,814 in 1820 to 1,634 in 1831.[6] Even though Béxar failed to experience the same population growth rate as the rest of Texas in the 1820s, its continued political significance made it the key town in the region. In a larger sense, about 2,000 Tejanos stood as cultural brokers between the expanding Anglo-American immigrant population to the northeast and the nascent government in Mexico City to the south. As the Anglo population continued to grow, immigrants developed their society outside of the oversight of government officials. New policies came about starting in 1829 in response to these developments. Through these policies and the Anglo-American re-actions, Bexareños experienced a series of changes in their relationship to the colonists. Rapid Anglo-American immigration forced Tejanos to recon-sider ethnic relations in the region, a move hastened by increasing political restrictions from Mexico City. Decades of brokering relations with indige-nous groups and Americans drove Tejanos to mediate these new changes and in the process cemented the importance of the borderlands to their identity.

By 1828, the opinions and directives of policy-makers in Mexico City began to directly affect Bexareño influence on colonization. Debates in Texas and Mexico City over the proper course of action regarding foreign immigration entered into the arguments between political factions. The strongest policy changes occurred following the arrival of General Manuel Mier y Terán and his commission to evaluate social conditions on the Texas frontier. Mier y Terán's reports resulted in laws curtailing American im-migration and political influence. These imposed policy changes began to limit what elite Tejanos could do for the region's future.

The roots of these tensions lay in the years before 1828, particularly with Haden Edwards's rebellion in 1826, also known as the Fredonian Re-bellion. The rebellion itself had only a minor impact on ethnic relations, since most Tejanos probably considered it anomalous rather than a general trend among Anglo-Americans. The support that Mexican troops received from Austin's colonists only reinforced this conclusion. Nevertheless, offi-cials in Mexico City read these events as reason for concern, or at least in-vestigation. For most Mexicans, the Texas frontier appeared worlds away, and the violent outburst caught many officials by surprise.

Based on the intensity of rumors making their way down to Mexico City, President Guadalupe Victoria decided to research the source of the vio-lence. He sent one of his most trusted and educated generals, Mier y Terán, to report on the immigrant situation and suggest a plan for keeping Texas in the Mexican nation.[7] Victoria's government established the Comisión de Límites, or Boundary Commission, ostensibly to delineate the border with the United States.[8] On November 10, 1827, Mier y Terán left Mexico City with a group that included, among others, a civil engineer, an artist, and a botanist. They reached Béxar in early March 1828. Mier y Terán spent that summer and the following year traveling through Texas, most of the time in Anglo-dominated towns. What he witnessed alarmed him.

By June, he began sending back his first observations of the state of affairs in Texas outside of Béxar. In a letter to the president, Mier y Terán noted the scarcity of Mexicans in the Anglo towns, and those living there were of "what people everywhere call the abject class [*la clase ínfima*], the poorest and most ignorant."[9] He went on to notice mutual cultural ignorance practiced by both Anglos and Tejanos, writing, "From this state of affairs an antipathy has emerged between the Mexicans and foreigners that is not the least of the volatile elements I have found to make me tell you that, if timely measures are not taken, Tejas will pull down the entire federation."[10] The other potential problems he referred to included the constant stream of Anglo-American immigrants of poor or criminal background and the growing controversy over slavery in Texas. In a later letter to the War Department, Mier y Terán began to express his suspicion that a more sinister motive lay behind the influx of Anglo immigrants, namely American imperialism. In it, he stated, "There is no power like that to the north, which by silent means has made conquests of momentous importance."[11]

Mier y Terán's comments provide a unique insight into the developing political and ethnic rift between Anglos and Tejanos in this period. While cultural brokering and cooperation still took place, the pressures of Anglo-American immigration began to shift the social terrain where these relations took place. Mier y Terán traveled to the towns and farms in Anglo-American *empresario* colonies where he observed the relative poverty of Mexicans' lives. As an outsider to Texas, Mier y Terán noted characteristics of Texas society possibly overlooked by many Tejanos. Mier y Terán's critical eye toward Texas allowed him to see a different trajectory of social relations on the frontier.

Mier y Terán's remarks on the social status of Tejanos in these Anglo colonies identified a significant transformation of race relations in Texas. Due to rapid Anglo population growth, Tejanos living to the northeast of Béxar were a political, economic, and cultural minority group. This ethnic shift took on both social and geographic manifestations. Because the Anglo towns were far away and difficult to get to, Bexareños either avoided or never knew about the inferior treatment of Tejanos there. Béxar became a frontier enclave of Tejano social power in the face of a still distant but encroaching Anglo-American migration. And as such, Béxar continued to be the pivot-point where relations between Anglos and Tejanos that shaped ethnic relations in Texas would be decided. But the new ethnic relations forged in the Anglo colonies of northeast Texas defined Mexican culture for a large portion of the Anglo-American immigrant population.

Mier y Terán's time in Texas represented a significant period of transition in the demographics of the territory. The Mexican government contracted the bulk of its Anglo-American land grants to *empresarios* in the four years from 1825 to 1828. Mier y Terán arrived in Texas at the latter part of that rush, and his presence may have influenced the government policy to halt this immigration. Still, while many of his comments characterized the Anglo presence in Texas as a threat to national integrity, Mier y Terán established close relations with a few Anglo Texans.

For example, during his investigation, Mier y Terán developed an especially close friendship with Austin. They initially corresponded about the environment and history of Texas.[12] Austin took the opportunity to propose policies on slavery and tariffs beneficial to Anglo-American immigrants. In one letter, Mier y Terán responded that "it is extremely difficult to reintroduce another law regarding slavery."[13] But political issues played a secondary role in Mier y Terán's interests, as most of the letter discussed his theories regarding the weather in Texas and the precise geographic coordinates of the territory.

The members of Mier y Terán's group faced a variety of obstacles hindering their ability to gauge the state of the colonies. At one point in June 1828, several of Mier y Terán's men, including botanist J. L. Berlandier, succumbed to fevers and were forced to return to Béxar.[14] Later, Mier y Terán met with a Cherokee chief to discuss the tribe's claims to land in Texas. In his role as commission leader, Mier y Terán lacked the authority to grant the Cherokees land; however, he commented to his superiors on indigenous relations, expressing his belief that every effort should be made to limit further immigration of indigenous peoples and to fortify the frontier against further migrations.[15]

By April 8, 1828, the commission had produced a preliminary report, but the final version would not be completed until January 6, 1830. At the conclusion of Mier y Terán's commission, the president named him comandante general of the northeastern Mexican states and stationed him in Matamoros. From his post, Mier y Terán could direct the legal and military response to perceived dangers presented by Anglo-Americans in Texas. In that period, Mier y Terán continued to believe Anglo-Americans posed a serious threat to the territorial integrity of Mexico. In a letter to the Minister of War and Navy in Mexico City, Mier y Terán warned that Anglo-Americans were settling in strategically important locations, such as river heads.[16] He made a similar point in a letter drafted to President Victoria on March 28, 1828, noting that none of the settlers "has requested permission or settled more than twenty leagues from the border. In the present state of affairs there is no one to demand that they obey the laws. . . . Acts of government cannot be carried out lest they provoke an uprising that inevitably will accomplish the expulsion of Mexicans from Texas."[17] His warning signaled that Anglo-American immigration and settlement would hinder any military response to rebellion.

The Colonization Law of April 6, 1830

The work done by Mier y Terán and the Comisión de Límites momentarily focused Mexican federal attention on Texas, leading to a series of policies and laws that forced Tejanos to further redefine their relationships with Anglo-Americans. The resulting laws raised the possibility of limits on slavery and further American immigration into Texas. Whether or not Mier y Terán understood Tejano attitudes toward Anglo-Americans, his observations and suggestions transformed the dynamic between the two groups. In particular, because he brought slavery to the fore, Tejanos could no longer turn a blind eye to the issue. Now Tejanos had to either justify the Mexican government's position or join Anglo-American protests against slavery and immigration limits. The maneuvering room that Bexareños enjoyed as cultural brokers in the region became narrower since limits on slavery and immigration loomed larger as the Anglo-American population increased.

As a result of these perceived security threats, many of Mier y Terán's recommendations for Texas centered on building military posts at strategic locations and sending increased numbers of troops to the region. Additionally, he believed the government needed to do more to encourage Mexicans to migrate north to Texas. The Mexican government established new posts at Tenoxtitlán, on the Brazos River, and at Anáhuac, on Galveston Bay. These outposts not only housed the Mexican military regulars but also became centers of contact between Anglo colonists and the Mexican government.

Through the Comisión de Límites, Mier y Terán noted adverse trends in Texas society and suggested policies that in turn affected that society. He might not have initially taken the diminished social status of Tejanos in east Texas as a sign of crisis, since he had greater military concerns on his mind, but as a general in the Mexican army, Mier y Terán would have been more cautious, wary of the loss of Texas to the United States.[18] He believed increasing the military presence in the region would not only prevent the secession of Texas but also facilitate and increase the migration of Mexicans from other parts of the nation.

The Mexican government reacted quickly to Mier y Terán's initial reports by sending soldiers and building forts along the Texas frontier. President Victoria's successor, Vicente Guerrero, complicated matters further when he issued a proclamation emancipating all slaves on Mexican territory, including Texas, on September 15, 1829, elaborating on the existing tradition where government officials freed convicts on Mexican Independence Day.[19] While Guerrero's decree appeared as the most comprehensive emancipation law, it emanated out of years of limits and conditions placed on slavery, starting in 1823.[20] Those laws ranged from limits on the importation and internal trade of slaves to the emancipation of enslaved people under fourteen. Coahuila's legislature added their own laws around slavery, including the emancipation of 10 percent of an estate's slaves upon sale or transfer and the establishment of ninety-nine-year indentures for Anglo-Americans to circumvent slavery restrictions.

Sensing the problems it would bring, the Béxar Ayuntamiento never published the decree and instead submitted a request to exempt Texas.[21] On several occasions previously, Tejano elites and the Béxar Ayuntamiento had quickly acted to prevent possible problems resulting from antislavery laws passed by the Mexican legislature. In a letter to Austin, José Antonio Navarro wrote, "You should believe that the most upstanding men of the State are against the Law which lacks Justice and good faith."[22] The Ayuntamiento's arguments included the need to honor the property rights of those immigrating into Texas.[23] But more important, Tejanos felt they needed to permit slavery in order to encourage slave owners to immigrate into Texas, since they brought a labor force to work the land and were wealthier immigrants.[24] A ban on slavery would deter large slave owners and leave only poorer southerners to migrate to Texas. Tejanos feared those immigrants would not help the state develop and would be more likely to foment revolution in Texas. Slavery gave elite Tejanos a way to attract Anglo-Americans of a higher social status to Texas.

While the Mexican government officially condemned slavery, it and other forms of bonded labor continued to exist in Mexico. Even though the agricultural slavery of southern Americans differed from Erasmo Seguín's domestic slaves, the similarities made it easier for Tejano elites to sympathize with Anglo immigrants on the issue of slavery. Even though state and federal governments placed various restrictions on slavery, Texas received an exemption as a special case. Much of this occurred through intense legislative lobbying efforts by Austin and various Béxar elites.[25] Tejanos not only tolerated slavery but also aided in enforcing the system. On June 12, 1828, Ramón Músquiz used his official capacity to post wanted signs around Béxar and La Bahía to locate a runaway slave.[26]

Just as the momentary crisis over the antislavery law calmed down, the Mexican government passed a new, more pointed law completely eliminating Anglo-American colonization: the Law of April 6, 1830. The legislation addressed issues raised by Mier y Terán by outlining new limits and policies on trade, security, immigration, and slavery.[27] While several articles of the law sought to increase Mexican colonists and the Mexican military presence in Texas, two articles in particular worried Anglo-American colonists. Article 10 directly addressed slavery, stating, "The federal government and the government of each state shall most strictly enforce the colonization laws and prevent the further introduction of slaves." The following article went further: "It is prohibited that emigrants from nations bordering on this Republic shall settle in the states or territory adjacent to their own nation." Article 10 singled out the carefully negotiated exemptions that Texas had secured regarding the limits to slavery and put an end to any future immigration of enslaved people. Article 11 responded to the threat of American expansion by effectively ending Anglo-American immigration into Texas, the territory adjacent to the United States. The article's language continued to allow other foreign immigration and American immigration into other parts of Mexico.

While Anglo-American colonization highly troubled Mier y Terán and he pushed to suspend it, he never suggested ending it altogether.[28] The Law of April 6, 1830, renewed and strengthened opposition to the Mexican government among Anglo-American colonists and fostered suspicion and sedition in the land grants. From this point on, Tejanos dedicated themselves to negotiating the deepening rift between Anglo-American colonists and the Mexican government. Through their experience with the intricate nature of ethnic relations in the region, Tejanos used their position as cultural brokers to smooth over tensions, particularly concerning slavery.

Anglo-American immigrants, on the other hand, interpreted the elements of the Law of April 6, 1830, that restricted further immigration as an indictment of their presence. The plans of many Anglo-American merchants and farmers depended on maintaining a connection with the United States as a market and supplier without the expenses of tariffs. In a letter intended for Minister of Foreign Relations Lucas Alaman, Austin expressed his concerns about the impact of the law on Anglos: "They [Austin's colonists] became Mexicans from choice[,] they have been faithful to this Government since they entered its territory, they wish to remain Mexicans, and it is their interest as well as their duty to remain—under this view of the subject is it good policy to sour their minds and alienate their affections?"[29] He continued, "The law of the 6 of April will have a fatal tendency if imprudently executed as you can easily perceive by taking a slight view of my colony."[30] In his letter, Austin bristled particularly at Article 10, restricting slavery, since he felt it would deny Anglo-American colonists their property rights. Austin continued to work in private to change the law, or at least soften its blow by advocating a generous interpretation of how it would be applied to existing *empresario* contracts.[31] In another letter to General Mier y Terán, Austin added, "It appears that the national Government will reward our loyalty and services with our destruction!!!"[32] These statements reveal Austin's complex attitudes regarding Tejanos and the Mexican government. While he maintained friendships with some Tejanos and supported keeping his Mexican citizenship, Austin privately showed frustration with the Mexican government.[33]

For Tejanos, the Law of April 6, 1830, overshadowed efforts to use local government to mediate and shield Anglo-Americans from opposition by the Mexican government. While the Ayuntamiento managed to keep Guerrero's law of 1829 hidden from public view, the broader Law of April 6, 1830, marked a more resolute and public stance against Anglo immigration by the Mexican government. Ramón Músquiz reacted by reiterating his support for Austin and his colonists, noting "that never have they [Austin's colonists] ignored the law or disobeyed the authorities of the country they have adopted as their nation."[34] Tejano elites still had an interest in maintaining Anglo-American immigration. They often expressed this interest in terms of increasing the population, expanding commerce, and even gleaning benefits from the American civic system.

Aside from Austin's colony, Mier y Terán saw greater problems with continued Anglo-American colonization. While the law of 1830 sprang out of Mier y Terán's attempts to increase domestic migration to counter Anglo dominance in Texas, he also understood the potential benefits of Anglo immigration. In an 1828 letter, he pointed to Austin's colony as a positive example, noting, "They are for the most part industrious and honest, and appreciate this country." But this did not mean that Mier y Terán fully supported colonization, either. Later he suggested, "If the colonization contracts in the territory of Texas by North-Americans are not suspended and if the circumstances of their settlement are not closely watched, it is necessary to say that it is definitively handed over to the foreigners, and for ignorance, which does not differ from treason, of selling the sacred interests of the Republic."[35]

Whether through persuasion or accommodation, Austin's private complaints against the law began to subside as he worked to publicly support the Mexican government.[36] Austin published an editorial in the *Texas Gazette* on June 26, 1830, seeking to allay fears among Anglo residents brought on by the new colonization law.[37] But pressure remained on Tejanos to continue to negotiate a middle road for Anglos in Texas.

The Law of April 6, 1830, sought to change the social landscape of Texas, moving it away from the threat associated with overwhelming Anglo-American colonization. The law managed to create change in Texas, but perhaps not in the direction government intended. The law strictly denied Anglo-Americans immigration while still encouraging Mexican and European migrations. The few Anglo-American *empresarios* who followed the colonization rules could finish the terms of their existing contracts. Only Mexicans received *empresario* contracts afterward, and few of those managed to attract any colonists. Of the six contracts granted in that period, two did go to joint ventures between Anglo-American and Mexican *empresarios*, namely Juan Antonio Padilla and Thomas J. Chambers, granted on February 12, 1830, for eight hundred families, and José María Royuela and J. C. Beales, granted on March 14, 1832, for two hundred families.[38] Only two of these six post-1828 contracts established viable colonies, those belonging to Lorenzo de Zavala and Martín de León. In these years, Anglo dissatisfaction with the Mexican system of government increased, leaving Tejanos in a more difficult mediation position.

Mexican *empresarios* began to take a more active role after Mier y Terán's reports. Even though the state legislature granted Lorenzo de Zavala a contract, it achieved a relative amount of success only after de Zavala joined with David G. Burnet and Joseph Vehlein to form the Galveston Bay and Texas Land Company.[39] Except in the case of Martín de León, Mexicans receiving land grants depended on Anglo-American *empresarios* and investors as well as on Anglo-American colonists.[40] De León received his *empresario* grant from the provincial government in Texas on April 13, 1824. His colony, based out of the town of Guadalupe Victoria, met its settlement quota with mostly Mexican migrants from Tamaulipas and with a handful of Anglo-Americans, Irish, French, and Germans.[41] It stands as a model colony, given the frequent defaults experienced with Anglo-American contracts.

Despite the lack of significant Mexican *empresarios* and colonists, Tejanos remained vital to the success of Anglo-American colonies. For instance, on November 25, 1830, Governor Músquiz appointed Miguel Arciniega commissioner for Austin's land grant. Six months later, Arciniega reported on the progress Austin had made over the last year toward completing the requirements of his contracts. By May 1831, Austin had settled two-thirds of the nine hundred families required by his contract.[42] While the Law of April 6, 1830, debilitated the *empresario* system, it didn't end it. Since the law encouraged non-American colonization, several groups of Irish took advantage of the opportunity and formed settlements. Irish *empresarios* James Power and James Hewetson received contracts to settle Irish families along the gulf south of de León's and Austin's colonies in 1829 and again in 1831.[43] Being Catholic, many Irish immigrants soon began to intermarry with Mexicans. The *empresario* system remained in place as the path to increasing the province's population and improving its economy.

Along with changes in the land grant process, the Law of April 6, 1830, also sought to increase the military presence in Texas through the creation of a new presidio, Tenoxtitlán, and by increasing the number of troops stationed at Béxar and La Bahía. Mier y Terán ordered the establishment of a fort at Tenoxtitlán on April 24, 1830.[44] He appointed Francisco Ruiz, a Bexareño and Indian agent, to build the fort and become its first commander. Strategically located on the Brazos River, on a major road between Béxar and the frontier town of Nacogdoches, the fort that Ruiz built was close to many of the large *empresario* grants. From this site, Ruiz and his men could oversee the adherence to the Law of April 6, 1830. The fort also provided a more proximate locale for Anglo colonists to access the Mexican government.

The establishment of Tenoxtitlán embodied Mier y Terán's strategy to bring the Tejano population into military oversight. Beginning with a fort aimed at controlling both indigenous peoples and Anglo-American enemies, his vision included bringing more Mexican families into a region of the nation he felt was Mexican in name only. Tejanos only partially embraced an "Indian fighter" ethos found in other parts of the northern frontier.[45] Instead, Tejanos strove to establish themselves as brokers of both merchandise and culture. Perhaps this explains why Tenoxtitlán was ineffective as a military fort yet prospered as a trading center for years after Mexican troops abandoned the town.

Tenoxtitlán served not only an economic role but a judicial one as well.

With its proximity to the largest *empresario* settlements in northeast Texas, the town provided Anglo-Americans closer access to people in the Mexican government. Tenoxtitlán temporarily displaced Nacogdoches as the point of contact between Mexico and immigrants to the frontier. Tenoxtitlán housed a few recently migrated Tejano families from Béxar and Mexican soldiers. Eventually, Mier y Terán believed families from farther south in Mexico would populate the town.

From the founding of Tenoxtitlán in 1830, Ruiz functioned as the representative for the Mexican government on the borderlands frontier. His role as supervisor of the fort exemplified how Tejanos functioned as cultural brokers. For example, in November 1830, a group of Anglo-American colonists from Tennessee arrived at the town with land contracts in hand. Unsure of the proper interpretation of the new colonization law, and probably amenable to the settlement of these colonists, Ruiz wrote to his superiors in the Mexican government regarding the application of the Law of April 6, 1830. They responded to Ruiz's inquiry, telling him to turn back the settlers. Ruiz never carried through on this order. Ruiz added in a letter to Austin, "I will continue to proclaim the advantages, that in my opinion, will result by admitting hard working and honest people, no matter what nation they are from . . . even hell itself."[46] Examples such as these show that cultural brokering meant more than serving as a conduit between two groups. Tejanos used their position to exert a degree of power and to carve out a political and social space for themselves in the region.

Ruiz used his post to maintain the delicate equilibrium between Anglos, indigenous groups, and Tejanos. At one point, Ruiz recruited the aid of a few members of local indigenous groups to punish a band of Wacos who had murdered an Anglo.[47] In another instance, local Anglos subdued another Anglo who had shot at a group of Choctaws, later taking him to San Felipe for trial.

Tejanos opposed the Law of April 6, 1830, in general, as they did the slavery restrictions. In December 1832, the Ayuntamiento of Béxar wrote a memorial to the president, exhorting him to change the law.[48] They stated that without continued Anglo-American support and immigration, Texas would cease to develop economically and politically. They also noted that Texas lacked the manpower to patrol the border and thereby enforce the law. They felt that as a result of the Law of April 6, 1830, the most honest Anglo-Americans would not come to Texas, leaving only those more willing to disregard Mexican authority. They concluded by reasserting the benefits of Anglo-American immigration, including elevated economic production,

increased peace with indigenous peoples, and improved commerce between the United States and Mexico. Nevertheless, the Law of April 6, 1830,
stood and Anglo-American challenges to Mexican laws increased, threatening the space Tejanos had carved out to develop their own social and
political identity.

Béxar and National Politics

While Anglo-Americans mounted challenges to Mexican legislation,
Tejanos continued to find ways to assert their voice in Mexican politics.
But changes in Mexico's political parties affected their ability to function
as cultural brokers, since the lines of authority kept changing. Struggles
mainly divided federalists demanding greater state autonomy and centralists favoring a strong executive government in Mexico City. In the latter
part of 1829, conservative leader Anastacio Bustamante led a revolt against
President Vicente Guerrero. Through the Plan de Jalapa, proclaimed on
December 4, 1829, Bustamante sought to concentrate power in a centralist
government. Mier y Terán had close ties with Bustamante and aided him
at several points in his career. But by 1832, Bustamante lost in a power
struggle to Manuel Gómez Pedraza, the constitutional president. One year
later, Antonio López de Santa Anna was elected president.

While turmoil proceeded on the national level, the Coahuila y Texas
legislature in Saltillo preoccupied itself with an internal power struggle
along lines mirroring national politics. These conflicts even resulted in
dual capitals in Saltillo and Monclova for a period in 1833. For Austin and
some Tejanos, this appeared as a good opportunity to suggest either dividing Texas from Coahuila or moving the capital to Béxar. Béxar not only was
more centrally located within the expanding region but also ensured that
colonization would remain in favor and a priority to the state government.

By summer 1832, Austin's reading of violence in Mexican politics led him
to believe that Santa Anna would soon come to power. He quickly asked political chief Ramón Músquiz to pledge Béxar's allegiance to Santa Anna and
against the Plan de Jalapa. Austin also organized a convention in San Felipe
to draft a petition to separate Texas from Coahuila y Texas. Fifty-eight delegates from around Texas met October 1–6, 1832; none were Tejano. The
meetings produced a set of demands that Anglo-American colonists believed needed to be brought to the attention of the Mexican government.
Their demands principally centered on changes and modifications in the
local government to allow for more autonomy and a distinct judicial sys-

tem. The cornerstone of these proposals appeared in their request for Texas statehood.

As he usually did, Austin advocated acquiescence and patience with the Mexican government along with direct demonstrations of loyalty. Nevertheless, he had to contend with pressures for immediate action from within his colonies. Anglo-American immigrants themselves were not monolithic in their support for any policy regarding the Mexican government. Their sentiments toward Mexico ranged from those wanting to secede and join with the United States to those content with being Mexican citizens.[49]

Upon his initial reading of the Anglo-Texan petition, Músquiz noted the possible illegality of requesting statehood for Texas. Austin understood the need for strong Tejano support if these changes were to take place, as seen when he wrote that Anglos should "harmonise [sic] with Béxar."[50] Austin's reliance on Tejano support differed from Tejano control over the terms and outcome of the political tensions. Tejanos understood the demands of negotiating a middle road between two political extremes. Tejano representatives needed to choose a stance that would alienate neither Anglo-American colonists nor the Mexican state. Had they joined in all of the Anglo-Texan demands, the Mexican government would label them rebellious. On the other hand, Tejanos could not reject the Anglo request outright, threatening the delicate relations between the two groups. Finally, many Tejanos affiliated themselves with federalists in national politics, so they agreed in principle with the need for political reforms.

But having veto power over the Anglo-American petition did not mean Tejanos enjoyed a privileged position in Texas during this period. To a large extent, the terms of the debate and the impetus for change emerged out of the Anglo-American meeting in San Felipe. The Tejano response to this meeting appears as a last-ditch effort to remain relevant as the cultural brokers between Anglo-Americans and the Mexican government. As long as Anglo-Americans remained interested in maintaining their allegiance to Mexico, they needed Tejanos.

As a result of Austin's request, the Ayuntamiento of Béxar gathered on December 19, 1832, to discuss the situation in Texas, especially in relation to problems with colonization. The committee sent a petition to the state legislature of Coahuila y Texas in Saltillo.[51] But unlike the Anglo-Texan resolution, the committee stopped short of requesting Texas statehood. Instead, the report delineated fourteen specific proposals on issues ranging from colonization to judicial reforms.

The Ayuntamiento proceedings began when six Bexareños—José Casiano, Angel Navarro, José Antonio Navarro, Refugio de la Garza, José María Balmaceda, and Erasmo Seguín—met to draft a petition to the state legislature. As noted previously, most of these Tejano elites associated closely with Anglo *empresarios* and often received benefits from the success of those ventures. But they also expressed a desire to see the province prosper and lamented the economic decline of several towns in Texas. They noted in their petition, "So it is that some towns have been destroyed while the rest have been unable to attain, even for a single day, that peace or those other guarantees which should have insured population and other resources for their development."[52] Here the Ayuntamiento addressed the circular problem of low populations and constant threats of Indian attacks. By stressing the desperate situation for Tejanos, the group sought to justify its calls for more dramatic action by government officials.

The committee's critique moved on to address the members' disapproval of the Law of April 6, 1830. "And what shall we say concerning evils caused by the general law of April 6, 1830 . . . ?" The Ayuntamiento added, "The law prevents immigration of some capitalists and of some industrious and honorable men who have refrained from coming because of it, but has left the door open to wicked adventurers and others who constitute the dregs of society."[53] The men went on to comment on the positive aspects of Anglo immigration into Texas. In particular, they noted the agricultural advances brought by Anglos resulting in the production of cotton and sugarcane on previously unfarmed land. They added, "Theirs [Anglos] is not a precarious existence, the only kind known in Mexican towns, which depend solely upon the troops' payroll that circulates so slowly among us."[54] Here the Béxar Ayuntamiento highlighted an underlying tension between Anglo-American frontier towns and the economic situation in Béxar. Currency was scarce in the northern frontier, and Béxar grew dependent on soldiers' wages to bring in money. The Ayuntamiento felt hampered by the Mexican political system, just as Miguel Ramos Arizpe had almost twenty years before. Rather than blaming the Crown and the colonial administration like Ramos Arizpe did, the Ayuntamiento presented an argument for the federalist opposition to the centralist Mexican government.

Although the Ayuntamiento did not recommend dividing Texas and Coahuila into two states, Austin continued his drive for Texas statehood. Austin called for a constitutional convention to be held in San Felipe to form the state constitution. Again, Béxar refused to join the Anglo-Texan colonists' call for separation, citing the illegitimacy of the political process initiated by the colonists. At the state level, legislators pointed to the dangers of an

Anglo-dominated state in order to justify the continued linking of Coahuila and Texas. They realized that demographically, the Anglo colonists in the state would always outvote the Tejano population. Historian Andrés Tijerina suggests that persistent support of Anglo-American immigration by Tejanos in the face of these problems indicates that they valued political self-determination and sought to respond to federal government efforts to limit their power.[55] Furthermore, other legislators feared that statehood would bring Texas one step closer to joining the United States.[56]

Bexareños found themselves once more pushed by Anglo-American colonists to respond to their request for statehood. In a letter to Congressman José Francisco Madero on April 6, 1833, Bexareño José María Balmaceda explained the political predicament the movement placed on Tejanos: "The political situation of the Mexican Texans, is now very difficult and compromised, and we all miss very, very much that the State government has not yet dictated any orders to preserve even a simulacrum of the laws and respect towards authorities that they are responsible for."[57] Balmaceda's comments portray the shaky position Tejanos found themselves in after the denial of Austin's request for statehood. Troubles within the ranks of the state government prevented the legislators from providing Balmaceda and other Bexareños the political support for reforming the political system in Texas.

Austin made several attempts at persuading Tejanos to support his view regarding Texas statehood. Austin's own admission of the importance of Tejano agreement for his proposal manifested itself in several personal visits to lobby elite Tejanos. Balmaceda noted that Austin traveled to Béxar, Goliad, and Nacogdoches at least three times in search of support. Aside from Austin's closest ally, Erasmo Seguín, Tejanos wavered in the face of this proposal. Balmaceda wrote, "[Austin] has been dealt a painful deception, seeing that only Erasmo feels the separation of Texas is justified."[58] Yet Austin persisted by whispering rumors and threats of Anglo-American revolts without statehood.[59]

Unable to get a definite agreement, Austin still set off for Mexico City to request Texas statehood. In an October 2 letter to the Ayuntamiento, Austin made known his intentions to circumvent the regional process and seek statehood if Béxar wouldn't take the lead.[60] The Ayuntamiento expressed shock at his decision and sent the letter to the state and federal authorities. The committee members' motivation remains unclear, though documenting their disapproval might have cleared them of charges of complicity with Austin or at least served to maintain their role as regional brokers. Austin might have also suffered the misfortune of sending the letter to Béxar at a time when Ramón Músquiz, his ally and the political chief, happened to be away. As Austin returned from a series of contentious meetings in Mexico City, government officials in Saltillo received his letters, considered his goals treasonous, and ordered his arrest. Federal officials detained Austin during a stop in Saltillo, and after waiting two weeks in Monterrey to receive orders, they marched him back to Mexico City in January 1834.[61] The statehood issue in Texas and Austin's arrest sufficiently raised the interest of the Gómez Farías administration to send another fact-finding expedition, this time led by Juan Nepomuceno Almonte.[62] Valentín Gómez Farías asked Almonte to identify any rebellious movements among Anglo-American colonists in Texas and to measure the impact of Austin's arrest on that population. These events evolved from the discussions introduced by Austin in the Béxar Ayuntamiento more than a year earlier.

The ambivalent stand on statehood taken by the Béxar Ayuntamiento resulted from the pressures Tejano elites felt from Anglo-American colonists on the one side and from their position in the shifting political situation in Mexico on the other. While several of the reforms brought up in the "Representación" to Saltillo refer to issues attributable to Austin's requests, other complaints address political points heavily debated in Mexico at the time. The Ayuntamiento specifically mentioned the alienation felt by Tejano elites after the Coahuila y Texas legislature signed on to Bustamante's Plan de Jalapa.[63] As a result, Tejanos lost much of their voice in the state's governance. Bustamante's government brought in many centralist and conservative policies, removing power from states and giving rise to the strength of landed elites and the church.[64] Furthermore, the Bustamante government approved of the unpopular Law of April 6, 1830.

From a political standpoint, Tejano elites ideologically allied themselves with the federalist groups in Mexican politics. At this point in late 1832, Santa Anna had already initiated an armed resistance to Bustamante and his Jalapista government. Despite Bustamante's attempts at reorganizing his government to share power with opposition groups, Santa Anna eventually gained power in coalition with Gómez Farías. By supporting Santa Anna and Gómez Farías, Tejanos probably anticipated receiving a greater voice in national politics through the federalist system. At the very least, they looked to regain the little representation they had possessed in the state legislature.

But personal politics might have also played a role in the Bexareño political stance. Most of the Tejano elite belonged to the York Rite Masons.[65]

As mentioned in chapter 3, the exclusively male setting of Masonic lodges acted as de facto political clubs throughout Mexico. Those in the York Rite, or *yorquinos*, mainly associated with the federalist wing of the political spectrum. While Bustamante's government contained mostly Scottish Rite Masons, Gómez Farías elevated the importance of *yorquinos* in politics. The borderland federalists received recognition, since Miguel Ramos Arizpe occupied a key position in Gómez Farías's government, bringing his connections with the Coahuiltexans to the center of Mexican politics.

Tejanos' participation in national politics elevated their political outlook beyond the local sphere. Not only did Tejano elites concern themselves with national debates, but they also desired a voice to influence the direction of national politics. While Tejanos developed a strong regional identity on the far northern borderlands of Mexico, internal and external forces compelled them to keep their political attention focused on Mexico City. Through Mexican politics, Tejanos expanded their identity beyond the region to include the nation. As frontier Mexicans lived a long distance from Mexico City, Mexican national identity was strengthened both by the proximity to the United States and by the resulting emigration from there. The local benefits gained from colonization, though, did not outweigh allegiance to the Mexican nation. The careful articulation produced by the men of the Béxar Ayuntamiento in their "Representación" pointed to their recognition of that balance. Yet a change was occurring, despite Tejano efforts to mediate the conflict. Their regional boosterism ran into growing polarization along ethnic lines. As time went on, Tejano political and ethnic options became limited, and the room to negotiate ran out.

Ethnicity in the Borderlands

By allowing Anglo-Americans into Texas, Tejanos not only considered their individual economic well-being but also projected a vision for the future of the entire province in the nascent Mexican nation. Since Texas was considered too weak to stand as an individual state, the Mexican legislature combined it with Coahuila to make one state with the capital far south, in Saltillo. Legislators also feared that Anglo-American demographic dominance would create an Anglo-American state, leaving ethnic Mexicans politically powerless. Yet for Tejanos, populating the province and making it economically productive made it of national significance. In this manner, Tejanos exhibited a strong sense of their local relevance to the nation.

Anglo-American immigration introduced ethnic consciousness into the

Tejano political culture by raising questions of group membership and national belonging. Assimilation of Anglo-Americans as Mexicanos did not occur right away. A letter dated 1822 addressed to Stephen F. Austin as the "estranjero Austin," or the "foreigner Austin."[66] Most documents from the 1820s and 1830s refer to immigrants from the United States as "Anglo Americanos." Through naming "Anglo Americanos," Tejanos took note of the immigrants' national and cultural differences. Rather than foreign invaders, Anglo-Americans became white ethnics within Mexican society.

Nevertheless, a certain amount of fluidity started to take place in Texas, and *estranjeros* became *ciudadanos*, or citizens. Evidence of the acceptance of Anglo-Americans appeared through the bilingual publication of the official state newspaper, *Correo de Tejas*, in 1823.[67] Anglo-American immigrants, required by law to be of good and honorable character, had the opportunity to participate as Mexican citizens. Supporting the Mexican government improved the standing of Anglo-Americans in Tejano eyes. As noted in the previous chapter, Juan Antonio Padilla's mention of *empresario* Reuben Ross's participation in the insurgency demonstrated the emphasis on rewarding physical risk in support of the nation. Oaths of allegiance to the Mexican nation taken by Anglo colonists also appear more frequently in this period. In May 1823, migrants from Austin's colony pledged to "defend at all costs the authority of the Constitution of the Mexican Nation" and later joined the Mexican army in resisting the Haden Edwards revolt.[68] By the mid-1820s, evidence appears in an official document that calls Austin "*ciudadano* Austin" rather than *estranjero*.[69]

But the cultural accommodation occurring on the Texas borderlands proved to be far from perfect. As much as Tejanos might have planned for a multi-ethnic province, few Anglo-Americans lived in Béxar. Instead, they preferred to remain separated in newly founded towns with their own government. This geographic and social distance prevented more Mexicans from interacting with Anglo-American immigrants.

By 1830, in response to increased Anglo-American immigration and suspicions about ulterior motives after the Edwards revolt, Tejanos shifted their expectations of the region's social and political future. Tejanos initially looked to Anglo-American colonization to encourage growth in the population and stature of their province in the Mexican nation. But as tensions increased around the Law of April 6, 1830, reality clashed with these aspects of Tejano aspirations. Texas increased in population and significance in the Mexican nation, although not economically, as Tejanos anticipated. Rather, Texas became an important pawn in the diplomatic struggle between Mexico and the United States. Also, the segregation of Anglo-American towns only further entrenched Anglo-American culture, hindering the process of Mexicanization. Any interactions took place on a limited scale, and primarily among Tejano and Anglo-American elites. These external events shaped the direction Tejano identity took over the next quarter century, from cultural brokers in the borderland to ethnic minorities in the American empire.

Despite the difficulties raised by separate and distant Anglo-American colonies, Tejanos managed to make connections between Anglo-Americans and Mexican government officials. Tejanos continued to bridge the divide between colonists and the government even as each side hardened negative stances toward each other. They carried out this function as cultural brokers unconsciously, rarely mentioning the significance of their actions.

Developments during this period of colonization placed a new emphasis and meaning on ethnic difference for Tejanos. Prior to this period, Tejanos primarily contended with indigenous peoples and their cultures. While initially, Tejanos might have considered Anglo-Americans culturally closer than Indians, colonization only exaggerated rifts between Anglo-Americans and Tejanos. These rifts not only shaped the government policy but also surfaced because of those policies. For instance, immigration restrictions in the Law of April 6, 1830, came out of the assumption that Anglo-Americans would never become either politically or culturally Mexicans. The law also created new lines of distinction and forced Tejanos to readjust their attitudes toward Anglo-Americans.

Tejanos also developed a unique borderlands identity that shifted from the isolated "character" of the late colonial period to the border condition of the early national period. In Spanish, *frontera* means both the far provinces and the border. In the early nineteenth century, Tejano experiences embodied both meanings, although to different degrees at different times. By the mid-1830s, though, the condition of being in-between shaped the lives and ideas of Tejanos the most. Tejanos, rather than being the first line of defense of Mexican civilization, moved and acted in a constantly shifting zone of transition in an increasingly complex economy and society. Nonetheless, even in 1832, many elite Tejanos still held a clear conception of the promises their land held for the future. In their petition to the state government, the members of the Ayuntamiento of Béxar noted, "Perhaps an entire volume would be insufficient to provide full and minute details of such a beautiful scene. And would not the inhabitants of Texas find it painful and even intolerable to continue envisioning how easily prosperity could be attained in this fertile land—with its mildness of climate, the plenty of its rivers, the abundance of its fish and game, which provides the most beautiful kinds of pelts[?]"[70] The articulation of these ideas by a Tejano in 1832 seems distant and untenable when contrasted with the tragic turn of events in 1835. Yet, Tejano elites seemed to work continuously to build a society where many people from differing cultures could live and profit. For Tejanos, the loss of Texas by Mexico was not inevitable. It might be easy to characterize conflicts between Anglo-Americans and Mexicans in nineteenth-century Texas as principally resulting from cultural differences, but that view fails to consider not only the constant material changes taking place in the region but also the heterogeneous populations and the dynamic qualities of culture and identity. For Tejanos, Anglo colonization didn't mean a sudden loss of land and status but rather a gradual redefinition of themselves and a slow contraction of their possible future.

Fellow citizens: You are covered with
scars, wounds from our grandparents.
—Angel Navarro, address to the
inhabitants of Béxar, October 14, 1835

Under existing circumstances, I consider
one fact plain and evident: that they who
are not for us must be against us.
—Henry Smith, December 12, 1835

Chapter Five

La Pérdida de Tejas

TEJANOS AND THE WAR OF TEXAS SECESSION, 1834–1837

In early fall of 1835, the citizens and government officials of Béxar gathered to prepare for the upcoming Independence Day celebration. For almost a decade since independence, Mexicans marked the origins of the independence movement beginning on the evening of September 15 and continuing through the next day. The decisions to commemorate the events of 1810 rather than 1821 signaled the popular disenchantment with the memory of Agustín Iturbide's government. A month before the celebration, fifty Bexareños gathered in the political chief's council hall to elect the *junta patriótica*, or patriotic commission, in charge of organizing the event.[1]

Ramón Músquiz emerged from the meeting as the president of the junta, elected by a margin of thirty-three votes to sixteen over Colonel Nicolas Condelle. Angel Navarro received the vote for vice president, over a larger field including Condelle, Gaspar Flores, and Lieutenant Colonel Nicolas Flores. Finally, José Arocha unanimously won the position of secretary of the group. The junta also included four *vocales*, or electors: Erasmo Seguín, Luciano Navarro, Colonel Francisco Sandoval, and Lieutenant Colonel Benito Garza. The men elected to serve in the junta included the most prominent civil and military elite in Béxar. Their desire to participate in the organizing committee attests to the importance of this event. Furthermore, as the formation of the junta through an election by the town's elite demonstrated, participation in the celebration served as an honor.

After its formation, the junta selected forty-four prominent citizens and officers to participate in six committees to plan, fund, and oversee various aspects of the Diez y Seis de Septiembre celebration.[2] For instance, Gaspar Flores headed the committee in charge of organizing the church services and lighting and decorating the main square. Condelle eventually headed the committee charged with decorating the other buildings and inviting the speakers and poets to address the gathering. But, of all the committees, the one in charge of the parade and floats appeared to contain several of the most elite citizens in Béxar, including Erasmo Seguín as its leader, José Antonio Navarro, Miguel Arciniega, and John W. Smith.

Along with the civic and religious celebrations, Bexareños planned two dances for the *fiestas patrias*. The first would be in the Plaza General and the second in the Plaza de Armas.[3] Béxar's military commander, Domingo de Ugartechea, along with Nicolas Flores led the committee for the first dance, in the Plaza General. Among the prominent Tejanos in his group was Juan N. Seguín, Erasmo's son. Captain Jorge Ledesma headed the second dance committee, with Ygnacio Arrocha and Antonio Menchaca on his committee. All six committees met several times over the week to plan the event and raise funds. By August 21, 1835, the junta gathered the committee reports and issued a schedule of events for the celebration.

After the parade, the crowds gathered around a podium erected at one end of the plaza to hear speeches on civics and elegies to the nation. Father Refugio de la Garza stood before the gathering to give the principal oration. Condelle's committee had spent the previous weeks soliciting "poetic compositions, regarding the celebration of that fateful day in 1810 of the proclamation in Dolores of the political Independence of the Nation."[4] The junta's request for submissions from the town at large suggests their sense that patriotism exists in all people, regardless of social status. Nationalism, in this case, appears as an emotion or sentiment that should inspire people to write lyrically in ways usually reserved for religious figures. The speeches ended with another salvo of rifle shots from the Béxar garrison.

Almost immediately, the escalation of violence and demands for Texas secession from Mexico put the meaning and strength of nationalism in the Independence Day parade to the test. Tejano participation on the side of what eventually became a secession movement underscores the limits of ideas like nationalism. When a group cheers an Independence Day parade together one day and fights against each other the next, then nationalism must be more complex than allegiance to a flag. In this case, external events constrained the choices and alliances available to Bexareños, forcing them to take sides on a growing borderland battle between two nations. In the long run, the changes resulting from the war of Texas secession strengthened the importance of ethnicity over nation or region as the central element of Tejano identity.

Tracing Tejano activities before and during the war of Texas secession puts nationalism in relative perspective regarding concerns. Many Bexareños present at the Independence Day celebration participated in a rebellion against the nation in the following months. Ultimately, nationalism operated at different levels within the Tejano community, dividing along lines of social class or family connection. The shared bonds that appeared during the Independence Day celebration can be understood as civic identity as much as nationalism. The range of Tejano responses to events that transpired between 1834 and 1837 demonstrates the variety and complexity of their identity. While they all claimed a Mexican identity, the political, cultural, and social meaning of that identity differed from person to person. The contours of those choices appear in their actions taken during the war of Texas secession, a war now reduced in the popular culture of our time to a single monument known as the Alamo.

After two days of celebration, the cold weather and harsh realities of Béxar's political situation in late 1835 began to set in. On September 21, Commander Ugartechea received reports of Anglo-American immigrant disregard of an order to return a cannon taken from Mexican troops in Gonzales. The cannon incident followed a string of problems with Anglo-American immigrants beginning with the Law of April 6, 1830, and leading to the imprisonment of Stephen F. Austin in Mexico City. These became the first steps in a revolt against the Mexican government led by Anglo-American immigrants, who began to call themselves Texians. This chapter describes the broader context necessary to understand the unfolding war in Texas and particularly Tejano participation in it. Throughout this period, the largely Mexican town of Béxar became the symbolic and strategic center of that war.

Attention turned to Béxar with the increased presence of federal troops led by General Martín Perfecto de Cos.[5] Within the span of a year, Béxar first would be invaded by Texian forces and later recaptured by the Mexican military. While the battle for Texas secession was largely Anglo-led, it also included significant Tejano participation. Among the Tejanos holding prominent roles in the Texan rebellion were several of the Bexareño elite who had planned the Diez y Seis celebration only months before. Juan N. Seguín and Manuel Flores led military units as commanding officers of the Tejano companies in the Texas Army.

The Texas rebellion and the secession of Texas from Mexico devastated the city of Béxar, leaving it in ruin and without much hope for the future. While present-day San Antonio serves as a central icon of Texas independence for Anglos, the town symbolized a much different reality for Tejanos over much of the nineteenth century. For Tejanos, Béxar stood at ground zero of the battle between Anglo-Texans and Mexico. These battles threatened to prevent Béxar and Bexareños from regaining the political importance they once held.

The variety of ways in which Tejanos participated for and against the secession of Texas along with the economic and social reorganization of the state reveal a shifting priority within Tejano identity: toward an ethnic and regional consciousness and away from the official nationalism displayed on Independence Day. While Tejano support for the Texian secession movement might appear anti-Mexican, the larger social and political context forces other interpretations to explain their participation. Growing disputes between centralist and federalist factions in Mexico provide the background for Tejanos' political identity. In the years before the war, Tejanos mediated between federalist leaders at the state level and their business interests developed with Anglo-American immigrants and Americans in Louisiana.

Just as Anglo-American immigration realigned notions of ethnic identity for Tejanos during the decade previous to the rebellion, the secession of Texas also reconfigured ethnic relations even further by affecting national sentiments. The choices Tejanos made during the centralist/federalist conflicts and the war of secession resulted both from a reaction to these external events and within the continuation of their existing social system that gave high value to honor and region. Instead of brokering disputes between Anglo-Americans and the Mexican government, elite Tejanos now officially and unofficially represented Tejanos in San Antonio and south Texas to the new Anglo-Texan power structure. Yet, even that role would constantly shift during the Republic period, as the politics and economics of Texas changed.

Federalism and the State Capital Schism

During 1834, two external issues began to take center stage in the world of Tejano politics. First, pressure and unrest from Anglo-American immigrants continued to increase since the turning point of the Law of April 6, 1830. As mentioned in chapter 4, Anglo-American demands for exemptions from federal legislation, particularly around slavery, and increased autonomy through Texas statehood put Tejano elites in increasingly more difficult positions relative to the government in Mexico City. Matters took a turn for the worse when Stephen F. Austin traveled to Mexico City to lobby directly and ended up imprisoned for much of 1834. And second, the growing conflict between centralist and federalist political factions on the national level began to reverberate in Béxar. Political leaders on the state level joined other states around the Republic in expressing their discontent with centralist policies emanating from Mexico City. Federalism became the prism that defined Tejano political action beginning in 1834.

After his release from Mexico City, Austin began to suggest his belief that Texas would one day join the United States.[6] Nevertheless, he felt the manner by which Texas would become an American territory depended more on increased immigration and political autonomy than on armed secession. Austin noted, "A gentle breeze shakes off a ripe peach. Can it be supposed that the violent political convulsions of Mexico will not shake off Texas as soon as it is ripe enough to fall?"[7] Austin suggested that if Mexico allowed Anglo-Americans to populate Texas and maintain their own political, cultural, and social institutions, an Americanized Texas would eventually become annexed to the United States. Austin led what some termed the "peace party" in the political split among Anglo-Texans.[8]

But in his correspondence with Tejanos and leaders in Béxar, Austin portrayed his political cause in terms of federalism versus centralism. He insisted that he and other Anglo-Americans had taken up arms to support the federalist constitution of 1824 and to resist the centralization of political power in Mexico. In one public letter to the inhabitants of Béxar, Austin wrote, "The People of Texas have declared themselves in favor of the constitution of 1824, the federal system and the territorial integrity of the Mexican Federation."[9] As a result of Austin's characterization of Anglo-American dissatisfaction, few Tejanos believed the growing Texian rebellion sought to totally separate Texas from Mexico, or worse, annex Texas to the United States. Instead, most Tejanos viewed the rumblings in their region as part of a larger Mexican movement already underway in Yucatán, San Luis Potosi, and Zacatecas. When Juan Martín de Veramendi and other Tejanos supported the federalist legislature's decision to move the capital of Coahuila y Texas, they situated their opposition with those other states.

During Austin's imprisonment in Mexico City, politics in Mexico and in Coahuila y Texas turned contentious. Tejanos found themselves embroiled in a national political schism between two parties: the federalists, advocating for greater autonomy at the state level, and the centralists, who looked to concentrate power in the presidency. From 1833 to 1835, General Antonio López de Santa Anna presided over a series of national coalition governments that negotiated power between the two factions.[10] On several occasions, Santa Anna managed to use his political savvy combined with his military skills to leave office and return as part of the opposition. In fact, he started his term in 1833 as a federalist but slowly moved toward the centralist faction.

Much of the power granted to the legislature of Coahuila y Texas resulted from a series of reform laws implemented by Vice President Valentín Gómez Farías in 1833 and 1834.[11] Even though Gómez Farías and Santa Anna entered the presidency under the same ticket, Santa Anna concentrated his efforts on organizing the Mexican military and personally leading the army in quelling rebellions throughout the provinces. Santa Anna entered his first lengthy stay as president in April 1834, almost a year after his election. By this time, though, he politically opposed Gómez Farías and managed to have him removed from office. This initiated a period of conservative backlash against the federalist reforms, resulting in clashes with the recently empowered state legislatures. In early 1833, a federalist faction, including Vice Governor Juan Martín de Veramendi and composed of a bloc from the towns of Parras, Monclova, and others in Texas, used their power to control the Coahuila y Texas legislature.

In a move to return the capital to its historic location and empower federalist legislators, the assembly voted that year to move the state capital from Saltillo north to Monclova.[12] Tejanos, along with a few Anglo-Texan representatives, provided key votes in putting together the new government and enjoyed increased prominence in the statewide political arena. Even before leaving Saltillo, the state legislature began repealing laws deemed offensive by Anglo-American immigrants and Bexareños in 1832.[13] The

Monclova legislature also increased the political voice of Texas by adding a district and increasing the number of representatives.

In April 1833, the Coahuila y Texas legislature opened its session in Monclova and continued to pass Texas-friendly laws. Santa Anna had just recently appointed his brother-in-law Martín Perfecto de Cos as the military commander for the northeastern interior provinces. Cos established his headquarters in Saltillo and manipulated the rift between Monclova and Saltillo in order to challenge the power of the federalist Congress in Monclova. Within a month, Cos sent troops to Monclova to arrest the governor and effectively end state opposition to Santa Anna's presidency.[14] With the backing of the federal government and the military, Cos attempted to place legislative power back in the hands of the conservative faction of the state government in Saltillo. In a proclamation on May 12, Cos acknowledged the importance of Texas by stating, "I shall not lose sight of the frontier settlements, which are more deserving of my consideration than their local authorities; in case that I should be compelled to remove some troops from the belt of Presidios, I shall leave them a sufficient protection against the savage tribes."[15] Cos's statement acknowledged concerns over stability and economic prosperity in Béxar. He understood the importance of Tejano support in enforcing any orders in the state. But instead of sensing increased support for their region, Bexareños resented the imposition of a new government and their lost voice in Congress.

The capital schism began to have a greater impact on Béxar in May 1835 when Cos decided to use the military to quiet the faction in Monclova. In Monclova, the legislature elected radical federalist Agustín Viesca to the governor's post. This caused Angel Navarro, brother of José Antonio Navarro and official link between the civilian authority of Béxar and the military command in northern Mexico, to bring Béxar leaders together to discuss what to do about the turmoil. Navarro's actions and letters of this period demonstrate the anguish and uncertainty Bexareños experienced during this time of partisan conflict at the state level. Navarro walked a narrow path between the two factions, asserting Bexareño power when possible without creating future problems for the town.

Navarro's actions during this crisis can be understood within the expectations of social prestige demanded of any member of the prominent Navarro family. Both Angel and José Antonio were the sons of Spanish merchant Angel Navarro and María Josefa Ruiz. Josefa connected the Navarro family to the prominent Ruiz family, particularly through her brother Francisco Ruiz.[16] Francisco Ruiz held public office in several capacities, including Indian agent and *empresario* commissioner. The Navarro brothers took on leadership roles at every critical juncture in Béxar's nineteenth-century history, from independence to colonization pressures. Despite being brothers, they often took conflicting positions at those moments, assuring the continued good standing of their family despite the outcome.

Along with other Bexareños, Angel Navarro feared reprisals from Cos for siding with the federalists during the Monclova government. Reports circulated in town that Cos had equipped a force of one hundred troops to enter Texas. In a letter to Cos on May 16, 1835, Navarro wrote, "I believe it to be my duty to beg you to state whether you are determined to make use of arms at the risk of shedding the blood of members of the Militia, and perhaps, that of the people of this Municipality who make common cause with them."[17] The militia he referred to was an armed force following orders of federalist leaders. Navarro's letter expressed not only his disagreement with centralists but also the fear of reprisals against federalists held by many Bexareños. Still, the letter hinted at Navarro's willingness to accept some limited federal military authority.

In another letter to the now-crumbling Viesca government, Navarro responded to Viesca's request for militia volunteers to support the federalist government in Monclova.[18] According to the letter, the citizens of Béxar raised a force of twenty-five men to aid Viesca. Significantly, only Béxar sent troops to Monclova, despite political support for Viesca from the Anglo-American-dominated districts in the north.[19] Navarro's decision to send militia stirred doubt and caused insecurity among the Bexareños and their leaders. The events of May 16 and 17 provide evidence not only of almost daily changes in the Tejano political situation but of the extremely careful, deliberate, and diplomatic process the leaders of Béxar undertook to fulfill their civic responsibilities without jeopardizing the future of the city.

Just as the militia had gathered and prepared to set off for Monclova, the Ayuntamiento received word that a squadron of the Mexican army would prevent the group from leaving. On the same day, Ramón Músquiz arrived in Béxar, having recently completed his term as vice governor. Navarro then wrote, "Desirous to preserve good harmony with the military authority, I sought, at once, an interview with the Commanding Officer, for the purpose of making with him some arrangements whereby our mutual responsibility might be covered, and the honor of both the Sovereign authorities of the State and the Federal Army, secured."[20] While Navarro failed to arrange the meeting, he managed to speak with the officer at the home of

Ramón Músquiz. Navarro employed the brokering skills available to him as an elite with prestige and made every effort to smooth relations with the military authorities, but to no avail. He agreed to send the militia out to Monclova that evening, despite the threat presented by Mexican troops. The local impact of Navarro's choices makes it difficult to mark them as pro- or anti-Mexican in nationalist terms. Instead, they highlight the importance of negotiation between competing interests with the larger goal of community survival. Historian Stephen L. Hardin has termed those taking ambivalent ideological stances in this period "conditional centralists" to emphasize their reaction to circumstances.[21] To that extent, whether or not national identity held any meaning would be measured in local terms.

The militia managed to avoid the Mexican troops but also failed to reach their goal of defending the Monclova government. Together with the Ayuntamiento and "several influential citizens," Navarro convened about seventy of the townspeople to decide what steps to take next. More might have attended, but many *vecinos* had already left for ranches in the countryside to avoid potential violence. Navarro wrote, "The meeting took place; but such was the popular excitement, that they resolved, at once, to make a bold attempt against the troops. However, the sound arguments of several intelligent citizens, and the advises [*sic*] of the old men, caused them to reconsider their first resolution, and to feel the rashness of such a step." Of the people remaining in Béxar, most opposed the military occupation of their region by conservative-led forces and advocated raising arms against them. But Tejanos seemed ill-prepared to do so. Navarro lamented the difficulty of following this course, writing, "Still I saw, at the time, no alternative left besides driving the troops out of town, or being driven off by them. The latter alternative was dreadful!—to have to abandon our families, and to withdraw on foot to Monclova, exposed to be attacked by the troops of this garrison sent to pursue us, and by those of Guerrero who would have attempted to cut off our passage!"[22]

Having reached an impasse, the group nominated a council of six citizens to select the most prudent course of action. The council elected to describe their dilemma to the governor and elicit further orders. Navarro added "that we should await patiently, the changes to be expected from the revolution, or the necessary support for solving this delicate question peaceably rather than by force, which is always fatal to society."[23] The tone of the letter might exaggerate enthusiasm for battle against the Mexican troops in order to convey support for the federalist faction and to justify the inaction taken in the end. Navarro's letters and actions taken later by the citizens of Béxar suggest the most desirable course appeared to be waiting to see the direction of change before making a choice. Meanwhile, Anglo-Americans in Texas began to increase their opposition to Mexican authorities, raising the stakes for Bexareño choices.

Events in other parts of Texas soon distracted the citizens and military in Béxar, turning their attention back to the Anglo-American colonists. On May 23, 1835, an Anglo-American militia attacked the customs house at Anáhuac, on the Texas coast, expelling the Mexican military from the fort.[24] Anáhuac had been the scene of previous protests in 1832 and a point for tax collection, and the military presence there represented the Mexican state to Anglo-Americans living on the frontier. The actions at Anáhuac amounted to a first strike against the Mexican army by the Texas militia. These actions raised the concerns of Angel Navarro, military commander Domingo de Ugartechea, and Martín Perfecto de Cos.

Now displaced from power, Viesca and other federalists attempted to make use of Anglo-American displeasure with the centralist government. Viesca exhorted Texans and Tejanos to join his cause and take up arms against the "unconstitutional government." In an open letter to the inhabitants of Texas in June 1835, he wrote, "Citizens of Texas, arise in arms or sleep forever! Thy dearest interests, thy liberty, thy properties, what is more, thy very existence depends on the deceitful capriciousness of thy most malevolent enemies."[25] Word of Viesca's appeal reached Austin and the Anglo-Texan rebels. But rather than act immediately to aid Viesca, they invited him, José Antonio Mexía, and Rafael Gonzalez to join in their resistance to Cos and Santa Anna and in their imposition of centralist policies on Coahuila y Texas.[26] Unlike Anglo-American participation in the 1813 insurgency against Spain, Anglo-American militias resisted subordination under a Mexican military commander.[27]

Despite the turmoil occurring on the state and national level in the summer of 1835, Bexareños still managed to come together, both civilian and military alike, to celebrate the independence of Mexico from Spain on September 16. In spite of the uncertainty of the future, or perhaps because of it, Bexareños threw the two-day fandango on a grand scale. Before the dust settled from the *fiestas patrias*, reports returned from the town of Gonzales that Anglo-American rebels refused to return a cannon to the local military commander.

Once again, Tejano citizens would be thrust into taking sides on an issue. But instead of choosing between federalist and centralist in Mexican politics, they faced the new option of a growing Anglo-American immigrant rebellion. Old tensions and distrust died slowly, though, and many Tejanos still resented the centralist military presence in Béxar. In a letter to Anglo-American colonists, Béxar resident and town engineer John W. Smith wrote concerning the mood among the *vecinos*. He noted, "The citizens of our town is red hot for a war and think the colonies does wrong in not making war. . . . They treat those officers with every respect and talk exactly crosswise."[28] Smith heard of an incident in Laredo where the Mexican army penalized Juan N. Seguín during the course of business in retaliation for Seguín's participation in the Monclova government. Smith himself served as something of a transition figure in Béxar, connecting himself to Tejano society by marrying a Tejana.[29] While Smith's comments might have been intended to instigate Anglo-Texan action, getting Tejanos to support the Mexican military directly against Anglo-American immigrants would be difficult at best.

Colonel Domingo de Ugartechea, the military commander in Béxar, employed his diplomatic skills to smooth over Anglo-American fears of Mexican military reprisals.[30] Nevertheless, Anglo-American insubordinates refused to give up their cannon at Gonzales and went on to overtake the Mexican military installation at Anáhuac as well. The men of the Texian militia achieved their first victory against the Mexican military, then used that event to organize their efforts into the Army of Texas and to plan a military strategy to install their government in Texas. That plan meant pushing loyal centralists farther south, out of the northern states. The first step involved capturing Béxar, the seat of local Mexican authority in the region. From the last two months in 1835 until March 1836, Béxar would be the central focus of the Texian rebellion against the Mexican government and of what became their drive for secession from Mexico.

Angel Navarro's efforts to maneuver through the changes in Mexican politics show that national politics mattered on a local level. Bexareños had to contend with their regional and state problems along with the increased demands from Mexico City. On the one hand, Anglo-Texan opposition to the centralist government provided a new avenue on which Tejanos could express their political desires. On the other hand, as tensions mounted between Anglo colonists and the federal government, Tejano room to negotiate became increasingly limited. These events created a rift in the balance Tejanos had struck between localism and nationalism.

Béxar's First Siege

Tejanos demonstrated their ability to negotiate through the treacherous terrain of partisan feuds in Mexican politics during the state capital schism in May 1835. By November, organized military pressures from Anglo-American rebels put Béxar in the front and center of a national challenge to Santa Anna's presidency. In order to respond more rapidly to problems in Texas, military commander Cos went to Béxar to lead the military response to immigrant colonist threats. For Bexareños, problems began to surface even before Cos's arrival.

Ugartechea encountered resistance from elite Tejanos unwilling to lend their homes to Cos during his stay. For separate reasons, both Angel Navarro and Erasmo Seguín refused to open their homes to Cos.[31] These actions indicated the extent of displeasure among Tejanos with the Mexican military and Santa Anna's centralist government. While Seguín and others stopped short of raising arms, they nevertheless opposed the centralist government and refused to accommodate its representatives while they dealt with the Anglo-American-led rebellion.

Some Tejanos joined the Texian militia at this early stage in the rebellion. José Antonio Padilla, from Victoria, decided to join the rebel cause on October 8, 1835, citing its defense of the constitution of 1824. He wrote in a letter to Austin, "I present my self to this Division as a soldier of the civil militia of Texas in defense of the constitution, and of its laws. I have made my testimony, and it is such; I have lived a long life, and lost much, it is disagreeable to live under the yoke of military rule."[32] Padilla, long an aid to the Anglo-American colonization project, had spent the previous years fighting murder charges in Saltillo before moving back to Texas.

The reasons Tejanos chose to fight with either the Texas militia or the Mexican military or to flee to the countryside during times of conflict were not always clear or uniform. Even when they articulated their reasons in writing, their personal situations often made it difficult to understand their motivations. Such was the case with Padilla. On the one hand, his friendships with Anglo-American immigrants and disagreements with state officials in Saltillo undergirded his decision to join the rebels. On the other hand, his stated support for the constitution of 1824 did not coincide with the shifting aims of the war from anti-centralism to secession.

Understanding Tejano choices during 1835 depends greatly on the narrative frame used to explain the Texas war. For Tejanos, the split between centralists and federalists created a civil war in Mexico. The split created a political space where opposition to the government could be voiced while maintaining loyalty and patriotism to the Mexican nation. Another narrative frame recalls years of trade and economic entanglements with Anglo-Americans, which led to cooperation and interdependence between Tejanos and the rebel Texians. Other narratives also explain Tejano choices, including family connections and obligations, *compadrazgo*, and survival. In all these cases, their choices appear less as either/or decisions and more as a complex and changing gray area reflecting political and social realities.

By the fall of 1835, Tejanos confronted difficult choices regarding the future of their homeland. Texians proposed an armed rebellion against the Mexican government. As a result, the Mexican government tapped into nationalist sympathies to maintain the allegiance of Tejano citizens who were in opposition. But a third choice existed. Tejanos could avoid the conflict altogether and leave their cities for ranches and farms in the hinterland. Most Tejanos chose this option, waiting for the political and military dust to settle, as they had done twenty years previously during the 1811 and 1813 insurgency battles. But, unlike the battles for Mexican independence, the results of this war prevented Tejanos from staking out a neutral stance during the clashes and reentering civil life just as they left it. In other words, while Tejanos faced complex decisions and made nuanced choices, postwar social and ethnic changes under Anglo-Texan rule reduced their actions to a simple yes or no on secession.

With the cannon incident at Gonzales, Anglo-Texans committed themselves to armed rebellion. In October 1835, Anglo-Texans attempted to raise an army to wrest Texas from the power of the centralist government. After the capture of the cannon, the Texian forces, called the "Army of the People" or the "Army of Texas," consisted of roughly 160 men.[33] Next, Texian forces set their sights on Béxar, the capital of the Mexican government in Texas. Preparations were made in November to mount a siege and invasion of the town. But the spontaneity and confusion at the start of the insurrection plagued attempts to impose a military structure on the Army of Texas. The troops continued to grow as they marched to Béxar. As one soldier noted, "Recruits were constantly arriving, singly and in squads, each squad being duly officered. . . . We soon had more officers than men."[34] The troops were to be led by John H. Moore, James Bowie, Austin, and Edward Burleson from the encampments outside of Béxar.

As tensions rose in anticipation of a Texian invasion, Angel Navarro attempted to stem the flight of Tejanos to rebel forces. On October 14, only days after Texian troops captured La Bahía, Navarro prepared a speech addressed to the inhabitants of Béxar. After informing the citizens of the fall of La Bahía, he defended the current Mexican government as magnanimous, especially in matters of religion. He turned around the Texian argument of oppression, noting, "They armed themselves and invaded our towns."[35] He continued by appealing to Bexareños to ignore the calls to battle made by Anglo-Americans and, rather, "not to hear among ourselves anything but the voice of the nation [*patria*], reason, and order." Throughout his speech, Navarro spoke in terms that united him with both the local population of Béxar and the Mexican nation as a whole. He concluded by calling the townspeople his countrymen and friends.

In addition to his appeal to patriotism, Navarro also evoked the specific history of Texas and Tejanos. He added, "Fellow citizens: You are covered with scars, wounds from our grandparents, the culture of war in defense of our properties in this frontier of lifelong incursions by barbarians [indigenous peoples] and enemies. And this time, acknowledge your patriotism."[36] Navarro's inclusion of fighting against indigenous peoples suggests that the people of Béxar considered this an integral part of their cultural memory. Navarro framed his plea by tapping into the early frontier ethos of the defense against Indian attacks and the border imperative of protecting Mexico against American invasion. How citizens responded was more complicated. As noted above, some Tejanos might have interpreted the centralist government as the invader and sided with the Anglo rebels. Yet, many Tejanos avoided armed conflict altogether, perhaps not equating either side with "barbarians" or peacefulness. Some, though, took up Navarro's call to defend the integrity of the nation.

Even before Cos arrived in Béxar, the military garrison under Ugartechea contained a cavalry company of about ninety locals. These troops remained loyal through the days leading up to the siege on Béxar. Whether because of Navarro's plea or mounting threats to the town or fear of American annexation, additional Bexareños enlisted in the Mexican military. Three days after Navarro's speech, several men presented themselves to Cos as volunteers. By October 20, Angel Navarro organized a militia company called "the volunteers of the Nation" to defend the city in case of an attack.[37] Other examples of Tejano support for the centralist authorities appear elsewhere in Texas. In the area around Victoria, Mexican officials recruited local Tejanos to form a loyalist unit called the Guardias Victorianas.[38]

But Navarro's call to support the Mexican government failed to sway

Juan N. Seguín. Seguín had already raised a company of Tejanos to aid in the Anglo efforts to oppose the Mexican army. On October 22, at an encampment near Salado Creek, Austin himself appointed Seguín captain in the Army of Texas to raise "a company of Mexicans."[39] The twenty-eight-year-old Seguín rode through the ranches outside of Béxar and into the city itself recruiting his boyhood friends to join him in the war against the centralist government. Four days prior, Mexican scouts made first contact with the rebel troops at Salado Creek. By this point, citizens and soldiers in Béxar knew a confrontation would occur. Between October 18 and 19, Cos offered Austin a chance to negotiate, and Austin responded with his resolve to fight. Cos had these letters read at each corner of the public square to the beat of a drum. An Anglo-American citizen of Béxar noted Cos's reaction to Austin's letter: "I want no more communications; let the damn rascals come."[40] When and where the battles would take place took longer to develop, due in part to the rebels' lack of a master plan or goal.

In preparation to defend Béxar, Cos managed to amass at least 750 troops in Béxar.[41] Their first test came in a battle on the southern outskirts of town, at Mission Concepción. On October 28, the Anglo and Tejano rebel groups managed to defeat Mexican troops and to establish a foothold at a strategic area around Béxar. A large contingent of Tejanos participated in the skirmish around Concepción, of which at least half came from Seguín's company. Thirty-two Tejano soldiers specifically listed fighting at Concepción in their pension applications, serving under the commands of James Bowie, Manuel Leal, Plácido Benavides, and Phillip Dimmitt as well as under Seguín.[42]

For the next month, Béxar remained in a state of siege, with the rebel companies camped on several sides of the city and Mexican troops struggling to bring in supplies and reinforcements. Soon after the battle of Concepción, more Texian troops arrived from the north to aid the rebels. Likewise, during this month, the numbers of Tejano participants in the rebellion also increased. Ninety-seven Tejanos listed themselves as fighting in the siege and battle of Béxar, up from thirty-two at Concepción.[43] Often, Tejanos residing in the area around the camp joined the Texian forces. Francisco Cuellar, an eighteen-year-old Tejano born on the grounds of Mission de Espada, allied himself with Seguín's company through Manuel Leal three days after the battle of Concepción.[44] Given Cuellar's connection to mission Indians by birth and the time he spent as a captive with the Comanches (he later went by the nickname "Comanche"), it appears that he considered himself of some indigenous identity.[45] His participation raises further questions about an Indian-Tejano fighting alongside Anglo-Americans for federalism or Texas secession.

Over the first two weeks of November, skirmishes continued to flare up in the outskirts of town.[46] Not only were the Texian forces biding their time to increase their strength and weaken Cos and the Mexican military, but they also used the time to convene a war council to plan their next move. The hardships on the Mexican soldiers resulted in several desertions out of Béxar. One deserter included a commander, José María Gonzales, who later assisted Austin in employing the language of federalism and constitutional reform to garner more support for the rebels.[47]

But, as the weeks passed, Anglo rebels grew weary of waiting for the attack. By November 22, Austin believed the time had arrived to capture Béxar. He abruptly halted the troop movements after receiving information that the attack might fail.[48] The next day, Austin left the Army of Texas to attend to Texas politics and raise interest in the Texas war in the United States. With Edward Burleson taking over the troops, the rebels prepared once again to make a move for Béxar. Burleson set the next attack for December 2, but once again the conditions seemed unfavorable and the Mexican army to have the advantage. This false alarm resulted in the abandonment of the war effort by somewhere between 250 and 300 Anglo volunteers.[49]

On December 4, another Mexican deserter arrived in the rebel camps and described the sorry state of Cos's troops. Burleson quickly readied the attack on Béxar, and the invasion began on December 5. The fighting lasted five days and occurred largely house-to-house and occasionally hand-to-hand. The rebel forces slowly gained ground a block at a time until they encircled the Mexican military. Reports from Texian soldiers fighting in the invasion occasionally mention aid they received from Bexareños living in the houses they occupied. One Texian wrote, "A Mexican woman discovered our Situation, and offered her services to get us a Bucket of Water, She got the water and on her return to the house which we occupied, was shot through the arm by the Mexicans."[50] His remarks indicate that a number of Bexareños opposed the presence of Cos and his troops in their city. Anglo-American accounts of Tejano participation need to be read with a critical eye, since they might have overstated or invented Tejano support. Timothy Matovina has pointed to contradictions between Antonio Menchaca's own memoirs and Anglo-American accounts of his activities.[51] In the Anglo-American telling, Menchaca fought mercilessly against Mexican troops in San Jacinto, while Menchaca himself describes providing solace

to Santa Anna after the battle. Even when Anglo-Americans believed Tejanos stood behind them, this support would soon come into question when
some Anglo leaders criticized and questioned Tejano allegiance.

Tired, depleted, and out-positioned, Cos raised the truce flag and negotiated a capitulation of Béxar. Cos later explained to Santa Anna that Béxar
could be won, but only after falling back to Laredo to regroup and bolster the
army.[52] The terms of surrender struck between Cos and Burleson allowed
Cos six days to prepare his troops to leave to the "interior of the Republic,"
with only enough provisions to make it to the Río Grande.[53] The deal stipulated that Cos's troops could choose to stay or go with their general and that
"nobody, whether military or civilian, can be harassed regarding the political opinions they expressed up to this day." The capitulation offered the
impression that Tejanos and Mexican soldiers could stay in Béxar to aid in
establishing the Texan government. But evicting the Mexican government
from Béxar only achieved a temporary victory for the Texian rebels, since
the full Mexican military had yet to respond to the secession attempt. From
this point forward, the war took on a decidedly different appearance in regard to both the Texan troops and relations between Anglos and Tejanos.

Four days after the surrender of Cos's troops, Burleson himself relinquished command of the Texian forces to Colonel Francis W. Johnson. The
month-long siege had exacted an economic toll on rebels and Bexareños
alike. An occupational government began to operate in Béxar while Bexareños slowly trickled back to town. Many Tejano soldiers also left Seguín's
company to attend to their homes and wounds. Francisco Cuellar fought
most of the battle for Béxar ill with a fever and chills.[54] After the capture
of Béxar, Cuellar returned to tend to his parents, who required assistance.
Like many Bexareños, Cuellar found the walls of his home pockmarked
with bullet holes and his city in shambles.[55]

The siege and storming of Béxar occupied most of November 1835,
with approximately 1,300 Texas separatist troops encamped at the outskirts
of town. Historian Paul Lack, who examined employee muster rolls and
service land grant records, notes the age, length of Texas residence, and
home of those volunteers in the Texas army in 1835.[56] These troops averaged thirty-one years of age, and almost 80 percent lived for some time in
Texas prior to the initiation of hostilities. However, a third of the army had
migrated to Texas within the previous five years, when their immigration
might be deemed dubious under the Law of April 6, 1830. And while at least
half of the troops came from the Brazos district of Texas, including Austin

TABLE 5.1. Tejano Participation in the War of Secession

Category	Number	%	Average Age
Born in Béxar	50	36	24.7
Not born in Béxar	88	64	25.9
Fought in siege of Béxar	97	70	25.5
Fought in battle of Concepción	25	18	24.1
Under Seguín's command	65	47	25.7

Source: John C. Barron et al., *Republic of Texas Pension Application Abstracts* (Austin: Austin Genealogical Society, 1987).

Note: 138 Tejano men were involved in the war of secession. Their average age was 25.4.

and Brazoria counties, 15 percent of the troops came from the largely Tejano Béxar district. These numbers gain significance when compared to the composition of the Army of Texas after the capture of Béxar. At that point, the army underwent a large demographic shift in both age and length of Texas residence, with marked increase of mercenaries and filibusters.

While historians acknowledge the presence of Tejanos in the Army of Texas, Lack notes that figures regarding the troop size at Béxar underestimate Tejano participation on the Texian side. In a letter from 1875, Juan N. Seguín remarked that approximately 160 Tejanos fought in the siege on Béxar.[57] An analysis of the pension applications for Texas Revolution veterans lists approximately 138 Tejanos who served during the entire rebellion, 97 (or 70 percent) of whom participated at some point in the siege on Béxar (see table 5.1).

Pension applications also offer insights into how and when Tejanos joined the Army of Texas during the 1835 uprising and to what extent they participated in the rebellion against the Mexican government. The pension applications themselves deserve a critical examination, given that benefits were being sought by the applicants. While most Tejanos probably avoided conflict and left the city, many joined the Army of Texas, principally under two commanders, Juan N. Seguín and Manuel Leal. But the composition of the two battalions indicates peculiarities in the method of organization and ideology of these troops. Foremost, the city of birth of the soldiers in these two units points to differences in their demographic makeup. Approximately 56 percent of the soldiers in Seguín's units were born in Béxar. Ethnic Mexican members of other battalions appear to be mostly from outside of Béxar (78 percent), a quarter overall migrating from within Mexico to Texas.[58] While it can be said that many Tejanos joined the Army of Texas to defend their homes in Béxar, a large portion participated for reasons that are more difficult to deduce.

Seguín's decision to support the Anglo-led rebellion stands as perhaps the single most influential factor in encouraging Tejanos to join the Army of Texas. The overwhelming participation of native Bexareños and Tejanos in Seguín's troops indicates the personal connection many of the troops shared when gathering as a force. Leandro Chavez's pension application described his experience in joining the army: "In mid-Nov[ember] while en route to the city with an ox cart, he was surrounded by a group of his friends and playmates who had armed themselves under John N. Seguín and they induced him to join them which he did."[59] The relative proximity in age between all the Tejano volunteers suggests that most of them grew up together in the intimate setting of Béxar.[60] Seguín's actions during this period began to define him as a political and social leader, no longer exclusively reliant on his father Erasmo's family prestige.

The search for reasons Tejanos entered in the service against the Mexican government reveals both personal and ideological motives. Personal ties heavily influenced the decision to fight on one side or the other. The rank and file under Seguín's command had shared the bonds of friendship since childhood. Furthermore, Seguín himself had spent much of his adolescent years with the family of Stephen F. Austin, both in Béxar and in northeast Texas.[61] These connections, between Seguín and his soldiers and between Seguín and Austin, established ties of trust that allowed these Tejanos to put their lives in danger under the direction of Anglo-American leaders. The personal connections forged in Texas elevated the importance of local concerns and region over ties to the nation at this crisis moment.

Tejanos also fought for political causes relating to their regional autonomy. In the weeks leading up to the siege on Béxar, Austin's exhortations to Tejanos often included calls to protect the federalist guarantees of the constitution of 1824. In an open letter to the inhabitants of Béxar, Austin wrote, "The People of Texas have pronounced themselves in favor of the Constitution of 1824, the federal system, and the territorial integrity of the Mexican Federation."[62] Indeed, antipathy toward the centralist Mexican government of Santa Anna gained strength throughout Mexico as federalist movements faced military reprisals for their efforts. For many Bexareños, resentment regarding Cos's centralist power grab in Monclova still lingered, especially since Cos now resided in Béxar. Even John W. Smith noted the growing resentment among Bexareños toward some government officials.[63] Knowing some Bexareños protested the government's position, certain Mexican officials abused their power and made life hard for those Tejanos. For many Tejanos joining the Texian forces, the battle for Texas meant the battle to uphold and defend the constitution of 1824.

Whether for friendship or for political ideology, many Tejanos chose to fight against Santa Anna's government and to expel the military from their hometown of Béxar. Unlike Anglo-Texans, Tejanos participating in the rebellion fought from within their own homes and homelands. Being Mexican, Tejanos stood to lose not only their homes but also their livelihoods in the event of defeat. During the rebellion, many Mexican political and military officials voiced vitriolic denunciations of Tejanos siding with Anglos. In a letter to Santa Anna, an official from Tamaulipas wrote, "Thousand curses on the Mexican who should be dastardly enough to join in that murderous and anti-national plot!"[64] In a proclamation to the citizens of Matamoros, an officer questioned the patriotism of Tejano rebels: "Generally, they are detested as I believe they should be for being such bad citizens."[65] Because they joined a rebellion identified with Anglo-Americans rather than simply oppose the centralist government, Tejanos were labeled by many Mexicans as secessionist collaborators rather than as government critics. But this label became difficult to pin on every Tejano who resisted the centralist government. While active in the early battles as a first lieutenant, Plácido Benavides eventually returned to his hometown of Victoria and sat out the last months of the war.[66]

On a more personal level, by fighting in their homeland, these Tejanos also alienated themselves from and fought against neighbors and family. Much of the eventual invasion of Béxar involved house-to-house battles. Places such as the Veramendi home and Zambrano Row became notable sites of crucial confrontations. The Navarro brothers, Angel and José Antonio, supported different sides in the battle. Francisco Esparza chose to fight in the Mexican army, while his brother Gregorio died fighting on the Texian side inside the Alamo.

To others, though, the reasons to choose sides defied generalization. In a letter to Austin, Cos wrote, "It is perhaps certain that some Mexicans, whether from private resentment or from private interest, or because no rule is without exception, will co-operate in the revolt of the Colonist; but the nation in general will oppose it with all her force; and that man must indeed be degraded who would not prefer death to base compromise."[67] The remarks by Cos put the Tejano dilemma in stark relief. While Tejanos sought to create a space in between the demands of the Mexican state, as was once possible on the frontier, external events limited their options. While most Tejanos chose to stay out of the conflict, Anglo-Americans and Mexican officials both interpreted inaction as disloyalty.

Many sought to avoid the difficult life associated with living in a town with a heavy military presence and potentially under siege. Two of Austin's commanders reported, "A large number of the citizens of Béxar and of this place, are now laying out, to prevent being forced to perform the most servile duties."[68] Some witnesses recounted rude behavior by Cos and his companies, although mainly toward suspected Texan sympathizers such as the Seguíns. Years later, Juan Antonio Chavez explained his family's flight from Béxar to a newspaper reporter: "Our home was right in the line of fire between Milam's men and the Mexican army.... On that occasion we were compelled to flee from home and seek refuge in the country."[69] Chavez's family returned to town after the battle, only to leave again upon word of the impending fight awaiting Santa Anna's arrival. Even after the rebellion, the apparent neutral position of avoiding conflict carried the weight of treason to the Texas Republic.

War irrevocably transformed the lives of Bexareños. They returned to their houses, but not to the same town. Choices they made in the early days of the conflict changed meaning as the war aims shifted. The battles of 1835 threw open the terms of ethnic and national identification by re-ordering ethnic relations along the lines dictated by the new Anglo-Texan-dominated political structure.

Occupation of Béxar and the Battle of the Alamo

Even though Anglo-Texans and Tejanos fought side-by-side in the siege and capture of Béxar, taking the town itself produced different results for each group. While Tejanos had aided in expelling Mexican officials from Béxar, they now lived under a new regime led by the Texian militia commanders. There did exist some opportunities for limited Tejano governance in Texian-controlled Béxar. Tejano elites availed themselves of their Anglo-American contacts and trust to secure these positions. Such was the case with Erasmo Seguín's appointment as justice of the peace during the occupation. In general, Anglo-Texans handled the occupation of Béxar as though they were invading foreign territory, as in a sense they were. Even while Tejanos fought for the Texas army, tensions between Anglo-Americans and Tejanos increased in the period prior to the entrance of Santa Anna's forces into Texas. As the hostilities escalated, Anglo-Texans demanded that Tejanos demonstrate their loyalty to the Texan cause. Moreover, Tejanos who supported the Texian cause in 1836 could no longer claim to fight in the name of the constitution of 1824.

The initial occupation of Béxar made readjusting to life after the siege difficult for Bexareños. The ambiguous and chaotic leadership structure of the Texian army created a confusing governing system in the town. Many Anglo-Texan soldiers were mercenaries from the United States who had no home or family to go to in Texas. Instead, they remained in Béxar at the command of charismatic captains. Unlike the relative racial harmony practiced by long-term Anglo-Texan residents, these recent arrivals into Texas strained relations between Anglo-Americans and Bexareños. They lacked prior contact with Mexicans and brought with them negative stereotypical views. As a result, the months between the fall of Béxar and the arrival of Santa Anna's army in March proved unsettling and even dangerous for the local population of Béxar. The political shifts also cloud the ability of historians to determine Anglo-American motivations behind the war of secession and to distinguish between negative racial attitudes toward Mexicans and political or economic opportunism.

As they had under the Mexican government, local Tejano elites continued to hold political seats in the town government. The range of their power and their ability to govern the city, though, depended on the cooperation and desires of the Anglo-Texan leaders. But political disorganization in the initial months of the Texas rebellion made finding even those limits difficult. One example of this situation appeared in mid-February, during a power struggle between Colonel James Bowie and Colonel William Barrett Travis.[70] After Bowie's men decided that Bowie should be the commander of the military post rather than Travis, Bowie decided to exert his prerogative and released several prisoners from the city jail. An observer described one prisoner, an Anglo-American convicted of mutiny, as walking out "with a Corporal Guard with Loud Huzzas." Bowie's volunteers seemed to be working themselves up into a public frenzy during these winter days.

The incident peaked when another prisoner, Antonio Fuentes, appeared before Erasmo Seguín, now justice of the peace for Béxar, requesting the return of his possessions. An outraged Seguín sent Fuentes immediately back to jail. Upon hearing that his order to release prisoners had been ignored, Bowie stormed over to Seguín and demanded Fuentes's release. Seguín responded by saying he would rather resign and let Bowie appoint another judge. An observer then noted, "Bowie immediately sent to the Alamo for troops and they immediately paraded in the Square, *under Arms*, in a tumultuously [*sic*] and disorderly manner, Bowie, himself, and many of his men, being drunk which has been the case ever since he has been in command."[71] After witnessing this spectacle, Travis apologized to Seguín and moved his troops to the edge of town on the Medina River.

By opening the prison door, Bowie revealed many of the problems facing Tejanos under the new regime. While Anglo-Texan officers rewarded with governing positions those Bexareños who participated in the rebellion, the Bexareños could act only with the oversight and support of Texian commanders. The behavior of Bowie's men also demonstrated a new problem facing Tejanos: recent Anglo-American immigrants. In the previous decade, a few Anglo-Americans had made some effort to learn Mexican culture and the Spanish language, and some even developed close friendships and business contacts with Tejanos. Those friendships and enterprises account for much of the eventual Tejano participation in the rebellion. But the recently arrived volunteers from Kentucky and Tennessee lacked such contact with Mexican people and instead developed negative impressions through the experience of war. As Paul Lack notes, "These views, generally expressed by men who had spent their time away from the front and who lacked first-hand knowledge of Tejano behavior, defined loyalty in terms of ethnic origin."[72] The recently arrived Texan volunteers relied on cultural and racial markers to determine who stood on their side of the conflict. Even when Tejanos fought with them, Anglo-Texans raised questions of mistrust or followed leaders who tapped into the suspicion of all Mexicans. Again, this general stance toward Tejanos raises questions about the racial nature of Texas secession. While not all Anglo-Texans shared the same views of Mexican people, the underlying resistance to fully embracing Mexican civil society resulted in some part from views of Mexicans as inferior.[73]

Not all Anglo-Texans shared or fueled these prejudices. By approaching Seguín and separating himself from Bowie's actions, Travis demonstrated that at least some Anglo-Texans felt it necessary to include Tejanos in the Texian movement. In another sign of support, the military commander of Béxar, Colonel Francis W. Johnson, issued a proclamation that continued to use the rallying cry of the 1824 constitution. Johnson also voiced the desire to include Tejanos in the Texan cause, stating, "They invite into their ranks all friends to freedom, of whatever name or nation. They invite them to unite in establishing on a firm and solid foundation, on Mexican soil, the banners of Morales and Hidalgo, inscribed with their own national mottoes."[74] Johnson's proclamation appears as a final attempt to bolster the rebels' attack by instigating a widespread revolt against Santa Anna by all federalists, including Tejanos. Johnson appealed to Mexican nationalism by evoking national heroes Father José María Morales and Father Miguel Hidalgo. Had he been in Béxar months before, he would have witnessed the popular celebration of these sentiments in the Independence Day parades.

Even with sizable Tejano participation in the siege of Béxar, many Anglo-Texans questioned Tejano loyalty. One of the staunchest anti-Tejano voices came from Henry Smith, who eventually served as the first American governor of Texas. In a letter to the governing council regarding his disagreement with a bill under consideration, Smith noted his suspicions by questioning whether to allow Tejanos representation in the Texan government. He commented on the events of the previous month in Béxar by noting, "Actions always speak louder than words; and a very great proportion of the inhabitants of Béxar afford fair examples. They have had, it is well known, every opportunity to evince their friendship by joining our standard. With very few exceptions they have not done so, which is evidence, strong and conclusive, that they are really our enemies."[75] In one move, Smith removed the possibility of neutrality or self-preservation from the list of acceptable Tejano actions. Smith summed up his feelings: "Under existing circumstances, I consider one fact plain and evident: that they who are not for us must be against us."[76] Once again, regardless of Tejano motivations, Anglo-Texans defined and limited the meaning and range of Tejano choices.

Smith concluded his letter by stating, "I therefore consider that they should neither be entitled to our respect or favor, and as such not entitled to a seat in our councils."[77] To be sure, Tejanos did hold official positions in government after the Texan victories, and they participated in important decision-making gatherings in this early period of the formation of the Texas Republic. For instance, on January 16, 1836, "a large and respectable meeting of the citizens and soldiers of this place" convened, forming a committee of seven headed by Colonel James Bonham and including both Juan N. Seguín and Gaspar Flores.[78] Ironically, this same committee—with the two Bexareños—issued a resolution to support Governor Smith in the face of charges of embezzlement and corruption.

Mexican participation in the rebellion extended to inclusion in the document marking the shift in the war from federalism to secession: the Texas Declaration of Independence. Two Tejanos and one Mexican politician attended as delegates to the convention at which the document was signed on March 2, 1836, the Tejanos being Bexareños José Antonio Navarro and Francisco Ruiz.[79] Lorenzo de Zavala, *empresario* and Mexican liberal party leader, also played an important role in the early era of the formation of the Texas Republic.[80] While de Zavala's *empresario* landholdings and previous dealing with the Galveston Bay and Texas Land Company as well as his experience in writing the constitution of 1824 partially explain his presence at the meeting, Navarro and Ruiz appear in the document more problematically. Regardless, the declaration they signed decidedly ended any policy of linking the Texan revolt with a federalist resistance movement in northern Mexico.

After the Texas Declaration of Independence, Tejanos could no longer rationalize their participation in the Texan war as upholding the constitution of 1824. This was now a war of secession. Perhaps Tejano leaders such as José Antonio Navarro, Juan N. Seguín, and Plácido Benavides continued their support of the Anglo-Texan movement since they had already raised arms against Mexico. In other words, the only two choices seemed full commitment to Mexico or to Anglo-Texans. Also, while de Zavala emerged from another part of Mexico, his important status as a founding father of the Mexican nation might have eased some of the apprehension held by Navarro and Ruiz. Most important, their participation in signing the Texas Declaration of Independence stood as the first step in a new direction of ethnic relations and Tejano politics. Tejanos still functioned as cultural brokers but, in this case, between Anglo-Texans in power and the rest of the Tejano population.

While Navarro, Ruiz, and de Zavala signed the Texas Declaration of Independence, it remains unclear how many Tejanos shared their opinions and political ideas. Being Tejano elites, they stood to gain materially from the success of the Anglo-Texan project. Most Tejanos, on the other hand, simply desired to be left alone by any invading army. The statements by Governor Smith, while inflammatory, point out the underlying fact that many Tejanos chose not to fight on either side of the Texan rebellion and abandoned the city for the countryside.[81] Later memorials recounting the battles of this period mention flight as a common reaction to violence in the city.

Since few Tejanos explained for posterity why they left Béxar, their actions need to be understood in the larger context of the rebellion. Most likely, Smith incorrectly asserted that avoiding the conflict equaled opposition to Anglo-Texan success. On a basic level, flight meant survival. Juan N. Seguín provided a company for those Tejanos who wanted an opportunity to participate in the Anglo-Texan cause. The choice by many not to join reveals the limits of allegiance to the constitution of 1824 among the general Tejano population. By refusing to raise arms against the Texian army, Bexareños might have anticipated some benefits or at least benevolence from the future Anglo-Texan government. Finally, Bexareños might have believed that Mexico would defeat the Anglo rebellion. In that case, joining the Anglo-Texans would result in severe punishment for treason.

When the Texian leadership met to write the Declaration of Independence, Bexareños returned to their town somewhat reluctantly. As Erasmo Seguín's brush with Bowie's men showed, they came back to a situation that remained uncertain and threatened to turn violent again. Three months after the retreat of Cos's army from Béxar, signs of another battle surfaced with reports in April of the return of the Mexican army led by Santa Anna. Once again, many Bexareños left town to avoid the ravages of war in the countryside. Unlike the first battle for Béxar, Seguín's Tejano company missed the second battle while on assignment in Gonzales.

After the siege and battle for Béxar in late 1835, most of the Tejano troops still in the Army of Texas went to Gonzales to regroup with the remainder of the Texas troops. A force of mostly Anglo-American soldiers remained in Béxar in the Alamo fort, a former mission. When Santa Anna's forces reached Béxar on February 23, 1836, Anglo-American calls for aid from Travis went unheeded. The events that transpired with the retaking of Béxar by the Mexican army, better known as the battle of the Alamo, have been recounted in dozens of monographs and from several perspectives.[82]

While most histories of Texas depict the second battle for Béxar in terms of a heroic last stand for independent Texas, few situate the conflict in the lives of Béxar's longtime citizens. The battle was less an act of self-defense against the Mexican army than a defense of conquered land by secessionist Texans. A few Tejanos were among the soldiers fighting on the Texan side of the second battle for Béxar, but in a much smaller proportion than in the first battle in December 1835.[83] One list contains five Tejanos as losing their lives.

Many Bexareños endured this second battle in the same way they did the first siege on Béxar: they simply fled to the countryside. Years after

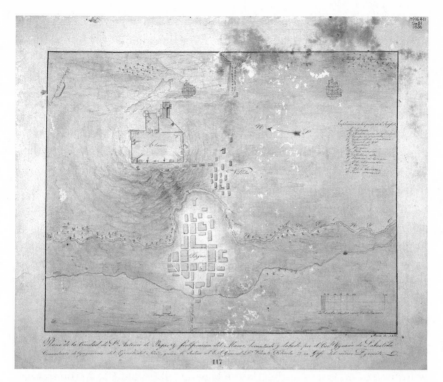

Map of Mexican battle plan by Ygnacio Labastida, commander of engineers of the Mexican army, 1836. This map illustrates the relation between the central plaza of San Antonio de Bexár, the Alamo presidio, and the San Antonio River. (Texas Map Collection, The Center for American History, The University of Texas at Austin)

the battles, Pablo Diaz, Juan Antonio Chavez, José María Rodríguez, and Antonio Menchaca each recalled that they fled the conflicts.[84] When a newspaper reporter asked Diaz why he stayed out of town, at Mission Concepción, during the second battle, Diaz replied, "I don't want war."[85] Family survival played a central role in the decision many Bexareños made regarding allegiances during the war. José María Rodríguez recalled his family's motivations: "My mother undertook to act for us and decided it was best for us to go into the country to avoid being here when General Santa Anna's army should come in."[86] Rodríguez's family feared a recurrence of the reprisals that federalists experienced after the Monclova statehouse schism. Enrique Esparza's wife and children missed an opportunity to leave town after a cart driver offered to take Esparza's parents and siblings to San Felipe during the hostilities.[87]

Other Tejanos stayed in Béxar either to defend the Anglo-Texan position or to provide services to the Mexican army. In either case, Tejano actions defy clear categorization as supportive of Anglo-Texans or Mexican troops. For instance, Juan Diaz told a newspaper reporter of his family's aid to Santa Anna, including feeding the staff officers.[88] Eulalia Yorba recalled: "We women were all terribly frightened. Every eatable in the house, all the cows, lumber and hay about the place were taken by [Mexican] troops."[89] Enrique Esparza's family turned to the Alamo for safety during the battle after missing the opportunity to leave the city. Bexareños also participated in the military confrontation on both sides of the second battle, though non-Tejanos made up the bulk of both forces.

In at least two cases, brothers struggled and fought on opposing sides. Among the Béxar elite, Juan Antonio Navarro continued his support of the Anglo separatists while his brother Angel worked with the Mexican troops. As noted above, Angel maintained his connections with the Mexican government in the hope of finding a peaceful solution to the problem. While neither brother appears to have raised arms, the two aided each side in the battles for Béxar. In later years, Francisco Esparza related the event of burying his brother Gregorio after the battle of the Alamo.[90] Gregorio, who also fought with Seguín's company in the first siege of Béxar, stood and died with the Texian forces in the Alamo. Having supported Cos in the siege of Béxar, Francisco was permitted by the Mexican generals to find his brother in the ruins. Francisco Esparza concluded his remarks by noting, "[I] have lived here ever since and done and performed all the duties of a good citizen, as all my neighbors can testify."[91] When summarizing his experience, Esparza put his connection to the local community above national and political causes.

The second battle for Béxar concluded with the Mexican army storming the Alamo on March 6, 1836. Historians and commentators have elevated the event to mythic proportions over the last century and a half.[92] Until recently, most accounts have almost exclusively focused on the Anglo-Texan soldiers rather than on the Tejano participants and inhabitants of Béxar.[93] The Battle of the Alamo itself appeared to be simply another disruption in the routines and commerce of Bexareños. Events of lasting significance to Tejanos took place soon after, with the defeat of the Mexican army at San Jacinto and the creation of the Republic of Texas. Those events immediately imbued the war of secession and the Alamo itself with new meaning for Tejanos.

At San Jacinto, the Texas army led a surprise attack on Santa Anna's troops, leading to the Mexican surrender. Tejano troops again participated in significant numbers in this battle.[94] Juan N. Seguín's company fought in the battle of San Jacinto, mostly in an area called Buffalo Bayou. In his social history of the Army of Texas, historian Paul Lack notes the shift of the troop composition from settler to more recent Anglo immigrants or mercenaries.[95] As a result, Tejanos made up a significant percentage of those Texas army troops at San Jacinto who had lived in Texas prior to 1835.

After their action in the battle of San Jacinto, the men of Seguín's company continued to aid the secessionist cause by escorting Mexican troops south.[96] Tejano troops seemed particularly suited to this task, functioning as liaisons between the Mexican and the Texan armies. Tejanos held a professional and practical relation with the defeated Mexican army. These contacts continued in later years as federalists in the Mexican north relied on Tejanos, such as Seguín, to pass on requests for Texan support.

Santa Anna's capitulation resulted in the secession of Texas from Mexico and the formation of the Republic of Texas. But acceptance of Texas secession by the Mexican government took several more years of skirmishes and another war. Battles continued in the Tejano homeland, as will be described in the next chapter. Nevertheless, Anglo-Texans initiated their independent government with an eye toward annexation with the United States. Tejanos who supported the Texan secession movement were rewarded for their loyalty with important government positions. Among these were such Bexareños as Erasmo and Juan Seguín and José Antonio Navarro. Juan Seguín had two companies of mostly Anglo-American soldiers added to his command.[97]

Yet, despite Tejano participation in the siege of Béxar and the battle of San Jacinto, many Anglo-Texan leaders still questioned their loyalty and allegiance. Broad ethnic stereotypes, such as those found in Henry Smith's comments after the siege of Béxar, continued to spread within the Anglo-Texan military leadership. Smith based his attacks on lack of Tejano involvement in Texan secession. While most Tejanos did avoid fighting, they did so for reasons that Smith did not consider. Sitting out the war was a typical response by residents across the region, Anglo-American and Tejano alike, not a declaration of opposition to Texan secession. As Lack notes, "For a people of such fabled militancy, the [Anglo-]Texans turned out for army duty in this period of crisis at a low rate of participation."[98] Over the course of the entire war of secession, a maximum of 3,685 out of about 40,000 Anglo-American immigrants fought in any battles, peaking at 60 percent of the Texian forces at any time. Most joined the army during the early months of the conflict. Perhaps Tejanos' lack of participation appeared more striking since a large part of the battles in the conflict occurred in the midst of Tejano homes. Nevertheless, it was Tejano loyalty and allegiance that remained suspect.

There remains room for interpretation regarding Bexareño motivations during these battles. Lack suggests that many Tejanos might have avoided fighting the Mexican army for fear of retaliation in the case of a Mexican victory. According to the apparent strength of Mexican troops, such a conclusion seems possible. Perhaps not choosing to fight functioned as a hedge against retaliation from either side. Regardless, Anglo-Texans quickly defined Tejano inaction as dangerous to the safety and stability of the Texas Republic. Tejanos and their towns remained the center of tension and conflict between Anglo-led Texas and Mexico for years after the battle of San Jacinto. This tension accelerated Tejano alienation from Texan authority over the years of the Texas Republic and into American annexation in 1845. As a result of these changes, Tejanos began to function in a new social context that defined their identity in primarily ethnic terms, though one where Mexican became the marker of difference.

Contingent Lives

Nearly a year after the Texan defeat in Béxar, Juan N. Seguín led a eulogy at a funeral service to bury the ashes of the Alamo dead.[99] With a band playing and the color flags of Texas flying, Seguín spoke in Spanish of the heroism displayed by the soldiers. He concluded that these men "preferred to die a thousand times rather than submit themselves to the tyrants['] yoke."[100] Major Thomas Western of Seguín's company also gave a speech in English. Seguín's eulogy took on added meaning at several levels. For instance, Seguín gave his speech in Spanish, in doing so displaying a sense of loyalty to Texas to serve as a model for other Bexareños. Also, Seguín's speech put a Tejano face on the commemoration of the battle. Finally, while Seguín referred to the government of Santa Anna with the word "tyrant," the question remains whether Santa Anna represented the entire Mexican nation.

Seguín's local take on nationalism or his critique of the nation-state put his participation in the war of secession in a unique context. Other Tejanos demonstrated the range of choices and stances taken toward Texan secession, basing their actions on a combination of local interests and national pressures. Unlike Seguín, Navarro, and Ruiz, several elite Tejanos chose to actively support the Mexican government in Texas and Béxar. Many Bexareños, elite and non-elite alike, simply chose to avoid the fray altogether. Should these stances be an indicator of a different conception of nation, particularly among Tejano elites? Under contemporary usage of the idea of nationalism, stances taken by Tejanos like Juan N. Seguín contradict the idea of being Mexican. The complex political context and borderlands social location made national identity a specific and fluid identity linked to a time and place.

The turn of events in Béxar from the fall of 1835 to the spring of 1837 indicates a more complex operation of national, local, and ethnic identification than simply Anglo, Texan, or Mexican. Family, friendship, business, violence, and history entered into the decision-making matrix for Tejanos. While the celebration of independence held on September 16, 1835, appeared as a unified expression of national identity, the differing actions taken by Tejanos during the war of secession exposed the contours of nationalism in Béxar during this period. To make room for such a contingent notion of nationalism requires modification of that identity to include various types of economic and social relations.

Rather than an absolute category, nationalism is but one factor of identity within the combination of family, friendship, politics, status, and history. Mexican nationalism not only was different in Béxar than in Mexico City or Guadalajara but also differed from person to person in Béxar itself. The various paths taken by Bexareños during this moment of crisis indicate that these differences had some connection to a shared notion of Mexican nationalism. Some might argue that those who either fled or fought with the Texians held other identities higher than nationalism, which influenced those actions. Yet those same Tejanos continued to refer to themselves as Mexican, just as those who supported the Mexican army did. Mexican identity must be expansive enough to make room for all those choices taken in 1835.

At this point, a deeper shift in the idea of Mexican identity in Texas was underway. These fissures in Mexican identity and reactions to Texan anger suggest "Mexican" shifts from a national identity to an ethnic/cultural identity. These changes provide evidence of an emergent culture developing in relation to the new social order presented to Tejanos.[101] However, though Bexareños turned their attention to the secessionist rhetoric of the Anglo-Texans, they still considered themselves Mexican for reasons that went beyond the issues of the moment. They continued to be the frontier people who built colonies in the rugged territory, made treaties with and fought against the indigenous populations, and participated in the protracted effort to attain independence from Spain. Those experiences, based on residual elements of culture extending from the previous decades, defined being Mexican for Tejanos.

By the end of 1836, Béxar and Bexareños changed as a result of circumstances outside of their world. While Bexareños had welcomed Anglo-American immigrants into Texas in the early years of the nineteenth century, their nation and city was transformed after the conflict between Anglo-Texans and Mexico. Materially, much of the town suffered from the scars of warfare, a result of two separate invasions. Ideologically, Tejanos now had to negotiate a new relationship between themselves and those in power. In this case, though, those in power considered themselves racially and culturally different. Anglo-American unfamiliarity with Tejanos and the suspicion raised by the war created an uneasy context for ethnic relations in the Texas Republic. Growing anti-Mexican sentiments influenced Tejano relations with Texans and redefined Tejano concepts of nationalism and ethnicity.

The range of Tejano activities during Texas secession again demonstrated their role as cultural brokers between new immigrants and the national government. Tejanos initially worked with the state to smooth over problems brought about by Anglo-American immigration. Once war broke out, many Tejanos, most supporters of Juan N. Seguín, enlisted to support the Anglo-Texans in opposing the centralist government of Santa Anna. Finally, other Tejanos avoided conflicts altogether, protecting themselves and their future. All these Tejano actions fall under the broad definition of Tejano political ideology. Characterizing Tejano identity, then, needs to take into account the multiple roles played by Tejanos and their underlying role as mediators in a culturally complex place.

Since Tejanos took such differing stances during this period, the concept of an essential Tejano identity itself falls into question. This fragmentation appears in the multiple paths taken by participants in the Independence Day celebration described at the beginning of this chapter. To a large extent, local and regional ties and interests took priority over national identity for most Tejanos. This shift can be attributed to either the circumstances of Texas politics or to turmoil and conflict in Mexico. In any case, those Tejanos who joined the Texan secessionists held a different understanding of their objectives than did Anglo-Texans. Tejanos continued to maintain a political position linking their identification with Texas and

Béxar to Mexican federalism, instead of with secession, as advocated by most Anglo-Texans.

After the dust and ashes from the Alamo settled, the people of Béxar stood at the beginning of a new chapter in the city's development. While change came gradually, Bexareños now had to deal more directly with Anglo-Americans on a daily basis. With their roles as cultural brokers between Anglo-Americans and the Mexican government gone, Tejano elites found themselves functioning as representatives of a Tejano constituency before the Anglo-Texan leaders. Béxar occupied an ethnically and socially reorganized borderland.

No longer a Spanish or Mexican city, Béxar also changed after the secession of Texas. The first visible change came when Anglo-Texans began playing a central role in local politics. Anglo-Texans moved into the city in increasing numbers over the coming decades. Nevertheless, Tejanos maintained their society and culture. While the Diez y Seis de Septiembre celebration in 1835 marked the last one with Béxar as a Mexican city, it would not be the final Mexican Independence Day celebration held by the Tejano community. Furthermore, the contest over who controlled Béxar both politically and functionally would be in flux until 1848. Tejanos now had a new nation to contend with, the Republic of Texas, and with it new articulations of political power and nationality along lines of ethnicity.

There was not one [family] who did not
lament the loss of a relative and, to crown their
misfortunes, they found their houses in ruins, their fields
laid waste, and their cattle destroyed or dispersed.
—Juan N. Seguín, *Personal Memoirs* (1858)

What were the results? The most depressing and ruinous.
The ingrate Texas colonists took our territory with impunity.
—*Alcance al Semanario Politico*, Monterrey, Mexico,
October 21, 1841

Chapter Six

Tejanos as a Suspect Class

THE END OF SECESSION, 1837–1848

After the loss at San Jacinto, General Antonio López de Santa Anna relinquished control of Texas to the Texan secessionists. For Anglo-Texans, the end of the war ushered in the Republic of Texas era. For Tejanos, though, the war's end brought only more uncertainty regarding their future. Their political and ethnic relation to Mexico stood at the center of that uncertainty. Mexicans continued to call for the reconquest of Texas, leading to two brief invasions of Béxar in 1842. During the second invasion, Mexican forces required Anglo-Texan inhabitants to sign an oath promising to "recommend to all Americans, who may come here after our departure, to treat the Mexican population residing in this place with lenience and kindness."[1] Why was this request necessary? What did it mean for the Mexican military to point out the mistreatment of Tejanos living in Béxar? Despite their participation in the war of Texas secession, Tejanos were marked by Anglo-Texans as Mexican and as such a suspect class. Even though "Mexican" was a national identity, the term functioned like an ethnic identity. Mexican identity brought together the residual tension and violence of the recent war with generalizations about an entire class of people.

The demographic and political identity of Béxar itself changed after the Mexican defeat at San Jacinto. Under the new Texas government, Béxar now took the name of its patron saint, San Antonio.[2] San Antonio, once almost exclusively a Mexican town, started to experience new waves of American and German immigrants. Instead of negotiating between somewhat geographically distant Anglo-American immigrants and the Mexican government, Bexareños witnessed increased proximity to Anglo-American social and political power. With the echoes of the war of secession still ringing between the Nueces and Río Grande, Tejanos' ability to carve out a space for their social and economic lives grew even more difficult in these years.

According to the terms of surrender under the Treaty of Velasco, a mostly Tejano contingent of the Army of Texas escorted the Mexican troops south beyond the Río Grande. While the war ended at San Jacinto, the battles continued over the next decade, mainly in Tejano-populated areas. Béxar occupied center stage of these battles, and Bexareños confronted new pressures and choices affecting their future. Recalling their history while looking toward the future, Tejanos attempted to negotiate through the pitfalls and uncertainties presented to them during the early years of the Texas Republic. They struggled to maintain the society and livelihood built over the previous century. An examination of the changes in San Antonio between the war of Texas secession and the American annexation of Texas reveals the social and economic effects of Tejano incorporation into the Texas Republic. How was Tejano identity affected by demographic changes in San Antonio, combined with continued military conflicts between Anglo-Americans and the Mexican government?[3] The undeclared continuation of the war of secession resulted in the inclusion of Tejanos as part of a suspect Mexican class, hindering their incorporation into the Texas Republic.

Of the few urban concentrations in Texas, San Antonio witnessed the most combat and suffered the greatest damage from the war of Texas secession.[4] Not only did most Tejano inhabitants leave the town during the battles, but invading armies on both sides fought from Tejano homes and indiscriminately pillaged them. After San Jacinto, Texan military leaders believed that although Santa Anna had capitulated, popular sentiment would fuel the fight to keep Texas within Mexico.[5] While hostilities died down, tensions still loomed over the city, putting its immediate future in question.

The full extent of the deterioration of the town's stature and the work confronting Tejanos appears in orders given by Texan general Felix Huston in March 1837 to abandon and completely raze San Antonio.[6] Huston's opinion represented the desire of a few Texan generals not only to erase the remnants of Mexican society in Texas but to extend the war into northern Mexico, exacting retribution and securing the southern border of Texas.[7] The order to destroy San Antonio appeared after Texan soldiers, entering the town, reported that "no shout of exultation welcomed our return to Béxar, the inhabitants plainly evidencing that their sympathies were with the enemy."[8] These reports had the effect of defining all Tejanos as enemies of Texas, even after the Mexican army retreated.

Juan N. Seguín had feared such anti-Mexican sentiments would arise among Anglo-Texans. Soon after the battle of San Jacinto, Seguín marched his troops into San Antonio on June 21, 1836, to evacuate the city. The *Telegraph and Texas Register* quoted Seguín as saying, "Fellow citizens: your conduct on this day is going to decide your fate before the general government of Texas. If you maintain your post as mere lookers-on; if you do not abandon the city and retire into the interior of Texas, that its army may protect you, you will, without fail, be treated as real enemies, and will suffer accordingly."[9] Few Bexareños responded to Seguín's call. Without an immediate threat, Tejanos probably wanted to stay at home, having been absent since November of the previous year.

After San Jacinto, Bexareños awoke to a beleaguered city to rebuild their homes and lives. But now it was a city in the Republic of Texas, and political and social life could no longer be the same. Seguín commented on the return of Tejano families to Béxar: "There was not one [family] who did not lament the loss of a relative and, to crown their misfortunes, they found their houses in ruins, their fields laid waste, and their cattle destroyed or dispersed."[10] Appointed Texan generals governed the city for a year until a city council and mayor were elected. Along with the military government, though, several *vecinos* continued to participate in the daily operation of the municipal government. Erasmo Seguín remained serving as a civic leader, sitting as the judge of Béxar County immediately after the war.[11]

The presence of Mexican troops at or near the Río Grande, though, kept Texan generals on edge as they anticipated renewed attacks by Mexican forces. Fearing the presence of a large Tejano population in San Antonio would encourage these raids, General Huston gave the order to evacuate and destroy the town.[12] Again, Bexareños refused to obey the order. This time, Juan N. Seguín supported the city, sending Blas Herrera to the Texan headquarters to request that Sam Houston spare San Antonio.[13] Herrera's message from Seguín persuaded Houston, saved the town, and secured for Herrera a position as a messenger for Houston's company. Far from being an arbitrary soldier for Seguín, Herrera came with family connections and a history of supporting roles. He was Francisco Ruiz's son-in-law and had escorted Ruiz and Antonio Navarro to sign the Texas Declaration of Independence.

Even though to Anglo-Texans, Tejanos appeared suspect and disloyal, Texas Republic officials carefully negotiated their relationship with Tejanos in an effort to maintain social order. Houston's response to Seguín's request to save San Antonio reiterated the grounds for support to Seguín and the Tejano population as a whole: "They shall remain at their homes, believing as I must that they will feel bound to return good faith and fidelity to our cause, for the humanity shown them."[14] Houston's support came with the expectation of loyalty, suggesting that not destroying San Antonio would be seen as an example of benevolence. Houston went on to direct Seguín to prove his patriotism by reporting enemies and aiding Texan officials, such as those sent to the town to make contact with indigenous groups. Houston concluded by noting his suspicions: "I need not suggest to you the necessity of sleepless vigilance, and increasing caution—You know the enemy whom you have to guard against—therefore I rely upon your ability, patriotism, and watchfulness to preserve the charge confided in you! Present my kind salutations to your relatives. Embrace your Father for me." Houston's comment that Seguín knew the enemy seems to refer to Seguín's continued contact with Mexican officials, as well as with Tejanos generally. Houston ended his letter with a familiar acknowledgment, conscious of the Seguín family's prestige within Tejano society. Houston's letter serves as an example of the shifting balance of power away from Tejanos into the hands of Anglo-Texans. These shifts point to a transformation in social relations underway in Texas, one where an ethnic connection to being Mexican stood in for a political connection to Mexico.

Through the efforts of Seguín and Herrera to block the destruction of San Antonio, Bexareños asserted political power over their destiny. It marked a new style that relied on personal connections of Tejano elites to advocate for their ethnic constituency. In this way, Tejano elites maintained their prestige in San Antonio's social order. After the summer of 1837, San Antonio incorporated its city council under the laws of the Republic of Texas.[15] With the exception of one individual, Tejanos made up the entire governing body on the eve of the first elections. The one exception, John W. Smith, stands out, since he held the position of president of

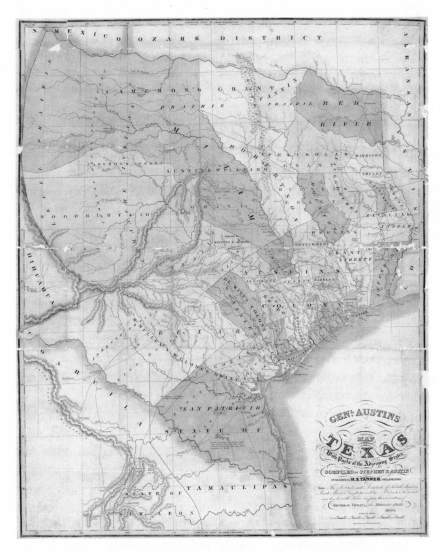

"General Austin's Map of Texas with Parts of Adjoining States, 1840," combining empresario *grants with new counties and Mexican and American states. (Map Collection, Archives and Information Services Division, Texas State Library and Archives Commission, 0424)*

the council. Unlike most commanders appointed to govern the city, Smith had lived in Béxar for several years before the rebellion.[16] He became somewhat integrated into elite Tejano society, going so far as to have the Spanish nickname "El Colorado."[17] Smith married María de Jesús Delgado Curbelo, a local Tejana, adding to the growing number of intermarriages discussed later in this chapter.[18] Naming Smith to the head of the council appeared to be a symbolic Tejano gesture of trust in the Republic government. Smith bolstered the Tejano voice in civic governance in the face of Anglo-Texan suspicions.

The *vecinos* of San Antonio voiced their support of Smith in an election held September 18, 1837. In an assembly of nineteen citizens, Smith received fifteen votes for president, over José Antonio Navarro, Francisco Antonio Ruiz (Francisco Ruiz's son), and J. Croco. All but one of the eight *regidores* named in the temporary council won their election by an overwhelming majority.[19] Finally, Erasmo Seguín and Father Refugio de la Garza oversaw and approved of the election itself. Politically, elite Tejanos still governed the city of San Antonio, but now within the laws and oversight of the Texas Republic.

In 1837, the city council emerged after a postwar hiatus of almost two years. Even while incorporated under a new nation-state, the city attempted to reconnect its municipal history and operation back to the Mexican period. First, the council decided to levy back-taxes on the property of *vecinos*, using a law established in 1832 under the state of Coahuila y Texas.[20] It then proceeded to explicitly extend the application of all ordinances of the "former Corporation."[21] Otherwise, the council concerned itself with the problems of a typical nineteenth-century frontier town.

In the council's first two years, many ordinances concerned taxation and social regulations. The council addressed public health by regulating abattoirs and garbage removal and demonstrated its class composition and elite values by passing vagrancy laws that required males to be employed "in decent things" or in the care of a proprietor or boss. All those found violating the ordinances would be sent out of the city. It appears council members directed such regulations at former Mexican soldiers who had deserted Santa Anna's army during the campaign in Texas. These laws also had their basis in Anglo-Texan fears of a Mexican invasion, or at least of Mexican spies living among the Tejano population. Tejano aldermen supported these vagrancy laws, demonstrating shared concern for stability and peace in their city with their new Anglo-Texan neighbors and political superiors.

Finally, the council instituted a license requirement for holding "private and subscription balls." The city required those throwing fandangos to pay one peso to the city treasury, or else pay a penalty of ten pesos. The ordinance also forced billiard halls to pay four pesos monthly.[22] The establishment of these ordinances and the payment of dance fees provide a glimpse of renewed social life in San Antonio after a year of battle conditions.[23] An Anglo-American visitor to the town in 1837 wrote, "The evening is spent by a large portion of the population at the fandango, a kind of Spanish waltz. There are seldom less than three or four of this description of dances during the night in different portions of the city."[24] These dances continued a civic tradition originating in the previous century. San Antonio remained culturally Mexican even after secession.

Anglo-Texans entered this Tejano world, becoming part of society and intermarrying. Writing to his wife, Sam A. Maverick commented on the dominance of Tejano elites in San Antonio society during the early Texas Republic period. He noted, "Our only society are Mexicans; two Irish families live in town but they are no society such home-people."[25] Once she arrived in the city, Mary Adams Maverick commented to her mother, "As for San Antonio, it is the same healthy and beautiful place as far as the gifts of nature go, as we have ever thought it."[26] Anglo-Texans found many of the same benefits and attractions in San Antonio as their Tejano and indigenous predecessors had. Though, noting the troubles plaguing this frontier city, Maverick added, "But oh! how condemned it is by the thieves and mean wretches who inhabit it."

San Antonio underwent a significant social transition during the Texas Republic period. For Tejanos in San Antonio, the period also meant an uncertain and shifting relation to Mexico. Mexico was at once a homeland and a barrier to inclusion constructed by Anglo-Americans now dominating Texas. Despite secession, political events in Mexico continued to affect Tejano society, particularly the debate around independent Texas and American expansion. For someone like Juan N. Seguín, a prominent role in the war of secession did not cut his ties to Mexico or the need to rely on them again.

Juan N. Seguín

Following the fortunes of Juan N. Seguín during this period provides a useful benchmark for gauging the effects of Anglo-American attitudes toward Tejanos. While Seguín's unique position in San Antonio society makes his case exceptional, he also serves as a symbol for the decline of Tejano power in the city. Seguín's story highlights the specific ways continued conflicts with Mexico affected Tejanos. The Mexican incursions in 1842 marked the turning point for Seguín, forcing him to leave his native city. While Bexareños interacted with and reacted to Anglo-Texans in a wide variety of ways, they all faced very similar circumstances as Tejanos living through a time of social and political changes. Their choices and obstacles shifted in a more accelerated manner as tensions rose between Mexico and Texas from 1838 to 1845.

In a memoir later in his life, Seguín wrote of his fall from Texan grace: "I had to leave Texas, abandon all, for which I had fought and spent my fortune, to become a wanderer."[27] Even though he had once held prestigious leadership positions in both the military and civilian life, threats against Seguín's life, family, and well-being resulted in his departure to Mexico in 1842. But Seguín's inclusion in the Texan political and military power structures once represented a form of Texan acceptance of Tejano authority.

Along with the Tejanos participating in city politics, Seguín and José Antonio Navarro served in the Texas legislature, Seguín as a senator and Navarro as a representative. Having been a commander in the Texan army, Seguín operated easily within the circles of Anglo-Texan political power. Starting his term in March 1838, Seguín submitted a bill for the relief of widows and orphans of the Alamo battle.[28] He served through two more terms, always conducting his business with the aid of an interpreter. Like his father Erasmo, Seguín began to take on the role of cultural broker, thus maintaining his family prestige.

While in Congress, Seguín and Navarro sat on several committees, using their positions to support the interests of Bexareños and Tejanos in general. As a member of several committees, Seguín claimed to protect the future of his fellow Tejanos. He articulated this desire in a speech before the Senate in February 1840. Regarding the inclusion of Tejanos in decision-making, he commented, "As a representative from Béxar, I never shall cease to raise my voice in effecting this object."[29] In particular, Seguín argued for funding the translation of Texas's laws and regulations. During the discussion of that item from the previous budget, Seguín noted, "My constituents have, as yet, not seen a single law translated and printed . . . , the dearest rights of my constituents as Mexico-Texians are guaranteed by the Constitution and the Laws of the Republic of Texas; and at the formation of the social compact between the Mexicans and the Texians, they had rights guaranteed them; . . . all of which they are ignorant, and in consequence of their ignorance of the language in which the Laws and the Constitution of the land are written."[30] Seguín's use of the language of rights and protections displayed his understanding of the liberal foundations of the Texan political system. But, in his delineation of the language barrier, Seguín laid out fundamental distinctions between Mexicans and "Texians." Enough differ-

Portrait of Juan N. Seguín from the Texas Republic period by Thomas Jefferson Wright. (Photograph by Perry Huston, Texas State Preservation Board, 1989.096)

ences existed and possible abuses lurked to justify Seguín's reliance on the broad protections under the Texas Constitution. The language issue surfaced again in April 1841 at a San Antonio city council meeting. Councilman Agustín Barrera suggested the council petition the Republic government to print its laws in Spanish.[31]

Seguín's role as cultural broker and interest in his constituency also appeared in the personal favors he extended to other Bexareños. A year after the war of secession, Seguín sent letters to President Sam Houston and Secretary of State James Pinckney Henderson vouching for the good character of José Cassiano.[32] Seguín's comments echoed standards of Tejano culture maintained during Anglo-American colonization. Seguín mentioned that from the time he first met Cassiano, "he has conducted himself in a manner worthy of a gentleman [*caballero*], and I have only seen him entirely dedicated to his own business as a merchant, his chosen employment." Regarding Cassiano's involvement in the war of secession, he wrote, "In the year 1835, the year the current Texas question began, he was the only citizen [*vecino*] of many to visit the camps of our troops surrounding this city and proclaimed himself in favor of our cause. And after we captured the plaza, he volunteered any aid we requested." Seguín's example shows his awareness that Anglo-Texans automatically assumed Tejanos were disloyal and suspect. Since much of the war occurred on land Tejanos occupied, their support had to be active rather than passive. Seguín concluded by noting, "For these reasons I believe no doubt remains that Cassiano is a true friend of Texas, and as such I recommend him to you to do me the favor of treating him as a good Texan with family in this nation." With this last statement, Seguín pushed his clout to improve the situation of Cassiano and other Bexareños.[33]

Seguín continued to press for access to the Texan political system by using moral grounds for the Tejano inclusion. He added in a speech, "The Mexico-Texians were among the first who sacrificed their all in our glorious Revolution, and the disasters of war weighed heavy upon them, to achieve those blessings which, it appears, [they] are destined to be the last to enjoy."[34] Four years after the war of Texas secession, Seguín recalled the damages done to the Tejano homeland. By evoking this legacy, Seguín alluded to the growing dissatisfaction among and abuse of Tejanos in San Antonio. Furthermore, Tejanos, or at least Seguín, understood the price they had paid during the war against Mexico and believed they continued to pay for being Mexican. Seguín's narrative of the Texas war directly responded to Anglo-American classification of Tejanos as a suspect class, in this case by emphasizing the sacrifice made by Tejanos.

Seguín met up with more controversy when he returned to San Antonio to take the position of mayor in January 1841. Several Anglos in town opposed Seguín's tenure and held personal grudges based on business deals and politics.[35] These tensions might have subsided over time, but military pressures and changing politics in Mexico intervened to further divide Tejanos and Anglo-Texans in San Antonio. For Seguín, the events of 1842 led to his eventual "expatriation" to Mexico. For this reason, it is important to understand the broader context of Mexican politics leading up to the incursions in 1842.

Seguín's fall from mayor to exile embodied the decline of Mexican ethnic relations with Anglos in Texas. Indigenous groups were also caught in the wave of Anglo-Texan land and power consolidation during the Republic period.[36] Militias formed to force all indigenous groups out of Texas, pushing them west and south into Mexican territory. Comanche groups found themselves extending their trading and raiding networks farther south into Mexico as a result of these pressures.[37] Once friendly relations between Anglo-Texans and Cherokee leaders also broke down following Texas secession, mirroring the relationship between Anglo-Texans and Tejanos. Problems for Cherokee groups came to a head in 1838, when rumors spread of a coordinated uprising by Cherokee warriors that was to coincide with a Mexican invasion of Texas. The apparent plot revolved around communications between the Cherokee chief Duwali and the former mayor of Nacogdoches, Vicente Cordova.[38] The threat of the so-called Cordova Rebellion resulted in increased violent attacks by Anglo-Texans against all indigenous groups and ethnic Mexicans living in the northeastern region of Texas. Locals attributed the massacre of an Anglo-Texan family to the Mexican-Indian plot. Through the Cordova Rebellion, Anglo-Texans linked suspicion of indigenous peoples with the distrust of Tejanos already visible in San Antonio.

Reconquista

After Santa Anna's defeat at San Jacinto, Mexican politicians and military officers continued to debate the legality and permanence of Texas's independence. Additional conflicts surfaced over the location of the Texas borderline, raising problems with the Treaty of Velasco.[39] These debates reached Texas Republic officials, often through information passed on by Tejanos. As a result, Texan military officials kept a close watch on Mexican maneuvers near the Río Grande. Despite these tensions, trade continued between Texas and Mexico, especially through San Antonio. Mexican pressures to reconquer Texas, or at least maintain a military threat on the border, along with Texan interest in New Mexico resulted in two invasions of San Antonio in 1842.

After suffering through these invasions and hearing of calls for a *recon-*

quista of Texas emanating from Mexico City, some Tejanos began to question the permanence of the Texas Republic. They may have even expected Texas to return to Mexico within a few years. This attitude, combined with Anglo-Texan suspicions of Tejanos, led to a heightened state of ethnic tension starting in 1842 and continuing through the annexation of Texas by the United States in 1845. Mexican threats on the Republic of Texas made Tejano identity a suspect class among Anglo-Texans.

While Santa Anna's capitulation terms at San Jacinto in 1836 had granted Texas its independence, many Mexican congressmen and political commentators questioned the legitimacy of the treaty.[40] Immediately after the secession of Texas, Mexico's territorial integrity became a key issue in Mexican politics. Over the next decade, talk circulated among politicians and military generals regarding the reconquest of Texas. They offered the *reconquista* as a unifying point during a time of division between centralist and federalist political factions. Already, threats of Texan designs on New Mexico began to circulate, reinforcing negative stereotypes of land-grabbing Anglo-Americans.[41]

Far from separating Tejanos from Mexican politics, the secession of Texas placed their future in a more significant position relative to Mexican debates. While Tejano opinions or desires never figured into the discussions around *reconquista*, its rhetoric continued to affect Tejano relations with Anglo-Texans. Also, Mexican attention to Texas was connected to a strong federalist movement in the northern states. Several federalist generals in the Mexican army raised troops and fought against the government throughout this period. The continuous movement of soldiers in northern Mexico along with the *reconquista* rhetoric worried the Texan government and added to their doubts about the loyalty of Tejanos to the Republic.

Mexican federalist politics were also meaningful for Bexareños. Fully aware that some Bexareños initially participated in the war of Texas secession to support the constitution of 1824, federalists made overtures requesting aid in their efforts against the Mexican government.[42] In August 1839, Erasmo Seguín, in his role as chief justice of San Antonio, wrote a letter to the secretary of state of Texas regarding a visit by General Juan Pablo Anaya. He noted that Anaya, commanding troops occupying the northeastern states, made overtures to those in power in Texas for financial and military support for upcoming conflicts with the Mexican government.[43]

A number of Tejanos who had supported the federalists during the war of secession continued to do so during the Texas Republic. In 1840, Juan N. Seguín went as far as loaning the federalist general Antonio Canales $3,000 to aid his cause.[44] The Anaya and Canales examples demonstrate another manner in which Tejanos acted as cultural brokers in Texas. In this case, Tejanos connected the interests of the federalist cause in Mexico with the goals of the Texas Republic. This bridge also served to inform Texas Republic officials of threats to Texas emerging from the calls for Mexican *reconquista*.

Seguín related his opinions about Mexican federalist efforts to Texas president Mirabeau Lamar in a letter of December 26, 1840.[45] Seguín informed Lamar of his visit to the Mexican towns of Mier and Monterrey, his meetings with Mexican generals, and rumors of a campaign to reannex Texas. Seguín met with Generals Canales and Isidro Reyes regarding requests for Texan soldiers to support the federalist forces in the north. Seguín noted, "During the three or four days that I was in that town, I heard frequent conversations relative to the approaching campaign against Texas. The chief Officers and Soldiers are all enthusiastic and anxiously desire the moment of undertaking the March to Texas."[46] Seguín's comments reflect the extent to which interest in the *reconquista* of Texas spread among the Mexican military. General Reyes approached Seguín to ask about the remaining national ties of Tejanos. Seguín added, "Genl. Reyes made many inquiries of me relative to the feelings of the old Colonists and their disposition to return to their former State of obedience to the Mexican Government under certain guaranteed privileges." Seguín did not provide his response to Reyes's question, though he carefully measured his words in a letter to the president of Texas.

Seguín provided Lamar with more information regarding Mexican designs on Texas. He quoted his discussion with General Mariano Arista, revealing Arista's plans. According to Seguín, Arista said, "I shall march upon my return from Saltillo to take possession of San Antonio and Goliad, for which place I shall offer the following terms to the Old Colonists—Lands to all who have not obtained it. Their ports free for 10 or 15 years and a State Legislature and Government. Should these propositions have no effect, I will continue the War until the country is subdued." Arista's comments imply that Tejanos might have believed that Anglo-Texans went too far by seceding from Mexico. Seguín also added information on troops and movements. Seguín ended by reaffirming his allegiance to the Texas cause, noting, "I should have required more information from Gen. Arista, but as soon as he observed that I did not coincide with his ideas, (for he had been induced to believe I was a friend of the Mexican cause) he withdrew from the conversation." Regardless of Seguín's opinion, Arista needed Seguín as a broker for continued contact with Anglo-Texans. The next year, Seguín escorted Rafael Uribe to the Texas capital at Arista's request.[47] Uribe approached the Texans to seek cooperation in fighting against indigenous groups. Seguín's role as an intermediary between the Texas government and Mexican federalists simultaneously aided the Texas government while proving Tejano loyalty.

While Seguín served as both a link between Mexicans and an informant for the Anglo-Texans, he may have unwittingly added to the general suspicions of Mexican motives. Less than two years after Texas secession, Seguín began warning Lamar about the possibility of a Mexican invasion. He wrote from New Orleans in 1838, "I am of the opinion that we will once again have a war in Texas in this year."[48] Two years later, Seguín added his observations of the mood in the Mexican north, noting, "The campaign against Texas is most certain, and I am sure we shall be attacked very soon. I have never witnessed such enthusiasm as that which exists amongst all classes of Mexicans against Texas."[49] Although Seguín held many connections among those in the Mexican military, his continued warnings also came from the increased discussions of *reconquista* in Mexican politics.

For Mexicans, the loss of Texas lay at the center of the debate about *reconquista*, especially the threat it posed to national integrity. While the Mexican discourse about Texas was mainly intended to garner support in favor of a political party, *reconquista* instilled a more concrete sense of Mexican nationalism among the general population. After all, rapid changes of government in Mexico since independence threatened even further loss of land and to possibly undo the nation. Furthermore, attention to a foreign threat could potentially put aside federalist/centralist divisions, or at least rally supporters to one side.

Reconquista rhetoric appeared frequently in the Mexican press beginning in 1837, starting in Mexico City and continuing later in the north. The newspaper *Imparcial*, founded in June 1837, devoted editorial coverage to Texas throughout its entire run of forty-five issues.[50] Later that year, a publisher in Puebla printed the pamphlet *Ligeras indicaciones sobre la usurpacion de Tejas*.[51] The pamphlet used racialized language to depict Anglo-Americans as inherently prone to enslaving people of other races and stealing land. By July 11, 1839, General José María Tornel wrote to the Mexican legislature from Monterrey that the government should "fix its sights on the Department of Texas, and understand that this opportunity to bring it back into the heart of the *gran familia mejicana* should not be passed up."[52] Tornel's language unquestionably situated Texas within the Mexican nation.

Plans for the *reconquista* met with the reality of Mexico's economic and political situation. Without directly opposing the idea of reconquest, *El Realtor*, published in Monterrey, presented a series of editorials critical of Mexico's ability to reincorporate Texas. In July 1838, the editor wrote, "The few colonists of Texas have enjoyed and reveled in their triumph, without a minimal effort in two years [by the Mexican government] to recover territorial integrity and national dignity."[53] Mexicans in Monterrey had experienced the war of Texas secession from a closer perspective and thus provided a different point of view regarding the possibility of reconquest. On the other hand, *La Luna*, printed in Chihuahua, provided a stronger argument in June 1841. The editors noted, "War with Texas and the expulsion of its usurpers is the necessity of the present and more than the present, the necessity of the future."[54] Pressures mounted on Mexican officials to take efforts to reclaim Texas, especially after Texan incursions into Mexico.

In the midst of these debates, the Republic of Texas government undertook a failed mission to establish trade with the Mexican town of Santa Fe, New Mexico, and in the process created an international incident. What became known as the Texan Santa Fe Expedition set off toward New Mexico with 320 Texans on June 20, 1841, with the stated goal of joining in the lucrative Santa Fe Trail trade between Santa Fe and Saint Louis.[55] President Lamar also entrusted the group with an ulterior motive: to attempt to regain claims to land believed to be part of Texas, or even bring New Mexico into the Republic. The organizers managed to convince José Antonio Navarro to join the expedition, conscious of the need for a Tejano to engage New Mexican officials and business upon their arrival. Bexareños like Navarro served as brokers and go-betweens for continued contact with Mexicans.

Tipped off to their impending arrival, New Mexican authorities arrested the expedition members when they reached Santa Fe. With the secession of Texas still fresh in their memory and still being debated, Mexican officials made an example of these Texans by imprisoning them and sending them to Mexico City. As historian Andrés Reséndez points out, subsequent publication of the misadventures of the expedition in the United States "generally exoticized Mexicans, hereafter associating their character with treachery, cruelty, and servility."[56] Reséndez links the anti-Mexican narratives of the expedition and of the battles of 1836 to a broader ethnic transformation hastened by print culture. For Anglo-Texans, the Texan Santa Fe Expedition served as a cautionary tale about suspicious Mexicans. On the other hand, Mexicans also read about the expedition and the arrests, seeing the trip as further adventurism by Anglo-Americans and their capture as some degree of retribution.[57] The affair brought renewed attention to Texas and the border.

Tales of the failed expedition fed into the *reconquista* debates' portrayal of Anglo-Texans and the Texan government in negative terms. Revealing their thoughts on Anglo-Americans, one newspaper noted New Mexican success in preventing Anglo-American colonization. New Mexicans, the journalist wrote, "figured out how to make those irritating adventurers that dream in their whisky vapor induced fantasies about conquering another territory, eat dirt."[58] Mexicans also feared an invasion by the Texas Republic, fueled by Anglo-Texan hunger for land. Upon hearing of rumors that Texas received funds from Havana, one paper wrote, "Certainly, Texans could not have found a better resource than one from the place where the first adventurers originated insurrections."[59] After the secession of Texas, most Mexicans believed the entire nation stood exposed to Anglo-American land-grabbing.

The rise in reports of theft and marauding by Anglo-Texans against Mexicans added to negative perceptions of Anglo-Americans and fueled the *reconquista* rhetoric. While normal trading between San Antonio and northern Mexican cities resumed soon after the war, Mexicans began to complain about horse thieves from Texas.[60] The reports noted that the horses would be sold to Anglo-Texans in exchange for clothing and tobacco, indicating the scarcity of these items on the Mexican side of the border. The market in stolen horses led General Arista to decree that those found participating in the trade would be pressed into army service for ten years and have their goods confiscated.[61] Arista added that even Tejanos caught facilitating the trade would meet the same fate. Beyond its attempt to reduce theft on the border, Arista's decree reinforced Mexico's claim to the Nueces River as the border. The decree demonstrated the impatience many Mexicans felt regarding the Texas question and provided Arista with a pretext to resume hostilities.

Arista's decree resulted in the capture and arrest of several Anglo-Texans, including the prominent Texan Philip Dimmitt. In June 1841, a Matamoros newspaper reported the arrest of twenty-three Anglo-Texan traders from San Antonio carrying tobacco and other merchandise.[62] Their goods were confiscated, in accordance with Arista's decree, and the violators sentenced to ten years' service in the presidial companies. Later the paper reported the arrest of fourteen others, naming several of them, including Thomas Pratt and James B. Onsby.[63] The newspaper reports identified these Texans as commanders in the battle of San Jacinto. These actions by Mexican military leaders both pushed Mexicans closer to a confrontation with Texas and situated the Mexican government as the protectors of Mexicans on both sides of the Río Bravo. A letter from General Pedro Ampudia appearing in the paper noted, "These officials from the impostor, land-grabbing republic, like so many of their compatriots, have for some time now been robbing livestock from the unfortunate villages of the North, from the left bank of the Rio Bravo to the Nueces."[64] Dimmitt died while imprisoned; vague reports attributed his death to either suicide or murder.[65]

Like the examples of Anglo-Texan transgressions across the border, Mexicans also participated in robbing and marauding, using the border as protection from capture. Reports emerged in January 1841 of a group of forty Mexican soldiers stealing cattle from ranches around San Antonio, including two hundred head from Juan N. Seguín.[66] Major George T. Howard was assigned to pursue the thieves, with the aid of Seguín and other Bexareños. Along with those reports, other accounts surfaced of large groups of marauders led by former Bexareños Agaton Quiñones, Manuel Leal, and Ignacio Garcia.[67] One Anglo-Texan attributed "robbing and pillaging" around the Nueces River since 1838 to these groups. As a result of the threats from Mexican thieves, the San Antonio city council passed an ordinance on September 9, 1841, requiring strangers to present themselves to the mayor.[68] Additionally, those found harboring strangers faced a fine of between twenty-five and one hundred dollars. Both the arrests of thieves by Mexican soldiers and the incursions by Mexican thieves raised the level of tension between Mexicans and Anglo-Texans.

Anglo-Texan military officers maintained their vigilance in the face of a possible invasion by Mexico.[69] One rumor of an invasion in December 1840 probably stemmed from Mexican military activity dealing with internal battles between federalists and centralists. Many of San Antonio's citizens carried on their business, belying Seguín's fear of an invasion mentality. In a letter to his wife, Samuel Maverick wrote, "I feel every confidence that no attempt of invasion will be made."[70] Yet, soon after the war of secession, General Felix Huston constantly pressured the Texas government to preemptively attack Mexican border troops.[71] Despite Huston's requests and perhaps from lack of funds, Texas president Lamar withheld using the Texas army in Mexico. Seguín's warnings, however, kept Anglo-Texans ready for renewed violence.

Whether rumor or fact, word of Mexican schemes to reconquer Texas heightened racial tensions in San Antonio. Anglo-Americans grew deeply suspicious of potential traitors living alongside them. One incident turned

Seguín from hero to villain and highlights the depth of doubt during this period. An Anglo-Texan blacksmith, James Goodman, demanded permission to set up his shop on property claimed by both him and the city. Goodman filed his petition in February 1840; it fell on Seguín, as mayor, to adjudicate the claim.[72] Seguín and the city council charged Goodman twenty-five dollars per month rent to occupy the residence and operate his business there. Known as a violent man, Goodman turned into one of Seguín's most vociferous opponents.[73] Goodman's complaint, along with the presence of rumors questioning Seguín's loyalty during the first raid on San Antonio, destroyed Seguín's political and social standing in the community.

Thefts and attacks in rural Texas increased anti-Mexican sentiment outside of San Antonio. Across Texas, more Anglo-Texans advocated removing all Tejanos, whether or not they opposed the Republic of Texas.[74] Some of these calls came from people who believed Tejanos hid their true thoughts and identity. P. H. Bell wrote in November 1841, "Mexicans disguised as Indians are formidable in depreciating on the property of Citizens on the Border.... In speaking of disguised Mexicans, I would by no means omit to mention that there are strong reasons to believe they have the co-operation of disguised Americans."[75] These sentiments and fears led to the creation of a police force to range across the region from the Nueces River to the Río Grande to take actions specifically against Mexicans. This police force became known as the Texas Rangers.

Despite these growing anti-Mexican sentiments, Tejanos continued to maintain their connections to the Anglo-Texan establishment. One example of this contact appears in an invitation to President Lamar to attend a ball in his honor in San Antonio.[76] Both Seguín and José Antonio Navarro signed the letter of invitation sent on May 15, 1841. A few days later, Navarro responded to Lamar's request for documents of Stephen F. Austin's life for a history. Regarding Austin, Navarro wrote that he was "one of my most gracious friendships."[77] He continued: "Stephen F. Austin was and shall be the most praised Anglo-American who will grace us with his respectable hands in our nation, and as a result the merited elegies of this eminent man shall as a consequence grow." Navarro concluded by asking for the documents back from Lamar in order to pass the memory of Austin on to his children. The ball itself served as a send-off to the failed Texan Santa Fe Expedition.

Tejanos also supported the Republic by participating in patrols of the region against Mexican and Anglo marauding. Texans launched one expedition in early 1841, in response to the robbery of two Tejano merchants,

Antonio Herrera and Francisco Granado. A company was organized by John "Jack" Coffee Hays, made up of twelve Anglo-Americans, led by Hays, and thirteen Tejanos, led by Antonio Perez.[78] Muster rolls from Hays's company contained several Tejanos, such as Francisco Longavilla, Damacio Galvan, Manuel Montalvo, Matias Curbier, Eusevio Farías, Matias Diaz, Antonio Garcia, Antonio Sanchez, Margil Salinas, Francisco Granado, Antonio Coy, and Crisanto Casanavo. Antonio Perez became an important co-captain with Hays in pursuing both thieves and suspicious indigenous bands in the Nueces strip. But, as Frederick Wilkins's study on the Texas Rangers notes, "This cooperative spirit began changing, very gradually, in 1840–1841."[79] He continues by pointing out the effects of anti-Mexican rumors, writing, "Various incidents showed that the Mexicans were encouraging Indian raids."

Tejanos also heard the rumors of a Mexican reconquest of Texas and began to consider the consequences of Mexican success. Perhaps Tejanos envisioned a strong Mexican army easily overpowering the Texan forces, especially since the young Republic paid little attention to San Antonio and south Texas.[80] The rapid sale of headright land certificates around this time may have signaled that some Bexareños held little stake in the future Texas Republic. Also, as seen below, many Tejanos cooperated with the invasions of San Antonio, some migrating south of the Río Grande after the incursions.

Reconquista *Expeditions*

Rumors turned to reality when General Rafael Vázquez invaded and occupied San Antonio March 5–7, 1842.[81] While the precise purpose of Vázquez's raid remains unclear, the timing hurt Tejano relations with Anglo-Texans, and especially Juan N. Seguín's status as a leader in the community. Seguín and three or four elite Tejano families sensed an imminent attack, leading them to once again retreat to the countryside a week before the occupation.[82] The remaining Anglo-Texan families stayed to defend the city for the Republic of Texas, but without troop reinforcements, they abandoned San Antonio. Mary Maverick noted in her journal, "Tuesday evening March 1 1842 we, the American families resident in San Antonio de Bejar run away from an advancing army of Mexicans—5 miles to arroyo Salado."[83]

More significantly, many Bexareños remained in the city and cooperated with Vázquez's occupation. Reports mentioned several natives of San Antonio among Vázquez's Mexican volunteers.[84] Furthermore, it appears that during the occupation, some Bexareños held a public meeting where they agreed to an unsigned petition for armed opposition to the Republic of Texas.[85] Vázquez and his troops remained in San Antonio only a few days. After destroying some public records in the San Antonio clerk's office, they returned to Mexico along with several Bexareño families.[86] While brief, Vázquez's raid raised fears and suspicions of Mexicans among Anglo-Texans. Conversely the raid reinforced the assumption held by some Tejanos that the Republic of Texas had a tenuous hold on San Antonio.

As Vázquez retreated to the Río Grande, Seguín joined up with Captain Jack Hays's soldiers to follow the troops. Manuel Flores, Ambrosio Rodríguez, Matias Curbier, and other Bexareños aided in the effort.[87] Their participation, however, failed to stop reports circulating in San Antonio that Seguín supported Vázquez's raid. Seguín later wrote, "On my return to San Antonio, several persons told me that the Mexican officers had declared that I was on their side. This rumor, and some threats uttered against me by Goodman, left me but little doubt that my enemies would try to ruin me."[88] While General Vázquez himself might have pushed the notion of Seguín's disloyalty and despite Seguín's support from prominent Anglo-Texans, few Anglo-Texans came to Seguín's defense. At one point, Goodman raised a group of thirty men to attack Seguín, wounding Matias Curbier in the process. For an officer of the war of Texas secession to fall so far in Anglo-Texan eyes suggests a rise in the level of animosity against Tejanos in the streets of San Antonio.

Although Seguín had some support from Anglo-Texans, including General Edward Burleson, the commander of Texas forces, Seguín resigned his position as mayor on April 18, 1842.[89] Fearing for his life, Seguín decided to move to northern Mexico and risk imprisonment there for his role in the 1835 war. In his memoirs, Seguín summarized his state at the time of his departure from San Antonio: "I left Béxar without any engagements towards Texas; my services paid by persecutions, exiled and deprived of my privileges as a Texan citizen, I was in this country a being out of the pale of society, and when she could not protect the rights of her citizens, they were privileged to seek protection elsewhere. I had been tried by a rabble, condemned without a hearing, and consequently was at liberty to provide for my own safety."[90] Seguín's comments pointed out not only his persecution but also the general problems of social and political marginalization facing all Tejanos. Furthermore, Seguín's departure highlights the tenuous political and ethnic situation in San Antonio, still reeling from the disruption of the war of secession. When Seguín left the city, San Antonio lost its most important cultural broker.

After the Vázquez invasion, the Republic government stationed more troops in San Antonio. But the increased troop presence along with returning Anglo-Texans created new problems for Tejanos. In a letter to President Sam Houston, the citizens of San Antonio requested that he "protect [us] not only from marauding Mexicans, but even from our own volunteers. We have been informed that some thieving volunteers, lately drove off nearly a thousand head of cattle towards the Colorado, belonging to citizens of Béxar. Messrs. Navarro, Flores, Erasmo Seguín, and others who have ever been faithful to our cause, have suffered greatly. Shame to the men who claim the name of soldiers and act the part of thieves, by robbing their own countrymen."[91] At least a few citizens of San Antonio started losing faith in the effectiveness of the Republic government. Their letter holds up prominent Bexareños as a barometer of how Anglo-Texans treated Tejanos. Finally, marauding by both Anglos and Mexicans in and around San Antonio cast a pall over the city's trade-based economy and underscores the uncertainty of control by the Republic government in south Texas.[92] Even after Vázquez and his troops and Tejano families continued to leave San Antonio in a steady stream, many Anglo-Texan families did not immediately return.

Despite Vázquez's raid, the Texas Congress failed to pass a bill in 1842 calling for a war with Mexico and an invasion of its border states. Texas lacked the resources to undertake an offensive war. This situation also encouraged discussions of annexation to the United States as a way out of these problems. The difficult economic and political situation of the summer of 1842 permeated south Texas. The *Telegraph and Texas Register* reported, "The Mexicans at Béxar were confident that Colonel Seguín would soon visit San Antonio with a large detachment of Mexican troops."[93] In this sense, Tejanos in San Antonio might have seen Mexican reconquest as a way out of their diminishing economic and political status.

Evidence of rising discord between Tejanos and Anglo-Texans in San Antonio began surfacing in the city council meetings during that summer. Prior to Seguín's departure, the ethnically mixed city council voted unanimously on many issues. But fissures surfaced at the council meeting of July 16, 1842, during the tenure of Seguín's replacement, John W. Smith.[94] At that meeting, the council, made up of three Tejano and five Anglo aldermen, voted to dismiss two Anglo councilmen with a split vote between Tejanos and Anglos. Smith declared the vote moot since the two aldermen had moved out of the city and called for the council to vote for two replacements.

The first vote for an aldermen position, between an Anglo (John Towhig) and a Tejano (Francisco Granado), again resulted in a split vote, with the three Anglos voting for Towhig and the three Tejanos for Granado. Smith, perhaps to decrease tensions, sided with Granado and the Tejano aldermen. In the vote for the second seat, between Towhig and Cornelius Van Ness, one Tejano alderman sided with the three Anglos in favor of Towhig. During the swearing-in of the new aldermen, Towhig declared himself unable to serve, calling for another vote for the final seat. The council considered Van Ness against Seguín's rival James Goodman. This time, with Granado on the council, Tejanos voted together, four to three, in support of Van Ness over Goodman.

During the same meeting, the council split along ethnic lines again in a vote to lower the tax for carts with goods entering the city.[95] With a majority, alderman Rivas introduced an ordinance cutting the tax in half. Tejano-driven horse-drawn carts were the principal means of transportation of merchandise in and out of the city. The tax decrease passed, with four Tejano councilmen voting for it and three Anglos voting against. These close votes and the divided opinions between Anglos and Tejanos on the council indicate deepening divisions even among the political elite of the city. The votes also threatened the new political and matrimonial bonds forged between Tejanos and their new neighbors. The bonds became strained again with a second invasion of San Antonio at the end of the summer of 1842.

On September 11, 1842, Mexican general Adrian Woll invaded San Antonio and occupied the city for a longer period than Vázquez did. Woll's invasion also met with stronger resistance. Texans organized two companies under Jack Hays to defend the city from Woll's attack. One company included seventy-five Anglo troops led by Chauncy Johnson, and the other consisted of one hundred Tejano troops led by Salvador Flores.[96] Hays had a lengthy history of cooperating with Tejanos and Mexicans.[97] But while Hays's soldiers put up some resistance, Woll's forces quickly overcame them. Mexican troops also captured several Tejanos under Hays, among them the prominent Bexareño Antonio Menchaca.[98] Menchaca managed to use his family connections to gain his release, vowing not to take up arms against Mexico again. After the invasion, Woll occupied San Antonio for over a week.

Woll's invasion of San Antonio also signaled the return of Juan N. Seguín, but now as commander of a company in Woll's army. Seguín's unit, named Defensores de Bejar, meant Tejanos once again found themselves fighting against other Tejanos. In his memoirs, Seguín explained that his participation in the raid resulted from a deal, made upon his return to Mexico, with General Mariano Arista.[99] Arista agreed not to prosecute Seguín as a traitor if Seguín led a company in an invasion of Texas. Arista hoped that the support of Seguín, recently a Tejano leader in San Antonio and a notable figure, might also turn Tejanos to aid in the Mexican effort. Seguín's company also included other prominent Tejanos, including José María J. Carrasco, Vicente Cordova, Leandro Arrieola, and Hays's former co-captain Antonio Perez.[100]

Woll's invasion reintroduced the tensions and choices Tejanos had experienced six years prior in the war of secession. Again, questions of national allegiance surfaced in choosing between fighting for or against the Mexican army. But unlike the war of secession, when some Tejanos had worked closely with Anglo immigrants, the recent violence and animosity between Anglos and Tejanos added new considerations for Tejanos to weigh. Seguín did not choose to support the Mexican side of the reconquest attempt until after Anglo-Texans forced him out of San Antonio.

Woll demanded that Anglo-Texan prisoners sign a letter acknowledging the likelihood that Tejanos would become even more suspect after the invasion. The entire statement is worth quoting since it gives a sense of how Mexicans perceived Anglo-Texan intentions:

> The undersigned, Americans, prisoners in the hands of the Mexican Army at this place, feel it to be a duty to recommend to all Americans, who may come here after our departure, to treat the Mexican population residing in this place with lenience and kindness. Up to the time of the unfortunate occurrence by which we were made prisoners nothing transpired to prejudice them in our estimation, and since our captivity they have been untiring in their kindness, supplying us in the most liberal manner with everything which could conduce in the least degree to our comfort. We do hope, therefore, should this place again fall into the hands of Americans, that for *our* sake the Mexican population here will not be in any way disturbed or injured either in person or property.[101]

Fifty-one Anglo-Texans signed the letter under duress of imprisonment. The letter portrayed Tejanos as people considerate of their neighbors and unfortunately caught in the midst of a diplomatic dispute between two governments. By stating that Tejanos treated Anglo-Texans kindly, the letter sought to preempt charges of disloyalty after Woll's withdrawal.

Woll attempted to transform San Antonio back into Béxar in his brief occupation of the city. As a step in this direction, Woll immediately reestablished Father Refugio de la Garza as the city priest.[102] Born in Béxar, Father Garza had established deep social and political roots in the Tejano community.[103] He participated in crafting the frontier colonization laws at the state and federal level and oversaw the secularization of Béxar's missions. By the 1830s, criticism of Garza began to surface over his management of the parish, though it was notoriously underfunded. After secession, Garza attempted to stay on as parish priest but was relieved of his position by the American Catholic church.

Another reminder of pre-1836 Béxar resulted from the invasion coinciding with the Mexican Independence Day celebration on September 16. The occupation army and Bexareños held a large citywide ball, recalling the glory of past celebrations. On September 20, 1842, Woll concluded his nine-day occupation of the city. The letter demanding better treatment for Tejanos suggests he planned for a brief invasion.[104]

Joining in Woll's retreat, two hundred Bexareño families left the city and went with Seguín to live south of the Río Grande. The retreating procession of soldiers also included 150 carts full of Bexareños' possessions. Woll commented on the fear of Anglo-Texan reprisals spreading among Tejanos. Woll wrote that Bexareños departed, "fearing that the volunteers on their return to the city after its evacuation by our troops might want to avenge their ignominious defeats on those defenseless families."[105] The treatment of Juan N. Seguín after the Vázquez raid served as enough warning to many Tejanos. Woll's departure almost halved the number of Tejanos at San Antonio. Most returned to Texas within six months, though, explaining their departure as fear of Mexican reprisals.[106]

The two invasions in 1842 and the departure of Tejanos from San Antonio changed the context in which Tejanos constructed their identity. Tejanos now had larger hurdles to clear to regain their social position in the city. Seguín himself paid a visit to San Antonio less than a month after Woll's departure.[107] Reports surfaced that he entered as a spy, but Seguín continued to have personal and business connections in San Antonio. The city's proximity to the Río Grande allowed Seguín and others to leave when their situation deteriorated. Some of the Bexareño elite, now in the Republic of Texas, apparently maintained their connections to Mexico.

Diplomatic tensions between Texas and Mexico ebbed a bit after Woll's invasion, due in large part to British intercession. British agents began lobbying for a general armistice in 1840 and succeeded in bringing about partial agreement between Santa Anna and Houston by 1843.[108] In a letter directed to President Houston, Woll promised to cease hostilities with Texas provided Houston recant the Texan Santa Fe Expedition. Obstacles remained on both sides relating to the release of the expedition prisoners, the location of the border on the Nueces, and Texas sovereignty.[109]

Woll's retreat from San Antonio did not signal the end of *reconquista* rhetoric in Mexico. In November 1844, Woll addressed his troops during a federalist uprising in Guadalajara and Zacatecas: "Eight years ago you came to this border encouraged by the sacred flame that every Mexican should fuel in their heart and with the hope of marching towards the reconquest of Texas!" He urged soldiers to "defend the border, uphold the Supreme Constitutional Government and employ your spent weapons for the recuperation of Texas!"[110] Talks of national reunification and military mobilization continued, especially after news that the U.S. Congress was considering the annexation of Texas. The editorial of a Monterrey newspaper reported, "Never has the heroic stance, opportunistic timing and insightful understanding of the Mexican Congress been more important to establish the measures necessary to conserve territorial integrity and the good name of the Nation."[111]

Against the backdrop of national politics and international tensions, Tejanos continued to participate in San Antonio politics and society. *Reconquista* politics and the increasing involvement of the United States in Texas accelerated the transformation of the ethnic Mexican population to that of minority status. Through this shift, Tejanos maintained their social world while capitalizing on their history of intercultural negotiation to carve out space for future generations.

Social and Political Transition

Despite the challenges posed by the invasions in 1842, San Antonio was now a city in the Republic of Texas. As such, the transition to an Anglo-dominated municipal political system took several years. Two Anglo-Americans held the mayor's seat: Smith, whose term lasted under a year, followed by William H. Daingerfield, who served for three months. Antonio Menchaca held the seat from July 20, 1838, through January 8, 1839, and as such became the first Tejano mayor in the Republic period. A year later, Juan N. Seguín became mayor for the second time, this time under the Texas flag. Soon after, Anglo-Texans began a campaign to discredit him and label him a traitor.[112] No Tejano held the seat of mayor in San Antonio for the remainder of the nineteenth century.[113] At a symbolic level, the position of mayor of San Antonio reflected the decrease in political significance of Tejanos across Texas.

Nevertheless, Tejanos continued to have a voice in the city's decision-making beyond 1842. Even with Anglo-Texan mayors, Tejanos still made up at least half of the eight aldermen through the end of 1847. In 1844 and 1845, Tejanos held five seats; in the following two years, they held four.[114] January 1849 marked the swearing-in of the first city council comprised of only three Tejano aldermen. At least twenty-six Bexareños served as city officials in the twelve years prior to 1849, with twenty-three serving more than one term (see table 6.1). In the twenty years after January 1849, only sixteen Tejanos served as city officials, with only eight lasting more than one term.

Not coincidentally, the years marked by striking decreases in power, 1842 and 1848, correlated with moments of international conflict: between Mexico and Texas in 1842 and between Mexico and the United States in 1848. The decline seen in electoral power also appeared in other facets of civic life. Tejano inclusion in juries fell precipitously through the 1840s, leveling off between 10 and 15 percent after 1850 (see figure 6.1). Tejanos continued to hold aldermen seats as well as judicial and administrative positions in the municipal government through the U.S.-Mexico War. Yet, the loss of explicit Tejano political power slowly overtook San Antonio in the years after 1836.

The loss of Tejano social and economic power occurred in different locations and at a different rate than the decline of political power. While representation in political positions serve as a benchmark for political power, social and economic indicators prove more complex and elusive. The transition of San Antonio from a Tejano city to an Anglo-Texan city requires an examination of changes in social interactions during the Republic period. Marriage records provide one window into social contact; in addition, land transactions in this period reveal the shift of economic significance and power from Tejano to Anglo-Texan hands. While these two areas demonstrate only a narrow slice of both social and economic life, they suggest Tejanos became increasingly displaced and marginalized in their own city.

TABLE 6.1. Tejano City Officials Serving More Than One Term, 1837–1873

Official	First Term	End of Last Term
Garza, Vicente	March 19, 1837	January 8, 1840
Ruiz, Francisco A.	September 19, 1837	January 9, 1841
Perez, Manuel	September 19, 1837	April 18, 1842
Flores, José	March 9, 1838	February 18, 1845
Garza, Rafael	March 9, 1838	February 18, 1845
Bustillo, Francisco	January 1, 1837	January 1, 1846
Cassiano, José	January 8, 1839	January 1, 1846
Delgado, Martín	March 30, 1844	January 1, 1846
Rivas, C.	April 18, 1842	January 1, 1846
Rodríguez, Ambrosio	March 9, 1838	January 1, 1846
Flores, Pedro	January 9, 1841	January 1, 1847
Veramendi, Marcus	January 9, 1841	January 1, 1847
Chavez, Ygnacio	February 18, 1845	January 1, 1848
Garza, R. C.	January 1, 1846	January 1, 1849
Manchaca, Antonio	February 9, 1838	January 1, 1849
Rodríguez, Antonio	January 1, 1846	January 1, 1849
Navarro, Luciano	January 8, 1839	January 1, 1850[a]
Herrera, Rafael	January 19, 1837	January 1, 1853[a]
Navarro, José Antonio	January 18, 1840	January 1, 1855
Urutia, Juan A.	January 9, 1841	January 1, 1858
Cassiano, F.	January 1, 1863	December 31, 1866
Yturri, Manuel	March 9, 1838	November 8, 1867[a]
Chavez, J. M.	January 1, 1858	March 28, 1870[b]

Source: May Richardson, "Alphabetical List of City Officials, 1837–1873," February 9, 1934, Center for American History, University of Texas, Austin.

[a]Two different terms in the time span listed.
[b]Last term served under military appointment.

Intermarriage

In the years following San Jacinto, Anglo-Americans slowly trickled into San Antonio. Evidence of the changes underway appeared in the city council meeting of June 22, 1844, when a resolution was adopted requiring that a public sign on the Main Ditch be posted in French and German in addition to Spanish and English.[115] While a few Anglos had lived in the city

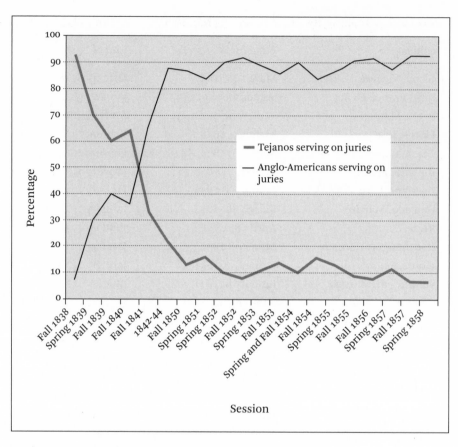

Figure 6.1. Jury Service by Ethnicity, 1838–1858
Source: *District Court (Bexar County), Civil Minutes, 1836–1907, microfilm (Salt Lake City: Genealogical Society of Utah, 1977).*

since the colonial period, their numbers began to rise after 1836. But their population did not boom overnight, and their appropriation of the social and political centers of San Antonio power occurred gradually over the next two decades. While Anglos held the state government positions and military control, Tejanos occupied the overwhelming majority of the aldermen seats and other bureaucratic offices in San Antonio. This governing arrangement suggests that Tejanos and Anglo-Texans negotiated a social balance despite mutual distrust.[116]

Beginning in 1837, in this complex social and political environment, Anglo-Texans and Tejanos began to intermarry. These marriages were almost exclusively between Anglo men and Mexican women. The unions reflected both the demographics of Anglo-American westward migration and the cultural and gender assumptions underlying interethnic relations. Men overwhelmingly made up the first waves of Anglo-Americans migrating to San Antonio.[117] Many carried visions of exotic women, as reported to them by previous visitors to San Antonio and the Mexican north.[118] Nevertheless, negative racial stereotypes countered these romanticized accounts, making intermarriage a challenge to both Anglo-Americans and Mexicans. Little is known about unsanctioned Anglo/Tejano cohabitation, yet officially recognized marriages provide a more complete view into legitimized and publicly acknowledged unions.[119]

Civil records from Béxar County indicate a noticeable number of Anglo/Tejano marriages from 1837 to 1860. More specifically, in the Republic period, twenty-three of the 294 marriages listed joined Anglo men and Mexican women.[120] These rates have been found to continue at between 8 and 9 percent of total marriages through 1860.[121] The marriages themselves were spread out evenly over the Republic period, never surpassing three in a given year without any significant gaps. Occurring at a rate below 10 percent, these marriages could be considered infrequent, but not rare. In other words, their continued presence throughout the period suggests an acceptance of the practice by both groups. The church-sponsored institution of marriage assumes acceptance at both state and religious levels.

Few clues exist regarding the motivations encouraging Tejanas to enter into these unions. Evidence from the records show about half of these brides came from elite Tejano families.[122] By analyzing the social class dimension of these marriages, both Anglo-Americans and Mexicans appeared to manipulate nuptials for mutual social or economic advancement. Elite Tejano families stood to gain from the cultural bridges with Anglo society or protection provided by an Anglo son-in-law, while Anglo men received inheritances of land or commercial legitimacy among Tejanos and Mexicans.[123] Furthermore, Tejanas might have perceived the benefits of Anglo parentage for their children; many offspring of these marriages left Texas for boarding school or college for lack of local schools.[124] One analyst of the 1860s intermarriages concludes, "Only the women and children with Anglo surnames, light skins, and wealth had a reasonable chance to escape the stigma attached to their Mexican ancestry."[125] But in the Republic period, that escape appeared less important and instead tied elite Tejanos to maintenance of their social status. An Anglo-American traveler in Texas noted what he called the savage dining habits of Mexican women who chose not to eat at the table with their Anglo husbands.[126] This observation suggests that Mexican women underwent little assimilation even after their marriages to Anglo-American men. Their children, though, were left to negotiate their own relation to San Antonio elite society.

These intermarriages also reveal facets of the interaction between gender and ethnicity among Tejanos and Anglo-Texans. Records show only Anglo men marrying Tejana women. While the lack of Anglo women alone may explain this phenomenon, ethnic assumptions and political power also shaped this outcome. Anglo-American conceptions of womanhood and cultural purity made marriage between Tejano men and Anglo women difficult. While Anglo-Texans and Tejanos shared the social and political stage, they still drew ethnic distinctions between each other. For Anglo-Texan men, consciously or not, marrying Tejanas stood as an additional step in the "conquest" of Texas.[127]

Taken together with political changes, intermarriages serve as an indicator of social transformation in post-secession San Antonio. Yet, at just under 10 percent of the married population, intermarriages fail to reveal a wholesale trend toward Americanization in the Tejano population. Rather, the consistent 10 percent interethnic marriage rate, even after increases in the Anglo-American population, and the principally elite nature of the existing intermarriages suggest that San Antonio Tejanos maintained their Mexican culture. Whether this occurred due to internal pressures or to external barriers to intermarriage is less clear. Few long-term trends can be deduced regarding changes in Tejano attitudes toward Anglo-Texans at this early point in San Antonio's transition to Anglo-American control. Several decades after secession and annexation by the United States, the demographic, economic, and political dominance of Anglo-Americans shifted the meaning of interethnic marriages from acculturation into Mexican society to survival in an Anglo-dominated town.

Headright Land Grants

The economic and political changes of the Republic period limited the stake Tejanos took in the future of Texas. Land speculation around headright grants awarded to Tejanos after the war symbolized the decline of Tejano influence on the Texas economy. Instituted to continue the colonization ethos from the Mexican period and reward Texans for their loyalty, headrights granted title to a portion of unplotted land to their recipients. Not attached to a measured parcel, the certificates served as shares in the public lands of Texas. Beyond simply exchanging the certificate for land, headrights infused the holder with a stake in the future of Texas. Con-

versely, selling or losing the headright mortgaged the recipient's investment in the future.

The Republic of Texas government granted these certificates of land to
citizens living in the territory prior to the war of secession. Families inhabiting Texas before March 2, 1836, received one league plus one *labor*
(approximately 4,606 acres), while single men gained one-third league (approximately 1,476 acres).[128] Those arriving in the state after March 2, 1836,
received less land, and those arriving after secession received even smaller
grants. The first category of headright grant, or the First Class Headright,
closely followed the amount granted to settlers under the colonization laws
of the Mexican state of Coahuila y Texas. Most Bexareños became eligible
to receive these First Class grants by nature of their historical ties to the
city. As a result, grantees obtained certificates for unpatented, or public,
land. To actually acquire a parcel of land required applying for a patent
from the government. Otherwise, the certificates simply granted ownership of an abstract parcel of land.

Beginning in April 1837, a few Anglo-Texans and Tejanos began buying
up large numbers of these certificates for land from Bexareños. At this early
date in the Republic era, Tejanos sold the most certificates exchanged in
San Antonio. In the first two years alone, these land speculators purchased
over two hundred headright certificates from the citizens of San Antonio.[129]
While these buyers did not identify themselves as speculators, they bought
these grants as commodities to resell and not to develop the land.

Even under uncertain terms, the headright certificates and their trade
signified a turning point for Tejano participation in the new Republic. The
headright grants served as abstract shares in the idea of Texas, an idea
perhaps not held by most Tejanos. On the one hand, the ease with which
Tejanos sold their certificates indicated their belief in the temporary nature
of the Texas Republic, or at least their lack of faith in its legal and business
practices. On the other hand, returning to a town in shambles, Tejanos
might have desired cash in the present over land in the future. In any case,
by selling their headright certificates, Tejanos lost a potential voice in the
making of Texas.

Two new residents of San Antonio, Ludovic Colquhoun and William H.
Steele, together and individually purchased a vast majority of these grants.
Of the 139 documented in the first two months, they bought 77 headright
certificates, all from Tejanos. While the information available in Béxar
County records identifies Colquhoun and Steele's activities, they provide
only sketchy details regarding their purpose and methods. Their purchases

ranged from certificates of a league and a *labor* to a third of a league; their payments ranged from $400 to $5,000 for the largest land parcels.[130] In those two months alone, Tejanos sold certificates worth nearly 300,000 acres of land to Colquhoun and Steele.

The circumstances surrounding those exchanges prove difficult to recreate, since the records reveal only the names and amounts involved in the transactions. Along with the buyer and seller, each transfer also indicates the name of a witness. Bexareño Ambrosio Rodríguez attended many of Colquhoun and Steele's purchases as both witness and translator. The receipts also note the signature of the seller, often bearing an "X" in the name of Tejanos. Assuming the "X" connotes illiteracy, 80 percent of Tejanos selling to Colquhoun and Steele could not sign their names.

The transaction receipts also include affidavits signed by the sellers reaffirming their residence in Texas prior to March 2, 1836. The affidavit includes a loyalty pledge, stating the signer never fled or took up arms against the Texan forces. Tejanos selling their headright grants signed or marked the standard statement as follows: "I do solemnly swear that I was a resident Citizen of Texas at the date of the declaration of Independence that I did not leave the Country during the Spring of 1836 to avoid a participation in the war and that I did not aid nor assist the enemy, that I have not previously received a title for my quantum of land and that I conceive myself to be justly entitled under the Constitution and laws to the quantity of land which I now apply."[131] Whether Tejanos signed the affidavit in affirmation of their fidelity in order to receive the money from the sale or without understanding the text, the land certificates served to reassure the Anglo-American government of Tejano allegiance to the new Republic. But the uncertainty of the process clouds our ability to understand Tejano motivations. By requiring Tejanos to sign the affidavit, Anglo-Texans made loyalty a significant requirement for belonging to Texas. Bexareños had to articulate their right to enjoy full citizenship in their hometown instead of assuming entitlement to such inclusion.

The unpatented certificates gave Colquhoun and Steele many options to turn a profit. They could patent the grant and keep the land or sell that patented land. Or, they could sell the certificates to another speculator. The certificates allowed the holder to survey and plot a parcel of public land in any county in Texas. But if the economy turned against land, speculators could be left holding the devalued merchandise. Mary Maverick noted in a letter, "Land here cheap as it has been, is getting down to nothing. My husband has been investing everything in land and is still dabbling in head rights and land; but he could not sell what he has bought for much more than half its cost."[132] Nevertheless, Texas continued to patent land from these grants as late as 1898.[133] As a result, thousands of acres granted by headright to Tejanos were converted into private holdings for land speculators and ranchers throughout Texas.

Several elite Tejanos also entered into the headright grant purchase market. José Antonio de la Garza purchased between eight and thirteen certificates, while Juan N. Seguín himself bought up ten.[134] Jesús F. de la Teja suggests that Seguín's involvement in headrights might have eroded his popular support among ordinary Tejanos. From a competitive standpoint, Seguín's activities could have also turned other grant buyers against him, including John W. Smith. As events unfolded during Seguín's tenure as mayor, the lack of support from both sides added to his problems. The shifting economic and political status of Tejanos accelerated once more as those calling for American annexation brought about the end of the Texas Republic.

Annexation and the U.S.-Mexico War

On March 1, 1845, the political status of Texas and San Antonio changed again when the U.S. Congress voted to annex the Republic of Texas as a state. Annexation challenged Mexico's claim to Texas and further pushed those in the government to carry out their goal of *reconquista*. Annexation led to the American militarization of the border and eventually to war and the invasion of Mexico. For Tejanos, these actions shifted the site of the contest away from the Tejano homeland and into the Mexican nation. As ethnic Mexicans, though, Tejanos remained to contend with the further vilification of their nationality in Anglo-American minds.

While the United States fought the U.S.-Mexico War over the possession of Tejano lands and the current American Southwest to California, the war itself did not directly involve Tejanos. Unlike the war of Texas secession, the American forces did not include Tejano companies or soldiers.[135] A few Tejanos, such as Chipita Sandoval from Corpus Christi, aided American efforts by carrying out spy missions across the Río Grande.[136] From the beginning, the goals of the American expedition into Mexico related to its objectives of expanding the nation westward.[137] Mexican party struggles influenced the war by destabilizing the nation, thus ensuring rapid American success. Tejano interest in the federalist movement became insignificant next to the larger national identification with either the United States or

Mexico. The American invasion of Mexico also put the war of Texas secession into new perspective, as part of American Manifest Destiny.

During the onset of hostilities, the Tejano company led by Juan N. Seguín participated in the resistance to the American invasion. Seguín's group, the Escuadron Auxiliar de Bejar, patrolled the Río Grande, crossing from Laredo north to Presidio Río Grande during these tense years.[138] Seguín's participation could be considered an extension of his impressed service requirement by Arista under General Woll. Yet, his conflicts with Anglo-Texans and support of Mexican federalists fed his anti-American sentiments. The conditions under which Seguín left San Antonio and his command of a Mexican unit made him a choice target for Texas Ranger companies fighting in the U.S.-Mexico War.[139] Ranger Ben McCulloch reported an instance when his company chased Seguín on the road to Monterrey. He wrote, "Seguín passed up San Juan a few days before we arrived. He had forty thieves and murderers from about San Antonio to kill which would be doing God a service it would be ridding the world of those that are not fit to live in it."[140] McCulloch's comment repeated the characterization of Tejanos as criminals and part of a suspect class. Apart from Seguín's *escuadron*, no other records exist of uniquely Tejano or Bexareño-Mexican companies during the war of 1846.

By 1846, the war between the two nations was underway, affecting the daily lives of Bexareños in other ways. San Antonio served as a launching point for several companies of American troops. General Zachary Taylor's plans involved organizing a battalion led by Brigadier General John E. Wool out of San Antonio, toward Saltillo and Monterrey.[141] The plan entailed amassing 2,500 troops in San Antonio beginning August 14, 1846. Wool quickly realized the city lacked the resources necessary to house and supply his soldiers for any significant time. As a result, his troops departed in two sections over the next two months. Other smaller companies, usually composed of Texans, also used San Antonio as a base of action during the war.[142]

The declaration of war between Mexico and the United States and the invasion of Mexico by American troops resulted in several turning points in the history and development of identity for Tejanos. The war shifted the limits and meaning of nationalism, materially affected interethnic relations, and permanently transformed the demographic and economic base of San Antonio. Ideologically, Tejanos faced the challenge of being both residents of Texas and ethnically Mexican. During the Republic period, these two identities coexisted, however tensely. The U.S.-Mexico War eliminated the flexibility and ambiguity of nationalism possible after the secession of Texas. The war linked being Mexican with the importance of territorial integrity. An editorial from *El Eco del Norte*, of Matamoros, Tamaulipas, noted the high stakes involved in resolving the "Texas Question" for all Mexicans: "The Texas question should not have taken the menacing threat that it now has, be prepared to dedicate yourself to all types of sacrifices, before permitting the loss of honor, in which our territory is dismembered, in which our very political existence lies in the balance, and our rights are exposed to the whims of a capricious usurper."[143] The editorial linked maintaining national territory to a deep sense of honor. Likewise, losing territory directly threatened Mexican honor and masculinity. While this editorial was written in northern Mexico, such a stance was not lost on Tejanos. In a sense, the contingencies and uncertainties of the Texas Republic allowed Tejanos to maintain some imagined connection to Mexico, due in part to the weak Republic government. Living in American Texas changed the meaning of being Tejano, making it even more distant from Mexican citizenship.

The war also exacerbated tensions between Tejanos and Anglo-Texans in San Antonio. Even the traditionally interethnic Ranger group led by Hays became segregated. As historian Frederick Wilkins notes, "Hays still used native tejanos as spies in checking on Mexican troop movements, but there were no longer large contingents of San Antonio men on his scouts."[144] Not only did anti-Mexican attitudes predominate among Anglo-Texan troops, but Tejanos might also have been reluctant to fight on Mexican soil. Relocating the conflict from Texas to Mexico changed the meaning of Tejano participation in those units. Unlike Tejanos fighting alongside Anglo-Texans to defend their homes and city during the Vázquez and Woll raids, invading Mexico meant taking their beliefs a step further. It meant repudiating Mexico's significance as a homeland in their identity.

Finally, the war resulted in a permanent change in the demographic and political face of San Antonio. While the population of San Antonio remained low and transient through the war years, the introduction of the American army led to a permanent federal military presence in the city. The establishment of the U.S. Army affected the city both physically, by the introduction of a base, and demographically, with soldiers stationed in the city. The San Antonio city council first considered donating land to the U.S. Army in a meeting on February 2, 1846.[145] Two weeks later, the city council approved the donation of one hundred acres to the army and noted, "The proposal . . . would greatly tend to the enhancing the value of Real Estate the increase of Population and the advancement of the best interest of this

City."[146] The city sought more immediate benefits from the army presence by charging the unit two dollars for every cord of wood cut within city limits. The U.S. military presence also raised the number of non-Tejanos living in San Antonio. Those numbers had already been changing before the war, as Anglo-Americans, French, and Germans started making the city their home. Despite the changes and the onset of war, the city raised much of its budget locally. For instance, the council reported revenues of $560 from fandango licenses for 1847. These changes are emblematic of political and social changes after the U.S.-Mexico War.

The storming and capture of Monterrey between September 20 and 24, 1846, and Santa Anna's last offensive at the battle of Buena Vista (also known as Angostura) on February 22, 1847, signified the end of large-scale military engagements in the Mexican north.[147] General Taylor's troops entered Mexico using brute force, caring little about their challengers or their reception among local people.[148] Northern Mexicans gave American troops an uneven but generally negative reception on their way to Monterrey. While some federalists and most Catholic clerics supported the American invasion, most Mexicans treated them coldly. During Taylor's occupation of Saltillo, in November 1846, merchants attempted to extort the invaders by selling necessities at inflated prices.[149]

At various points during the war, Americans and Mexicans attempted to establish a settlement to end the war. For the most part, the Mexican insistence on the Nueces River as the southern border of Texas caused negotiations to fail.[150] When negotiations deadlocked on September 7, 1847, a temporary armistice ended, resulting in General Winfield Scott's occupation of Mexico City. American control of Mexico City effectively ended the war by making Mexican interest in settlement terms more agreeable to the United States.

On February 2, 1848, Mexico and the United States agreed to the Treaty of Guadalupe Hidalgo, establishing a new border between the two nations and ending Mexico's claim to Texas. For Bexareños, the treaty also closed off the possibility of the city returning to Mexico. It also secured their status as citizens of the United States.[151] In a sense, the treaty served as the culmination of the war of Texas secession.

Aside from the territorial exchange, the treaty affected the lives of Tejanos in the areas of landholding and citizenship. Officials from both countries spent a considerable amount of time negotiating and debating the terms under which property rights would be transferred for existing landholders.[152] The resulting treaty, which was ratified by both nations' legislatures, left many of the questions pertaining to land titles to the American courts. In the case of Texas, the United States rejected a reassessment of titles from the Mexican period, claiming the Texas Republic had already adjudicated its land claims.[153]

Article IX of the treaty gave Mexican citizens the choice of keeping their citizenship or declaring themselves Americans, "to the enjoyment of all the rights of citizens of the United States according to the principles of the Constitution."[154] But Tejanos and Mexicans in other annexed territories also had the opportunity to migrate south beyond the new border. Mexico sought to encourage this resettlement to increase the population of northern states and to decrease the threat of conflict with indigenous peoples.[155] A significant number of families—about 150—left the state under the Mexican offer.[156] The issue of citizenship also became clouded regarding the transference of rights to Mexican indigenous peoples.

Transformation Completed

The years of the Texas Republic extended the uncertain position of Tejanos in San Antonio. Following the surrender of Santa Anna at San Jacinto, Tejanos determined to continue their society in San Antonio in the face of some Anglo-Texan opposition. San Antonio escaped destruction after the war, as Seguín pointed out in his memoir, and Tejanos continued to participate in local and state government. In the San Antonio city council, Bexareños held the majority position through the first years. Some Tejanos, especially within the elite, took the step of joining with Anglo-Americans through marriage. This combined not only their material fortunes but also their social and political futures. Tejanos also maintained commercial ties with Mexico after the war, keeping the lines of communication open for federalist generals to contact Texan officials. Through these political, social, and economic means, Tejanos carved out their position as cultural brokers in Anglo-Texas while negotiating their new status as a suspect class.

This position parallels historian David Montejano's "peace structure," which is, he writes, "a general postwar arrangement that allows the victors to maintain law and order without constant use of force."[157] According to Montejano's analysis, both intermarriage of elites and the subordination of Tejano politicians established a social system permitting the entrenchment of Anglo-Texan power over San Antonio. While some would argue that Tejanos who joined in these arrangements did so in their own self-interest, the results support Montejano's theory.

But, the history of San Antonio does not strictly conform to Montejano's characterization of Anglo domination. The events that transpired over the Republic period in San Antonio tested the limits and crossed the line of the peace structure. The peace structure came to an end in San Antonio when newly arrived Anglo-Americans forced Juan N. Seguín to leave his city and move to Mexico. While Tejanos participated in civic life in San Antonio, that inclusion was always contingent on oaths of loyalty and proof of allegiance. Tejanos lived under a cloud of suspicion. Statements Tejanos signed in order to sell their land certificates included claims of allegiance. The politics of loyalty attached conditions on Tejano inclusion in civic and social life. The tense relation between Tejanos and Mexico and the threat of Mexican invasion put more pressure on Tejanos to actively assert their loyalty to Texas.

While the politics of loyalty served as a central aspect of the peace structure, violence also entered into the establishment of Anglo-American power in San Antonio. The combination of anti-Mexican Ranger attacks and the invasions of San Antonio by Mexican troops in 1842 created a tone of distrust regarding Tejanos and a desire for vengeance. The split votes in the city council in 1842 underscored those new divisions. This situation led two hundred families to leave the city with General Woll's retreating troops after the second invasion. Their departure during this time raised the question of belonging to a place. The conflicts during the Republic period created contradictions for Tejanos, who were ethnically Mexican in an Anglo-American nation. For the first time in the century, Tejanos felt alienated from their homeland.

As Bexareños returned to San Antonio after Woll's retreat and during the U.S.-Mexico War, the city regained its commercial and social vibrancy. Tejanos continued to hold seats in the city council and other civic positions, but their dominance of San Antonio waned. No longer Béxar, San Antonio changed permanently in more than name. Now that the city was part of the United States, Tejanos had a new political system to learn and a more difficult struggle ahead in asserting their significance in the city's future. The next chapter details the changes in San Antonio's demographics at the 1850 census and the Tejano role in city politics prior to the American Civil War.

Chapter Seven

Voting and Violence

TEJANOS AND ETHNIC POLITICS, 1848–1861

The morning of September 12, 1857, began like countless others for Bexareño cart driver Nicanor Valdez.[1] He and a convoy of twelve Mexican teamsters continued their haul of American military supplies on the public road between San Antonio and the port on the Gulf of Mexico at Lavaca. Only this time, the convoy encountered an attack by a group of heavily armed bandits from Helena, in Karnes County. The attackers, about forty men in masks and painted faces, leveled their shotguns and six-shooters at the Mexican cart drivers. Without warning, the men began firing at the teamsters. Valdez's partner Antonio Delgado received fourteen shots, which killed him instantly. Valdez himself took a bullet in the shoulder. His brothers Esteban and Mariano were each wounded by pistol and shotgun fire as well. The convoy managed to make it back to San Antonio and report the attack to the justice of the peace. Valdez told the judge he recognized two of the assailants, having seen them in Helena only hours before the ambush.

What appeared as a random attack to Valdez amounted to an organized effort by the Anglo-Texans of Karnes County to disrupt Mexican cart traffic. Other ambushes took place in both Karnes and Goliad counties with enough violence and planning to be known publicly as the "Cart War." The Cart War and its racial overtones drew the attention of the San Antonio press, Texas state authorities, and the national governments of Mexico and the United States. The Cart War stood as a test of the recently annexed Texas state government. More important for Tejanos, the Cart War signaled mounting anti-Mexican sentiments and tested the government's ability and willingness to respond to these changes. Texas governor Elisha Marshall Pease issued a report on the violence and provided protection for the cart drivers, indicating his desire to save face at a diplomatic level and revealing the new role of Tejanos in state politics.

To understand the strong reaction to the Cart War by the San Antonio press and the governor requires an examination of the emerging ethnic identity among Tejanos. The Treaty of Guadalupe Hidalgo finalized the incorporation of San Antonio within the United States and presented Bexareños with the option of claiming either American or Mexican citizenship. While some Tejanos left the city and moved to Mexico, most remained, choosing to carve out a future as culturally Mexican American. Those Tejanos stayed in a city changed by migrations, battles, and new nations. Yet, the city was still their birthplace and home.

Analyzing the demographic, political, and social composition of the city provides insight into the forces shaping Tejano political and ethnic identity. Rather than simply question why Tejanos remained in San Antonio, it is also important to ask how they lived after annexation. Answering this exposes the accommodations Bexareños made to maintain their home in San Antonio. While the United States incorporated the political character of the city, Tejanos protected their Mexican culture and society. An exploration of antebellum San Antonio reveals the areas of conflict and compromise between these Mexican and American national cultures and political ideologies. When Texas voted to secede from the Union, local attention momentarily shifted away from defining Mexican ethnicity. Mexico itself served as a conduit for Confederate cotton and resources, and Tejanos became potential allies or enemies. Likewise, the Civil War and Indian wars resulted in the increased militarization of San Antonio, making it a center for federal authority in the borderlands.

While the history of San Antonio between 1848 and the Civil War lacks the drama of the previous twenty years, the effects of American annexation resulted in significant changes to Tejano culture. These changes appeared in several social historical texts, such as the 1850 census, city council records, and newspaper reports. Each of these sources aids in understanding the maintenance of Tejano society while the citizens became American in a newly American city. The role Tejanos initiated during this period lasted in some form or another into the next century.

Demographic Shift

After annexation to the United States, San Antonio experienced a boom in commerce and population. The city's tax base doubled every year from 1850 to 1855. A report in one newspaper attributed this prosperity to the end of Indian depredations and a peaceful frontier.[2] The amount of farmland and its cash value grew in the decade of the 1850s by 489 percent.[3] San Antonio's remarkable expansion was also reflected in the first two American censuses of the city in 1850 and 1860. The city experienced an increase of 136 percent during the decade, from a population of 3,488 to 8,235.[4] Béxar County as a whole similarly rose 139 percent, from 6,052 to 14,454. This jump appeared as the largest percentage increase for the entire nineteenth century. In terms of ethnic composition, Anglo-Americans grew to become the dominant group, socially, economically, and, by 1860, demographically. In the decade 1850–60, Tejanos went from composing almost half of the city's population—47 percent Tejano to 48 percent Anglo-American (including Germans)—to making up only 35 percent, compared to 64 percent Anglo-American.

Even though the Tejano population dropped as a percentage of the city's population, their numbers increased over the decade of the 1850s.[5] Tejanos went from approximately 2,749 to 4,211, an increase of 53 precent.[6] Closer analysis by age cohort reveals variations in the increase, suggesting an influx of Mexicans or Tejanos into the city in addition to the natural birth rates. While most age cohorts showed little if any growth during the decade, the 11–20-year-old group rose from 647 in 1850 to 1,166 as the 21–30-year-old group in 1860. The increase was more pronounced among the male population, although this was offset by a larger female rise in the 6–10-year-old group in 1850 to the 16–20-year-old group in 1860 figures. The rise in this age cohort also helps explain an increase in the percentage of children 0–10 as a percentage of the Tejano population over the decade. The rise in the Tejano population in the childbearing cohort mirrored the entire county's growth, although the 1850 21–30-year-old cohort also witnessed a similar spurt. This latter growth was not reflected in the Tejano figures, pointing to an area where Anglo-American and German immigrant growth outpaced growth among Tejanos.

These figures show that Tejanos faced a changed and reorganized San Antonio. Not only had their majority disappeared, but their voting age proportion also dropped. The general Tejano population did increase, suggesting Tejanos maintained an interest in remaining in the city and others chose to migrate to there. The newcomers appear to be principally laborers, with the census showing an increase from 0 in 1850 to 394 in 1860. Tejano farmers also increased in the decade, from 0 to 183. All other occupations either remained the same or increased slightly, with the position of cart man leading these other occupations, from 197 to 229. Tejano jobs listed in the census show a diverse population of tradesmen and merchants. The census lists carpenters, silversmiths, cigar makers, bakers, shoemakers, saddle makers, masons, blacksmiths, and merchants as professions with double-digit Tejano affiliation. The economic significance of Tejanos, along with their third of the population, made ignoring their concerns and disenfranchising their population difficult for the Anglo-American leadership.

Their continued social significance in the city's character appeared in the continued ties between Mexicans and Anglo-American elites, especially with intermarriages. Mary Adams Maverick, the wife of former mayor Sam A. Maverick, mentioned her friendships with Mexican women of prominent Tejano families. Referring to the Tejana elites, Maverick commented, "They dressed nicely and were graceful and gracious of manner."[7] Although intermarriages between elite Tejano and Anglo families continued, marriage records indicate a drop in those figures. Marriages between Tejanas and Anglos moved from roughly 10 percent, as noted in the previous chapter, to about 5 percent of the total marriages from July 1852 to July 1855.[8] These changes can be attributed to the overall drop in Tejanos as a percentage of the city's population.

Political life also reflected a loss of influence among Tejanos. As noted in chapter five, after the 1848 term, when three Tejanos served on the city council, the council had one or no Tejano representatives.[9] Tejanos also experienced a sharp drop in inclusion on the grand and petit juries of Béxar County.[10] Nevertheless, Tejanos found ways of remaining politically pertinent in the face of declining power. Through a combination of political negotiation as well as external circumstances, Tejanos carved a political space in the new Anglo-Texan social order.

Know-Nothing Threat: Tejanos in Party Politics

While Tejano representation as a percentage of the city council dropped precipitously after 1848, Tejano involvement in city politics remained central to power struggles and debates among the new Anglo-American leadership. The issue of Tejano rights and citizenship overtly surfaced during city elections in 1854 through 1856. In those years, the surging Know-Nothing Party presented a serious challenge to the Democratic Party officeholders. Emerging from a national nativist platform, the Know-Nothing Party combined aspects of a secret society with xenophobic and anti-Catholic rhetoric to foster discontent with incumbent politicians.[11] Know-Nothings surprised Democrats and won several seats on the 1855 San Antonio city council, including mayor. During their election campaigns, year in office, and subsequent loss of power, Know-Nothing candidates directly attacked Bejareño culture and religion. The Democratic response to Know-Nothing challenges reveals several aspects of the importance and position of Tejanos in city and state party politics.

Since annexation, Democrats held most political offices in San Antonio and throughout Texas. If nothing else, the Know-Nothing victory exposed the presumption by most San Antonians that Democrats would succeed regardless of their participation levels. Still, the large Mexican and German populations of San Antonio along with their Catholic associations made the Know-Nothing nativist rhetoric appealing to some. While nativism and anti-foreign sentiments found a voice in many nineteenth-century political parties throughout the United States, the Know-Nothing Party saw national success in the years between 1854 and 1856.[12] In San Antonio, Know-Nothing candidates ran with a similar nativist message against the Democratic Party. Several prominent San Antonians sided with the Know-Nothings, using the *San Antonio Herald* to advocate for their positions. Ironically, an immigrant from Nova Scotia, James P. Newcomb, served as the paper's publisher and led the charge against the influence of foreigners and Catholics.[13]

Being an unknown element in the state and holding meetings in secret allowed the Know-Nothings to creep up on San Antonio Democrats, electing James R. Sweet as mayor and enough councilmen to pass ordinances in the city. In January 1855, the Know-Nothings were sworn in and quickly voted on several changes to the city code. Two ordinances appeared to be directly aimed at the city's Tejanos: the elimination of Spanish translations of city publications and the banning of bull- and cockfighting and gambling.[14] The bilingual publication of local laws had existed since the Mexican period, with the migration of Anglo-Americans. Soon after the passage of the law eliminating Spanish translations, Democratic Party supporters founded the newspaper *El Bejareño*, published in Spanish.[15] In its first issue, the editors of the paper, X. Debray and A. A. Lewis, declared that one of the paper's objectives was to translate and publish the city's laws in Spanish. Otherwise, the paper noted, Tejanos would learn about these laws only after they violated them.

Banning bull- and cockfighting (passed on January 30) and gambling (passed on May 17) also struck at the core of Tejano society in San Antonio. Not only had the city been collecting significant revenues by regulating these activities over the previous twenty years, but Tejanos and Anglo-Texans of all classes socialized through these public events. Know-Nothing politicians sought to eliminate the public presence of cultural difference. The city also maintained a ban on fandangos that had been initiated five years earlier. The council deemed these activities a "public nuisance."

The loss of political seats set in motion a response by the full Democratic Party apparatus in the city and state and introduced new methods of securing the party's base. Democrats immediately mobilized the Tejano population, recognizing their size and vilification by Know-Nothings. Besides founding a Spanish-language newspaper, Democrats also held meetings led by and for Tejano Democrats. Through these means, Democrats earned the allegiance of San Antonio Tejanos while recognizing their significance and differences. The Democratic Party relationship with Tejanos, built in response to the Know-Nothing attack, served as a first step in a long-term pattern of Anglo political organizing among Tejanos.

Published to serve "la población Méjico-Tejana," or the Mexico-Texan public, *El Bejareño* sought to counter the Know-Nothing expansion in San Antonio while attempting to include Tejanos in the American political system. The paper mixed reports on activities by both parties and American and Mexican news with lengthy histories of Texas, Mexico, and the United States as well as American civics lessons. Little is known of the paper's circulation and precise readership, but the publishers' names and the advertisements indicate a largely Anglo-Texan ownership. While it cannot be called a "Tejano" paper, *El Bejareño* claimed to advocate positions to benefit Bejareños, including support for Tejano rights under the U.S. Constitution, public schooling for Tejano children in Spanish and English, and translation of all laws and ordinances, and to oppose the idea that Tejanos were not morally fit to be American citizens.[16] The broad range of news story coverage, both north and south, assumed a connection Tejanos held to events in the United States and Mexico.[17]

The paper also reported on events affecting local Tejanos more directly. Early in its run, *El Bejareño* included reports on attacks made against Tejano cart drivers. The paper noted that three carts owned by Rafael de Herrera were shot at and robbed on their way through southeast Texas.[18] The article added that the town of Seguín had voted to evict "Mexican *peones*" living in the town on August 21, 1854. Tejanos began writing to the paper, giving accounts of problems they faced with Anglo-Texans in nearby ranch areas. On June 26, 1855, another cart driver, Pedro Rodrígues, wrote a letter to the editors detailing an attack on his carts on the way to the coastal ports. He began by stating, "Dear Sirs, I expect from you impartiality that you will print in your newspaper the following account of a travesty committed against me."[19] Not only did the paper report these incidents, but the Democratic Party also responded in support of Tejanos. The newspaper also published reports on several meetings held by the Béxar County Democratic Party and the "Junta Democratica de los Ciudadanos Mejico-Tejanos del Condado de Bejar," or the Democratic Committee of Mexican-Texan Citizens of Béxar County. *El Bejareño*'s coverage informed Tejanos of the Democratic Party's plans to regain power in the city government and to strengthen their hold in statewide elections.

Reports from the newspaper reveal the Democratic Party's interest in cementing their ties with Tejanos. Such interest extended to the organization and running of the party. This newfound attention to Tejanos coincided with Juan N. Seguín's return to San Antonio soon after the U.S.-Mexico War.[20] He quickly reentered politics, winning two terms as county justice of the peace beginning in 1852. At the party leadership level, the Béxar County Democrats named Seguín as one of the two vice presidents under Sam A. Maverick's chairmanship. Democrats sought Tejano participation more directly through meetings led and attended by the county's Tejanos. The first of these meetings took place on June 23, 1855, at the home of Señor Flores.[21] Narciso Leal served as the meeting's chair with Juan M. Chaves as secretary.

Leal called the meeting to order and declared that the aims of the meeting were to "expose the 'Know-Nothing' Party and realize the imminent necessity to drown them in their nascent stage, before they take hold in our State."[22] Then Leal appointed a committee to write the meeting's resolutions, which—approved unanimously by the group—principally attacked the Know-Nothing Party and supported the Democratic candidates.[23] The document lambasted Know-Nothings as intolerant, secretive, xenophobic, and anti-Catholic. While these Tejano Democratic Party leaders discredited Know-Nothings, they also articulated their entitlement to rights and participation in the political process as American citizens. One resolution began, "As sons of Texas, citizens of the United States, and zealous lovers of free institutions, we cannot look . . . with anything but indignation and disdain upon the secret political association commonly called 'Know-Nothings.'"[24] This statement goes beyond simply establishing Tejano citizenship by claiming a native connection to political rights with the use of "sons of Texas" in the preface. These sentiments appear again in the next resolution: "That we hold as a singular sentiment and desire to bear witness to the Honor, the Glory and the Prosperity of the country of our birth and the land of our affections; simultaneously contrast our obedience to the law [and] our interest in the welfare of Texas, against those that portend to take away our unalienable rights, and who, for the most part, are foreigners to this land, with at the most four years of residence in our State."[25] Not only did Tejano Democrats assert their political rights as native Texans; they made claims based on deeper, almost primordial connections to place, regardless of the nation-state it pertained to. They declared the Know-Nothing attack as a violation of that connection and used the language of honor and defense to mobilize Tejanos emotionally. Turning the nativist attack on its head, the resolution called Know-Nothings the foreigners in this conflict.

Similar sentiments of deeper connections to the land surfaced in a letter written by José Antonio Navarro and read by Leal at the second meeting of the Tejano Democrats of Béxar County.[26] The letter deserves extensive quotation to reveal Navarro's language situating Tejanos in the American polity. Navarro began by acknowledging the residual tension from San Antonio's history of conflict between Mexicans and Anglo-Americans: "Divine Providence and subsequent events have permitted that the 'Patria' that our fathers left their footsteps on, now belongs to another government and another prodigious race in the social order of human things." Navarro's comments, though, removed blame or malice toward Anglo-Americans concerning their annexation of Texas and placed the United States on equal moral footing with Mexico regarding rule over Texas. He continued, "It was not our fault, nor is it our current disgrace: it was one of those High dispositions that was out of our hands to prevent, . . . making us adoptive sons of a great and free nation." In each of these statements, Navarro incorporated a notion of divine destiny regarding Tejano political status. Navarro's expla-

José Antonio Navarro. (McArdle Notebooks, Archives and Information Services Division, Texas State Library and Archives Commission)

nation here seems to be pointed at dispelling any tensions introduced by Know-Nothing anti-Mexican rhetoric. His statements deflected animosity and encouraged cooperation and participation in the American political system.

Know-Nothing attacks against Tejano loyalty threatened Navarro's sense of honor and standing as an American. Navarro believed that voting with the Democrats would restore the status of Tejanos. He wrote, "Then, let us be true Americans in the name of reason and especially for the future." For Navarro, the entitlement of citizenship sprang from the historical connection Tejanos held to their homeland, over and above larger ties to nations. He added, "Let us throw off the vestiges of foreignerism: let us forget the pride of nationalism: this is where we live, where we have our homes: this government protects and sustains us, it gives and defends our rights." Navarro's rhetoric indicates his belief that Tejanos could choose to identify as American or foreign. While Anglo-Americans employed these terms, Tejanos could appropriate them to their benefit. Tejanos, then, were foreigners in their own land as long as they considered themselves as such. Navarro concluded, "Why not become purely American in order to gain the benefits of its institutions? Then we cannot be frightened by that bogeyman that we are of foreign origin." Navarro's comments must be taken in the context of his consistent participation in the Anglo-Texan political system dating from the first days of the Texas Republic and even to the maintenance of *empresario* grants in the Mexican period. Nevertheless, the article noted that applause punctuated several points of Leal's reading of Navarro's letter.

After making the claim that he was American, Navarro turned his attention to the upcoming statewide elections of August 6, 1855, and the effort to defeat the Know-Nothing candidates. He echoed the critique that Know-Nothings sought to exclude Tejanos from full participation as American citizens. But instead of leaving that attack at the level of rights, he elevated opposition to Know-Nothing ideology to a matter of honor. At one point in the letter, Navarro mentioned all personal friendships with Know-Nothing adherents should be put aside during questions of public policy. He surmised, "Things of the public sphere are worth honor, reputation, good name and notoriety. Things of the private and business sphere are worth 'pesos y daimes.'" Yet Navarro's definition of honor and Americanism did not mean stripping off Tejano culture. Rather, true Americanism meant maintaining the traditions and beliefs held by Tejanos over the generations. He concluded, "The die has been cast; Mexican-Texans are Catholics, they should be proud of their parents' faith, and defend it hand to hand, from the infamous aggression." Navarro went one step further, tying voting to personal honor in the next issue of *El Bejareño*, writing, "Do not sell your votes, for that is to sell your honor. And he who sells that goddess, is better off not having been born."[27]

Through *El Bejareño*, the Democratic Party supported Navarro's call for a democratically informed American Tejano political ethic. The paper ran a series of dialogues aimed at exposing Know-Nothing campaign propaganda and providing Tejanos with examples of how to be a voting citizen. These efforts, along with the Tejano Democrat meetings described above, sought to modify Tejano political culture along the lines of American politics. Interpreting Democratic Party actions and Tejano participation is clouded by the unstated interests each had in this political process. Democrats needed Tejanos to retain power in San Antonio. Their loss to Know-Nothing candidates indicates the erosion of their base among Anglo-Texans. The question remains whether the Tejano Democrat meetings and *El Bejareño*, along with the inclusion of Tejanos in leadership roles, functioned as part of Democratic machine politics or held a deeper meaning and impact on the San Antonio Tejano community.

According to the Know-Nothing press, Democrats manipulated and deceived Tejanos to maintain their power. Know-Nothing opinions appeared in the pages of the English-language *San Antonio Herald*.[28] In a series of articles published just before the August elections, the *Herald* argued that Democratic propaganda misled and wrongly characterized the American Party, as the Know-Nothings also called themselves.[29] "MEXICANS BEWARE," the editors wrote. "Do not pay attention to those who say that the Know Nothing Party wishes to proscribe you on account of your race or religion."[30] But without a Spanish-language mouthpiece or membership among the city's elite Tejanos, the Know-Nothing response reached few Tejano voters. Know-Nothing candidates suffered crushing losses in the August 1855 elections, setting up their defeat in the subsequent municipal elections that December. San Antonians elected a popular Democrat, J. M. Devine, for a third term.[31] One Tejano, G. Soto, was elected to the city council during Devine's term.[32]

After the election, the pages of the *Herald* filled with vitriolic attacks, depicting Tejanos as ignorant saps following the Roman Catholic Church and Democratic Party leadership. One article noted, "By deception, falsehood and misrepresentation thousands of good men and true have been led to believe that Americanism is whiggery in disguise."[33] Another article added specific evidence of Tejano manipulation, noting, "Many [Mexicans] stated that they were voting for the Catholic religion."[34] Along with accusing the Democrats of using propaganda, the *Herald* also claimed Democrats rigged the elections by bringing in people from Mexico to vote. They used this belief to support their call for registry laws.[35]

The claims by Know-Nothing candidates of unfair elections turned to more direct ethnic attacks against Tejanos and Mexicans in general. The paper made the point clear from the onset by stating, "We still maintain that AMERICANS SHALL RULE AMERICA—that to prevent native Americans from being out-numbered and overpowered by those of foreign birth, it is necessary to limit immigration and extend the term of naturalization."[36] This statement exemplifies the fearful tone the paper used to create a "Mexican scare." A reprint from the *Austin State Times* report on the election exposed even deeper racial sentiments espoused by the Know-Nothing Party. The article, comparing national elections, stated, "Either these ignorant, vicious, besotted *greasers,* who have swelled to such an unprecedented extent the majority of the anti-American party in Béxar county are wrong, or the seventy thousand intellectual, educated and refined Virginians who supported the American ticket at the late election in that State, are in error."[37] The reprint also blamed the Catholic church for manipulating Tejanos. Their ability to be swayed seemed to be evidence of their unworthiness to be full citizens of the United States. The article concluded by characterizing the Know-Nothing defeat as "a triumph of the guests over the host, it is the rout of the American by a foreign party—it is a political defeat of Texians by the very men whom their valor defeated on the ensanguined field of battle."

As noted in previous chapters, anti-Mexican sentiments were not new to Bexareños. In light of those comments, the efforts by Anglo-Texan Democrats to increase Tejano participation in the political process are more significant. The Know-Nothing statements after the election also indicated the growing ferocity of the anti-Mexican position, which turned to violence against cart drivers in the state's hinterland. The next section of this chapter delves further into those attacks and their direct and indirect impact on Bexareños. Regarding the city's political process, though, the Know-Nothing statements and actions add meaning to Tejano participation in the Democratic Party. The political context of the time broadens the explanation of Tejano participation beyond Anglo-Texan manipulation to negotiation within a complex and dynamic set of choices.

The presence of Tejano Democrat meetings along with Democratic Party interest in Tejano issues to counter the Know-Nothing campaigns suggest greater levels of Tejano assertion in local politics rather than Tejano manipulation by the Anglo-Texan political establishment. Further examinations into voting patterns might reveal more specific information on the extent of this participation. Evidence from *El Bejareño* provides insight into participation at the organizational level of party politics. As such, Tejano participation serves as an example of both "boss rule" by a nascent Democratic Party machine and an avenue for asserting Tejano interests in an increasingly hostile environment. Tejano Democrats went beyond simply approving the party's platform; they also formed an election vigilance committee and articulated a Tejano Americanism. The first Tejano Democrat meeting set up the vigilance committee to "guard our fellow Mexico-Tejano citizens against the character and tactics of that perverse and dangerous party that 'knows nothing of that which is just, liberal and generous;' and . . . impede the submission of illegal votes, and to encourage our fellow citizens to make every honest and legal effort to frustrate those 'dim' candidates."[38] The subsequent meeting appointed twelve Tejanos to the committee, including Juan N. Seguín, José Antonio Navarro, and Francisco Herrera.[39]

While Tejanos organized under the banner of the Democratic Party, the separate meetings placed this organization at a transitional stage of Tejano entrance into the American political system. Separate institutions, though, limited the degree of participation by Tejanos in the party leadership. Tejano Democrats acknowledged these separate meetings to be a necessary part of the transition. During their second meeting, they accepted the following resolution:

Being the case, that our imperfect grasp of the English language impedes our ability to actively participate in the Meetings of the Béxar County Democratic Party.

Be it resolved, that informed of their conventions, we declare our cordial adherence to their resolutions.

Resolved, that having full confidence in our Democratic brothers, we support the candidates they chose, and despite the differences in our language forcing separate meetings, we will always march under the same banner.[40]

The wording of this resolution appears to have made the Tejano Democrat convention a rubber stamp of the Democratic Party platform. But the

Juan N. Seguín after his return to Texas from Mexico. (McArdle Notebooks, Archives and Information Services Division, Texas State Library and Archives Commission)

issues of trust and language imply a more complex relationship. When Tejanos described the "full confidence" they held in the Democratic Party, they suggested a level of trust that their decisions would protect the interests of Tejanos. Personal friendships along with overt support of Tejanos in the face of Know-Nothing attacks served as important elements in building that trust. Also, pointing to language as the largest obstacle to full membership suggests larger social and cultural barriers to Tejano inclusion in the Democratic Party. These separate conventions served as opportunities in American politics for Tejanos, perhaps with the expectation of full incorporation in the near future.

The following year, Democratic Party meetings incorporated Tejanos, indicating a degree of integration in the party.[41] In order to include Tejanos in the proceedings, interpreters translated during the meeting. Tejano participation at this level resulted in having a voice, however limited, in the decision-making process. For instance, the 1856 nominating committee of the Béxar County Democratic Party included José Antonio Navarro for precinct one, Narciso Leal and J. Urrutia for precinct two, and B. Lopez in precinct three.

The various Democratic Party conventions, the civics lessons present in *El Bejareño*, and the rhetoric exhibited in José Antonio Navarro's letter all make up parts of the Tejano political culture after annexation by the United States. Over the previous twenty years, many Tejanos had begun to learn the lessons of American politics. Despite many structural barriers to participation, such as poverty, low education, citizenship status, language, and restrictive voting laws, Tejanos continued to assert themselves in the new political system. Navarro's lengthy participation in the political system made him the appropriate person to deliver the remarks on being a "Tejano-American" citizen. Yet these meetings occurred under the eye of the Democratic Party, suggesting the party held an interest in encouraging Tejano participation. Magnanimity aside, did Tejano Democrat conventions and Tejano political education serve the purpose of exploitation or inclusion?

Tejano participation rarely extended to significant participation in elective bodies. Navarro and the Tejano Democrats mostly voted for Anglo-Texan candidates, since so few Tejanos could or did run for office. The few Tejanos who achieved elected positions stood in a controversial position. Historian Arnoldo De León has observed that "Anglo politicians saw the Mexican [elected official] as one to be 'voted' by them in the interest of maintaining white supremacy."[42] Yet Navarro's articulation of the problems introduced with Know-Nothing politics suggests limits to the manipulation and oppression of Tejanos. These constraints occurred when Tejanos asserted their interests and threatened to withhold support at election time. To count on Tejanos, Democrats at least had to talk in pro-Tejano language, if not open their political process to allow Tejano participation.

With the conclusion of the statewide elections, *El Bejareño* turned to the approaching local elections and more quotidian matters of interest to the Tejano readership. Minor changes in the content of the weekly happened as the Democratic Party worried less about Tejano support in upcoming elections. While the paper reported on several more meetings by both Tejano and Anglo-Texan Democrats, stories appeared on Mexican subjects, both in San Antonio and throughout the United States and Mexico. One article provided news of the lynching of Mexicans and Chileans in California.[43] Several accounts of stabbings and fights within San Antonio also appeared in its pages.[44] The report on one knife fight at a fandango reveals the writer's consciousness of a Bejareño readership. In identifying the individuals involved in the fight, the paper added the phrase "son of this city" to Antonio de la Garza's name and "from the other side of the Rio Grande" to Ignacio Garcia's.[45] In the two years of the paper's run, it seems to have responded more directly to the Tejano readership's day-to-day concerns.

This personal connection appeared in a poem submitted to the paper by J. Y. Barrera in February 1856. Barrera's elegy touched on the importance of the paper to Tejanos within the Anglo-Texan city. Berrera wrote:

Al Bejareño	To the Bejareño
El sueño fatal de mi memoria,	The fatal dream of my memory
Tus gratos echos lo despiertan luego;	Your graceful works then awake;
Entonces lleno de placer y gloria,	Then I am filled with pleasure and glory,
Abre los ojos cual *Longino* el ciego.	Opens the eyes of the blind man Longino.
Si tus columnas beo cuidadoso,	If I read your columns carefully,
En ellas encuentro sin porfia,	Without a doubt I find in them,
Que aquel que se hallaba dudoso,	That he who found himself doubtful,
Despierta con tu ciencia cada dia.	Awakes with your science every day.
En gratos recuerdos sean envueltos,	In graceful memories shall be wrapped,
Los pasados pliegos que has cedido,	Pages of the past that you have given,
Que en ellos queda dispuesto	That in them remains disposed
Nuestro grande y sabio *Partido*.	Our grand and enlightened Party.

De celica Deidad y Hermosura,	From heavenly Deity and Beauty,
Te colme sin fin el alto cielo,	I filled without end the heavens above,
Cual flor que llena de ternura,	That flower that fills you with pride,
Reparte sus perfumes en el suelo.	Distribute your scent to the earth.[46]

Barrera's poem deserves attention for the way it combines Mexican poetic devices with a description of a traditional American newspaper holding overt political goals. The presence of the poem provides a window into the ties some readers made with the paper. The author used grand images and hefty notions of the heavens and beauty, characteristic of the Mexican poetic style of the time, to describe the significance of an otherwise everyday subject. The newspaper is described as "awaking" and giving sight, referring to the basic knowledge and information provided in its pages. But other phrases suggest that the paper's information made life richer. In particular, the image of the flower leaving a fragrance on the earth suggests that aspects of the newspaper might have made life more pleasant and meaningful. While the newspaper made many efforts to shape Tejano political ideology, it also provided Tejanos with a sense of inclusion in the dominant political and social system and an avenue to express their concerns about the future.

The paper presented several stories that together show the range of problems that faced Tejanos in this period. One item described the dilapidated and inhumane condition of the section of town known as Laredito.[47] Tejanos also confronted the city's growing military presence. An article on February 23, 1856, reported on a group of disorderly American soldiers who began shooting their weapons in the street.[48] *El Bejareño* also chronicled the deteriorating situation for Tejanos in the city's hinterlands. One report noted the shooting of a Mexican by Anglos near the town of Victoria, on the road to the Texas coast.[49] Yet another commented on the decision by the citizens of Caldwell County to expel all Mexicans from their county under the pretext that they would seduce their slaves.[50] The paper condemned the county's action and added, "Do not make a mockery and theater of liberty granted in the jury system of the State Law—just because you are the strongest." The paper, and later the Democratic Party, began to take notice of these problems in the outlying counties.

Broader issues of importance to Tejanos also appeared in the newspaper. These ranged from news from other Latin American nations to reports from the short-lived Republic of the Sierra Madre in northern Mexico.[51] After the paper presented a lengthy, episodic history of the United States, it added a history of Mexico. In the midst of presenting these histories, the paper took the opportunity to critique a recently written history of Texas by H. Yoakum.[52] The review surveyed the scope of Texas history with an emphasis on the Spanish and Mexican struggles of the previous century. It then turned to Yoakum's work and denounced it for glossing over this early history: "We feel that it leaves much to be desired in reference to the first years of the history of Texas, and would be better entitled, 'History of the Americans in Texas.'" The review goes on to note a number of factual mistakes in sections on the Mexican period, pointing out that Tejanos like José Antonio Navarro were available to provide the correct information from their firsthand experience.

Near the end of *El Bejareño*'s run, Angel Navarro's name appears on the masthead as co-publisher/editor.[53] The son of José Antonio Navarro, Angel had only recently returned to San Antonio from California, where he had practiced law.[54] His presence in the management of the newspaper came during the paper's increased attention to Tejano issues. While enjoying only a brief run, the paper served as a vehicle for Tejano mobilization in the face of increasing attacks from inside and outside the city. Tejanos witnessed themselves being "written out" of significance in the state, much like in Yoakum's history book. The response found in the pages of *El Bejareño* not only chronicled these alarming changes but also claimed Tejano entitlement to political and social inclusion on moral and historical grounds. These claims grew more important as the political effects of violence against Tejanos were debated in the city and state government.

Cart War: The Limits of Participation

The scattered reports of violence against Tejanos on the ranges outside San Antonio grew more frequent in the beginning of 1857. The attacks focused on oxen-drawn carts, which were the principal mode of mercantile transportation, and their mostly Tejano teamsters. The violence became so frequent, explicit, and pointed that people began calling it the Cart War. While the Cart War took place outside of San Antonio, the attacks affected Bexareños both directly, since many worked in the trade, and indirectly, by challenging and shaping the role of Tejanos in state and local politics. The Cart War became a reminder to Tejanos that increasing physical threats and anti-Mexican animosity limited their modest gains of inclusion in the social and political system of San Antonio. Nevertheless, the Democratic

Oxcarts on Commerce Street, 1882. (San Antonio Light Collection, UTSA's Institute of Texan Cultures, No. L-1228-H, courtesy of the Hearst Corporation)

Party and media response demonstrated some acceptance of Tejanos as permanent members of the civic polity.

Cart transportation provided a critical service to two of San Antonio's most important industries of the time, trade and agriculture. As a mercantile center, the city depended on the movement of goods and produce in and out of the city. Tejanos played a central role in the city's commerce with their dominance in the horse-cart business. Their presence as cart drivers was so pervasive as to elicit the remark by Frederick Law Olmsted that "almost the entire transportation of the country is carried on by [Mexicans] with oxen and two-wheeled carts."[55] The 1850 census of San Antonio indicated that 58 percent of the Tejano heads-of-household were employed as cart drivers.[56]

Cart drivers (*arrieros*) contributed the skill and work that built and maintained commercial routes radiating in and out of San Antonio. Carts served this function until railroads were built in south Texas after the Civil War. San Antonio boomed as a warehouse distribution center in the American period. Merchants depended on *arrieros* to keep the flow of goods and produce constant and timely. *Arrieros* principally drove their loads along a route between San Antonio and the Gulf Coast of Texas, making the city an inland port of sorts. *Arrieros* also derived a great deal of business from trade with Mexico, adding to the paths through south Texas. It was mainly along these routes that Anglo-Texans from towns and ranches in those areas began menacing Tejano *arrieros* as well as Tejanos living there.

Signs of violence toward cart drivers surfaced as early as 1855, when a driver, Pedro Rodrígues, wrote to *El Bejareño* regarding an incident on the road to the Gulf Coast.[57] He described an instance when a rancher, J. J. Golman, refused to hand over two oxen with Rodrígues's brand. Golman claimed that one of Rodrígues's drivers owed him fifty pesos. Golman then reached over and grabbed Rodrígues by the throat, while twenty to twenty-five of Golman's men surrounded him. Golman then threatened to have Rodrígues jailed or killed to get the fifty pesos. Rodrígues wrote, "In order to avoid greater problems, in the presence of those infuriated people who already spoke of lynching me, I had to sign an I.O.U. to pay the fifty pesos within three months. Golman stated among other things that being Justice of the Peace, he didn't care a straw for me, nor a dime for my sort, and he didn't give a damn if my body dammed up the creek." Rodrígues left the ranch without his oxen, a crucial element of his cart-driving business. He concluded, "It is not the first act of aggression perpetrated in this part of the land." Nor would it be the last.

Over the next two years, attacks on cart drivers escalated until the summer of 1857, when popular outrage against the attacks began to take shape in San Antonio. For the most part, newspapers and politicians in San Antonio defended the interests of the Tejano teamsters. This stance resulted in a wave of resentment from the townships where the violence was taking place. A letter to the *San Antonio Herald* from the *Goliad Express* noted the regional differences between Anglo-Texans involved in the matter.[58] The editors wrote, "But you want us to sympathize *with your Mexicans.* . . . When wrongs are done to *us* by your Mexicans, you not only want us to overlook them, but to take the wrongdoers by the hand." Rural Anglo-Texans in the southeastern section of the state felt the defense of Tejano cart drivers by San Antonio's political establishment not only intruded on their self-governance but also imposed an external attitude toward Tejanos held by San Antonians.[59]

The defense of these cart drivers in San Antonio follows along with the shift seen after the Know-Nothing victory. Supporting Tejano cart drivers improved both the business prospects for San Antonio merchants and Anglo/Tejano relations in the city. Other commentators elevated the Cart War issue to a higher moral and ideological level, tied to the definition of American. In a response to a negative editorial in a rural paper, the *Herald* published a letter anonymously signed "A Citizen of San Antonio."[60] The author described the Cart War as a "war on the principles of a true American." His letter began by explicitly placing the Cart War within the larger conflict, emphasizing the importance of land issues in south Texas. He characterized the writer of the rural article as a man who "may own more land with original Mexican titles, than all the unfortunate Mexican Texans who are now suffering the diabolical outrages that are now being perpetrated." This comment noted both the grounds for ethnic tension in south Texas and the rapid change of status by Tejanos, away from landowners. "Citizen" continued by emphasizing Tejano entitlement and rights as full American citizens. He wrote, "The citizens who were born on this soil without distinction of color, and are not touched by the late decision of the Supreme Court of the United States—that they are citizens, as good as their rights under the law are involved, and that we are bound to respect them, if we value our own." Here the author made a claim for racial parity by noting where Tejanos stood in relation to the Dred Scott decision; in other words, they were not "Negro." As a result, the actions by Anglo-Texans in attacking the cart drivers violated the equality and protections outlined in the Constitution. By making these statements, the writer attempted to close the gap between Tejanos and Anglos under a common notion of "American."

While Anglo politicians in San Antonio and Austin lined up to defend Tejanos in the Cart War, the Mexican government began to take notice of the violence. The Mexican envoy in Washington, D.C., responded by sending letters to the U.S. secretary of state, drawing these localized conflicts into an international arena. The letters sent on October 14 and 19, 1857, figure into a growing pattern of the Mexican government's official interest in the rights and treatment of Mexicans living in the United States, regardless of their citizenship status.[61] By acting in this manner, the Mexican government acknowledged the complex nature of national identity, considering Tejanos Mexicans, regardless of their official political status. An ambiguous identification of citizenship status resulted from the fluid border in the region during this period. Border crossing was largely unregulated and undocumented. Questions of citizenship surfaced only during elections and in dealings with the judicial system.

Manuel Robles y Pezuela, the Mexican envoy to the United States, wrote

American secretary of state Lewis Cass to inform him of the organized nature of the attacks on Mexican cart drivers. He added, "It is also affirmed that from the town of San Antonio de Béxar, the residents of Mexican origin have been expelled, living there in a peaceable manner, under the protection of the laws of the United States and of the treaties subsisting between the two governments."[62] Robles y Pezuela's remarks referred to a large-scale, violent campaign against Mexicans in Texas. His use of "residents of Mexican origin" indicated indifference to citizenship in addressing people whose welfare concerned his government. Mexican nationals as well as longtime Tejano families, now American citizens, deserved protection as Mexicans. Robles y Pezuela concluded with a request that the United States "apply the corrective, and take all such measures as are demanded by justice, the law of nations and the honor of the United States."

Cass forwarded his concern to Texas governor E. M. Pease, adding, "I need not inform your Excellency that the least aggravated of these outrages is a glaring violation of the rights guaranteed to these people both by law and by treaty."[63] Cass's response made clear that the actions against Mexicans in south Texas were subject to both American legal jurisdictions and international diplomatic agreements. Governor Pease responded quickly to Cass's letter, issuing an official report on the Cart War on November 11, 1857.[64]

In his response, Pease presented the interests of the state of Texas in terms of fundamental political rights. He pointed out that violence against "any class of citizens" was unjustified as long as laws and a judicial system existed to remedy problems. Such vigilantism would erode any confidence in the state's ability to protect its people and property. Pease also noted that these transgressions could lead to larger racial conflicts in the state. He wrote, "A profound hostile mood against citizens of Mexican origin prevails over many of the surrounding counties, and there has been an imminent danger of reprisals on their part, if allowed to begin would inevitably lead to a civil war between the races."[65] Citing such a danger, Pease organized a patrolling force of seventy-eight men to protect the cart traffic through south Texas. Appointing such a force displayed Pease's distrust of the local authorities in those counties and elevated the stakes involved in Tejano politics.[66] By taking steps to directly address what he perceived as a "civil war between the races," Pease seemed to suggest that regardless of being "untouched" by the Dred Scott decisions, Tejanos were still treated as a race apart.

Pease vocalized his support for Tejanos by publicly noting, "The large majority of [people of Mexican origin] are as orderly and obedient of laws as any other person in the state."[67] Despite Pease's statement, the attacks on cart drivers indicated the rising levels of animosity toward Mexicans. His solution points to the growing importance of the government to ensure at least minimal levels of protection to Tejanos. Angel Navarro, now a representative in the state legislature, underscored the distrust of local protection of Mexican interests by proposing a law to extend the jurisdiction of cases relating to attacks on carts to two hundred miles from the place of the attack.[68] The legislature passed a law giving the governor permission to send a military force to protect the cart drivers.[69]

The efforts of the governor and legislature apparently had the effect of ending the Cart War. Statewide attention tempered the actions of local authorities in Karnes and Goliad counties, but not without some resistance on their part. In a letter to the *San Antonio Herald*, the chief justice of Karnes County stated, "To a man, almost all the citizens along the road, are in favor of stopping the carts, driving the Mexicans out of our county, and many are not very choice as to the means adopted to effect it."[70] To him, by sending the state militia into the county, the governor took the side of the electoral concentrations in the cities over the countryside. Indeed, the votes in cities such as San Antonio provided a critical base of support for state politicians. And, as the Know-Nothing challenge revealed, the Tejano vote played a crucial role in swinging the urban vote. The 1859 campaign for governor introduced the importance of the Tejano vote once more.

Antebellum San Antonio

The importance of Tejanos in statewide politics appeared once again during the Texas gubernatorial campaign of 1859. The Union Democratic Party presented a slate of candidates, including the nomination of Sam Houston for governor. Under new ownership, the *San Antonio Daily Herald* supported the ticket and also endorsed candidates for local House and Senate seats.[71] The party nominated Angel Navarro for state representative, acknowledging the importance of Tejanos to the political future of Texas. The tensions building between northern and southern politicians nationwide echoed in the Texas campaign, with the Union Democratic Party rejecting both secession and the reopening of the African slave trade.[72] For San Antonians, the inclusion of Tejanos in the state's future also lay in the balance. In particular, Tejanos experienced a moment where the debates around race and society referred to African Americans in the South and avoided directly defining Tejano status. This created a space for Tejano participation and a degree of access that briefly passed for white.[73]

The *Daily Herald* published several articles expressing its beliefs in the benefits to Tejanos of electing Houston. The paper also noted that his opponent, Hardin R. Runnels, stood opposed to the rights of Mexicans, especially regarding land claims, writing, "There is no doubt that Gov. Runnels is a bitter and uncompromising enemy to the confirmation of all old Mexican land grants."[74] His opposition to these grants would, the *Herald* continued, lead to the alienation of Tejano voters. "If they expect the Mexican vote, they will be sadly disappointed." On the other hand, the paper supported Houston's position regarding Tejano rights. "Their lands will be protected under and by his administration, their taxes reduced, their lives insured, and every care taken of their interest and property, as much as the proudest national American citizen. . . . Gen. Houston will cross the San Antonio [River], coming from the Rio Grande with more than THREE THOUSAND MAJORITY." The remarks highlight not only the benefits to Mexicans but, more important, the votes Houston stood to receive. The concentration on Tejanos as a voting bloc simultaneously indicates their significance in politics as well as their marginal position.

The *Herald*'s comments also suggest that the issue of landownership had not been settled among Tejanos. Unlike Mexicans living in territories annexed by the Treaty of Guadalupe Hidalgo in 1848, Tejanos had already faced a decade of land adjudication under the Texas Republic. The issue appeared to affect choices Tejanos made to support a candidate or political party. Old allegiances also played a role in decisions, as evidenced by José Antonio Navarro's support for Houston.[75] Navarro's significance as an elder statesman of San Antonio appeared in the general, non-Tejano tone his support of Houston took. With the lessons of the Know-Nothing victory in 1854 in hand, Anglo Democrats could not ignore Tejano voters. Yet on a statewide level, Tejano issues constituted only one of a myriad of issues.

While Tejanos mattered in state politics, their fate would be decided by the larger Anglo polity or by sympathetic politicians. Politicians courted Tejano votes, considering them an early interest group, but participation in the core of the government eluded Tejanos. Their survival depended on maintaining their ties to the Anglo-Texan power structure. This explanation suggests one possible motivation for Tejano enlistment in the Confederate army, only two years after the 1859 elections.

While Navarro and other Tejanos supported Houston and the Union Democratic ticket, they put aside their differences regarding the state's future to join in the Texas battalions of the Confederate army. Their participation in the Confederacy demonstrates their close connection with the Democratic Party and the local Anglo leadership. The example of San Antonio stands in contrast to the many Tejanos who enlisted in the Union in other areas of south Texas.[76] Historian Jerry D. Thompson attributes south Texas Tejanos' choice to join the Union to the effects of alienation and disenfranchisement in the rural sections of the region. On the other hand, Tejanos in urban areas such as Laredo and San Antonio participated overwhelmingly in the Confederacy, indicating a degree of cooperation between Tejanos and Anglo-Texans, or perhaps reliance by Tejanos on Anglos.

In San Antonio, Tejanos joined the Confederate army in large numbers. Tejanos constituted 37 percent of the indigent families of Confederate soldiers in Béxar County for February 27, 1865, making up a significant portion of the San Antonio Confederate forces.[77] Tejanos enlisted in five different regiments.[78] Portions of the Second Texas Mounted Rifles and the Third, Sixth, and Eighth Texas Infantries contained Tejano soldiers or entire Tejano regiments. Often, these regiments were led by Tejano officers, such as Manuel Yturri II, Joseph De La Garza, Joseph M. Peñaloza, Angel Navarro, Sexto E. Navarro, Erasmo J. Chavez, Antonio Bustillos, Eugenio Navarro, and Clemente Bustillos. In more than one case, such as Trevanion T. Teel's artillery company and Charles L. Pyron's company, Tejanos served directly under Anglo-Texan commanders. The majority of Tejano soldiers enlisted between April and June 1861. Their ages ranged from sixteen to forty-six, most falling between twenty-five and thirty.[79] The troops in Bustillos's company also listed their occupation, with most Tejanos indicating they were laborers. Tejano Confederate soldiers fought in a few battles during the war, in Texas and as far away as Tennessee and Georgia.

Tejano participation in the Confederacy differed from that of Tejanos in the Texas army during the war of Texas secession. In 1835, Tejano soldiers had mostly joined with secessionists to oppose the centralist government. In contrast, Tejanos had little to gain from taking sides in the Civil War. Though individual ties to Anglo-Texans also played a role in joining in 1835, those allegiances carried an even greater weight over ideology in the decision to join the Confederacy. The ties forged between Anglos and Tejanos during the decade of the 1850s best explain the motivations behind Tejano participation in the Confederacy. Perhaps inclusion in the Democratic Party and the overtures in favor of Tejanos during the Cart War invested Tejanos with a stake in the future of Texas. In a sense, a national debate over race and social status began to redefine or at least influence the politics of race and whiteness at the local level.

Cultural Persistence

The 1860 census, conducted on the eve of the Civil War, revealed that San Antonio had transformed over the previous half century. The ethnic and economic demographic composition described in that census would remain similar for the next fifty years. The changes initiated by the Texas Revolution were fairly complete by 1860.

San Antonio remained the most populous city in Texas in the antebellum period. Its position as the economic capital of south Texas and as the port of trade with Mexico maintained its strategic importance to the state and to the Confederacy. The city's stature in the state's economy brought its political and social issues to the attention of state officials. Political leaders had to address Tejano civic issues to solidify their positions.

The organizing and posturing surrounding the Democratic Party and the Cart War described above serve as examples of a continued Tejano presence in San Antonio's shape and character. On the other hand, Tejanos grew increasingly poor and held less land from year to year. Furthermore, while Tejano votes mattered to politicians, Tejanos had negligible direct representation or voice in governing. Many Tejanos weathered the changes in their city and nation brought by Anglo-American colonization and annexation. The 1860 census demonstrated the shrinking significance of Tejanos in the city and the state.

In the years between 1850 and 1860, the population of San Antonio more than doubled. Yet as historian Arnoldo De León has noted, the Tejanos as a percentage of the city's population decreased during that same decade.[80] San Antonio's growth came from an increase in the Anglo population and from a large influx of German and other European immigrants. Once the leadership and majority of the town they founded, Tejanos became a minority ethnic group in less than a generation.

Tejanos carved out the space to survive in the dominant Anglo-Texan society. Far from cloistering themselves, Tejanos maintained a slight degree of political clout even while experiencing increased economic and social oppression and segregation. Tejanos did not disappear after 1836, only to reappear as workers in the early twentieth century.

Ideas, commodities even, refuse the bounds
of a nation. All are inextricably connected,
so that each is needed to explain the others.
—Frederick Jackson Turner,
"The Significance of History," 1891

I went to Texas on my own initiative, there I spoke of
the Mexican nation to the humble workers of those border
areas, and while I believed that seventy years of banishment
had extinguished any trace of patriotism, I found noble Mexican
souls filled with a fervent love for their homeland [patria],
augmented and transmitted from generation to generation,
as do all people who are oppressed by their conqueror.
—M. Romero Palafox, 1909

Conclusion

Challenging Identities

TRANSNATIONAL BECOMES LOCAL

This book started with Diez y Seis de Septiembre and ends with the same celebration, only seventy-five years later. On September 16, 1910, Mexicans marked the centennial of their independence with larger versions of the annual parades and celebrations. The Mexican government established a centennial commission to oversee the work of local organizing *juntas patrioticas* formed across the nation. The juntas extended into the borderlands area of the United States, with groups forming in San Antonio and south Texas as well as in Los Angeles, Tucson, and El Paso.[1] Mexican Independence Day celebrations continued an existing tradition in these areas. By including Mexicans living in the United States in the centennial planning, the commission acknowledged an idea of nationalism that extended beyond the nation, a "Mexico de afuera" in a sense.

Celebrations of foreign patriotic festivals by ethnic groups in the United States are common. But those festivities take on a different meaning in the U.S.-Mexico borderlands where history and demographics complicate traditional beliefs about nation, nationalism, and patriotism. As M. Romero

Palafox noted in a letter to the commission, the Tejanos he interviewed in 1909 identified Mexico as their homeland.[2] Many of them felt this way despite never having lived on Mexican soil. The Mexican homeland, or *patria*, served as an identity that Tejanos held well after the secession of Texas and its subsequent annexation by the United States. The meaning of *patria* and its relation to national identity changed for Tejanos from Mexico's founding through Anglo-American colonization and the secession of Texas. That change reflected the shifting political boundary and new ethnic demographics of the borderlands. Those external alterations set in motion the development of Texas-Mexican borderlands identity, initially based on regional culture and eventually settling into more recognizable patterns of ethnic identity seen in 1850s San Antonio.

Palafox's observations on Tejano Mexican nationalism in 1908 and the subsequent organization of celebratory juntas take on added meaning in the context of growing discontent with the presidency of Porfirio Díaz. Indeed, Palafox himself points out that the juntas served "for them [Tejanos] to make an objective study of the state of affairs in our country, with the goal of preventing the perverse slander by the Magons, the Sarabias, etc."[3] Patriotic celebrations organized by officially sanctioned juntas served different goals from those organized through more popular means. For instance, the organizing junta in Corpus Christi involved the leadership of several *sociedades mutualistas* and unions in their celebration plan.[4]

Such a split took place for San Antonio's Independence centennial celebration as two separate groups formed competing week-long celebrations.[5] One group, led by the Grand International League of Mexico, held its functions in Central Park, while the other, composed of several *mutualistas* and the Grand Liga Mexicana, held its events in San Pedro Park. The festival in San Pedro Park seemed better attended, due perhaps to the sponsoring organizations' larger membership and popular base of support. Also, prior to the split, San Antonio's Tejanos usually held the main independence celebration in San Pedro Park.[6] In 1895, over 5,000 attended the closing evening dance and fireworks at that location.[7] This split continued through 1917, in the midst of the Mexican Revolution, when class divisions between the celebrations became more apparent. In that year, Mexican elites held their independence celebration in the casino, highlighted by the singing of arias and ballroom dancing to the sounds of a full orchestra.[8]

By the turn of the century, the festival had transformed into a civic event that incorporated the entire city, regardless of ethnicity. Of the 1895 celebration, the *San Antonio Daily Express* noted, "To judge from the nationality of the people who were on the grounds it would be hard to tell exactly what kind of a celebration was in progress." The centennial parade in 1910 included several regiments of American soldiers alongside city officials, Mexican delegates, and "nearly all the Mexican mutual societies in the city." The parade route wound through downtown San Antonio, from Milam Square to San Pedro Park. On the occasion of the centennial parade, the *Daily Express* observed that "the reception by both Americans and Mexicans on the streets traversed by the [American] troops was notably enthusiastic."[9] Following the soldiers came leaders from a wide variety of Mexican organizations such as the Gran Circulo de Obreros, the Union Sociedad Ignacio Allende, and Club de Trabajadores. Diez y Seis de Septiembre had established itself as a significant recognition of the history and continued presence of Mexicans in San Antonio.[10]

In the years between the celebrations in 1835 and 1910, social relations had dramatically transformed for the Mexican community in San Antonio. Despite sweeping changes in their citizenship, political power, and social status, Tejanos continued to identify as Mexican. But because of the material changes as well as cultural shifts in the prior decades, the meaning of Mexican identity differed for Bexareños in 1835 and Mexican Americans in 1910. New features of the independence celebration itself, such as the class split or the inclusion of the American military, show that the meaning of Mexican ethnic and national identity were in the process of negotiation and development. This book followed those identities over the critical period 1821 to 1861, demonstrating how identity influenced decisions and changed with social and political realities. Mexican identity seems like a moving target for historians to capture. It was much that way for Mexicans in nineteenth-century Texas as well.

In short, this book serves as an examination of identity through the reconstruction of the context where that identity is forged. Each chapter presented an element of that context or the shifting social landscape where Tejanos defined their identity. Part 1 developed the three larger social worlds that formed the basis for that context around the time of Mexican independence. The insurgency in Béxar provided the backdrop to situate the relationship between nation-state formation and local issues and concerns. The broad sweep of indigenous identities went further in marking the geographic and ideological location of Béxar in the northern frontier. Finally, large-scale Anglo-American immigration into Texas elevated the importance of cultural brokering among elite Tejanos, establishing a pattern that recurred through the next decades.

Part 2 described the shifting context as secession, expansion, and nation-state consolidation interrupted the social development underway in Béxar. The changing nature of the borderlands brought about by American westward expansion and Mexican renegotiation of immigration in the Law of April 6, 1830, began to reshape the meaning of Tejano actions. When secession escalated, Tejanos once again took a variety of stances in the dual contexts of Mexican federalist politics and local violence. The tense years following secession and before annexation forced Tejanos into the newly created suspect category of Mexican. After American annexation, Tejanos maintained their Mexican identity as an ethnic group in the new American political context.

To understand the context and shifting ground where identity takes root requires historians to move beyond their comfort zones and training specialties into multiple languages, national histories, and historiographies. Historians taking a transnational approach to their work have pointed to methodologies and analytical approaches that make it possible to untangle the complex web of identities in borderland regions and other places of cross-cultural contact.[11] Taking a transnational approach means writing history from a starting point beyond a single nation, consciously seeking and including sources, ideologies, and frameworks from multiple nations. This approach stands in contrast to international or area studies that examine national interaction at the level of state actors such as diplomats.[12]

Transnational history recasts the meaning of national and international categories by examining their cultural relevance to daily life at the local level. One summary notes, "In short, instead of framing the 'local' and the 'global' in binary opposition, the transnational 'optic' is a bifocal one which views the nation-state and transnational practices as 'mutually constitutive.'"[13] Perhaps it is counterintuitive to focus on the local level rather than on the geopolitical to fully understand the extensive web of ideas, cultures, peoples, and commodities across nations. But using San Antonio de Béxar and Bexareños as the pivot- or reference point for this book reveals as much about their connection to ideas, cultures, and politics outside the region and nation as about their internal social structure.

The current interest in transnational history stems from critiques of globalization in the twenty-first century. Social scientists and cultural critics realized that traditional or official concepts of nation failed to explain the global movement of people and capital and the identities produced by that movement. Transnational, for these scholars, defines an identity based on connections and displacement in a global context.[14] Transnational history makes the assumption that national histories limit a historian's ability to trace social, cultural, and economic connections and movements implicit in migrations and colonization. To transcend national histories, a transnational approach requires three commitments by practitioners: engage with outside primary sources, often in a second language; converse with multiple historiographies and narratives that serve to define the nation; and write a new narrative that develops these connections and conversations to produce a rich transcript of social and economic interaction.

The decision to explore Mexican archives and Spanish language sources was not a difficult one when it came to writing about nineteenth-century San Antonio. After all, Texas was both a Spanish and Mexican territory. The larger problem came in how to contextualize the sources within a larger body of history. The challenge of writing the history of nineteenth-century San Antonio was in bridging the gap between Mexican historiography and American historiography. As Mexican history, the story of San Antonio de Béxar fits in the larger narratives of Spanish frontier settlement and the incorporation of indigenous communities.[15] The Mexican narrative begins to falter in its attempt to integrate American westward expansion and conquest over the northern frontier territories.[16] This oversight extends beyond the nineteenth century by, at times, failing to include continued imperial conquest by American neocolonialism to the present.[17]

Conversely, the established American narrative struggles to address cultures and societies west of the Appalachian Mountains for the colonial period.[18] The narrative normalizes American territorial acquisition without exploring contradictions and inequalities in the process of expansion, such as those posed by indigenous claims to land. In that sense, the story of San Antonio is absent from the American narrative until Anglo-Americans appear on the scene. San Antonio enters the story in medias res, without a sense of how previous history and social development might explain subsequent events. Such myopia toward alternate ethnicities and concepts of nationalism within American borders continues to confound social and political observers.

The history of San Antonio challenges these national narratives to go beyond their "safety zone" to make room for contradictions and identities that disrupt the integrity of the national narrative. Historian Thomas Bender describes such a project of transnational history as "deprovincializing the narrative of American history."[19] He surmises, "One aim of destabilizing the nation must be to defamiliarize the stories that make up American history, thus inviting a fresh curiosity that is not prompted by the ever more refined and increasingly technical analyses of long-established themes and questions."[20] Institutional and cultural momentum makes embarking on these transnational projects difficult. While the organization of traditional academic units discourages such comparative work, larger obstacles exist to incorporating transnational research into survey courses and general history books. Part of the problem stems from how "American" and "world" histories are defined individually and against each other. The contradictions raised by the transnational approach and by the lives of those engaging in what Dipesh Chakrabarty calls "the politics of despair" have the potential to destabilize these categories by exposing their role in maintaining the social order.[21]

The destabilization of the American narrative produced by transnational history resonates with the aims of Chicano/a history and ethnic studies in general. Based on academic engagement with identity politics, ethnic studies began as a response to exclusion and marginalization in the production of knowledge. For instance, Chicanos/as demanded histories that reflected their experiences and told the story of the growth and struggles of their communities. This critique held that Chicano/a exclusion in American history supported continued economic and political exploitation while subordinating Chicano/a self-worth and identity. Both from a critical narrative perspective and because of the importance of multiple national contexts, ethnic studies and Chicano/a history in particular are largely transnational.

Areas exist where ethnic studies and transnational history can learn from each other and benefit from an expanded view. Transnational history often lacks insight into the political dimensions of identity formation, particularly from the perspective of relatively powerless people. Though its central concerns stem from incongruences in identity formation, transnational analysis quickly turns to an examination of the faults and weaknesses of national worldviews. An ethnic studies approach, however, keeps the focus on transnational communities to describe their responses to exclusion and forms of economic and cultural survival. But because of the historic connection to political struggles in the American civil rights movement, ethnic studies have labored to move beyond the disciplinary bounds of American history. Transnational history brings a comparative framework as well as the consideration of multiple national narratives to the field of ethnic studies. Recent migrations and economic shifts brought on by global politics, seen in policies such as the North American Free Trade Agreement, have popularized transnationalism while forcing ethnic studies programs to reconsider their constituency and mandate.

Both transnational history and ethnic studies seek to bring contemporary insight and relevance to the study of the past. The identity of the Mexican-origin community of San Antonio continues to evolve as economic and political conditions change. On Saturday, September 13, 2003, San Antonians once again observed Mexican Independence Day with a parade, as they had in 1835 and 1910.[22] The parade's sponsoring organization, the Avenida Guadalupe Association, estimated 100,000 people participated in all the festivities, including the parade, street carnival, and historic reenactments. The festival reflected changes in San Antonio's Mexican community as well as continuities with previous celebrations. The parade theme, "Saluting San Antonio's Heroes," echoed the sizable presence of Mexican American soldiers in the U.S. military and the military's dominance in the city's economic landscape. Organizers named Staff Sergeant Eric Alva, a Marine from San Antonio who lost his leg in the Iraq war, grand marshal. The parade's American patriotism casts a different light on the celebration of Mexican independence, in this case elevating Mexican cultural and ethnic heritage over nationalism. By the turn of the twenty-first century, Mexican-origin people made up over half of the city's population, and migrants from Mexico and Central America have continued to move to San Antonio in increasing numbers over the past twenty years. Many recent immigrants joined the military during the Iraq war while still Mexican citizens.[23] Some of those migrants who were killed in action received American citizenship posthumously.

Mexican citizens fighting in the U.S. Army and marching in the Mexican Independence Day parade held in San Antonio crisscross the political and ideological borders of nationalism several times simultaneously. Far from a static category, national identity continues to raise questions and cut across other identities, as it has for generations. Juan N. Seguín's story—fighting for Texas secession alongside Anglo-Americans seeking annexation with the United States—contains contradictions similar to Eric Alva's story. Nationalism will continue to confound and confuse our ability to understand identity and motivations. The continued dominance of national narratives requires historians and cultural critics to explore the ways these narratives limit a full and deep explanation of the meaning people give to their words and actions.

Notes

Abbreviations

AGEC   Archivo General del Estado de Coahuila, Coahuila, Mexico

AGN   Archivo General de la Nación, Mexico City, Mexico

AMSPM   Archivo Municipal de Saltillo, Ramo Presidencia Municipal,
        Saltillo, Mexico

AP   Eugene C. Barker, ed., *The Austin Papers*, vols. 1 and 2
        (Washington: Government Printing Office, 1924, 1928);
        vol. 3 (Austin: University of Texas, 1927)

BA   Béxar Archives, University of Texas, Austin

BLAC   Benson Latin American Collection, University of Texas, Austin

BMWA   Beinecke Rare Book and Manuscript Library, Western Americana,
        Yale University, New Haven, Conn.

CAHUT   Center for American History, University of Texas, Austin

PTR   John H. Jenkins, ed., *The Papers of the Texas Revolution, 1835–1836*,
        10 vols. (Austin: Presidial Press, 1973)

TSA   Texas State Archives, Austin

Introduction

1. Junta Patriotica notes, Béxar, August 22, 1835, BA.

2. José Antonio Navarro, *Defending Mexican Valor in Texas: José Antonio Navarro's Historical Writings, 1853–1857*, ed. David R. McDonald and Timothy M. Matovina (Austin: State House Press, 1995).

3. Junta Patriotica notes, Béxar, August 22, 1835, BA.

4. "Bexareño" means a person from Béxar. I will use that term to describe ethnic Mexicans from Béxar. "Tejano" means a person from Texas. That term will be used to describe people broadly from the region, not just Béxar. Béxar becomes San Antonio, Texas, after 1836, so Tejano is used more commonly after that date unless the subject uses the term as well.

5. Junta Patriotica notes, Béxar, August 22, 1835, BA.

6. On the unique history of Tlascaltecan migrants to northern Mexico, see David B. Adams, "The Tlaxcalan Colonies of Spanish Coahuila and Nuevo León: An Aspect of the Settlement of Northern Mexico" (Ph.D. diss., University of Texas, Austin, 1971).

7. T. R. Fehrenbach, *Lone Star: A History of Texas and the Texans* (New York: Collier Books, 1968), 289, 320. Fehrenbach suggests Mexicans in San Antonio never politically progressed because they lacked initiative. He also claims San Antonio didn't become an economic center until 1850, with the arrival of Germans.

8. There exists a rich social science literature on the concept of identity. For a detailed history of the academic uses of identity, see Philip Gleason, "Identifying Identity: A Semantic History," *Journal of American History* 69, no. 4 (March 1983): 910–31. For the purposes of this study, I use the term "identity" in the sense that social scientists define "social identity." See Jan E. Stets and Peter J. Burke, "Identity Theory and Social Identity Theory," *Social Psychology Quarterly* 63, no. 3 (2000): 224–27. Sociologists debate the nature of social identity as between primordial or inherited and optionalistic, where its import depends on specific situations. Gleason, "Identifying Identity," 919. This study falls on the side of the optionalists by noting that identities come and go with changing social and political circumstances. This doesn't mean that prior identities disappear but rather that they are mediated and transformed in the present.

9. George J. Sanchez, *Becoming Mexican American: Ethnicity, Culture and Identity in Chicano Los Angeles, 1900–1945* (New York: Oxford University Press, 1993), 3–14; Michael Omi and Howard Winant, *Racial Formation in the United States: From the 1960s to the 1990s* (New York: Routledge, 1994), 15.

10. My use of "nation" here is based on a cultural and ideological reading of the term rather than a strict juridical or territorial definition. See Benedict Anderson, *Imagined Communities: Reflections on the Origin and Spread of Nationalism* (New York: Verso, 1991), 17–40.

11. Eric John Hobsbawm, *Nations and Nationalism since 1780: Programme, Myth, Reality* (Cambridge: Cambridge University Press, 1992), 46–48.

12. Anderson, *Imagined Communities*, 17.

13. Omi and Winant, *Racial Formation*, 14–23.

14. Juan Mora-Torres, *The Making of the Mexican Border: The State, Capitalism, and Society in Nuevo León, 1848–1910* (Austin: University of Texas Press, 2001), 1–7.

15. Jeremy Adelman and Stephen Aron, "From Borderlands to Borders: Empires, Nation-States, and the Peoples in Between in North American History," *American Historical Review* 104, no. 3 (June 1999): 816.

16. Peter Sahlins, *Boundaries: The Making of France and Spain in the Pyrenees* (Berkeley: University of California Press, 1989), 9.

17. Ibid., 110–13.

18. Richard White, *The Middle Ground: Indians, Empires, and Republics in the Great Lakes Region, 1650–1815* (New York: Cambridge University Press, 1991), 50–60.

19. Other recent studies incorporating and modifying these approaches include James Brooks, *Captives and Cousins: Slavery, Kinship, and Community in the Southwest Borderlands* (Chapel Hill: University of North Carolina Press, 2002); Andrés Reséndez, *Changing National Identities at the Frontier: Texas and New Mexico, 1800–1850* (New York: Cambridge University Press, 2005); and Samuel Truett and Elliott Young, eds., *Continental Crossroads: Remapping U.S.-Mexico Borderlands History* (Durham: Duke University Press, 2004).

20. For a broad sweep of the development of the Chicano/a history field, see the following: Arnoldo De León, *They Called Them Greasers: Anglo Attitudes toward Mexicans in Texas, 1821–1900* (Austin: University of Texas Press, 1983); Albert Camarillo, *Chicanos in a Changing Society: From Mexican Pueblos to American Barrios in Santa Barbara and Southern California, 1848–1930* (Cambridge: Harvard University Press, 1979); David G. Gutiérrez, *Walls and Mirrors: Mexican Americans, Mexican Immigrants, and the Politics of Ethnicity* (Berkeley: University of California Press, 1995); Deena J. Gonzalez, *Refusing the Favor: The Spanish-Mexican Women of Santa Fe, 1820–1880* (New York: Oxford University Press, 1999); Ramón A. Gutiérrez, *When Jesus Came, the Corn Mothers Went Away: Marriage, Sexuality, and Power in New Mexico, 1500–1846* (Stanford: Stanford University Press, 1991); Douglas Monroy, *Thrown among Strangers: The Making of Mexican Culture in Frontier California* (Berkeley: University of California Press, 1990); Vicki L. Ruiz, *Cannery Women/Cannery Lives: Mexican Women, Unionization, and the California Food Processing Industry, 1930–1950* (Albuquerque: University of New Mexico Press, 1987); and Matt Garcia, *A World of Its Own: Race, Labor, and Citrus in the Making of Greater Los Angeles, 1900–1970* (Chapel Hill: University of North Carolina Press, 2001). For an overview of the field, see David G. Gutiérrez, "Significant to Whom? Mexican Americans and the History of the American West," *Western Historical Quarterly* 24, no. 4 (1999): 519–39; and Tomás Almaguer, "Historical Notes on Chicano Oppression: The Dialectics of Racial and Class Domination in North America," *Aztlan* 5 (Spring and Fall 1974): 27–56.

21. Sanchez, *Becoming Mexican American.*

22. Cuauhtémoc Velasco, "Historiografía de un territorio perdido," *Historias* [Mexico] 40 (1998): 21–27.

23. Ibid., 23.

Prologue

1. Letter dated January 1, 1778, in Juan Agustín de Morfi, *Diario y Derrotero, 1777–1781*, ed. Eugenio del Hoyo and Malcolm D. McLean (Monterrey: Publicaciones del Instituto Tecnológico y de Estudios Superiores de Monterrey, 1967), 215.

2. Luis Berlandier, "Diario del viage de Luis Berlandier—1828," *Registro Oficial del Gobierno de los Estados-Unidos Mexicanos*, January 26, 1831, 101.

3. Ibid.

4. For recent conceptualizations and debates over the loaded term "frontier," see the following essays: Jeremy Adelman and Stephen Aron, "From Borderlands to Borders: Empires, Nation-States, and the Peoples in Between in North American History," *American Historical Review* 104, no. 3 (June 1999): 814–41 (for critiques of Adelman and Aron, see the subsequent forum in *American Historical Review* 104, no. 4 [October 1999]: 1222–39); Samuel Truett and Elliott Young, "Introduction," in *Continental Crossroads: Remapping U.S.-Mexico Borderlands History*, ed. Samuel Truett and Elliott Young (Durham: Duke University Press, 2004), 1–33; William Cronon, Jay Gitlin, and George Miles, "Becoming West: Toward a New Meaning for Western History," in *Under Open Sky: Rethinking America's Western Past*, ed. William Cronon, Jay Gitlin, and George Miles (New York: Norton, 1992), 1–16.

5. Jesús F. de la Teja, *San Antonio de Béxar: A Community on New Spain's Northern Frontier* (Albuquerque: University of New Mexico Press, 1995), 7–8.

6. Ibid., 10–11.

7. Morfi, *Diario y Derrotero*, 216; Alicia V. Tjarks, "Comparative Demographic Analysis of Texas, 1777–1793," *Southwestern Historical Quarterly* 77 (1974): 298.

8. Peter Gerhard, *The North Frontier of New Spain* (Norman: University of Oklahoma Press, 1993), 24; Tjarks, "Comparative Demographic Analysis," 299. Tjarks also provides an excellent analysis of census estimates by contemporary and present-day writers on the region as well as ethnic data.

9. José Felix Menchaca, "Census of Individual Families," December 31, 1795, in *Residents of Texas, 1782–1836*, 3 vols. (San Antonio: University of Texas Institute of Texan Cultures, 1984), 1:193–221.

10. Nettie Lee Benson, "A Governor's Report on Texas in 1809," *Southwestern Historical Quarterly* 71 (April 1968): 611.

11. Miguel Ramos Arizpe, *Report Presented to the August Congress on the Natural, Political and Civil Condition of the Provinces of Coahuila, Nuevo León, Nuevo Santander, and Texas of the Four Eastern Interior Provinces of the Kingdom of Mexico, November 7, 1811*, ed. and trans. Nettie Lee Benson (Austin: University of Texas Press, 1950), 16.

12. J. C. Clopper, "Journal of J. C. Clopper, 1828," *Southwestern Historical Quarterly* 13 (1909): 74.

13. On New Mexico, see Deena J. Gonzalez, *Refusing the Favor: The Spanish-Mexican Women of Santa Fe, 1820–1880* (New York: Oxford University Press, 1999); Ross H. Frank, *From Settler to Citizen: New Mexican Economic Development and the Creation of Vecino Society, 1750–1820* (Berkeley: University of California Press, 2000); and Andrés Reséndez, *Changing National Identities at the Frontier: Texas and New Mexico, 1800–1850* (New York: Cambridge University Press, 2005).

14. Figures also cited in Tjarks, "Comparative Demographic Analysis," 331–37. Census reports for Texas in 1793 found in the Béxar Archives.

15. This information can be found in baptismal books 3 and 4, San Antonio de Valero, Cathedral of San Fernando, Bexar County Archives, San Antonio, Texas.

Though only a few marriage records exist, see Tjarks, "Comparative Demographic Analysis," 317.

16. The idea of a Norteño sensibility or regional character has been developed by several historians and cultural critics. Miguel Leon-Portilla, "The Norteño Variety of Mexican Culture: An Ethnohistorical Approach," in *Plural Society in the Southwest*, ed. Edward H. Spicer and Raymond H. Thompson (New York: Interbook, 1972), 77–114; José Cuello, ed., "Allende las 'borderlans' se encuentra el norte de Mexico colonial: un comentario autocritico sobre el estudio del norte de Mexico y el suroeste de los Estados Unidos por historiadores estadounidenses," in *El norte, el noreste y Saltillo en la historia colonial de Mexico* (Saltillo: Archivo Municipal de Saltillo, 1990), 15–52. Both works include environmental and geographical elements in their explanations of these differences. Americo Paredes ("El folklore de los grupos de origen mexicano en Estados Unidos," *Folklore Americano* 14 [1966]: 146–63) and other borderlands historians have also taken this approach, including the interaction with Anglo-American culture and society, in their analyses of Norteño culture. Finally, Mexican historians with a focus on region have provided insight into the peculiar history of this area. Ana Maria Alonso (*Thread of Blood: Colonialism, Revolution, and Gender on Mexico's Northern Frontier* [Tucson: University of Arizona Press, 1995]) and Hector Aguilar Camin ("The Relevant Tradition: Sonoran Leaders in the Revolution," in *Caudillo and Peasant in the Mexican Revolution*, ed. D. A. Brading [New York: Cambridge University Press, 1980], 90–114) have both inserted the Norteño culture and tradition of Sonora into larger events in Mexican history.

17. Arizpe, *Report*, 16. Also "Testimonio del Poder, e Ynstrucciones que se Dieron al Señor Doctor Don Miguel Ramos, y Arizpe como apoderado en Cortes Extraordinarias del Supremo Consejo de Regencia, dado por el Ayuntamiento Capitular de esta Villa de Saltillo, como adentro se expresa. Año de 1811," September 24, 1810, AMSPM.

18. David J. Weber, "Turner, the Boltonians, and the Spanish Borderlands," in *Myth and the History of the Hispanic Southwest*, ed. David J. Weber (Albuquerque: University of New Mexico Press, 1988), 33–54. Weber comments on the lack of a "Mexican Turner" thesis that notes the impact of this northern character on the Mexican national character.

19. James E. Crisp, "Anglo-Texan Attitudes toward the Mexican, 1821–1845" (Ph.D. diss., Yale University, 1976); Reginald Horsman, *Race and Manifest Destiny: The Origins of American Radical Anglo Saxonism* (Cambridge: Harvard University Press, 1981); David J. Weber, *The Spanish Frontier in North America* (New Haven: Yale University Press, 1992); Arnoldo De León, *They Called Them Greasers: Anglo Attitudes toward Mexicans in Texas, 1821–1900* (Austin: University of Texas Press, 1983). Referring to the Black Legend of Spanish monarchic rule of New Spain, commentators then, as now, frequently emphasized the cultural traits inhibiting independent action and local improvisation. More recently, some historians have attributed Anglo-American success in Texas to these same cultural assumptions. One notes, "The successful

movement for the independence of Texas from Mexico began long before the first public meeting of protest or the first shot was fired in anger. It came along as a part of the cultural baggage of Anglo-American immigrants . . . because *these* Americans inherited their identity as a birthright from their Revolutionary parents." Archie P. McDonald, "Lone Star on the Rise," in *Texas: A Sesquicentennial Celebration*, ed. Donald W. Whisenhunt (Austin: Eakin Press, 1984), 59–61. John Francis Bannon further develops these stereotypes, writing, "The lazy, easy going, romantic California of the padres and the rancheros they transformed most profoundly, uncovering and developing its riches, publicizing its beneficent climate and turning it to advantage for a legion of modern industries." Bannon, *The Spanish Borderlands Frontier, 1513–1821* (New York: Holt Rinehart and Winston, 1970), 232.

20. De la Teja, *San Antonio de Béxar*, 119–38.

21. Ibid., 105–7. De la Teja notes, "The same mule trains that brought flour, chocolate, and cloth into Béxar left with jerked meat, candle tallow, and hides."

22. Arizpe, *Report*, 17; Alonso, *Thread of Blood*, 16–17. Alonso places warfare at the center of Norteño ideology in her analysis of the insurgency and revolution in Chihuahua, although she criticizes those theories that emphasize environmental factors as necessarily or "naturally" producing an "ethos" or character.

23. Vito Alessio Robles, *Coahuila y Texas en la época colonial* (México City: Editorial Cultura, 1938), 613. Although Alessio Robles thought Texas separated itself from the esprit de corps found among the other three provinces, he attributes this to Texan commerce along the Louisiana border, providing it with a place to turn other than Mexico City.

24. On the colonial history of the Provincias Internas, see Edmundo O'Gorman, *Historia de las Divisiones Territoriales de Mexico* (Mexico: Editorial Porrua, 1966), 15–25. De Croix's authority excluded Nuevo Reino de León and Nuevo Santander.

25. "Testimonio del Poder," September 24, 1810, AMSPM, 3–4.

26. Arizpe, *Report*, 40.

27. Ibid., 41.

28. Ibid., 24.

29. Ibid., 23–24.

30. Ibid., 21.

31. Reséndez, *Changing National Identities*, 93–95.

32. Arizpe, *Report*, 12.

33. Ibid., 40.

34. Clopper, "Journal," 70.

Chapter One

1. Félix Almaráz, "Governor Antonio Martinez and Mexican Independence in Texas: An Orderly Transition," *Permian Historical Annual* 15 (December 1975): 45–54.

2. James E. Crisp, "José Antonio Navarro and the Problem of Powerlessness," in *Tejano Leadership in Mexican and Revolutionary Texas*, ed. Jesús F. de la Teja (College Station: Texas A&M University Press, forthcoming), n.p.

3. Navarro quote in ibid., n.p.

4. David McDonald, "Juan Martin de Veramendi: Tejano Political and Business Leader," in *Tejano Leadership in Mexican and Revolutionary Texas*, ed. Jesús F. de la Teja (College Station: Texas A&M University Press, forthcoming), n.p. For names of insurgents in 1811, see also Nemisio Salcedo to [Manuel Salcedo], October 13, 1811, BA, 49:300–302.

5. John Tutino, *From Insurrection to Revolution in Mexico: Social Bases of Agrarian Violence, 1750–1940* (Princeton: Princeton University Press, 1986), 138–64.

6. Along with Tutino, several Mexican historians put the Bajio region in perspective by looking at other regions of the national movement. For example, see Brian Hamnett, *Roots of Insurgency: Mexican Regions, 1750–1824* (New York: Cambridge University Press, 1986); Peter F. Guardino, *Peasants, Politics, and the Formation of Mexico's National State: Guerrero, 1800–1857* (Stanford: Stanford University Press, 1996); and Isidro Vizcaya Canales, *En los albores de la independencia: las Provincias Internas de Oriente durante la insurrección de don Miguel Hidalgo y Costilla, 1810–1811* (Monterrey: Instituto Tecnológico y de Estudios Superiores de Monterrey, 1976). Their work attempts to explain not only the motivations behind those seeking independence from Spain but also the reasons others did not follow. The research on regional histories attempts to understand the activities of the insurgency over its decade-long struggle. Hamnett states, "What needs to be explained is how a political entity such as New Spain managed to cohere at all." Hamnett, *Roots of Insurgency*, 2.

Nevertheless, most authors conclude their studies with an analysis explaining the resulting unified nation, not one broken up into fragments. See recent scholarship by Timothy E. Anna (*Forging Mexico: 1821–1835* [Lincoln: University of Nebraska Press, 1998]) and Florencia E. Mallon (*Peasant and Nation: The Making of Postcolonial Mexico and Peru* [Berkeley: University of California Press, 1995]). They note that the experiences of postcolonial Latin America do not fit within the modern notion of nationalism based on nation-states. The work of these historians seeks to turn nationalism into a dialogue between elite articulations of nation and peasant actions fitting under nationalism.

7. This account has been taken from Francisco Travieso's testimony in "Alta Traicion Contra.—Don Juan Baptista Casas Capitan retirado por haber alzado la vos de la insurreccion en esta San Fernando de Béxar a 22 de Enero," in *Texas in 1811: The Las Casas and Sambrano Revolutions*, ed. Frederick C. Chabot (San Antonio: Yanaguana Society, 1941), and from the narrative described in Julia Kathryn Garrett, *Green Flag over Texas: A Story of the Last Years of Spain in Texas* (New York: Cordova Press, 1939). See also Jesús F. de la Teja, "Rebellion on the Frontier," in *Tejano Journey, 1770–1850*, ed. Gerald E. Poyo (Austin: University of Texas Press, 1996), 15–30.

8. "Alta Traicion Contra. —," 59.

9. M. Salcedo to the Faithful Inhabitants of Texas, January 6, 1811, BA; Garrett, *Green Flag*, 38–39.

10. For the insurgency in the northeast, see Vizcaya Canales, *En los albores de la independencia*; and Vito Alessio Robles, *Coahuila y Texas en la época colonial* (México City: Editorial Cultura, 1938), 42–45. Specifically on San Luis Potosi, see analysis in Tutino, *Insurrection*, 151–64.

11. De la Teja, "Rebellion," 19.

12. Garrett, *Green Flag*, 73; de la Teja, "Rebellion," 17–19.

13. De la Teja, "Rebellion," 19.

14. "Diligencias seguidas en averiguacion de unas voces que oyeron, como principio de revolucion," Miguel Diaz de Luna, San Fernando de Béxar, December 19, 1810, BA. Surprisingly, one of the people interviewed by Luna regarding the disturbance was Juan Bautista de las Casas.

15. "Fieles Habitantes de la Prova. de Texas," Manuel de Salcedo, Béxar, January 6, 1811, BA. See also Félix Almaráz, *Tragic Cavalier: Governor Manuel Salcedo of Texas, 1808–1813* (Austin: University of Texas Press, 1971), 115.

16. "Fieles Habitantes de la Prova. de Texas," Manuel de Salcedo, Béxar, January 6, 1811, BA.

17. The *audencia* in Guadalajara rejected the choice of Salcedo and required another election, this time of a local person. De la Teja, "Rebellion," 18.

18. "Fieles Habitantes de la Prova. de Texas," Manuel de Salcedo, Béxar, January 6, 1811, BA.

19. Diana Balmori, Stuart F. Voss, and Miles Wortman, *Notable Family Networks in Latin America* (Chicago: University of Chicago Press, 1984), 4.

20. Frederick C. Chabot, *With the Makers of San Antonio* (San Antonio: Artes Graficas, 1937), 202–3.

21. See, for instance, the classic Oscar Lewis, *The Children of Sanchez: Autobiography of a Mexican Family* (New York: Vintage Books, 1961); and William B. Taylor, *Drinking, Homicide and Rebellion in a Mexican Village* (Palo Alto: Stanford University Press, 1979), as examples of the genre.

22. Balmori, Voss, and Wortman, *Notable Family Networks*, 2.

23. Ibid., 6.

24. Ibid., 8.

25. Mark Wasserman points to the ranching, banking, and manufacturing empire of the Terrazas-Creel families in *Capitalists, Caciques and Revolution: The Native Elite and Foreign Enterprise in Chihuahua, Mexico, 1854–1911* (Chapel Hill: University of North Carolina Press, 1984); and Alex M. Saragoza looks at the breweries and steel mills of the Monterrey Group, including the Garza-Sadas, in *The Monterrey Elite and the Mexican State, 1880–1940* (Austin: University of Texas Press, 1988). See also Stuart F. Voss, *On the Periphery of Nineteenth-Century Mexico: Sonora and Sinaloa, 1810–1877* (Tucson: University of Arizona Press, 1982).

26. Becerra de Seguín to Seguín, October 18, 1824, BA.

27. The remaining discussion of the 1813 rebellion comes from Garrett and de la Teja unless otherwise noted.

28. Garrett, *Green Flag*, 184.

29. "Informe del comandante del Ejercito Republicano del Norte de Mexico y director de la revolucion en las provincias internas de oriente," José Alvarez de Toledo, New Orleans, February 10, 1815, Hernandez y Davalos Manuscript Collection, BLAC. Toledo comments on the disorder and chaos among the insurgent ranks and places the blame on Gutiérrez's ambition.

30. Bernardo Gutiérrez de Lara, "To the Mexican Congress," in *The Papers of Mirabeau Buonaparte Lamar*, ed. Texas State Library (Austin: A. C. Baldwin, 1921–27), 1:9.

31. Ibid., 11.

32. Ibid., 16.

33. "Fieles Habitantes de esta Capital," Governor Manuel Salcedo, Béxar, August 18, 1812, BA.

34. Timothy M. Matovina, *Tejano Religion and Ethnicity: San Antonio, 1821–1860* (Austin: University of Texas Press, 1995), 17.

35. Almaráz, *Tragic Cavalier*, 163.

36. Garrett, *Green Flag*, 183. Of the two Americans, Masscott and Hale, Garrett notes that Shaler identified Masscott as French.

37. Ibid., 223. Garrett suggests that Toledo's reorganization of the troops into separate companies, one Anglo and the other Mexican and Indian, led to their defeat, in contrast to their victory as a united company at the battle of Alazan.

38. "Relacion de las Casas de Piedra y Paja, Labores y Ranchos qe. tenian los Ynsurgentes qe. salieron fugitivos de esta Capital," José Antonio Saucedo and Luis Galán to Governor Cristóbal Dominguez, Béxar, September 24, 1813, AGEC, fondo colonial (hereafter FC), c.27, e.54.

39. Dennis Glenn Medina, "El Jacalito: History and Images of the Jacal House Type in Texas" (M.A. thesis, University of Texas, Austin, 1997).

40. Eric Van Young has found similar economic figures in his analysis of Mexican insurgents. Van Young notes that 34 percent of those participating were white-collar or skilled laborers, while 66 percent were small merchants, other laborers, and farmers. "La otra rebelion: Un perfil de la insurgencia popular en Mexico, 1810–1815," in *Los ejes de la disputa. Movimientos sociales Y actores colectivos en American Latina, siglo xix*, ed. Antonio Escobar Ohmstede and Romana Falcon (Madrid: AHILA-Iberoamericana-Vervuert, 2002), 25–55.

41. Arredondo to Dominguez, October 10, 1813, BA. See also de la Teja, "Rebellion," 23–24.

42. Summary judgment, Monterrey, October 29, 1814, BA.

43. "Suplicaciones al alcalde D. Antonio Martinez, le restituyan las propiedades que le confiscaron al huir a la frontera Anglo-Americana el año de 1813, cuando el

Brigadier d. Joaquin de Arredondo reconquisto la capital," Béxar, August 3, 1820, AGEC, FC, c.36, e.17.

44. Arredondo, Monterrey, February 29, 1815, AMSPM, c61/1, e66.

45. "Sumario Ynformacion sobre la conducta que observo en el tiempo de la Revolucion el Paizano Pedro Procela, alias Pedro Chino, que ha benido a acorerse al Yndulto," Béxar, August 27, 1817, AGEC, FC, c.32, e.41. This document contains an explanation of the actions of Procelas, a farmer from Nacogdoches, during the revolt.

46. "Moradores de estas quatro provincias de oriente . . ." Monterrey, February 12, 1821, BA 2:523; Arredondo, Monterrey, March 13, 1821, BA.

47. Reservado, Arredondo to Viceroy Venadito, February 9, 1821, AGN transcripts, CAHUT, PI, V.251, p. 222.

48. Varela to Arredondo, Béxar, May 22, 1814, BA.

49. Ayuntamiento to Varela, Béxar, February 1, 1816, BA.

50. Reservado, Arredondo to Viceroy Venadito, February 9, 1821, AGN transcripts, CAHUT, PI, V.251, 222.

51. "Sumario . . . Pedro Procela," Béxar, August 27, 1817, AGEC, FC, c.32, e.41.

52. Reservado, Arredondo to Viceroy Venadito, February 9, 1821, AGN transcripts, CAHUT, PI, V.251, 222.

53. Béxar, May 4, 1814, BA.

54. Letter to Brigadier General Gaspar Lopez, Béxar, March 23, 1823, AMSPM.

55. Sometimes spelled Veramendi.

56. Robert H. Jackson, *Race, Caste, and Status: Indians in Colonial Spanish America* (Albuquerque: University of New Mexico Press, 1999).

57. Ann Twinam, *Public Lives, Private Secrets: Gender, Honor, Sexuality, and Illegitimacy in Colonial Spanish America* (Palo Alto: Stanford University Press, 1999).

58. Ibid., 43.

59. Ibid., 44–45.

60. Court proceedings, June 28, 1824, Béxar, BA.

61. Chabot, *With the Makers*, 32–33.

62. Court proceedings, June 28, 1824, Béxar, BA.

63. Twinam, *Public Lives*, 44.

Chapter Two

1. José Francisco Ruiz, *Report of observations and additional information about Indians living in the Department of Texas*, 1828, in *Report on the Indian Tribes of Texas in 1828*, ed. John Canfield Ewers (New Haven: Yale University Library, 1972), 7.

2. Historian Juliana Barr explains the codes and rituals of honor and masculinity in her recent work on Spanish/Indian relations in eighteenth-century Texas, *Peace Came in the Form of a Woman: Indians and Spaniards in the Texas Borderlands* (Chapel Hill: University of North Carolina Press, 2007), 207–46.

3. See John Canfield Ewers, introduction, in *Report on the Indian Tribes of Texas in 1828*, ed. John Canfield Ewers (New Haven: Yale University Library, 1972), 1.

4. "Sumaria contra los yndividuos que se hallan en lo interior de esta provincia . . . ," Don Feliciano Ramirez, Jues Fiscal, La Bahía, October 1814, BA.

5. Many books describe Indian violence on the frontier. See Rupert Norval Richardson, *The Comanche Barrier to South Plains Settlement: A Century and a Half of Savage Resistance to the Advancing White Frontier* (Glendale: Arthur H. Clark Company, 1933); and Mildred P. Mayhall, *Indian Wars of Texas* (Waco: Texian Press, 1965).

6. A more appropriate approach would use the terms "indigenous" instead of "Indian" and "group" instead of "tribe" or "nation" since "Indian" and "tribe" change meaning in different uses and contexts.

7. One major distinction between America and Mexico, though, is the infrequent use of a mixed-race category, such as mulatto, in the United States. Mexico developed a major mixed category in mestizo. For the lack of the use of "mulatto" in the United States, see Bruce R. Dain, *A Hideous Monster of the Mind: American Race Theory in the Early Republic* (Cambridge: Harvard University Press, 2003).

8. Alvar Nuñez Cabeza de Vaca, *The Account: Alvar Nuñez Cabeza de Vaca's Relacion*, annotated and trans. Martin A. Favata and José B. Fernandez (Houston: Arte Publico Press, 1993); Donald Chipman, "In Search of Cabeza de Vaca's Route across Texas: An Historiographical Survey," *Southwestern Historical Quarterly* 91, no. 2 (1987).

9. Curtis Marez lays out the intricate, decentered place of indigenous identity in Mexican identity in his article "Signifying Spain, Becoming Comanche, Making Mexicans: Indian Captivity and the History of Chicana/o Popular Performance," *American Quarterly* 53, no. 2 (June 2001): 267–307.

10. Ana Maria Alonso, *Thread of Blood: Colonialism, Revolution, and Gender on Mexico's Northern Frontier* (Tucson: University of Arizona Press, 1995), 7–9.

11. Raúl A. Ramos, "Finding the Balance: Béxar in Mexican/Indian Relations," in *Continental Crossroads: Remapping U.S.-Mexico Borderlands History*, ed. Samuel Truett and Elliott Young (Durham: Duke University Press, 2004), 35–65.

12. José María Cortés y de Olarte and Elizabeth Ann Harper John, *Views from the Apache Frontier: Report on the Northern Provinces of New Spain* (Norman: University of Oklahoma Press, 1989), 34.

13. Elizabeth A. H. John, *Storms Brewed in Other Men's Worlds: The Confrontation of Indians, Spanish, and French in the Southwest, 1540–1795* (College Station: Texas A&M University Press, 1975), provides one of the best histories of Indian relations but covers mostly the eighteenth century and areas west of Texas. William W. Newcomb, *The Indians of Texas: From Prehistoric to Modern Times* (Austin: University of Texas Press, 1961), presents the most comprehensive treatment of Texas Indians but concentrates on their tribal histories with only one brief chapter on the relations Indians carried out with European colonists. Edward H. Spicer, *Cycles of Conquest:*

The Impact of Spain, Mexico, and the United States on the Indians of the Southwest, 1533–1960 (Tucson: University of Arizona Press, 1962), also covers the period in his overview of both Mexican and American Indian policies. Historians of Mexico have touched on the subject more often, such as Cuauhtémoc Velasco Avila, "Historiografía de una frontera amenazada. Los ataques comanches y apaches en el siglo XIX," in *Indio, Nacion y Comunidad en el México del Siglo XIX*, ed. Antonio Escobar Ohmstede and Patricia Lagos Preisser (Mexico: Centro de Estudios Mexicanos y Centroamericanos/Centro de Investigaciones y Estudios Superiores en Antropologia Social, 1993); and David B. Adams, "Embattled Borderlands: Northern Nuevo León and the Indios Bárbaros, 1686–1870," *Southwestern Historical Quarterly* 95 (1991): 205–20. Ramón A. Gutiérrez, *When Jesus Came, the Corn Mothers Went Away: Marriage, Sexuality, and Power in New Mexico, 1500–1846* (Stanford: Stanford University Press, 1991).

14. Spicer, *Cycles*, 16.

15. Cecilia Sheridan, *Anónimos y desterrados: la contienda por el "sitio que llaman de Quauyla", siglos XVI–XVIII* (Mexico: CIESAS, 2000), 353.

16. Eric R. Wolf, *Sons of the Shaking Earth* (Chicago: University of Chicago Press, 1959); David J. Weber, *The Spanish Frontier in North America* (New Haven: Yale University Press, 1992).

17. Vito Alessio Robles, *Coahuila y Texas en la época colonial* (México City: Editorial Cultura, 1938), 422–23.

18. The *encomienda*, or labor tax on the indigenous people, existed in other parts of the northern regions, especially New Mexico. But it never took hold in Texas.

19. Sheridan, *Anónimos*, 7.

20. See Hatcher's translation of Juan Antonio Padilla's "Report on the Barbarous Indians of the Province of Texas" in Mattie Austin Hatcher, trans., "Texas in 1820," *Southwestern Historical Quarterly* 23 (July 1919): 47.

21. Ibid., 47.

22. Ibid.

23. David J. Weber, "American Westward Expansion and the Breakdown of Relations between Pobladores and 'Indios Barbaros' on Mexico's Far Northern Frontier, 1821–1846," in *Myth and the History of the Hispanic Southwest*, ed. David J. Weber (Albuquerque: University of New Mexico Press, 1988).

24. To get a sense for the networks and scope of the Comanche sphere of influence, see Pekka Håmålåinen, "The Western Comanche Trade Center: Rethinking the Plains Indian Trade System," *Western Historical Quarterly* 29 (Winter 1998): 485–513. Brian DeLay has taken this observation further by reconstructing Comanche attacks in Texas to make the case for their impact and influence on historical events in Texas in the mid-nineteenth century. Brian DeLay, "Independent Indians and the U.S.-Mexican War," *American Historical Review* 112, no. 1 (2007): 40–48, and "The Wider World of the Handsome Man: Southern Plains Indians Invade Mexico, 1830–1848," *Journal of the Early Republic* 27, no. 1 (2007): 83–113.

25. *Gaceta del Gobierno Imperial de Mexico*, January 30, 1823, 1:14, 51, BLAC; Thomas W. Kavanagh, *Comanche Political History: An Ethnohistorical Perspective, 1706–1875* (Lincoln: University of Nebraska Press in cooperation with the American Indian Studies Research Institute, Indiana University, Bloomington, 1996), 195–99; James Brooks, *Captives and Cousins: Slavery, Kinship, and Community in the Southwest Borderlands* (Chapel Hill: University of North Carolina Press, 2002), 183–84. "Pisinampe" is Kavanagh's spelling.

26. *Gaceta del Gobierno Imperial de Mexico*, January 30, 1823, 1:14, 52, BLAC.

27. Ibid.

28. The fact that some captives would choose not to return raises the interesting issues regarding acculturation into indigenous life. James Brooks describes those captives as cultural bridges between Spanish/Mexican society and indigenous societies in *Captives and Cousins*, 35–36, and in "'This Evil Extends Especially to the Feminine Sex': Captivity and Identity in New Mexico, 1700–1846," in *Writing the Range: Race, Class, and Culture in the Women's West*, ed. Elizabeth Jameson and Susan Armitage (Norman: University of Oklahoma Press, 1997), 97–121.

29. *Gaceta del Gobierno Imperial de Mexico*, January 30, 1823, 1:14, 52, BLAC. My emphasis.

30. Ibid.

31. For discussions on Mexican liberalism, see Charles A. Hale, *Mexican Liberalism in the Age of Mora, 1821–1853* (New Haven: Yale University Press, 1968).

32. Felipe de la Garza to Colonel D. José Felix Tres Palacios, October 11, 1823, BMWA.

33. Håmålåinen, "Western Comanche Trade Center," 507–8.

34. Robert H. Jackson, *Race, Caste, and Status: Indians in Colonial Spanish America* (Albuquerque: University of New Mexico Press, 1999), 51–52.

35. For further discussions of *casta*, see Susan Kellogg, "Depicting Mestizaje: Gendered Images of Ethnorace in Colonial Mexican Texts," *Journal of Women's History* 12, no. 3 (2000): 69–92; Patricia Seed, "Social Dimensions of Race: Mexico City, 1753," *Hispanic American Historical Review* 62, no. 4 (1982): 569–606; Ross Frank, "'They Conceal a Malice Most Refined': Controlling Social and Ethnic Mobility in Late Colonial New Mexico," in *Choice, Persuasion, and Coercion: Social Control on Spain's North American Frontiers*, ed. Jesús F. de la Teja and Ross Frank (Albuquerque: University of New Mexico Press, 2005), 77–94; and Gerald E. Poyo, "Social Identity on the Hispanic Texas Frontier," in *Recovering the U.S. Hispanic Literary Heritage*, vol. 3, ed. Maria Herrera-Sobek and Virginia Sanchez Korrol (Houston: Arte Publico Press, 2000), 384–401.

36. R. Jackson, *Race*, 97.

37. For a discussion of *calidad* in New Mexico from 1964 to 1846, see Gutiérrez, *When Jesus Came*, 193–206. Gutiérrez notes that usage of these classifications fell out of the marriage records beginning in 1799. He concludes, "A person's social status — calidad — was a summation of various measures of social worth within the com-

munity: religion, race, ethnicity, legitimacy, occupation, and ownership of land" (205).

38. Here I emphasize the importance of racial practices in defining race. For discussion on race practices, see David Montejano, *Anglos and Mexicans in the Making of Texas, 1836–1986* (Austin: University of Texas Press, 1987), 4–7; and Marez, "Signifying Spain," 297.

39. *Residents of Texas, 1782–1836*, 3 vols. (San Antonio: University of Texas Institute of Texan Cultures, 1984), 2:153–84.

40. Martha Menchaca, *Recovering History, Constructing Race: The Indian, Black, and White Roots of Mexican Americans* (Austin: University of Texas Press, 2001), 111–12.

41. Jesús F. de la Teja, *San Antonio de Béxar: A Community on New Spain's Northern Frontier* (Albuquerque: University of New Mexico Press, 1995), 28.

42. R. Jackson, *Race*, 104.

43. Menchaca, *Recovering History*, 110–12.

44. Juan Agustín de Morfi, *Viaje de indios y diario del Nuevo Mexico* (Mexico: Manuel Porrua, 1980), 351.

45. See chapter 1 for a discussion of a *limpieza de sangre* case. Court proceedings, June 28, 1824, Béxar, BA.

46. Carlos Eduardo Castañeda, *Our Catholic Heritage in Texas, 1519–1936*, vol. 5 (New York: Arno Press, 1976), 40; Félix D. Almaráz, "San Antonio's Old Franciscan Missions: Material Decline and Secular Avarice in the Transition from Hispanic to Mexican Control," *The Americas* 44, no. 1 (July 1987): 1; Jesús F. de la Teja, "Indians, Soldiers, and Canary Islanders: The Making of a Texas Frontier Community," *Locus* 3, no. 1 (Fall 1990): 81.

47. Félix D. Almaráz, *The San Antonio Missions and Their System of Land Tenure* (Austin: University of Texas Press, 1989), 3–4.

48. Almaráz, "San Antonio's Old Franciscan Missions," 2.

49. Almaráz, *San Antonio Missions*, 2–7.

50. Cynthia Radding, *Wandering Peoples: Colonialism, Ethnic Spaces, and Ecological Frontiers in Northwestern Mexico, 1700–1850* (Durham: Duke University Press, 1997).

51. Donald Worster, *Rivers of Empire: Water, Aridity, and the Growth of the American West* (New York: Pantheon Books, 1985), 88–92.

52. Béxar, November 12, 1826, BA.

53. Almaráz, *San Antonio Missions*, 17–18, 38–40, 50–52.

54. Weber, *Spanish Frontier*, 306.

55. Gilberto M. Hinojosa and Anne A. Fox, "Indians and Their Culture in San Fernando de Béxar," in *Tejano Origins in Eighteenth-Century San Antonio*, ed. Gerald Eugene Poyo and Gilberto Miguel Hinojosa (Austin: Published by the University of Texas Press for the University of Texas Institute of Texan Cultures at San Antonio, 1991), 119.

56. "General Census Report of the City of Béxar and Its Missions: Barrios Valero, Sur, Norte, Laredo, Jan. 1, 1820," in *Residents of Texas, 1782–1836*, 2:153–84.

57. While more work remains to be done on Indian identification in the late colonial/early national period, Lisbeth Haas describes the continuity of a new identity as mission Indians lasting into the twentieth century among the people of San Juan mission in Orange County in *Conquests and Historical Identities in California, 1769–1936* (Berkeley: University of California Press, 1995).

58. Sheridan and Radding both use the concept of ethnogenesis to describe the complex process of ethnic identity category development throughout the colonial period.

59. Almáraz, *San Antonio Missions*, 39.

60. Antonio Cordero to Nemisio Salcedo, Béxar, October 30, 1807, BA Translations, v.30, 139.

61. Dianna Everett, *The Texas Cherokees: A People between Two Fires, 1819–1840* (Norman: University of Oklahoma Press, 1990), 5, 57. Everett goes into detail about the relations between Mexico and the Texas Cherokees, particularly explaining the Cherokee perspective on their actions.

62. Ibid., 11.

63. Ibid., 73, notes the Cherokees carried this sort of policy in their negotiations with the Republic of Texas in 1836, calling the groups "associated bands."

64. Letter from Peter Ellis Bean to General Manuel de Mier y Terán, July 11, 1828, from AGN, Guerra y Marina, transcribed, AGN transcripts, CAHUT, V.329, 303–6.

65. Letter from Bean, 303. The political chief, or diplomacy chief, was most probably Gatunwali ("Hard Mush"), as noted in Everett, *Texas Cherokees*, 57.

66. Everett, *Texas Cherokees*, 60, notes the Cherokees often fought against the Tawankawas and Wacos.

67. Letter from Bean, 305.

68. Ibid.

69. March 15, 1827, BA.

70. Dickson to Clay, Béxar, July 1, 1827, Dispatches from U.S. Consuls in Texas, 1825–1844, National Archives—Department of State, Washington, D.C.

71. Cortés y de Olarte and John, *Views from the Apache Frontier*, 7.

72. Padilla, "Report," 53–54.

73. Robert S. Weddle, *The San Sabá Mission: Spanish Pivot in Texas* (Austin: University of Texas Press, 1964). In 1758, Comanches burned down the mission and killed several missionaries and Apaches living there. The attack has mainly been attributed to Apache-Comanche conflict. Those Apaches living in the mission were thought to be seeking Spanish protection from Comanche attacks. More recently, Juliana Barr places Apaches in the larger context of eighteenth-century Texas in *Peace Came*, 159–96.

74. Luis Aboites Aguilar, "Poblamiento y Estado en Mexico, 1830–1835," in *Indio, Nacion y Comunidad en el México del Siglo XIX*, ed. Antonio Escobar Ohmstede and

Patricia Lagos Preisser (Mexico: Centro de Estudios Mexicanos y Centroamericanos/ Centro de Investigaciones y Estudios Superiores en Antropologia Social, 1993), 303–13.

75. October 4, 1825, August 22, 1825, BA.

76. November 11, 1825, BA.

77. February 13, 21, 1824, April 21, 1825, BA.

78. Elizabeth A. H. John, "Nurturing the Peace: Spanish and Comanche Cooperation in the Early Nineteenth Century," *New Mexico Historical Review* 59, no. 4 (1984): 363–64; Nemisio Salcedo to Governador Interino de Texas (Simon Herrera), Chihuahua, September 17, 1811, BA.

79. Salcedo to Herrera, BA.

80. John, "Nurturing the Peace," 347.

81. Elizabeth A. H. John, "Independent Indians and the San Antonio Community," in *Tejano Origins in Eighteenth-Century San Antonio*, ed. Gerald E. Poyo and Gilberto M. Hinojosa (Austin: Published by the University of Texas Press for the University of Texas Institute of Texan Cultures at San Antonio, 1991), 126.

82. John, "Nurturing the Peace," 351.

83. Simon Herrera, Béxar, December 15, 1811, BA.

84. John, "Nurturing the Peace," 364–65.

85. Ibid.

86. Brooks, *Captives and Cousins*, 186. Historian Juliana Barr has also examined the enslavement of Comanche women in the eighteenth century. Juliana Barr, "From Captives to Slaves: Commodifying Indian Women in the Borderlands," *Journal of American History* 92 (2005): 3.

87. Radding refers to this as ethnogenesis. Radding, *Wandering Peoples*, 8.

88. Menchaca, *Recovering History*, 113.

89. John Davidson, "Coahuiltecans," *San Antonio Express News*, April 1, 2001, p. 1H.

90. Weber, "American Westward Expansion."

91. DeLay, "Independent Indians," 48–68.

Chapter Three

1. Quoted in Eugene C. Barker, "Native Latin American Contribution to the Colonization and Independence of Texas," *Southwestern Historical Quarterly* 46 (1943): 318; *AP*, vol. 3, May 9, 1833.

2. Arnoldo De León and Kenneth L. Stewart, *Tejanos and the Numbers Game: A Socio-Historical Interpretation from the Federal Censuses, 1850–1900* (Albuquerque: University of New Mexico Press, 1989), 1–5.

3. For a brief overview of these two strains in American immigration history, see George J. Sanchez, *Becoming Mexican American: Ethnicity, Culture and Identity in Chicano Los Angeles, 1900–1945* (New York: Oxford University Press, 1993), 2–14.

4. This chapter uses "Anglo-Americans" to refer to American immigrants. Tejanos used this term in documents from the nineteenth century. While not all immigrants were Anglo-Saxons, the use of "Anglo" before "American" also highlights the need to think of them as ethnics in Mexico.

5. Juan Mora-Torres suggests the Mexican state did not consolidate power over the frontier regions until 1867 in *The Making of the Mexican Border: The State, Capitalism, and Society in Nuevo León, 1848–1910* (Austin: University of Texas Press, 2002), 52–84.

6. Daniel K. Richter, "Cultural Brokers and Intercultural Politics: New York–Iroquois Relations, 1664–1701," *Journal of American History* 75 (June 1988): 40–67; Richard White, *The Middle Ground: Indians, Empires, and Republics in the Great Lakes Region, 1650–1815* (New York: Cambridge University Press, 1991); Margret Szasz, *Between Indian and White Words: The Cultural Broker* (Norman: University of Oklahoma Press, 1994); Frances E. Karttunen, *Between Worlds: Interpreters, Guides, and Survivors* (New Brunswick, N.J.: Rutgers University Press, 1994), 165–69.

7. Eric Wolf, "Aspects of Group Relations in a Complex Society: Mexico," *American Anthropologist*, n.s., 58, no. 6 (December 1956): 1075.

8. Jacqueline Peterson, "Many Roads to Red River: Métis Genesis in the Great Lakes Region, 1680–1815," in *The New Peoples: Being and Becoming Métis in North America*, ed. Jacqueline Peterson and Jennifer S. H. Brown (Lincoln: University of Nebraska Press, 1985), 37–72.

9. Governor Martinez to Trudeau, Béxar, February 26, 1821, *AP* 1:382, which commissioned Erasmo Seguín to inform Moses Austin of his land grant.

10. Barker, "Native Latin American Contribution"; Jesús F. de la Teja, "The Colonization and Independence of Texas: A Tejano Perspective," in *Myths, Misdeeds, and Misunderstandings: The Roots of Conflict in U.S.-Mexico Relations*, ed. Jaime E. Rodríguez O. and Kathryn Vincent (Wilmington: SR Books, 1997), 79–95; Le Roy P. Graf, "Colonizing Projects in Texas South of the Nueces, 1820–1845," *Southwestern Historical Quarterly* 50 (April 1947): 431–48. De la Teja suggests Tejanos sought to elevate the importance of the state in the nation through colonization.

11. Mattie Austin Hatcher, *The Opening of Texas to Foreign Settlement, 1801–1821* (Austin: University of Texas Press, 1927), 44–59.

12. Official communications from Don Antonio Martinez, governor of Texas, to Moses Austin, Béxar, February 8, 1821, reprinted in H. P. N. Gammel, *The Laws of Texas 1822–1897* (Austin: Gammel Book Co., 1898), 1:25–27.

13. One *labor* equals approximately 177 acres and one *sitio* approximately 4,400 acres.

14. Martinez to Austin, *Laws of Texas*, 26.

15. Several questions remain unanswered regarding the origins of Anglo-American colonization. Why didn't Mexicans migrate northward? Why did Mexicans accept Anglo-Americans even though their policy aimed to stop American expansion? Answers to these questions are mostly speculative at this time.

16. Josefina Zoraida Vázquez and Lorenzo Mayer, *Mexico frente a Estados Unidos: Un ensayo historico 1776-1988* (Mexico: Fondo de Cultura Economica, 1989), 41-43.

17. Colonization Law of the State of Coahuila and Texas, Saltillo, March 24, 1825, reprinted in H. P. N. Gammel, *The Laws of Texas 1822-1897* (Austin: Gammel Book Co., 1898), 1:41.

18. James E. Crisp, "Anglo-Texan Attitudes toward the Mexican, 1821-1845" (Ph.D. diss., Yale University, 1976), 4-15.

19. Ibid., 3-6. Crisp singles out criticism of Eugene Barker's reliance on cultural differences as the root cause of the Texas Revolution.

20. Ibid., 12-20.

21. Letter from Peter Ellis Bean to General Manuel de Mier y Terán, July 11, 1828, from AGN, Guerra y Marina, transcribed, AGN transcripts, CAHUT, V.329, 303-6.

22. Bernard W. Sheehan, *Seeds of Extinction: Jeffersonian Philanthropy and the American Indian* (New York: W. W. Norton, 1973), 97-101.

23. For Southern suspicions of Northern limits on slavery and expansion, see Eugene Genovese, "Origins of Slavery Expansionism," in *The Causes of the American Civil War*, ed. Edwin Charles Rozwenc (Lexington, Mass.: Heath, 1972).

24. Mark E. Nackman, "Anglo-American Migrants to the West: Men of Broken Fortunes? The Case of Texas, 1821-46," *Western Historical Quarterly* 5 (1974): 445-48.

25. Reginald Horseman, *Race and Manifest Destiny: The Origins of American Racial Anglo-Saxonism* (Cambridge: Harvard University Press, 1981).

26. Andreas Reichstein, *Rise of the Lone Star: The Making of Texas* (College Station: Texas A&M University Press, 1989), 16-19, 23-24.

27. Bertram Wyatt-Brown, *The Shaping of Southern Culture: Honor, Grace, and War, 1760s-1890s* (Chapel Hill: University of North Carolina Press, 2001), 35-38, 56-63.

28. Slave sale from Luisa Gertrudis to V. Blanco, May 20, 1820, BA. Other mentions of Tejano slave ownership appear scattered throughout the Béxar Archives; see July 8, 1807 and July 15, 1820, BA.

29. From the January 1, 1820, census in *Residents of Texas, 1782-1836*, 3 vols. (San Antonio: University of Texas Institute of Texan Cultures, 1984), 2:167.

30. Ibid., 162, 167.

31. Manuel Yturri Castillo, Certification of Emancipation for María Rosa de la Rosa, Béxar, July 19, 1823, BA.

32. Governor José Felix Trespalacios, Certificate of Emancipation for Phil, Béxar, January 8, 1823, BA.

33. Several historians have developed a variety of definitions and manifestations of honor in the borderlands. See Ramón A. Gutiérrez, *When Jesus Came, the Corn Mothers Went Away: Marriage, Sexuality, and Power in New Mexico, 1500-1846* (Stanford: Stanford University Press, 1991); Ana Maria Alonso, *Thread of Blood: Colonialism, Revolution, and Gender on Mexico's Northern Frontier* (Tucson: University of Arizona Press, 1995); James Brooks, *Captives and Cousins: Slavery, Kinship, and Com-*

munity in the Southwest Borderlands (Chapel Hill: University of North Carolina Press, 2002); and Juliana Barr, *Peace Came in the Form of a Woman: Indians and Spaniards in the Texas Borderlands* (Chapel Hill: University of North Carolina Press, 2007).

34. Navarro to Austin, *AP*, 2:147.

35. Andrés Reséndez, *Changing National Identities at the Frontier: Texas and New Mexico, 1800–1850* (New York: Cambridge University Press, 2005), 100.

36. Discussions of the colonization process can be found in David J. Weber, *The Mexican Frontier, 1821–1846* (Albuquerque: University of New Mexico Press, 1982), 158–78; Mary Virginia Henderson, "Minor Empresario Contracts for the Colonization of Texas, 1825–1834," *Southwestern Historical Quarterly* 31, no. 4 (1928): 301; and Eugene C. Barker, "Native Latin American Contribution."

37. Historians of Mexico have explored many dimensions of Mexican nationalism during this period. For a concise overview, see Alan Knight, "Peasants into Patriots: Thoughts on the Making of the Mexican Nation," *Mexican Studies—Estudios Mexicanos* 10, no. 1 (1994): 135–61.

38. Frederick C. Chabot, *With the Makers of San Antonio* (San Antonio: Artes Graficas, 1937).

39. *Handbook of Texas Online*, "Juan Martín de Veramendi," <http://www.tsha .utexas.edu/handbook/online/articles/VV/fve6.html> (accessed September 6, 2005).

40. Jack Jackson, *Indian Agent: Peter Ellis Bean in Mexican Texas* (College Station: Texas A&M University Press, 2005), 6–11.

41. Ibid., 55, 99. Jackson notes that Bean never divorced his first wife from Tennessee and continued to represent himself as married to her when in Texas. He became widely known as a bigamist. Bean also kept his Mexican army officer status through the war in 1835.

42. Martha Menchaca, *Recovering History, Constructing Race: The Indian, Black, and White Roots of Mexican Americans* (Austin: University of Texas Press, 2001), 36–42.

43. Reséndez, *Changing National Identities*, 61–70.

44. *Handbook of Texas Online*, "Juan José María Erasmo Seguín," <http://www .tsha.utexas.edu/handbook/online/articles/SS/fse7.html> (accessed September 6, 2005).

45. Erasmo Seguín to Governor Martinez, August 10, 1821, *AP*, 1:406.

46. Born in Dutch Guiana, Bastrop lived in Spanish Louisiana and moved to Béxar in 1806. He was appointed to the Ayuntamiento of Béxar in 1810. Bastrop also played an important role in securing Moses Austin's contract. *Handbook of Texas Online*, "Baron de Bastrop," <http://www.tsha.utexas.edu/handbook/online/articles/ BB/fbaae.html> (accessed September 6, 2005).

47. Seguín to Austin, Béxar, August 30, 1821, *AP*, 1:411.

48. Becerra to Austin, Béxar, April 20, 1824, *AP*, 1:767, and September 20, 1824, 1:899.

49. Becerra to Austin, September 20, 1824, *AP*, 1:899.

50. Gregg Cantrell, *Stephen F. Austin: Empresario of Texas* (New Haven: Yale University Press, 1999), 159–62.

51. "General Census Report of the City of Béxar and Its Missions, January 1, 1820," in *Residents of Texas, 1782–1836*, 1:167.

52. Seguín to Austin and Bastrop, Mexico, January 14, 1824, *AP*, 1:723.

53. Seguín to Bastrop, Mexico, March 24, 1824, *AP*, 1:757.

54. See Padilla's "Report on the Barbarous Indians of the Province of Texas" in Mattie Austin Hatcher, trans., "Texas in 1820," *Southwestern Historical Quarterly* 23 (July 1919).

55. *Handbook of Texas Online*, "Juan Antonio Padilla," <http://www.tsha.utexas .edu/handbook/online/articles/PP/fpa6.html> (accessed September 6, 2005).

56. Padilla to governor of Coahuila y Texas, Saltillo, August 21, 1826, BMWA.

57. Ibid., May 11, 1826.

58. Arizpe to secretary de Estado y Relaciones, Saltillo, February 12, 1827, BMWA.

59. Cameron to governor of Coahuila y Texas, Leona Vicario, August 18, 1828, BMWA.

60. Padilla to Austin, Saltillo, January 12, 1828, *AP*, 2:6.

61. Ibid., April 9, 1828, *AP*, 2:30–31, and May 3, 1828, *AP*, 2:34–36.

62. *AP*, 2:94–96.

63. Padilla to Austin, Saltillo, August 9, 1828, *AP*, 2:90.

64. Chabot, *With the Makers*, 202–3; *Handbook of Texas Online*, "José Francisco Ruiz," <http://www.tsha.utexas.edu/handbook/online/articles/RR/fru11.html> (accessed September 6, 2005).

65. Navarro to Austin, Saltillo, May 17, 1828, *AP*, 2:41.

66. "Form of Contract for Introducing Servants into the State of Coahuila and Texas," *AP*, 2:46.

67. *AP*, 2:147.

68. Edward A. Lukes, *DeWitt Colony of Texas* (Austin: Jenkins Publishing Co., 1976), 94. In his biography of Navarro, Joseph Martin Dawson asserts, "But for [Navarro's] influence with Austin, in truth the whole Anglo colonization effort would have collapsed, all because of a reckless, presumptuous man from the United States named Edwards." Joseph Martin Dawson, *José Antonio Navarro: Co-Creator of Texas* (Waco: Baylor University Press, 1969), 38.

69. *Handbook of Texas Online*, "Ramón Músquiz," <http://www.tsha.utexas.edu/ handbook/online/articles/MM/fmu20.html> (accessed September 6, 2005).

70. Músquiz to Austin, Béxar, January 22, 1828, *AP*, 2:9.

71. Ibid.

72. Ibid., June 26, 1828, *AP*, 2:55.

73. Ibid., November 27, 1828, *AP*, 2:146–47.

74. Austin to Zavala, San Felipe de Austin, June 24, 1828, *AP*, 2:48–49.

75. Músquiz to Austin, Béxar, January 22, 1828, *AP*, 2:9.

76. Austin to Viesca, Béxar, May 31, 1830, *AP*, 2:398.

77. Arciniega to Austin, Saltillo, May 17, 1828, *AP*, 2:41–42.

78. Músquiz to Austin, November 25, 1830, *AP*, 2:540.

79. Several authors have explored how honor shaped Spanish/Mexican culture. James Brooks examines the role of shame, or *vergüenza*, in *Captives and Cousins*, 8–9. Ramón Gutiérrez looks at honor in constructing ideas of masculinity and in Spanish acculturation of indigenous peoples. He divides honor between its role in social status and its importance in social control. Gutiérrez, *When Jesus Came*, 177–80. Alonso also looks at honor, adding its function in ethnic difference along with social control and elite status. Alonso, *Thread of Blood*, 52–55, 79–98.

80. Alonso writes on the importance of Indian fighting in the construction of masculinity through a system of honor. Alonso, *Thread of Blood*, 80–82.

81. Austin to Samuel M. Williams, January 12, 1834, *AP*, 1:1026.

82. Lukes, *DeWitt Colony*, 73–74.

83. Austin to citizens of Victoria, January 1, 1827, *AP*, 1:1558–59; Austin to Austin Colony, January 5, 1827, *AP*, 1:1570–72.

84. February 19, 1826, BA.

Chapter Four

1. Frederick C. Chabot, *With the Makers of San Antonio* (San Antonio: Artes Graficas, 1937), 243–48.

2. J. Villasana Haggard, "Epidemic Cholera in Texas, 1833–1834," *Southwestern Historical Quarterly* 40, no. 3 (1937): 216–30.

3. Mary Virginia Henderson, "Minor Empresario Contracts for the Colonization of Texas, 1825–1834," *Southwestern Historical Quarterly* 31, no. 4 (1928): 301.

4. Despite Austin's friendships with elite Tejanos, David J. Weber and Arnoldo De León have identified anti-Mexican, racist remarks Austin made in several letters. See David J. Weber, "'Scarce More Than Apes': Historical Roots of Anglo-American Stereotypes of Mexicans," in *Myth and the History of the Hispanic Southwest*, ed. David J. Weber (Albuquerque: University of New Mexico Press, 1988); and Arnoldo De León, *They Called Them Greasers: Anglo Attitudes toward Mexicans in Texas, 1821–1900* (Austin: University of Texas Press, 1983). Historian James E. Crisp has critiqued Weber's and De León's interpretation of Austin and Anglo-American motivations generally. He questions the racial basis for Texas secession in "Race, Revolution, and the Texas Republic: Toward a Reinterpretation," in *The Texas Military Experience*, ed. Joseph G. Dawson III (College Station: Texas A&M University Press, 1995), 34–38. Crisp calls for a more nuanced analysis of Anglo-American racial attitudes, choosing to characterize the conflict as a "war of racial disruption," 43.

5. Jesús F. de la Teja and John Wheat, "Béxar: Profile of a Tejano Community, 1820–1832," *Southwestern Historical Quarterly* 89 (1985): 10–11; Andrés Tijerina, *Te-*

janos and Texas under the Mexican Flag, 1821–1836 (College Station: Texas A&M University Press, 1994), 12; 1834 statistic from Juan N. Almonte, "Informe . . . ," Mexico, November 25, 1834, in Celia Gutiérrez Ibarra and Juan Nepomuceno Almonte, *Cómo México perdió Texas: análisis y transcripción del Informe secreto (1834) de Juan Nepomuceno Almonte* (México, D.F.: Instituto Nacional de Antropología e Historia, 1987), appendix.

6. Tijerina, *Tejanos and Texas*, 12. Figures fluctuate throughout the decade. The differences might be attributable to the scope of the census or to differences in the methodology. For discussion of the divergent figures, see Alicia V. Tjarks, "Comparative Demographic Analysis of Texas, 1777–1793," *Southwestern Historical Quarterly* 77 (1974):291–338.

7. Alleine Howren, "Causes and Origin of the Decree of April 6, 1830," *Southwestern Historical Quarterly* 16 (1913): 391.

8. Manuel de Mier y Terán, *Texas by Terán: The Diary Kept by General Manuel de Mier y Terán on His 1828 Inspection of Texas*, ed. Jack Jackson, trans. John Wheat (Austin: University of Texas Press, 2000), 1–3.

9. Mier y Terán to the President of Mexico, Nacogdoches, June 30, 1828, in ibid., 97.

10. Ibid., 98.

11. Mier y Terán to Minister of War, November 24, 1829, in ibid., 178.

12. Austin to Mier y Terán, May 24, 1828, *AP*, 2:42–45, and June 30, 1828, *AP*, 2:59–60; Mier y Terán to Austin, June 24, 1828, *AP*, 2:51–54.

13. Mier y Terán to Austin, June 24, 1828, *AP*, 2:52.

14. Mier y Terán to Minister of Foreign Relations, June 9, 1828, AGN, Guerra y Marina, V.327, Transcripts, University of Texas, Austin, TX.

15. Mier y Terán to Minister of Foreign Relations, June 9, 1828, in Mier y Terán, *Texas by Terán*, 91–95.

16. Mier y Terán to Minister of War and Navy, December 14 1829, Hernandez y Davalos Manuscript Collection, BLAC.

17. Mier y Terán to President Guadalupe Victoria, Béxar, March 28, 1828, in Mier y Terán, *Texas by Terán*, 32. The editor notes not finding evidence that the letter was received by Victoria, 27.

18. Mier y Terán, *Texas by Terán*, 177–79.

19. Randolph B. Campbell, *An Empire for Slavery: The Peculiar Institution in Texas, 1821–1865* (Baton Rouge: Louisiana State University Press, 1989), 25.

20. Sean Kelley, "Mexico in His Head: Slavery and the Texas-Mexico Border, 1810–1860," *Journal of Social History* 37, no. 3 (2004): 714–15.

21. Howren, "Causes," 389; Eugene C. Barker, "Native Latin American Contribution to the Colonization and Independence of Texas," *Southwestern Historical Quarterly* 46 (1943): 323–26; Navarro to Austin, Béxar, October 29, 1829, *AP*, 2:277.

22. Navarro to Austin, Béxar, October 29, 1829, *AP*, 2:277.

23. Ramón Músquiz to governor, October 25, 1829, *AP*, 2:273–75.

24. Barker, "Native Latin American Contribution," 326–30; Ayuntamiento de Béxar, "Representacion dirijida por el ilustre Ayuntamiento de la ciudad de Béxar," December 21, 1832, in *Troubles in Texas, 1832: A Tejano Viewpoint from San Antonio*, ed. David J. Weber and Conchita Hassell Winn (Dallas: DeGolyer Library of the Southern Methodist University, 1983).

25. Campbell, *Empire*, 17–21.

26. Músquiz, June 12, 1828, *BA*.

27. Law of April 6, 1830, translated in Howren, "Causes," 414–17.

28. Howren, "Causes," 418.

29. Austin to Lucas Alaman, May 18, 1830 (copy of letter not sent), *AP*, 2:383.

30. Ibid., 384.

31. Gregg Cantrell, *Stephen F. Austin: Empresario of Texas* (New Haven: Yale University Press, 1999), 219–24.

32. Austin to Terán, San Felipe de Austin, May 18, 1830, *AP*, 2:381.

33. Cantrell, *Austin*, 130–31.

34. Músquiz to governor, Béxar, July 4, 1830, BA; Músquiz to governor, *AP*, 2:441.

35. Mier y Terán to Minister of Foreign Relations, June 9, 1828, AGN; Mier y Terán, December 1829, Hernandez y Davalos Collection, BLAC.

36. Cantrell, *Austin*, 222–23.

37. Stephen F. Austin, June 26, 1830, *AP*, 2:431.

38. Henderson, "Minor Empresario," 300.

39. A detailed description of the formation and limited operation of the company can be found in ibid., 302–15.

40. For the De León contract, see Ana Carolina Castillo Crimm, *De León: A Tejano Family History* (Austin: University of Texas Press, 2003), 74–95.

41. Ibid., 84–86.

42. Arciniega to Músquiz, Villa de Austin, May 4, 1831, *AP*, 2:659.

43. Castillo Crimm, *De León*, 98–103.

44. The most thorough treatment of the presidio appears in Malcolm D. McLean, "Tenoxtitlan, Dream Capital of Texas," *Southwestern Historical Quarterly* 70 (July 1966): 23–43.

45. Various sides of the warrior ethic are outlined in Raúl A. Ramos, "Finding the Balance: Béxar in Mexican/Indian Relations," in *Continental Crossroads: Remapping U.S.-Mexico Borderlands History*, ed. Samuel Truett and Elliott Young (Durham: Duke University Press, 2004).

46. McLean, "Tenoxtitlan," 27–28. Also Ruiz to Austin, Tenoxtitlan, November 26, 1830, *AP*, 2:541–42.

47. McLean, "Tenoxtitlan," 29.

48. Ayuntamiento de Béxar, "Representacion," 16.

49. Paul D. Lack, *The Texas Revolutionary Experience: A Political and Social History, 1835–1836* (College Station: Texas A&M University Press, 1992), 10–16, 156–82.

50. Austin to Samuel M. Williams, Mexico City, January 12, 1834, *AP*, 1:1026.

51. Ayuntamiento de Béxar, "Representacion," 16.

52. Ibid.

53. Ibid., 19.

54. Ibid., 20.

55. Tijerina, *Tejanos and Texas*, 130–33.

56. José Francisco Madero, letter to the Gaceta del Gobierno Supremo del Estado de Coahuila y Tejas, 1:9, May 27, 1833, in Gutiérrez Ibarra and Almonte, *Cómo México perdió Texas*, 45.

57. Ibid.

58. Ibid.

59. This appears in various letters from Austin to other Anglos regarding the Texas problem. See, for instance, Austin to Mary Austin Holley, April 20, 1833, *AP*, 2:954–56; Austin to Convention, April 1, 1833, *AP*, 2:934–40; and Austin to Wily Martin, May 30, 1833, *AP*, 2:977–81.

60. Cantrell, *Austin*, 277.

61. Ibid., 277–79.

62. Juan N. Almonte, *Almonte's Texas: Juan N. Almonte's 1834 Inspection, Secret Report and Role in the 1836 Campaign*, ed. Jack Johnson (Austin: Texas State Historical Association, 2003).

63. For the text of the plan, see Thomas B. Davis and Amado Ricon Virulegio, *The Political Plans of Mexico* (Lanham, Md.: University Press of America, 1987), 223–25.

64. An excellent analysis of this period can be found in Torcuato S. Di Tella, *National Popular Politics in Early Independent Mexico, 1820–1847* (Albuquerque: University of New Mexico Press, 1996), chap. 8.

65. Cantrell, *Austin*, 122–23.

66. Governor of Texas to Bustamante, Béxar, September 18, 1822, BA.

67. Rafael Fernandez to Gov of Texas, Béxar, May 26, 1823, BA.

68. Letter to governor of Texas, Punta Palaria, May 18, 1823, BA.

69. Minutes of the Ayuntamiento of Béxar, February 12, 1825, BA.

70. Ayuntamiento de Béxar, "Representacion," 21.

Chapter Five

1. Meeting Notes, Béxar, August 17, 1835, BA.

2. The names on the list of participants appear in Comisiones, Béxar, August 21, 1835, BA.

3. The Plaza de Armas is now known as Military Plaza, and the Plaza General is probably now where city hall sits in modern-day San Antonio. For a discussion on the town's layout, see Jesús F. de la Teja, *San Antonio de Béxar: A Community on New Spain's Northern Frontier* (Albuquerque: University of New Mexico Press, 1995), 31–48.

4. Al Respetable Publico, Béxar, August 22, 1835, BA.

5. James E. Crisp points to indications that Bexareños found the presence of Cos unwelcome and hostile, perhaps constituting a first invasion. Crisp, "Race, Revolution, and the Texas Republic: Toward a Reinterpretation," in *The Texas Military Experience*, ed. Joseph G. Dawson III (College Station: Texas A&M University Press, 1995), 41. He refers to a letter from John Linn to James Kerr noting Tejano support for their cause as rooted in opposition to Cos. Linn to Kerr, July 30, 1835, *PTR*, 1:288. It is hard to know on what Linn based his observations.

6. Paul D. Lack, *The Texas Revolutionary Experience: A Political and Social History, 1835–1836* (College Station: Texas A&M University Press, 1992), 33.

7. Austin to Samuel M. Williams, August 22, 1835, *PTR*, 1:534; Gregg Cantrell, *Stephen F. Austin: Empresario of Texas* (New Haven: Yale University Press, 1999), 307.

8. William Travis uses this terminology in a letter in 1835. Travis to Bowie, July 30, 1835, *PTR*, 1:454.

9. Austin to inhabitants of Béxar, November 18, 1835, *PTR*, 1:1230.

10. Torcuato S. Di Tella, *National Popular Politics in Early Independent Mexico, 1820–1847* (Albuquerque: University of New Mexico Press, 1996), chap. 8.

11. Ibid., 232–33.

12. Andrés Tijerina, *Tejanos and Texas under the Mexican Flag, 1821–1836* (College Station: Texas A&M University Press, 1994), 134; Vito Alessio Robles, *Coahuila y Texas, desde la consumación de la independencia hasta el tratado de paz de Guadalupe Hidalgo*, 2 vols. (México: Editorial Porrua, 1945), 1:441–45.

13. Alessio Robles, *Coahuila y Texas*, 1:445.

14. In January 1835, three months previous, Santa Anna personally led a military expedition to cease a similar liberal government in Zacatecas. That time, he left Barragan as the vice president in charge rather than Gómez Farías. Alessio Robles, *Coahuila y Texas*, 1:486–87.

15. Cos Proclamation, May 12, 1835, *PTR*, 1:176.

16. James E. Crisp, "José Antonio Navarro and the Problem of Powerlessness," in *Tejano Leadership in Mexican and Revolutionary Texas*, ed. Jesús F. de la Teja (College Station: Texas A&M University Press, forthcoming), n.p.

17. Angel Navarro to military commander, May 16, 1835, *PTR*, 1:184.

18. Angel Navarro to the secretary of state of Coahuila y Texas, Béxar, May 18, 1835, *PTR*, 1:189.

19. Alessio Robles, *Coahuila y Texas*, 1:536.

20. Navarro to the secretary of state of Coahuila y Texas, Béxar, May 18, 1835, *PTR*, 1:189.

21. Stephen L. Hardin, "Efficient in the Cause," in *Tejano Journey, 1770–1850*, ed. Gerald E. Poyo (Austin: University of Texas Press, 1996), 64.

22. Ibid.

23. Ibid.

24. Navarro to Gonzales, May 24, 1835, BA.

25. Translated in Tijerina, *Tejanos and Texas*, 136, from Alessio Robles, *Coahuila y Texas*, 2:22.

26. See several letters from Austin to Viesca and Mexía, November 1835, *PTR*, 2:1025, 1199, 1228, 1229, 3:1491.

27. It might also be safe to assume that Anglos didn't want to fight for Viesca's cause but rather for their own independence. When given the chance to fight for federalism, they refused.

28. John Smith to Chambers, September 2, 1835, *PTR*, 1:576.

29. Timothy M. Matovina, "Between Two Worlds," in *Tejano Journey, 1770–1850*, ed. Gerald E. Poyo (Austin: University of Texas Press, 1996), 80.

30. Many letters between Ugartechea and Gritten, *PTR*, 1:331, 336, 338, 351, 361, 391, 497, 511.

31. Angel Navarro to Ugartechea, September 13, 1835, BA; Erasmo Seguín to Ugartechea, September 15, 1835, BA.

32. Padilla to Austin and Zavala, Victoria, October 8, 1835, *PTR*, 2:786.

33. Lack, *Texas Revolutionary Experience*, 112.

34. Noah Smithwick, *The Evolution of a State, or Recollections of Old Texas Days* (1900; Austin: University of Texas Press, 1985), 73; quote cited in Lack, *Texas Revolutionary Experience*, 112.

35. Navarro to inhabitants of Béxar, October 14, 1835, *PTR*, 2:859.

36. Ibid.

37. Lack, *Texas Revolutionary Experience*, 166. Navarro presented Cos with a list of volunteers noted in a letter, October 20, 1835, BA. Another list dated October 27, 1835, contains thirty-four names, seven of whom volunteered without any pay. Muse Collection, BLAC.

38. Hardin, "Efficient in the Cause," 62.

39. Austin to Dimmitt, October 22, 1835, *PTR*, 2:943.

40. Samuel A. Maverick, *Notes on the Storming of Béxar in the Close of 1835*, ed. Frederick C. Chabot (San Antonio: Artes Graficas, 1942).

41. Alwyn Barr, *Texans in Revolt: The Battle for San Antonio, 1835* (Austin: University of Texas Press, 1990), 20.

42. Data gathered from John C. Barron et al., *Republic of Texas Pension Application Abstracts* (Austin: Austin Genealogical Society, 1987).

43. Ibid.

44. Barron et al., *Pension Application Abstracts*, 91.

45. Harbert Davenport, "Captain Jesus Cuellar, Texas Cavalry, Otherwise 'Comanche,'" *Southwestern Historical Quarterly Online* 30, no. 1 (1926): 56–63, <http://www.tsha.utexas.edu/publications/journals/shq/online/v030/n1/article_7.html> (accessed January 26, 2007). Davenport notes that Cuellar disappeared after 1841, but his appearance in the pension records suggests he lived into the 1850s.

46. Most of the descriptions of the siege and battle of Béxar herein come from

A. Barr, *Texans in Revolt*. Barr provides a rich and detailed military history of this aspect of the Texas war.

47. Gonzales, December 10, 1835, *PTR*, 3:1435.

48. A. Barr, *Texans in Revolt*, 36.

49. Maverick, *Notes on the Storming of Béxar*.

50. Mag Stiffs, "Account Taking of San Antone," November 8, 1835, *PTR*, 3:1680.

51. Timothy Matovina, "Menchaca's Memoirs: Narrating a Tejano Life," in *Tejano Leadership in Mexican and Revolutionary Texas*, ed. Jesús F. de la Teja (College Station: Texas A&M University Press, forthcoming), n.p.

52. Cos to Santa Anna, December 27, 1835, *PTR*, 3:1624.

53. "Capitulacion celebrada . . . ," December 11, 1835, Carlos Garcia y Arriaga Papers, BLAC.

54. Barron et al., *Pension Application Abstracts*, 91.

55. Description of post-battle San Antonio in Andrew Forest Muir, ed., *Texas in 1837; an Anonymous, Contemporary Narrative* (Austin: University of Texas Press, 1958), 97.

56. Lack, *Texas Revolutionary Experience*, 115.

57. Seguín et al. to Stephen H. Darden, January 12, 1875, in James M. Day, "Letters and Documents," *Texana* 5 (Spring 1967): 81–82.

58. Data gathered from Barron et al., *Pension Application Abstracts*.

59. Ibid., abstract of Leandro Chavez.

60. The average age of the troops in Seguín's unit was 25.6 years, with a median age of 25 and a standard deviation of 5.7. Those who came from Béxar averaged 25.5 years of age, with a median age of 25.5 and a standard deviation of 5.2. Meanwhile, troops outside of Seguín's unit had a standard deviation of 6.8 for the average and a median age of 25.1 and 24.5, respectively.

61. See discussion of relations between Seguín and Austin in chapter 3.

62. Austin to inhabitants of Béxar, November 18, 1835, *PTR*, 2:1230. My translation.

63. Smith to Chambers, September 2, 1835, *PTR*, 1:576.

64. Gregorio Gomez to Santa Anna, October 17, 1835, *PTR*, 2:892.

65. Guerra Proclamation, Matamoros, November 12, 1835, *PTR*, 2:1159. My translation. José Mariano Guerra, *Proclama*, Matamoros, November 12, 1835, Muse Collection, BLAC.

66. Stephen L. Hardin, "Plácido Benavides: Fighting Tejano Federalist," in *Tejano Leadership in Mexican and Revolutionary Texas*, ed. Jesús F. de la Teja (College Station: Texas A&M University Press, forthcoming), n.p.

67. Cos to Austin, October 18, 1835, *PTR*, 2:902.

68. Bowie and Fannin to Austin, Béxar, October 22, 1835, *PTR*, 2:945.

69. Juan Antonio Chavez, December 15, 22, 1907, interviewed by Charles Merritt Barnes, in *The Alamo Remembered: Tejano Accounts and Perspectives*, ed. Timothy M. Matovina (Austin: University of Texas Press, 1995), 95–96.

70. J. J. Baugh to Henry Smith, February 13, 1836, *PTR*, 4:2076.

71. Ibid.

72. Lack, *Texas Revolutionary Experience*, 160.

73. A debate among historians has resulted over this point. Arnoldo De León has staked out a position attributing a large part of Texas secession to racial motivations. James E. Crisp, on the other hand, has emphasized the political differences driving secession, setting the conditions for racism. Yet a third approach describes the conflict as a "clash of cultures" as presented by Samuel H. Lowrie. My approach tends to focus on the almost complete absence of Tejanos in Anglo-American-dominated areas of Texas. Three elements stand out in regard to Anglo-American attitudes: first, they chose not to follow Mexican laws and civic practices; second, according to Mier y Terán's report, those Tejanos in their midst were treated poorly; and finally, many Anglo-Americans created a generalized negative attitude toward people of Mexican origin after the Law of April 6, 1830. Arnoldo De León, *They Called Them Greasers: Anglo Attitudes toward Mexicans in Texas, 1821–1900* (Austin: University of Texas Press, 1983), 12; James E. Crisp, "Race, Revolution, Republic," 34–48; Samuel H. Lowrie, *Culture Conflict in Texas, 1821–1835* (New York: Columbia University Press, 1932).

74. Johnson Proclamation, San Felipe de Austin, January 10, 1836, *PTR*, 3:1752.

75. Henry Smith to council, December 12, 1835, *PTR*, 3:1459; Lack, *Texas Revolutionary Experience*, 160.

76. Ibid.

77. Henry Smith to council, December 12, 1835, *PTR*, 3:1459.

78. San Antonio meeting, January 16, 1836, *PTR*, 4:1925.

79. Texas Declaration of Independence, March 2, 1836, *PTR*, 4:2226.

80. Margaret Swett Hanson, *Lorenzo de Zavala: The Pragmatic Idealist* (Fort Worth: Texas Christian University Press, 1996).

81. Timothy M. Matovina, ed., *The Alamo Remembered: Tejano Accounts and Perspectives* (Austin: University of Texas Press, 1995), 7.

82. Something of a cottage industry has developed around Alamo history. Retellings of this battle and the surrounding events come second only to the American Civil War in popular interest. Paul Hutton has suggested that this appeal might be to blame for the paucity in academic treatments of the period. Paul Andrew Hutton, "The Alamo as Icon," in *The Texas Military Experience*, ed. Joseph G. Dawson III (College Station: Texas A&M University Press, 1995), 15. A sampling of only a few histories published in the last decade can give a sense of the continued exploration of the events and myths surrounding the Alamo: H. W. Brands, *Lone Star Nation: How a Ragged Army of Volunteers Won the Battle for Texas Independence — and Changed America* (New York: Doubleday, 2004); William C. Davis, *Three Roads to the Alamo: The Lives and Fortunes of David Crockett, James Bowie, and William Barret Travis* (New York: Harper Perennial, 1999); Stephen L. Hardin, *Texian Iliad: A Military History of the Texas Revolution* (Austin: University of Texas Press, 1996); Jack Jackson, *The*

Alamo: An Epic Told from Both Sides (Austin: Paisano Graphics, 2002); Michael Lind, *The Alamo: An Epic* (Boston: Houghton Mifflin, 1997); Frank T. Thompson, *The Alamo* (Denton: University of North Texas Press, 2005); Lon Tinkle, *13 Days to Glory: The Siege of the Alamo* (College Station: Texas A&M University Press, 1996); Richard Bruce Winders, *Sacrificed at the Alamo: Tragedy and Triumph in the Texas Revolution*, Military History of Texas Series, No. 3 (Abilene: Mcwhiney Foundation Press, 2004).

83. "List of Mexicans who fell in the Alamo . . . ," Béxar, 1840, Lamar Papers, Texas State Archives, Austin, no. 2427.

84. Matovina, *The Alamo Remembered*, 72–76, 113–19.

85. Ibid., 97.

86. Ibid., 115.

87. Ibid., 68–70.

88. Ibid., 94.

89. Ibid., 54–55.

90. Ibid., 33–34.

91. Ibid., 34.

92. The most recent example can be found in Lind, *The Alamo*. Several scholars have examined the social and cultural processes that elevated the Alamo to mythic and socially symbolic status. See Holly Beachley Brear, *Inherit the Alamo: Myth and Ritual at an American Shrine* (Austin: University of Texas Press, 1995); Richard Flores, *Remembering the Alamo: Memory, Modernity, and the Master Symbol* (Austin: University of Texas Press, 2002); and Randy Roberts, *A Line in the Sand: The Alamo in Blood and Memory* (New York: Free Press, 2001).

93. Recent work by Timothy M. Matovina (*The Alamo Remembered*) and the republication of Adina De Zavala's 1917 work *History and Legends of the Alamo and Other Missions In and Around San Antonio* (Houston: Arte Publico Press, 1996) have done much to change that narrative.

94. Exact numbers are broken down in Lack, *Texas Revolutionary Experience*, 130.

95. Ibid.

96. Pedro Ampudia to Erasmo Seguín, Cienega de Contrabandos, May 2, 1836, CAHUT.

97. Juan N. Seguín, *A Revolution Remembered: The Memoirs and Selected Correspondence of Juan N. Seguín*, ed. Jesús F. de la Teja (Austin: State House Press, 1991), 148–51. The document lists the muster rolls of Seguín's regiment on December 31, 1836.

98. Lack, *Texas Revolutionary Experience*, 132.

99. Seguín, *Revolution Remembered*, 32.

100. Matovina, *The Alamo Remembered*, 156.

101. Raymond Williams, *Culture and Materialism: Selected Essays* (New York: Verso, 2005), 40–42.

Chapter Six

1. William E. Jones and others to the American officers and citizens, San Antonio, September 14, 1842, in *Telegraph and Texas Register* (San Felipe de Austin), September 28, 1842.

2. Regarding the town name, see Jesús F. de la Teja, *San Antonio de Béxar: A Community on New Spain's Northern Frontier* (Albuquerque: University of New Mexico Press, 1995), 8–11. From this point, Béxar will be referred to as San Antonio, which was the name used with increasing frequency after 1836. Tejano residents of San Antonio, though, will continue to be identified as Bexareños throughout this study.

3. Several historians have begun to broach the question; see Timothy M. Matovina, *Tejano Religion and Ethnicity: San Antonio, 1821–1860* (Austin: University of Texas Press, 1995), 24–48; David Montejano, *Anglos and Mexicans in the Making of Texas, 1836–1986* (Austin: University of Texas Press, 1987), 24–49; and Arnoldo De León, *The Tejano Community, 1836–1900* (Albuquerque: University of New Mexico Press, 1982), 23–49.

4. Much of this chapter relies on the detail provided by the comprehensive volumes on the Republic period in southern Texas by Joseph Milton Nance, *After San Jacinto: The Texas-Mexican Frontier, 1836–1841* (Austin: University of Texas Press, 1963), and *Attack and Counterattack: The Texas-Mexican Frontier, 1842* (Austin: University of Texas Press, 1964).

5. Nance, *After San Jacinto*, 11–20.

6. Ibid., 13; Juan N. Seguín, *A Revolution Remembered: The Memoirs and Selected Correspondence of Juan N. Seguín*, ed. Jesús F. de la Teja (Austin: State House Press, 1991), 111. Nance refers to Felix Huston as a "turbulent and overbearing soldier of fortune from Kentucky" (17).

7. Nance, *After San Jacinto*, 20.

8. Ibid., 35.

9. September 21, 1836, quoted in ibid., 13.

10. Seguín, *Revolution Remembered*, 89.

11. Nance, *After San Jacinto*, 66.

12. Ibid., 17–20, 32–36; Seguín, *Revolution Remembered*, 111.

13. John C. Barron et al., *Republic of Texas Pension Application Abstracts* (Austin: Austin Genealogical Society, 1987), entry for Blas Herrera.

14. President Sam Houston to Juan Seguín, Camp Independence, January 16, 1837, in Seguín, *Revolution Remembered*, 152–53.

15. Minutes of the City Council of the City of San Antonio from 1837 to 1849, Journal Book "A," San Antonio City Clerk's office, transcript, September 20, 1837, 1, CAHUT (hereafter "Journal Book 'A'").

16. The name Juan Smith appears in the July 9, 1830, census report of Béxar and is listed as married, age thirty-seven, artisan with one horse. Census report of Barrio

Sur, July 9, 1830, Ignacio Chavez, transcribed in *Residents of Texas, 1782–1836*, 3 vols. (San Antonio: University of Texas Institute of Texan Cultures, 1984), 2:280.

17. Frederick C. Chabot, *With the Makers of San Antonio* (San Antonio: Artes Graficas, 1937), 274.

18. M. L. Crimmins, "John W. Smith, the Last Messenger from the Alamo and the First Mayor of San Antonio," *Southwestern Historical Quarterly* 54 (January 1951): 344–46.

19. Journal Book "A," Béxar, September 18, 1837, 3–4.

20. Ibid., October 7, 1837, 12.

21. Ibid., March 13, 1838, 18–19.

22. Ibid.

23. This contradicts the view that Tejano families stayed out of San Antonio until 1848. Charles Ramsdell, *San Antonio: A Historical and Pictorial Guide* (Austin: University of Texas Press, 1959), 32–33.

24. Andrew Forest Muir, ed., *Texas in 1837; an Anonymous, Contemporary Narrative* (Austin: University of Texas Press, 1958), 104.

25. Sam A. Maverick to Mary Adams Maverick, Béxar, August 25, 1838, Maverick Family Papers, CAHUT.

26. Mary Adams Maverick to her mother, San Antonio de Bejar, September 8, 1839, Maverick Family Papers, CAHUT.

27. Seguín, *Revolution Remembered*, 118.

28. Ibid., 33.

29. Juan N. Seguín, *Austin City Gazette*, February 5, 1840, cited in ibid., 174.

30. Ibid.

31. Journal Book "A," Béxar, April 28, 1841, 98.

32. Juan N. Seguín (signed John) to Sam Houston, Béxar, June 21, 1837, TSA.

33. Seguín also added regards from his father, Erasmo Seguín, to Houston.

34. Juan N. Seguín, *Austin City Gazette*, February 5, 1840, cited in Seguín, *Revolution Remembered*, 174.

35. Seguín, *Revolution Remembered*, 35–39.

36. W. W. Newcomb Jr., *The Indians of Texas: From Prehistoric to Modern Times* (Austin: University of Texas Press, 1961), 348–54.

37. Ralph A. Smith, "Indians in American-Mexican Relations before the War of 1846," *Hispanic American Historical Review* 43, no. 1 (1963): 34–64.

38. Dianna Everett, *The Texas Cherokees: A People between Two Fires, 1819–1840* (Norman: University of Oklahoma Press, 1990), 89–97.

39. The Mexican government took action on this claim by patrolling the Nueces strip, the land between the Río Grande and the Nueces River, beginning April 13, 1841. Mariano Arista to his troops, April 13, 1841, Lund Collection, BLAC; and Nance, *After San Jacinto*, 447.

40. Josefina Zoraida Vázquez, "The Texas Question in Mexican Politics, 1836–1845," *Southwest Historical Quarterly* 89 (1986): 314.

41. Andrés Reséndez, *Changing National Identities at the Frontier: Texas and New Mexico, 1800–1850* (New York: Cambridge University Press, 2005), 229–30.

42. Letters from Mexía, cited in Seguín, *Revolution Remembered*, 39.

43. Erasmo Seguín to secretary of state, Béxar, August 30, 1839, TSA.

44. Juan N. Seguín to president of the Republic, December 26, 1840, TSA. See also Seguín, *Revolution Remembered*, 176.

45. Juan N. Seguín to president of the Republic, December 26, 1840, TSA.

46. Ibid.

47. Nance, *After San Jacinto*, 432.

48. John N. Seguín to M. B. Lamar, vice president, New Orleans, January 2, 1838, TSA.

49. Juan N. Seguín to president of the Republic, December 26, 1840, TSA.

50. Vázquez, "Texas Question," 317.

51. *Imparcial* (Puebla, Mexico), November 11, 1837, La Fragua collection, Universidad Nacional Autónoma de México.

52. Tornel to Diputados y secretarios, July 11, 1839, Lund Collection, BLAC.

53. *El Realtor* (Monterrey), July 23, 1838, 3, Lund Collection, BLAC.

54. *La Luna* (Chihuahua), June 29, 1841, 2, Lund Collection, BLAC.

55. Reséndez, *Changing National Identities*, 197–214.

56. Ibid., 213.

57. Ibid., 229–31.

58. *La Gaceta de San Luis Potosi*, San Luis Potosi, November 14, 1841, Lund Collection, BLAC.

59. *Seminario Politico* (Monterrey), January 13, 1842, Lund Collection, BLAC. Reporting from Havana, October 2, 1841.

60. Governor Jesus Garza Gonzalez to Prefecto Linares, Monterrey, N.L., September 18, 1840, Lund Collection, BLAC.

61. Mariano Arista to his troops, April 13, 1841, Lund Collection, BLAC.

62. *El Ancla* (Matamoros, Tamaulipas), June 7, 1841, Lund Collection, BLAC.

63. Ibid., June 28, 1841. Nance, *After San Jacinto*, 466–67, provides names from reports from American sources.

64. Andres de Saldaña to Alcalde de Camargo, Matamoros, December 24, 1824, Lund Collection, BLAC.

65. Nance, *After San Jacinto*, 469.

66. Ibid., 409.

67. Ibid. cites a report from R. M. Potter in the *Telegraph and Texas Register*, June 9, 1841.

68. Journal Book "A," Béxar, September 9, 1841, 89; Nance, *After San Jacinto*, 419. The ordinance is assumed to be directed at Mexicans since the second article exempts all inhabitants of the Republic of Texas.

69. Nance, *After San Jacinto*, 382.

70. Samuel A. Maverick to Mary Adams Maverick, Béxar, March 13, 1838, Maverick Family Papers, CAHUT.

71. Support for Huston's efforts extended throughout the American South, with meetings held to finance Huston's ventures. Nance, *After San Jacinto*, 481, mentions a meeting in Mississippi on July 4, 1842.

72. Journal Book "A," Béxar, February 20, 1840, 55, and April 26, 1841, 77.

73. Seguín, *Revolution Remembered*, 43.

74. Nance, *After San Jacinto*, 490–92.

75. P. H. Bell to B. T. Archer, November 21, 1841, in *The Papers of Mirabeau Buonaparte Lamar*, ed. Charles Adams Gulick et al. (Austin: A. C. Baldwin Printers, 1921) 3:592, quoted in Nance, *After San Jacinto*, 489.

76. J. N. Seguín et al. to Lamar, San Antonio de Béxar, May 15, 1841, TSA.

77. José Antonio Navarro to M. B. Lamar, Béxar, May 18, 1841, TSA.

78. Nance, *After San Jacinto*, 410–11. Nance cites lists from John S. Ford's *Memoirs*, 2:242–47. The Militia Rolls, January 20–May 20, 1841, TSA, also include Luis Castano, Leandro Garcia, Raphael Garcia, Canato Parez, Pablo Parez, and Melchor Travena.

79. Frederick Wilkins, *The Highly Irregular Irregulars: Texas Rangers in the Mexican War* (Austin: Eakin Press, 1990), 19.

80. Tejanos received little military support from the Texas army. President Houston ignored Mayor Seguín's requests for aid in the case of a Mexican invasion. Nance, *Attack and Counterattack*, 11–12. Seguín wrote the letter January 30, 1842. Seguín, *Revolution Remembered*, 43.

81. Nance, *Attack and Counterattack*, 18–30.

82. Seguín, *Revolution Remembered*, 44; Nance, *Attack and Counterattack*, 18.

83. Mary Adams Maverick, Diary 1836–1895, Maverick Family Papers, CAHUT.

84. Nance, *Attack and Counterattack*, 27.

85. Ibid., 37.

86. Ibid., 47–48; Journal Book "A," Béxar, August 13, 1842, 126–27.

87. Seguín, *Revolution Remembered*, 44; Nance, *Attack and Counterattack*, 52.

88. Seguín, *Revolution Remembered*, 94.

89. John H. Jenkins and Kenneth Kesselus, *Edward Burleson: Texas Frontier Leader* (Austin: Jenkins Publishing Company, 1990), 126–27; Seguín, *Revolution Remembered*, 44.

90. Seguín, *Revolution Remembered*, 119.

91. Editor of *Morning Star Newspaper*, *Telegraph and Texas Register*, June 15, 1842, cited in Nance, *Attack and Counterattack*, 204.

92. Nance, *Attack and Counterattack*, 222–24. The *Telegraph and Texas Register*, June 15, 1842, wrote, "Business is at a stand and the gloom of desolation seems to rest over the devoted city. Poor Béxar, her history is replete with disaster and misfortune."

93. September 7, 1842, cited in Nance, *Attack and Counterattack*, 282.

94. Journal Book "A," Béxar, July 16, 1842, 120.

95. Ibid., 122.

96. Nance, *Attack and Counterattack*, 306.

97. Wilkins, *Highly Irregular Irregulars*, 18. Wilkins writes, "Hays had another leadership quality: the ability to work with diverse groups."

98. Timothy Matovina, "Menchaca's Memoirs: Narrating a Tejano Life," in *Tejano Leadership in Mexican and Revolutionary Texas*, ed. Jesús F. de la Teja (College Station: Texas A&M University Press, forthcoming), n.p.

99. Seguín, *Revolution Remembered*, 45, 97–98.

100. Nance, *Attack and Counterattack*, 326.

101. William E. Jones and others to the American officers and citizens, San Antonio, September 14, 1842, in *Telegraph and Texas Register*, September 28, 1842; also in Samuel A. Maverick Papers, cited in Nance, *Attack and Counterattack*, 327.

102. Nance, *Attack and Counterattack*, 351.

103. Robert E. Wright, O.M.I., "Father Refugio de la Garza," in *Tejano Leadership in Mexican and Revolutionary Texas*, ed. Jesús F. de la Teja (College Station: Texas A&M University Press, forthcoming), n.p.

104. Some suggest the attack served as an incentive for Texans to re-annex with Mexico, as Santa Anna had recently sent peaceful overtures. Vázquez, "Texas Question," 336.

105. *Expedicion hecha en Tejas por una parte de la Division del Cuerpo de Egercito del Norte* (Monterrey: n.p., 1842), 40–43, cited in Seguín, *Revolution Remembered*, 48.

106. Nance, *Attack and Counterattack*, 385.

107. Ibid., 431.

108. Doyle to Elliot, Mexico, May 27, 1843, Woll to Houston, Matamoros, July 16, 1843, Hill to Woll, Washington on the Brazos, July 29, 1843, in "Correspondence from the British Archives Concerning Texas, 1837–1846, VII," ed. Ephraim Douglass Adams, *Southwestern Historical Quarterly* 17 (1913): 67–92; McLeod to Elliot, Galveston, November 26, 1843, in Ephraim Douglass Adams, ed., "Correspondence from the British Archives Concerning Texas, 1837–1846, X," *Southwestern Historical Quarterly* 17 (1914): 415–27.

109. Specific requests were made to British go-betweens for the release of José Antonio Navarro. McCleod to Elliot, Galveston, November 26, 1843, and Elliot to Aberdeen, Galveston, November 29, 1843, in Adams, "Correspondence X," 415–27.

110. *Seminario Politico*, November 28, 1844, Lund Collection, BLAC.

111. Ibid., April 3, 1845.

112. Seguín, *Revolution Remembered*; Nance, *Attack and Counterattack*, 52–54.

113. Montejano, *Anglos and Mexicans*, 27.

114. Journal Book "A," Béxar, March 30, 1844, to December 29, 1845, 132–51.

115. Ibid., June 22, 1844, 140.

116. David Montejano refers to this arrangement as the "peace structure." Montejano, *Anglos and Mexicans*, 8, 34–41.

117. Jane Dysart, "Mexican Women in San Antonio, 1830–1860: The Assimilation Process," *Western Historical Quarterly* 7 (October 1976): 365; Jacqueline Peterson, "Women Dreaming: The Religiopsychology of Indian-White Marriages and the Rise of a Metis Culture," in *Western Women: Their Land, Their Lives*, ed. Lillian Schlissel, Vicki L. Ruiz, and Janice Monk (Albuquerque: University of New Mexico Press, 1988), 53–56.

118. Dysart, "Mexican Women," 367; Muir, *Texas in 1837*, 104; George Wilkins Kendall, *Narrative of the Texan Santa Fe Expedition* (New York: Harper and Brothers, 1844), 1:46–48; Josiah Gregg, *Commerce of the Prairies* (Norman: University of Oklahoma Press, 1954).

119. Dysart, "Mexican Women," 368.

120. Marriage Records, Book "A," Bexar County Archives, San Antonio, Texas, transcribed in *The San Antonio Genealogical and Historical Society Newsletter*, 1959–1960, San Antonio, Texas.

121. Dysart, "Mexican Women," 369–70.

122. Marriage Records, Book "A," presents 10 of 23; Dysart, "Mexican Women," 369–70 nn. 42, 88.

123. Several recent works have been published on the way Mexicanas negotiated the social and economic changes taking place in the face of American westward expansion. See Miroslava Chavez-Garcia, *Negotiating Conquest: Gender and Power in California, 1770s to 1880s* (Tucson: University of Arizona Press, 2004); and Deena J. Gonzalez, *Refusing the Favor: The Spanish-Mexican Women of Santa Fe, 1820–1880* (New York: Oxford University Press, 1999).

124. Dysart, "Mexican Women," 374. Dysart also notes Protestant conversions and Anglicized names as evidence of Tejano loss of ethnic identity.

125. Ibid., 375.

126. Muir, *Texas in 1837*, 108.

127. Gonzalez, *Refusing the Favor*, 3–16.

128. Texas General Land Office, Archives and Records Division, "Categories of Land Grants in Texas," 1996.

129. John Bost Pitts III, "Speculation in Headright Land Grants in San Antonio, 1837–1842" (M.A. thesis, Trinity University, 1966), appendix.

130. Transcribed Record Book A1, 1837, County Clerk's Office, San Antonio, Texas.

131. Ibid.

132. Mary Adams Maverick to her mother, San Antonio de Béxar, September 8, 1839, Maverick Family Papers, CAHUT.

133. *Hogue v. Baker* (1898) declared the end of vacant public land in Texas.

134. Transcribed Record Book A1, 1837; Seguín, *Revolution Remembered*, 38.

135. Barbara S. Wolfe, *Index to Mexican War Pension Applications* (Washington: Heritage House, 1985). The index does not include any Spanish surnames from Texas.

136. A. Brooke Caruso, *The Mexican Spy Company: United States Covert Operations in Mexico, 1845–1848* (Jefferson, N.C.: McFarland and Co., 1991), 80–92.

137. Congressional discussions centered on the effects of expansion on sectional conflicts. See John S. D. Eisenhower, *So Far from God: The U.S. War with Mexico, 1846–1848* (New York: Random House, 1989); and Robert Walter Johannsen, *To the Halls of the Montezuma: The Mexican War in the American Imagination* (New York: Oxford University Press, 1985).

138. Seguín, *Revolution Remembered*, 48.

139. Wilkins, *Highly Irregular Irregulars*, 20, 52, 64–70.

140. McCulloch Family Papers, Library of Daughters of the Republic of Texas, San Antonio, Texas, quoted in Wilkins, *Highly Irregular Irregulars*, 64–65.

141. Eisenhower, *So Far from God*, 155–57.

142. Ibid., 154.

143. *El Eco del Norte de Tamaulipas* (Matamoros), August 11, 1845, Lund Collection, BLAC.

144. Wilkins, *Highly Irregular Irregulars*, 20.

145. Journal Book "A," Béxar, 157.

146. Ibid., 159.

147. Charles M. Robinson III, *Texas and the Mexican War: A History and a Guide* (Austin: Texas State Historical Association, 2004), 66–69, 80–83.

148. Eisenhower, *So Far from God*, 91.

149. Ibid., 168.

150. Richard Griswold del Castillo, *The Treaty of Guadalupe Hidalgo: A Legacy of Conflict* (Norman: University of Oklahoma Press, 1990), 34.

151. Article IX, Treaty of Guadalupe Hidalgo, in ibid.

152. Griswold del Castillo, *Treaty*, 40.

153. Ibid., 47–49.

154. Article IX, Treaty of Guadalupe Hidalgo, in ibid., 190.

155. Griswold del Castillo, *Treaty*, 63–64.

156. Ibid., 65.

157. Montejano, *Anglos and Mexicans*, 34.

Chapter Seven

1. Affidavit in Elisha Marshall Pease, *Informe del Gobernador del Estado de Tejas i documentos relativos a los asaltos contra los carreteros mejicanos* (Austin: John Marshall and Co., 1857), CAHUT.

2. *El Bejareño* (Béxar), December 1855. The report noted the total value of property in the city, including slaves, rose from $918,408 in 1850 to $5.3 million in 1855.

3. Arthur James Mayer, "San Antonio, Frontier Entrepot" (Ph.D. diss., University of Texas, 1976), 285.

4. Ibid., 275.

5. V. K. Carpenter, comp., *The State of Texas Federal Population Schedules Seventh Census of the United States, 1850* (Huntsville, Ark.: Century Enterprises, 1969), 1:111–89; *Population Schedules of the Eighth Census of the United States, 1860* (Washington: The National Archives, 1967), 1288:1–192a.

6. Based on Spanish-surnamed individuals.

7. Quoted in Dorothy Kelly Gibson, "Social Life in San Antonio, 1855–1860" (M.A. thesis, University of Texas, 1937), 17.

8. "Marriage Records, Book C: June 29, 1852 to July 1, 1855," Béxar County Courthouse, San Antonio, Texas, compiled by Elizabeth M. Morey, n.d., n.p., Perry Castañeda Library, University of Texas, Austin.

9. See chapter 5, table 5.1.

10. District Court (Bexar County), Civil Minutes, 1836–1907, microfilm (Salt Lake City: Genealogical Society of Utah, 1977).

11. Sister Paul of the Cross McGrath, "Political Nativism in Texas, 1825–1860" (Ph.D. diss., Catholic University, 1930).

12. Ibid., 24.

13. Mayer, "San Antonio," 130–31.

14. Timothy M. Matovina, *Tejano Religion and Ethnicity: San Antonio, 1821–1860* (Austin: University of Texas Press, 1995), 70; "Charter and Digest of Ordinances of the City of San Antonio," March 19, 1857, CAHUT.

15. *El Bejareño*, February 7, 1855.

16. Ibid.

17. Benedict Anderson stresses the importance of newspapers in building connections in nations made of different regions. Benedict Anderson, *Imagined Communities: Reflections on the Origin and Spread of Nationalism* (New York: Verso, 1991).

18. *El Bejareño*, February 17, 1855, 2.

19. Ibid., July 7, 1855, 3.

20. Juan N. Seguín, *A Revolution Remembered: The Memoirs and Selected Correspondence of Juan N. Seguín*, ed. Jesús F. de la Teja (Austin: State House Press, 1991), 50–51.

21. *El Bejareño*, July 7, 1855, 2.

22. Ibid., 3.

23. The committee was composed of Agustín Chaves, Antonio Montes, Clemente Bustillos, Mariano Garcia, Antonio Gutierres, Juan Barrera, and Julian Vasquez.

24. *El Bejareño*, July 7, 1855, 3.

25. Ibid.

26. Ibid., July 21, 1855, 2–3.

27. Ibid., July 31, 1855, 2.

28. Arnoldo De León, *Apuntes Tejanos* (Austin: Texas State Historical Association/

UMI, 1978), 1. This book contains an index of nineteenth-century Tejano-related articles in the *Herald* and *Express*.

29. *San Antonio Herald*, July 10, 1855, 2; July 24, 1855, 2.

30. Ibid., July 10, 1855, 2; cited in De León, *Apuntes Tejanos*, 191.

31. Devine also served as mayor from 1849 to 1850 and in 1853.

32. *San Antonio Herald*, January 5, 1856.

33. Ibid., August 14, 1855, 2.

34. Ibid.

35. De León notes that registry laws and poll taxes combined to disenfranchise Tejano voters. Arnoldo De León, *The Tejano Community, 1836–1900* (Albuquerque: University of New Mexico Press, 1982), 25.

36. *San Antonio Herald*, August 14, 1855, 2.

37. Ibid.

38. *El Bejareño*, July 7, 1855, 3.

39. Ibid., July 21, 1855, 13.

40. Ibid.

41. Ibid., May 23, June 7, 1856.

42. De León, *Tejano Community*, 25.

43. *El Bejareño*, January 5, 1856.

44. Ibid., February 16, May 17, 1856.

45. Ibid., February 16, 1856.

46. My translation.

47. *El Bejareño*, April 26, 1856.

48. Ibid., February 23, 1856.

49. Ibid., January 26, 1856.

50. Ibid., May 3, 1856.

51. Ibid., May 17, 1856.

52. Ibid., April 19, 1856.

53. Ibid., June 14, 1856.

54. Ibid., May 31, 1856. Angel Navarro also left the city to pursue his education at Harvard University.

55. Frederick Law Olmstead, *Journey through Texas* (New York: Dix, Edwards, 1857), 160. De León, *Tejano Community*, 88–90, provides a detailed listing of the goods carried by these carts.

56. De León, *Tejano Community*, 88. Statistical analysis of the census conducted by De León.

57. *El Bejareño*, July 7, 1855, 3, letter dated San Antonio, June 26, 1855.

58. *San Antonio Herald*, August 8, 1857.

59. Larry Knight, "The Cart War: Defining American in San Antonio in the 1850s," *Southwestern Historical Quarterly* 91, no. 3 (2006): 327.

60. *San Antonio Herald*, August 22, 1857.

61. These actions would be repeated over and over again. See David G. Gutiér-

rez, *Walls and Mirrors: Mexican Americans, Mexican Immigrants, and the Politics of Ethnicity* (Berkeley: University of California Press, 1995), chap. 1.

62. *San Antonio Daily Herald*, November 28, 1857, letter dated New York, October 14, 1857.

63. Ibid., letter dated Washington, October 24, 1857.

64. Pease, *Informe del Gobernador*, 1.

65. Ibid., 4.

66. L. Knight, "Cart War," 332.

67. Pease, *Informe del Gobernador*, 5.

68. *San Antonio Herald*, December 17, 1857, 2.

69. Ibid., December 19, 1857, 2.

70. J. M. Lowrie of Helena, Texas, in *San Antonio Herald*, October 22, 1857, 2.

71. The newspaper changed hands and political affiliations several times in its history. The original owners, James Pearson Newcomb and J. M. West, supported the Know-Nothing Party. John D. Logan and G. W. Palmer purchased the paper in 1856. *Handbook of Texas Online*, "San Antonio *Herald*," <http://www.tsha.utexas.edu/handbook/online/articles/SS/ees4.html> (accessed May 24, 2007).

72. *San Antonio Daily Herald*, July 15, 1859, 2.

73. There exists a debate in Mexican American history over the use of "whiteness" to categorize political and social action. See Neil Foley, *The White Scourge: Mexicans, Blacks, and Poor Whites in Texas Cotton Culture* (Berkeley: University of California Press, 1999); and Carlos K. Blanton, "George I. Sanchez, Ideology, and Whiteness in the Making of the Mexican American Civil Rights Movement, 1930–1960," *Journal of Southern History* 72 (2006): 569–604.

74. *Herald*, July 22, 1859, 2.

75. Ibid., 2.

76. Jerry D. Thompson, *Vaqueros in Blue and Grey* (Austin: Presidial Press, 1976), 25–29.

77. Linda Mearse, *Confederate Indigent Families Lists of Texas: 1863–1865*, n.p., 1995, TSA.

78. J. Thompson, *Vaqueros*, 26–29.

79. Confederate Muster Role Index Cards, TSA.

80. De León, *Tejano Community*, 88.

Conclusion

1. Romero Palafox to the Honorable National Commission of the Independence Centennial, Mexico City, October 4, 1909, Gobierno, 2a, AGN. Palafox is a resident of Del Rio. My translation.

2. Ibid.

3. Ibid.

4. Ibid.

5. *San Antonio Daily Express*, September 15–16, 1909; September 13–18, 1910.

6. Judith Berg-Sobré, *San Antonio on Parade: Six Historic Festivals* (College Station: Texas A&M University Press, 2003), 89.

7. *San Antonio Daily Express*, September 18, 1895.

8. *La Prensa* (San Antonio), September 15, 1917; *San Antonio Express*, September 15, 1917. On the class and musical differences in San Antonio's Mexican community, see Richard Garcia, *Rise of the Mexican American Middle Class: San Antonio, 1929–1941* (College Station: Texas A&M University Press, 1991).

9. *San Antonio Daily Express*, September 18, 1895; September 13, September 18, 1910.

10. Berg-Sobré, *San Antonio on Parade*, 82–98.

11. Recent works have taken a transnational approach, especially in the nineteenth-century American West and Mexican north. See Adam McKeown, *Chinese Migrant Networks and Cultural Change: Peru, Chicago, Hawaii, 1900–1936* (Chicago: University of Chicago Press, 2001); Elliott Young, *Catarino Garza's Revolution on the Texas-Mexico Border* (Durham: Duke University Press, 2004); Andrés Reséndez, *Changing National Identities at the Frontier: Texas and New Mexico, 1800–1850* (New York: Cambridge University Press, 2005); Sam Truett, *Fugitive Landscapes: The Forgotten History of the U.S.-Mexico Borderlands* (New Haven: Yale University Press, 2006); and Omar Valerio, *River of Hope: Identity and Nation along the Rio Grande, 1749–1890* (Durham: Duke University Press, forthcoming).

12. Thomas Bender, "Historians, the Nation, and the Plenitude of Narratives," in *Rethinking American History in a Global Age*, ed. Thomas Bender (Berkeley: University of California Press, 2002); Micol Seigel, "World History's Narrative Problem," *Hispanic American Historical Review* 84, no. 3 (2004): 442.

13. Brenda S. A. Yeoh et al., "Introduction: Transnationalism and Its Edges," *Ethnic and Racial Studies* 26, no. 2 (March 2003): 208.

14. Ibid., 208–12.

15. John Tutino, "Globalizaciones, autonomías y revoluciones: poder y participación popular en la historia de México," in *Crisis, reforma y revolución: México: historias de fin de siglo*, ed. Elisa Servin and Leticia Reina (Mexico City: Editorial Taurus, 2002), 25–85.

16. Cuauhtémoc Velasco, "Historiagrafía de un territorio perdido," *Historias* [Mexico] 40 (1998): 21–27.

17. John Mason Hart, *Empire and Revolution: The Americans in Mexico since the Civil War* (Berkeley: University of California Press, 2002).

18. One recent attempt to correct this trend is Alan Taylor, *American Colonies: The Settling of North America* (New York: Penguin, 2002).

19. Bender, "Historians," 5–6.

20. Ibid., 11.

21. Dipesh Chakrabarty, "Postcoloniality and the Artifice of History: Who Speaks for 'Indian' Pasts?" *Representations* 37 (Winter 1992): 23. He writes, "I ask for a his-

tory that deliberately makes visible, within the very structure of its narrative forms, its own repressive strategies and practices, the part it plays in collusion with the narratives of citizenships in assimilating to the projects of the modern state all other possibilities of human solidarity. The politics of despair will require of such history that it lays bare to its readers the reasons why such a predicament is necessarily inescapable."

22. "S.A. Set to Mark Diez y Seis with Parade, Festival and More," *San Antonio Express-News*, September 11, 2003, 8B; "Parade Hails Independence of Mexico: Participants Celebrate Their Culture and Reaffirm Their Roots," *San Antonio Express-News*, September 14, 2003, 1B.

23. "Iraq War Shows Growing Latino Role in U.S. Military," *Houston Chronicle*, April 3, 2003.

Index

and stereotypical attitudes toward Mexicans, 154, 155, 156, 161, 266 (n. 73); mercenaries as, 154, 155, 161; participation rate in war of Texas secession, 161–62; success in Texas, 243–44 (n. 19). *See also* Mexican/Anglo-American relations; Tejano/Anglo-American relations; Texians

Anglo-Texans. *See* Texians

Apaches, 15, 53, 55, 56, 60, 63, 73, 253 (n. 73)

Arciniega, Miguel, 50, 102–3, 121, 134

Arista, Mariano, 179–80, 182, 189, 200

Army of Texas: and Alamo, 2, 160; and Tejanos, 14, 136, 150–51, 154, 158, 161–62, 164, 168, 265 (n. 60); structure of, 143, 145, 154; and Juan N. Seguín, 147, 151, 158, 164, 174; characteristics of troops, 149–51, 161–62, 265 (n. 60); and San Jacinto, 160–61

Arocha, Ignacio, 103, 134

Arredondo, Joaquín de, 39, 41, 44, 46, 47–49, 55

Arrieola, Leandro, 189

Assimilation, 7, 56, 82, 129–30

Austin, James, 82, 96

Austin, Moses, 84, 86, 96

Austin, Stephen F.: and Erasmo Seguín, 81–82, 83, 84, 89, 94, 96–97, 100, 104, 126; and Anglo-American immigrants, 81–83, 84; and Juan N. Seguín, 82, 101, 147, 151; and José Antonio Navarro, 93, 100, 184, 258 (n. 68); and Juan Antonio Padilla, 99; and Ramón Músquiz, 101–2, 123, 124, 127; and Tejano elites, 105, 112, 121, 122, 124, 126, 259 (n. 4); and Edwards, 106; and Mier y Terán, 115; and slavery, 115, 118, 119; and impact of colonization laws, 118–19; and Mexican government, 120, 123–24; and Plan de Jalapa, 123–24; request

for statehood, 123–27, 137, 262 (n. 59); arrest and imprisonment of, 127, 135, 137, 138; and lack of assimilation, 129; and war of Texas secession, 145, 147, 148, 151, 152–53

Balmaceda, José María, 125, 126

Balmori, Diana, 36, 37

Barr, Juliana, 248 (n. 2), 254 (n. 86)

Barrera, J. Y., 220–21

Bastrop, Baron de, 50, 95, 96, 97, 257 (n. 46)

Battle of San Jacinto, 160–61, 162, 167, 168

Bean, Peter Ellis, 70, 71, 95, 257 (n. 41)

Becerra de Seguín, María Josefa, 37, 96–97

El Bejareño, 210–11, 215, 217, 219, 220–22, 224

Benavides, Plácido, 147, 152, 157

Bender, Thomas, 235–36

Béxar, Texas: and Mexican independence, 1–2, 3, 27–28, 32, 33–35, 38, 49–52, 133–35, 142, 165; and war of Texas secession, 4, 13, 135, 136, 146, 157–58, 164; Anglo-American representations of, 5; national transitions in, 6, 11–12, 27–28; cross-cultural contacts in, 9, 24; and New Spain's northern expansion, 10–11, 15; landscape of, 15, 17; location on frontier, 17, 18–19, 21, 24, 27, 28, 52, 55, 235; population of, 18, 19, 23, 64–65, 112, 260 (n. 6); economy of, 20–21, 22, 139, 149; and contraband trade, 22; militarization of, 23, 47–48, 121, 136, 143, 147, 152, 153; social order of, 27–28, 33, 35, 48, 49–52; importance of prestige in, 35–38; Anglo-American immigrants in, 43, 129; political leadership of, 49–50; missions of, 56, 63, 67–69, 78; and Mexican/indigenous relations, 60, 62, 74–76; and trade with Comanches, 62, 76, 78; census figures for, 64–65, 69; and *empresario* colonization, 90; and political issues, 112, 123–28, 143; and Tejano social power, 114; and national politics, 123–28; Texians' invasion of, 136, 143; siege of, 144–53, 156, 161, 264–65 (n. 46); Tejano flight from violence in, 145, 153, 157–59, 168; Texian occupation of, 153–54; and battle of Alamo, 158–59; and Texian political structures, 165; Mexican invasions of, 167; demographics of, 168; renaming of, 168, 268 (n. 2). *See also* San Antonio, Texas

Béxar Ayuntamiento, 117, 119, 122, 124–28, 130–31, 141

Bexar County, Texas, 169, 207, 208, 211, 212, 216

Bexareño elites: and Mexican independence celebrations, 3, 133–34; and Anglo-American colonization, 13, 89, 94–97, 164; and prestige, 28, 35–38, 51, 52; and insurgency of 1811, 30–31; and insurgency of 1813, 45; and *limpieza de sangre*, 50–51; interrelations among, 51; and power relations, 52, 136; and Mexican/indigenous relations, 63; racial composition of, 66; and secularization of missions, 68; and slavery, 92, 118; and war of Texas secession, 136, 163

Bexareño identity, 6–8, 10, 11, 13, 14, 21, 50, 66

Bexareños: social practices of, 2, 3, 7, 9, 49, 50–52; and political issues, 2–3, 7, 8, 9, 38, 49, 58–59, 170, 203; and Anglo-American immigrants, 3, 10, 11, 28, 35, 43, 52, 113; and indigenous identities, 8, 50, 52, 56–58; and

Mexican ethnic identity, 8, 206, 233; and indigenous groups, 10, 11, 28, 35, 52, 55–56, 63, 76, 82; and frontier life, 19, 20–21; dissatisfaction with Spain, 28, 31, 32, 33–34, 45; and insurgency of 1811, 31, 37; Salcedo's appeal to, 33–35, 43–44; and insurgency of 1813, 37, 41, 44; and federalist/centralist debates, 58, 137, 139–42, 159, 178; and nationalism, 82, 163; and Anglo-American colonization, 90, 93, 113; flight from violence in Béxar, 145, 153, 157–59, 163, 168, 185; and war of Texas secession, 146, 148, 150–52, 153, 163, 265 (n. 60); and occupation of Béxar, 154; and Texian political structure, 155, 165; and battle of Alamo, 158–59, 160; Anglo-American mistreatment of, 167, 176; Juan N. Seguín, 169, 174, 176; and invasions of San Antonio, 185–86, 190; and headright land grants, 197, 198; and U.S.-Mexico War, 200; and Treaty of Guadalupe Hidalgo, 202; accommodations made by, 206; and Know-Nothing Party, 209; and Cart War, 216, 222; and Mexican identity, 233; as ethnic Mexicans from Béxar, 239 (n. 4)

Black Legend of Spanish colonization, 20, 243–44 (n. 19)

Bonded servitude, 56, 117

Bonham, James, 156

Borderland region: and cross-cultural contacts, 8, 9; and nationalism, 8, 12, 163; and ethnicity, 8, 128–31, 165; and middle ground, 9, 12; Béxar as frontier town of, 17, 18, 27, 28, 43; colonial policy toward, 22; and insurgency of 1811, 32; and insurgency of 1813, 39; and Anglo-American filibusters, 48; and social order, 52;

control of Béxar area, 15, 63, 75; and Tejanos, 54–55; Mexican relations with, 56, 57, 60, 61–63, 72–78; treaties with, 61–63, 72, 75–76; and San Sabá mission, 73, 253 (n. 73); Americans' trade of arms to, 98; and Anglo-American colonization, 98–99; and Texas Republic, 177

Comisión de Límites, 113–16

Compadrazgo, 38, 52, 111, 145

Condelle, Nicolas, 133, 134

Confederate army, 228, 229–30

Constitutional Congress of 1824, 97, 144, 151, 152, 154, 155, 157, 158, 178

Cordova, Vicente, 177, 189

Cordova Rebellion, 79, 177

Cos, Martín Perfecto de, 136, 139–40, 142, 144, 152–53, 158, 263 (n. 5)

Crisp, James E., 89, 256 (n. 18), 259 (n. 4), 263 (n. 5), 266 (n. 73)

Croix, Teodoro de, 18, 21

Cross-cultural contacts, 3, 6, 7, 8, 9, 12, 28, 55

Cuba, 39–40

Cuellar, Francisco, 147–48, 149, 264 (n. 45)

Cultural brokers: Tejano elites as, 12–14, 81–88, 93, 95, 97–106, 112–14, 116, 118, 120–24, 130, 157, 164, 165, 179–81, 233; Ruiz as, 55, 122; Bexareños as, 59; Cherokees as, 70; role of, 83

Curbier, Matias, 185, 186

De la Garza, José Antonio, 50, 51, 103, 199

De la Garza, Refugio, 111, 125, 134, 172, 190

De la Teja, Jesús F., 33, 199

De León, Arnoldo, 219, 230, 259 (n. 4), 266 (n. 73), 276 (n. 35)

De León, Martín, 120, 121

Democratic Party, 209–12, 214, 215–17, 219–20, 222–23, 227–29, 230

De Witt, Green, 100–101

De Zavala, Lorenzo, 120, 157

Díaz, Porfirio, 232

Dimmitt, Phillip, 147, 182–83

Diplomacy, 60, 70–73, 143, 206

Dominguez, Cristóbal, 44, 47

Dred Scott decision, 225, 226

Economic issues: and Anglo-American immigrants, 4, 83, 84–88, 89, 90–92, 93; and Tejano elites, 14, 25, 84–89, 92, 93, 103, 117, 119, 122, 128–31, 136, 192, 196; Texas as Mexican province, 21–22; and frontier, 21–22, 125; and regional identity, 22, 24; and *empresario* system, 86, 121; and Mexican national identity, 163; and *reconquista*, 181

Edwards, Haden, 98, 105–6, 112, 113, 129, 258 (n. 68)

Empresario colonization: and Tejano elites, 85, 86–88, 90, 93, 94–97; and Stephen F. Austin, 96, 97, 112, 121; and Ross, 97–98; and Edwards, 98, 105–6, 112; and De Witt, 100–101; and José Antonio Navarro, 100–101, 214; and Mexican/Anglo-American relations, 114, 115, 120–21; and de Zavala, 120, 157

Encomienda labor system, 59, 250 (n. 18)

English language: and Tejanos, 82

Environment, 19, 21, 60, 244 (n. 22)

Esparza, Francisco, 152, 160

Esparza, Gregorio, 152, 160

Ethnic identity, 7, 8, 9, 14. *See also* Mexican ethnic identity

Ethnicity: meaning of, 3, 8; ethnic minorities, 3, 11, 114, 130, 191, 230; and borderland region, 8, 128–31, 165;

and Anglo-American immigrants, 13, 129; and national identity, 43; ethnic creation, 78; ethnic difference, 85, 130, 162, 164

Ethnic studies, 236–37

European identity: and Bexareños, 8, 50

Farías, Eusevio, 185

Federalist/centralist debates: and Mexican nationalism, 14, 123, 124, 125, 127, 136; and Bexareños, 58, 137, 139–42, 159, 178; and Tejanos, 136, 138, 142–45, 152, 161, 164–65, 178–79, 234; and war of Texas secession, 136, 151–52, 156, 157, 229; and Texians, 142, 143, 145, 264 (n. 27); and *reconquista*, 178, 180, 183; and U.S.-Mexico War, 200, 202

Fehrenbach, T. R., 240 (n. 7)

Flores, Gaspar, 30–31, 37, 38, 50, 101, 102, 133, 134, 156

Flores, Manuel, 136, 186, 187

Flores, Nicolas, 133, 134

Florida, 88, 91

Franciscan missionaries, 67–69, 73, 78–79

Fredonian Rebellion, 105–6, 112, 113, 129

Frontera: meaning of, 130

Frontier: and Mexican independence, 12; and location of Béxar, 17, 18–19, 21, 24, 27, 28, 52, 55, 235; and Norteño identity, 19–22, 243 (n. 16); and indigenous groups, 21, 23; and economic issues, 21–22, 125; and Anglo-American expansion, 23; and insurgency of 1811, 32; and strains of insurgency, 35; Arredondo's maintaining of, 48; securing of, 59; and Mexican/indigenous relations, 60, 63, 72, 73, 121; social

hierarchy on, 65, 66; and missions, 67; Mexican government's control of, 83, 103, 113, 255 (n. 5); cooperation and coexistence on, 84; Spain's policies on colonization of, 86, 88; and Tejano/Anglo-American relations, 89, 101, 103, 104; and Mexican/Anglo-American relations, 90; and honor, 98; and military, 117; and Mexican national identity, 128, 163–64; and Tejano identity, 130, 146; Cos on, 139; and location of San Antonio, 173

Fuentes, Antonio, 154–55

Galán, Luis, 44, 45, 92

Galveston Bay and Texas Land Company, 120, 157

Garcia, Ignacio, 183, 220

Gift-giving: and Mexican/indigenous relations, 60, 62–63, 71–72, 74–78

Globalization, 234–35

Golman, J. J., 224

Gómez Farías, Valentín, 127, 128, 138

Gómez Pedraza, Manuel, 123

Gonzales, José María, 148

Goodman, James, 184, 186, 188

Granado, Francisco, 185, 188

Guerrero, Vicente, 117, 119, 123, 141

Gutiérrez, Ramón, 251–52 (n. 37), 259 (n. 79)

Gutiérrez de Lara, Bernardo, 37, 38, 39–41, 42, 44, 97–98, 247 (n. 29)

Hays, John "Jack" Coffee, 185, 186, 188, 201, 272 (n. 97)

Herrera, Blas, 169–70

Herrera, Simon, 30, 31, 40

Hidalgo, Miguel, 28, 31, 32, 33, 34, 39, 156

Hinojosa, Gilberto M., 69

Honor: and Anglo-American immi-

citizenship, 212, 214, 228, 230; in
south Texas, 225; and *patria*, 232;
and indigenous groups, 235
Law of April 6, 1830, 2, 118–23, 125, 129,
130, 135, 137, 149, 234, 266 (n. 73)
Leal, Manuel, 147, 150, 183
Leal, Narciso, 211, 212, 214, 219
Limpieza de sangre, 50–52, 66–67
Lind, Michael, 267 (n. 92)
Local government, 36, 49, 119, 123–24,
126, 128
Local identity, 3, 7–8, 9, 31
Local interests: and national identity, 3,
4, 7, 9, 14, 28, 49; and regional autonomy, 59; and Tejano elites, 128,
141, 143; and national politics, 143;
and war of Texas secession, 151, 160,
162; and Mexican national identity,
164; and transnational narratives,
234
Lopez, Mariano, 92
Louisiana, 22, 32, 39, 40, 88, 90, 98, 136
Louisiana Purchase, 23, 70, 87, 91

Marriages: in Béxar, 19; and prestige,
36, 37; Bexareño/indigenous intermarriage, 55, 56; and *casta* identification, 64, 65; and cultural brokers, 83, 85; and Tejano elites, 94,
195, 203, 208; and Mexican/Anglo-
American relations, 95; and Tejano/
Anglo-American relations, 171–72,
173, 192, 193–96, 203, 208
Martinez, Antonio, 86, 104
Masculinity, 53, 83, 92, 95, 104, 201, 259
(n. 79)
Masonic lodges, 95–96, 99, 100, 127–28
Maverick, Mary Adams, 173, 185, 198–
99, 208
Maverick, Samuel A., 173, 183, 211
McCulloch, Ben, 200

Menchaca, Antonio, 134, 148–49, 159,
188, 191–92
Mestizaje, 12, 55, 58, 59, 63, 64–67, 78,
95
Mestizos, 19, 56, 64, 65, 69
Mexía, José Antonio, 142
Mexican/Anglo-American relations:
and Mexican government, 2, 13, 81,
225; and development of region, 4;
and Béxar as Spanish colony, 81; and
Anglo-American immigrants, 81,
83; and Mexican national identity,
88; and class, 89; and indigenous
aspects of Mexican identity, 89; and
race, 89; and ethnic identity, 107,
181–82; Mier y Terán on, 114, 119,
266 (n. 73); and Mexican military,
115, 116–17, 143; and war of Texas
secession, 148; and mistreatment of
Mexican population, 167; and *reconquista*, 180, 183; in San Antonio, 183–
84, 187–89. *See also* Tejano/Anglo-
American relations
Mexican ethnic identity: persistence
of symbols of, 2; Anglo-American
definition of, 5; and Bexareños, 8,
206, 233; and Tejano identity, 52, 84,
105, 106–7, 118, 128–31, 136, 162, 167,
204, 206; and indigenous identities,
58, 79; and *mestizaje*, 64–67; fluid
nature of, 66; and Anglo-American
immigrants, 82, 83, 84, 85, 88; and
Tejano/Anglo-American relations,
106–7, 113, 114, 128–29, 154, 164, 167,
177, 196, 199, 200; and war of Texas
secession, 136, 163; and Mexican
national identity, 170
Mexican government: colonization
laws of, 2, 12, 13, 85, 97, 98, 102,
105–6, 112, 113, 118–21; and Mexi-
can/Anglo-American relations, 2, 13,

81, 225; and Anglo-American immigrants, 2, 13, 85–86, 88, 91–93, 101, 103, 118, 119, 121–24, 129, 130; and states, 21; constitution of 1824, 49; and citizenship, 58, 71; and alliances with indigenous groups, 61–63; and census of Indian subjects, 64; and secularization of missions, 67–68; and Mexican/indigenous relations, 71; and domestic migration to Texas, 116, 117, 119, 120, 122; and European migration to Texas, 120; and Stephen F. Austin, 120, 123–24; and Texas secession, 161; territorial integrity of, 178, 180–81, 201; and *reconquista*, 199; and Cart War, 225–26; and *juntas patrioticas*, 231–32

Mexican history, 11, 12, 78, 235, 243 (n. 16)

Mexican identity: indigenous aspects of, 2, 3, 56, 66, 89; transformation of, 2–3, 167–68; and Mexican independence, 43, 58, 164; and *mestizaje*, 63, 64–67, 78; and Tejanos, 63, 135, 163; flexibility of, 95. *See also* Mexican ethnic identity; Mexican national identity

Mexican independence: and Béxar, 1–2, 3, 27–28, 32, 33–35, 38, 49–52, 133–35, 142; celebration of, 2–3, 117, 133–35, 163, 231–33, 237; changes associated with, 12, 49, 63; and Hidalgo, 28, 31; dynamics of, 29, 245 (n. 6); Salcedo on, 33–35; Anglo opposition to, 42; and social order, 49–52; and Anglo-American colonization, 82; and Erasmo Seguín, 83–84

Mexican/indigenous relations: and Tejanos in Comanchería, 54–55; violence of, 56; and Comanches, 56, 57, 60, 61–63, 72–78; and indigenous identities, 58, 59, 70–71; and peace, 62, 63, 70–71, 73, 75–78, 123; and Anglo-American immigrants, 79, 123; Mier y Terán on, 115, 121; and raids, 185; and Treaty of Guadalupe Hidalgo, 203

Mexican military: and Mexican/indigenous relations, 60, 73–74, 75; and Mexican/Anglo-American relations, 115, 116–17, 143; and colonization laws, 121; and Angel Navarro, 140–41, 146, 264 (n. 37); and Tejano elite, 144, 162; and war of Texas secession, 148, 149, 152–53, 169; and battle of Alamo, 159–60; and battle of San Jacinto, 160–61; and Anglo-American mistreatment of Bexareños, 167; and Treaty of Velasco, 168; and deserters, 172; and *reconquista*, 179, 180, 183, 185–91

Mexican national identity: persistence of symbols of, 2; emergence of, 7, 106; and Bexareños, 14, 28; regional identity contrasted with, 85; and Tejanos, 85, 88, 93, 106, 107, 128, 141, 163, 164, 199–200, 232; colonization's expansion of, 88; fluid nature of, 163; and Mexican ethnic identity, 170

Mexican nationalism: and federalist/centralist debates, 14, 123, 124, 125, 127, 136; meaning of, 89; and cross-ethnic alliances, 105, 107; and Mexican independence celebrations, 134–35, 163; complexities of, 135, 163; and Tejanos, 135, 163, 232; and Johnson, 156; and *reconquista*, 180

Mexican Revolution, 232

Mexico/Texas Republic relations: conflict in, 173–74, 187; and Texas Republic border, 177, 182–83,

269 (n. 39); and invasions of San Antonio, 177–78, 185–91; and *reconquista*, 177–85, 191; and Texan incursions into Mexico, 181, 182, 183; and Texas annexation, 187; and Santa Anna, 191, 272 (n. 104)

Mexico/United States relations, 130, 192, 199–201

Mier y Terán, Manuel, 53, 99, 113–16, 118–23, 266 (n. 73)

Mission Concepción, 147, 159

Mission Indians, 12, 53, 56, 60, 67–69, 72, 78–79, 87

Mission San Francisco de la Espada, 68

Monclova, Mexico, 19, 32, 101, 123, 138–41, 152

Monroe, James, 39, 42

Montalvo, Manuel, 185

Montejano, David, 203–4, 273 (n. 116)

Morales, José María, 156

Mora-Torres, Juan, 8, 255 (n. 5)

Morfi, Juan Agustín de, 15, 18

Mulattoes, 19, 51, 64, 65, 66, 249 (n. 7)

Músquiz, Ramón, 93, 101–3, 105, 118–19, 121, 123–24, 127, 133, 140–41

Nacogdoches, Texas, 18, 19, 22–23, 42, 45–46, 55, 106, 122, 126

Natchitoches, Louisiana, 46, 47, 48

Nation: meaning of, 7, 240 (n. 10); elite articulations of, 245 (n. 6)

National identity: and local interests, 3, 4, 7, 9, 14, 28, 49; and Tejanos, 4, 52, 85; and regional identity, 8; and local identity, 8, 9; and family history, 36; and ethnicity, 43; complex nature of, 225, 237. *See also* Mexican national identity

Nationalism: meaning of, 3; local and regional identities as subset of, 7–8; and borderland region, 8, 12, 163; and Tejano identity, 8, 52, 85;

163–64, 200–201, 214; and Anglo-American expansion, 11, 13; and Mexican independence, 12, 231, 245 (n. 6); and Anglo-American immigrants, 13, 82, 83; and insurgency of 1813, 39, 41; multiple nationalisms, 82, 231; and Anglo-American historical narratives, 235; political borders of, 237; and peasant actions, 245 (n. 6). *See also* Mexican nationalism

Nativism, 209, 212

Navarro, Angel (father of José Antonio Navarro), 36, 50, 111, 125, 133, 139–47, 152, 160

Navarro, Angel (son of José Antonio Navarro), 222, 227, 229

Navarro, José Angel, 28

Navarro, José Antonio: as insurgent, 28; and Iturbide, 50; and indigenous groups, 63; and Stephen F. Austin, 93, 100, 184, 258 (n. 68); and land titles, 100–101; as cultural broker, 105; and slavery, 117; and Béxar Ayuntamiento, 125; and patriotic commission, 134; and war of Texas secession, 152, 157, 160, 162; and Texas Declaration of Independence, 157, 170; and Texas Republic, 161, 174; and San Antonio government, 172; and Texan Santa Fe Expedition, 181, 272 (n. 109); persecution of, 187; and Tejano citizenship, 212, 214–15, 219–20; and election vigilance committee, 217; and Democratic Party, 219; and histories of Texas, 222; and Houston, 228–29

Navarro, Luciano, 133–34

Negotiation: and Anglo-American immigrants, 10, 11; in borderland regions, 12; and Béxar's social order, 48; and Tejano identity, 58; and Mexican/indigenous relations, 63,

70–71, 72; and Cherokees, 79, 177, 253 (n. 63); and Tejano elites, 90, 141

Newcomb, James P., 209, 277 (n. 71)

New Mexico, 10, 74, 75, 177, 178, 182, 251–52 (n. 37)

New Spain: northern expansion of, 10–11, 15; internal migrations within northern region of, 19, 22, 23; governing structure of, 21, 31, 245 (n. 6); and prestige, 35; and Anglo-American colonization, 90; and honor, 94

Norteño identity, 8, 14, 19–22, 94, 243 (n. 16)

North Atlantic Free Trade Agreement, 236–37

Nueces River, 182, 183, 184, 202

Nuevo León, Mexico, 21, 23

Oso Ballo (Comanche leader), 75–76, 77

Padilla, Juan Antonio, 60, 73, 97–100, 102, 104, 105, 120, 129, 144

Palafox, M. Romero, 231–32

Palmer, G. W., 277 (n. 71)

Peace: and Mexican/indigenous relations, 62, 63, 70–71, 73, 75–78, 123; peace structure, 203–4, 273 (n. 116)

Pease, Elisha Marshall, 206, 226–27

Peonage, 92, 107

Pereyra, Francisco, 33, 34

Perez, Antonio, 185, 189

Perry, Henry, 48

Plan de Jalapa, 123, 127

Political issues: and Anglo-American immigrants, 84, 86, 90; and ethnic difference, 85, 130; and frontier issues, 90; and Tejano elites, 94, 95, 97, 99, 103, 122–29, 136–37, 170, 173; and Anglo-American colonization, 99, 102, 103; and Stephen F. Austin, 112, 120, 123–24, 125, 126–27; and

Béxar, 112, 123–28, 143; and Tejano/Anglo-American relations, 124, 130, 157, 165, 191–93, 194, 206, 227, 229; and power relations, 164, 191–92, 204, 207–8, 209; and *reconquista*, 181

Power relations: and historical narrative, 12; women's role in, 37; and Bexareño elites, 52, 136; and Texian political structure, 164; and political issues, 164, 191–92, 204, 207–8, 209; and Texas Republic, 170

Prestige: and social order, 27, 28, 35–38, 42, 48, 50, 52; of Tejano elites, 28, 36, 90, 93, 94, 103, 104, 112, 139, 141, 151; and *limpieza de sangre* hearings, 51; and Anglo-American immigrants, 83

Proto-nationalism, 7–8

Race: and social order, 13, 50, 51, 52, 66; in Béxar, 64–65; Anglo-American ideas of, 72, 86, 88–89, 92, 99, 107; Tejano ideas of, 86, 99; transformation of race relations, 114; and Texas secession, 155, 259 (n. 4), 266 (n. 73); and Cart War, 225; and African Americans in South, 227–28; politics of, 230. See also *Mestizaje*

Ramos Arizpe, Miguel, 18, 19–24, 40, 49, 125, 128

Rancherias, 46, 75

Reconquista: and invasions of 1842, 177–78, 185–91; and Mexico/Texas Republic relations, 177–85, 191; and Texas annexation, 199

Regional identity, 7–8, 22, 24, 85, 93, 128, 136

Regional interests: of Mexican independence, 29, 49, 245 (n. 6); and indigenous identities, 66–67; and Anglo-American immigrants, 83, 90; and Mexican ethnic identity, 128;

in, 53, 60, 70–71, 72, 79; *casta* identification in, 64; and Mexican/in-
digenous relations, 74, 78; mission
system in, 75; as border state with
United States, 88; Mier y Terán's investigation of, 113–16; demographics
of, 115; and Stephen F. Austin's request for statehood, 123–27, 137, 262
(n. 59); and Louisiana, 244 (n. 23).
See also War of Texas secession
Texas, state of: historical narratives of,
4, 5, 10, 11, 78; annexation of, 13,
89, 90, 100, 137–38, 161–62, 178, 187,
191, 199; Mexican attempts to reconquer, 14, 167; secession from United
States, 206, 227
Texas Declaration of Independence, 55,
157, 158
Texas Rangers, 10, 184, 185, 200, 201,
204
Texas Republic: and Tejanos, 13, 160,
161, 165, 168, 203; and Gutiérrez de
Lara, 39, 40–41; Ruiz as senator in,
55; and Mexican/indigenous relations, 77; and Cherokee negotiations, 79, 177, 253 (n. 63); and Mexi-
can/Anglo-American relations, 95;
Tejanos involved in formation of,
156; and Tejanos' loyalty, 162, 168,
170, 172, 176, 177, 178, 180, 183–86,
198, 204; securing southern border
of, 169, 177; social order of, 170;
power consolidation in, 177; and
headright land grants, 196–99; land
claims of, 203, 228. *See also* Mexico/
Texas Republic relations
Texas Revolution, 4, 256 (n. 19). *See also*
War of Texas secession
Texians: and revolt against Mexican
government, 135, 142–43, 145; invasion of Béxar, 136, 143; and peace
party, 137; Tejanos allied with, 144,

145, 152–62 passim; and war of
Texas secession, 147–49; political
structure of, 153–55, 158, 164, 165;
and Texas annexation, 161; and Tejano loyalty, 168, 176, 183–85; Mexican portrayals of, 178, 182–83
Thompson, Jerry D., 229
Tijerina, Andrés, 126
Tjarks, Alicia V., 242 (n. 8)
Toledo, José Alvarez, 39–40, 41, 44, 47,
247 (nn. 29, 37)
Trade: with Anglo-American immigrants, 22, 35, 43, 48, 86, 90, 98;
contraband trade, 22, 48–49, 86,
90, 98; with indigenous groups, 22,
55, 58, 96, 177; and Mexican/indige-
nous relations, 62, 63, 76, 78; and
Tejano elites, 88; slave trade, 91, 117,
227; and Tejano/Anglo-American
relations, 93; limits on, 118; and
Tenoxtitlán, 121; and Mexico/Texas
Republic relations, 177, 182; and
Texas Republic, 181; and cart traffic,
223–24
Transnational historical narratives,
234–37, 278 (n. 11), 278–79 (n. 21)
Travieso, Francisco, 30–31, 32, 38
Travis, William Barrett, 154–55, 158
Treaties: with indigenous groups, 55,
56, 60, 61–63, 70–72, 75–76; and
Anglo-American expansion, 70
Treaty of Guadalupe Hidalgo, 202–3,
206, 228
Treaty of Velasco, 168, 177, 178
Trespalacios, José Felix, 50
Turner, Frederick Jackson, 19
Tutino, John, 245 (n. 6)
Twinam, Ann, 51

Ugartechea, Domingo de, 1, 134, 135,
142, 143, 144, 146
Union Democratic Party, 227–29

Uribe, Rafael, 180
Urrutia, J., 219
U.S.-Mexico War, 13, 79, 106, 192, 199

Valdez, Nicanor, 205–6
Van Young, Eric, 247 (n. 40)
Vázquez, Rafael, 185–87, 190, 201
Vecinos, 42, 51, 63, 104, 141, 143, 169, 172
Velasco Avila, Cuauhtémoc, 11, 250 (n. 13)
Veramendi, Juan Martín de, 28, 50, 94, 111, 138
Veramendi, Ursula de, 111
Victoria, Guadalupe, 113, 115
Viesca, Agustín, 139, 140, 142, 264 (n. 27)
Voss, Stuart F., 36, 37

Wacos, 71, 73, 74, 122
Warfare, 53, 244 (n. 22)
War of Texas secession: and Tejanos, 4, 13, 135–38, 144–45, 150–57, 159–60, 162, 229; as Anglo-led, 136, 143; and federalist/centralist debates, 136, 151–52, 156, 157, 229; and Mexican ethnic identity, 136, 163; and Béxar's first siege, 144–53, 156, 264–65 (n. 46); and Texas Declaration of Independence, 157; and battle of Alamo, 158–61; and battle of San Jacinto, 160–61; and Texas Republic era, 167; undeclared continuation of, 168, 177–85; and American Manifest Destiny, 200; and Treaty of Guadalupe Hidalgo, 202
Weber, David J., 243 (n. 18), 259 (n. 4)
White, Richard, 9, 12
Wilkins, Frederick, 185, 201
Woll, Adrian, 188–90, 191, 200, 201, 204
Women: role in power relations, 37; and Mexican/indigenous relations, 73; and Tejano/Anglo-American marriages, 195–96, 273 (n. 123)
Wortman, Miles, 36, 37

Zambrano, Juan José, 32, 33, 50